"This is an excellent interdisciplinary book, capturing the complex, changing and multi-dimensional relationship between religion and sexuality. Page and Shipley are key international scholars in the field and intertwine their multi-sited research, over a 15-year period, illustrating religious-sexual citizenship, embodiment, practice, identity – and more – beyond enduring problematic binary thinking. An impressive range of methodological and theoretical approaches are used, framed in conversation with queer feminist perspectives, and returning the reader to intersectional endeavours and potentials. This book constitutes an extensive and impressive overview of 'where we are now', pushing important questions of 'what next?' for sexuality and religion studies."

*– Yvette Taylor, University of Strathclyde, UK*

"This timely text provides a meticulous, in-depth and critical interrogation of a wide range of theories and methodologies on religion and sexuality, substantially enriched by empirical insights drawn from the authors' own research projects. Offering a thorough mapping of the current terrain and authoritative directions for future research, this expansive and exhaustive text is a must-read for scholars investigating religion and sexuality."

*– Andrew Kam-Tuck Yip, University of Nottingham, UK*

"Building from their own research projects, Page and Shipley offer an innovative and inclusive approach to the study of religion and sexualities, where both central topics are seen as complex, lived, and multi-layered. Using a queer feminist lens, the book explores various regulatory relationships between sexualities and religion, moving beyond the 'straight time' conceptions of the supposedly typical life pattern to an examination of how religion and sexualities intersect in multiple and often unpredictable ways, making this a substantial and valuable contribution to the expanding field of studies in religion and sexuality."

*– Pamela Dickey Young, Queen's University, Canada*

# RELIGION AND SEXUALITIES

This book examines key themes and concepts pertaining to religious and sexual identities and expressions, mapping theoretical, methodological, and empirical dimensions. It explores the ways in which debates around sexuality and religion have been framed, and what research is still needed to expand the field as it develops. Through the deployment of contemporary research, including data from the authors' own projects, *Religion and Sexualities* offers an encompassing account of the sociology of sexuality and religion, considering theoretical and methodological lenses, queer experiences, and how sexuality is gendered in religious contexts. This comprehensive text will act as an essential accompaniment to scholars and students across the social sciences and humanities, whether they have a general interest in the field or are embarking on their own research in this area.

**Sarah-Jane Page** is Senior Lecturer in Sociology at Aston University, UK, and the co-author of *Religious and Sexual Identities: A Multi-faith Exploration of Young Adults* and *Understanding Young Buddhists: Living Out Ethical Journeys*.

**Heather Shipley** is Project Manager for the Nonreligion in a Complex Future Project at the University of Ottawa, Canada. She is co-author, with Pamela Dickey Young (Queen's University, Kingston, Canada) of *Identities Under Construction: Religion, Gender and Sexuality among Youth in Canada* and editor of *Globalized Religion and Sexual Identity: Contexts, Contestations, Voices*.

# RELIGION AND SEXUALITIES

## Theories, Themes, and Methodologies

*Sarah-Jane Page and Heather Shipley*

LONDON AND NEW YORK

First published 2020
by Routledge
2 Park Square, Milton Park, Abingdon, Oxon OX14 4RN

and by Routledge
52 Vanderbilt Avenue, New York, NY 10017

*Routledge is an imprint of the Taylor & Francis Group, an informa business*

© 2020 Sarah-Jane Page and Heather Shipley

The right of Sarah-Jane Page and Heather Shipley to be identified as authors of this work has been asserted by them in accordance with sections 77 and 78 of the Copyright, Designs and Patents Act 1988.

All rights reserved. No part of this book may be reprinted or reproduced or utilised in any form or by any electronic, mechanical, or other means, now known or hereafter invented, including photocopying and recording, or in any information storage or retrieval system, without permission in writing from the publishers.

*Trademark notice*: Product or corporate names may be trademarks or registered trademarks, and are used only for identification and explanation without intent to infringe.

*British Library Cataloguing-in-Publication Data*
A catalogue record for this book is available from the British Library

*Library of Congress Cataloging-in-Publication Data*
A catalog record has been requested for this book

ISBN: 978-1-138-50427-1 (hbk)
ISBN: 978-1-138-50428-8 (pbk)
ISBN: 978-1-315-14594-5 (ebk)

Typeset in Bembo
by Deanta Global Publishing Services, Chennai, India.

# CONTENTS

| | |
|---|---|
| *Acknowledgements* | *viii* |
| Introduction | 1 |
| 1 Situating sexualities and religion: Place, space, and the body | 10 |
| 2 Understanding sexualities and religion through censure and control | 29 |
| 3 Identity, sexualities, and religion | 47 |
| 4 Methodological insights: Researching religion and sexualities | 68 |
| 5 Conceptualising the "normative": The straight time model | 93 |
| 6 Navigating the "normative": Constituting safe and unsafe space | 111 |
| 7 Gendering sexuality and religion | 129 |
| 8 Gendered bodies: Reproductive and sexual control | 146 |
| 9 Institutional contexts: Religion and state processes | 167 |
| *Conclusion: Managing religion and sexualities* | *191* |
| *Bibliography* | *196* |
| *Index* | *222* |

# ACKNOWLEDGEMENTS

This book has been made possible by the huge collaborative potential generated through the *Religion and Society* funded *Religion, Youth and Sexuality* project and the *Religion and Diversity Project* funded *Religion, Gender and Sexuality among Youth in Canada* project. Without these projects, we no doubt would not have met as soon as we did, nor have been enabled to meet so much as we have been able to. Indeed, these projects gave us the potential to develop a strong working relationship over a number of years to enable this book to come to fruition. As part of those projects, we are indebted to the Principal Investigators of those projects – Prof. Andrew Kam-Tuck Yip in the UK and Prof. Pamela Dickey Young in Canada. Both have supported us unconditionally and have been invaluable in their guidance and mentorship over the years.

We are also grateful to the various professional associations and groups to which we belong. Sarah-Jane is thankful for the various spaces where she has been able to test ideas and debate issues within the discipline, such as the Sociology of Religion Study Group, the Maternal Identities Group, the Shiloh project, and the Australian Association of Buddhist Studies network. Heather is grateful to the Canadian Society for the Study of Religion, the Association for the Sociology of Religion, the Society for the Scientific Study of Religion, and all the colleagues and friends who have shared their ideas, feedback, and support throughout the years.

We cannot name everyone who has helped us on this journey as the list could nearly fill a whole chapter (and keeping to the word count in this book has been a struggle!). But special thanks to all those in academia who have kept up our spirits when things have been challenging, often over a glass of wine or gin, and all of those people who enabled the projects we use in this book to be possible.

Personally, Sarah-Jane would like to thank her long-suffering family, especially for all the times she has worked evenings and weekends to meet the book

Acknowledgements  **ix**

deadline. Projects such as this are not solely the labour of the authors on the front of the book, but envelop those who enable the writing to be sustained. Sarah-Jane is especially grateful to her family in this regard.

Heather would personally like to thank her family, for daring to continue asking questions about what she is writing and for always responding with interest. Heather would also like to thank her partner, Peter, who has supported the process of the creation of this book and has experienced the endless hammering of typing over the course of its writing.

# INTRODUCTION

## Understanding religion and sexualities

The relationship between religion and sexuality is complex and multidimensional. Drawing on our combined expertise – spanning numerous projects – we hope to give an insight into various sociological dimensions to the topic. While this book will cover a lot of ground and offers a window into the relationship between religion and sexuality, it does not hope to cover all aspects, examples, and contexts, as this would be too vast for one book to contemplate. We are operating from particular geographical and disciplinary perspectives – one author as a sociologist of religion in the UK, and another as a religious studies scholar in Canada – and many of our insights will be framed with these contexts in mind. However, we do hope to offer a guide to readers in situating the study of religion and sexualities, its theories, methodologies, and forms of empirical investigation.

The first question that arises concerns what we mean by sexuality. This can be narrowly defined – as pertaining to particular genital acts – or it can be more encompassing. We take the broader view. Sexuality relates to more than just something called "sex"; indeed, it is more than intimate activities such as holding hands and kissing (Brintnall, 2016). As McGuire says:

> That prevalent idea of sexuality is far too focused on artificially binary ideas of properly masculine or feminine sexuality, conceived merely in genital and/or erotic terms. This limitation prevents us from appreciating other possible expressions of human sexuality, such as nursing a baby, giving birth, enjoying a caress, or even practicing celibacy.
>
> *(2008, p. 180)*

**2** Introduction

This book will explore how intimate relationships are organised to contribute to broader structured organising systems such as heteronormativity. This is important so that we can account for how power is operationalised through sexuality norms. Sexuality therefore pertains to more than sexual expression and relates to many other elements of life (Jackson and Scott, 2010). Heterosexual forms of sexuality have come to dominate our conceptualisation of social life, with heterosexuality underpinning how much of our social life is ordered, through institutions such as marriage, and how "the family" is conceptualised (e.g. until very recently, marriage was only understood in cross-sex terms). While heterosexuality is premised on a particular narrowly defined genital act (usually penetrative vaginal sex between a man and a woman – where procreative potential is emphasised), heterosexuality actually relates to a much broader system of social relations, codifying gendered behaviour. As Jackson and Scott articulate, 'As an institution, heterosexuality is, by definition, a gender relationship, governing relations between women and men, ordering not only sexual life but also domestic and extra-domestic divisions of labour and resources' (2010, p. 85). Therefore, the success of heterosexuality does not depend on the genital acts assumed to underpin it, but by a whole raft of mechanisms that support its existence, which become routinised through day-to-day social practices. Those not subscribing to heterosexual patterns of behaviour are excluded, constructed in non-normative terms, and in some cases, as an explicit threat to the rest of society. Non-heterosexual sexualities have traditionally been considered in terms of deviancy, with associated forms of punishments and regulation such as imprisonment. Given the recent liberalising of legislation in a number of Western contexts such as Canada, England, Wales, and Scotland to recognise same-sex marriage, it might be assumed that the dominance of heterosexuality is waning. But a number of authors have specified how, by co-opting same-sex relationships into embedded forms and symbols of heterosexuality such as marriage, extends, rather than contests, heterosexuality. Instead, same-sex couples come to be recognised and included so long as they adhere to a strict heterosexually recognised code of conduct (e.g. a commitment to monogamous and lifelong partnerships – Duggan, 2002; Jackson, 2006; Richardson, 2018). Meanwhile, constraints remain against those unwilling to comply. In other contexts, punishments against non-heterosexual forms of sexuality have intensified and become harsher, such as the recent negative legislation towards sexual minorities in Nigeria and Uganda (Van Klinken and Chitando, 2016). Therefore, when certain forms of sexuality become visible, further mechanisms of censure emerge, whether explicitly or in more subtle forms.

How we conceptualise a schema of sexualities invokes certain hierarchies. For much of the 20th century, the homosexual/heterosexual binary loomed large; individuals were understood as situated on one side or another, despite the efforts of sexologists like Alfred Kinsey to challenge this assumption. The gay liberation movement from the 1960s, predominantly read through the lens of gay men, did start the acknowledgement of a broader array of sexualities, and the "LGBT" acronym – lesbian, gay, bisexual, and trans – was forged. Yet even through its claims of inclusivity, this acronym had its own hierarchy, with gay men prioritised. Meanwhile, bisexual and trans experiences were often ignored (Daniels, 2012; Richardson and Monro, 2012). More recently, other identities such as queer and intersex have been recognised, but this has created its own tensions, regarding how meaningful it is to keep adding letters to the mix, and what it means to structure our understanding of sexuality through discrete identity labels. In this text, we will use the term "queer" wherever possible to denote non-heterosexual forms of identity, to try to elicit inclusivity, while maintaining the preferences of other researchers using different terminology. To understand sexualities in plural ways may mean that we recognise identity markers such as heterosexual, gay, lesbian, and bisexual. But lived sexualities are far more complicated and messier than such categorisations would suggest:

> there are those who identify as straight, but who regularly indulge in homoeroticism, and of course there are those who claim the identity of gay or lesbian but engage with heterosexual sex. In addition, some people identify themselves sexually but don't actually have sex, and there are those who claim celibacy as a sexual practice.
>
> *(Takagi, 1996, p. 245, quoted in Neitz, 2000, p. 388)*

Starting with the individual reveals the complexity and fluidity embedded in how individuals navigate the terrain of sexuality. And the same can be said for the sphere of religion. While religion is typically thought of in bounded terms, as split between pre-determined categories such as Christianity, Judaism, and Buddhism, each with its own concerns and predilections regarding sexuality, we take a more expansive view. Following Brintnall (2016), we are not assuming that any religion has a singular narrative on topics such as masturbation, abortion, or queer identities, for any religion is comprised of various strands and influences, with practitioners living out those religious traditions in various and diverse ways. As Beckford argues, 'all too often theorists have taken religion as a relatively unproblematic unitary and homogenous phenomenon that can be analysed and compared across time and space' (2003, p. 15). But religion is more complex than this, and we therefore reject static understandings which argue, for example, that 'Islam says this' about masturbation, or 'Buddhism says that', to instead focus on the heterogeneous ways that religion is lived (Ammerman, 2014; McGuire, 2008; Orsi, 2007).

Goldenberg argues that 'social and political agendas and institutions construct "religion" in different times and places in relation to other equally unstable concepts such as secular and profane' (2007, p. 1). Social and political agendas therefore construct the place and role of religion at any given time. Attending religious services is often used to define an affiliation with a religious community, but this is a very narrow conceptualisation.

**4** Introduction

In social scientific literature and the humanities, the category of religion has historically been left unproblematised. Although much recent work, such as that referenced here, pushes for nuance in the study of religion and religious identity, much research (especially in psychology) still use narrow and often Christian-centric categories and markers for analysis. Psychological studies often determine religiosity to be a set of behaviours that can be measured, such as the frequency of prayer or church attendance (see for example Koenig *et al.*, 2001; Pargament, 1997). There are problems with limiting religious belief or being religious to types of actions. One problem is the Christian-centric framework because not all religious groups or individuals would count prayer or institutional attendance as being primary or even as constituting any part of the expression of their faith tradition. Further, the National Household Survey in Canada (2011) shows that the category of "religious nones" (no religious affiliation) is on the rise (from 16% in 2001 to 23.9% in 2011). Understanding better the relationship of non-religion to social, political, and legal contexts is an emerging and critical area of study. While "religion" is frequently blamed for anti-queer attitudes, non-religious and "secular" spaces continue to restrict, harm, and disavow non-heterosexuality.

Narrow categorisations of religious affiliation as related to a rigid set of behaviours also ignores the conscientious application of ethical and moral belief systems that do not uphold the same rules or doctrine as determined by particular forms of mainstream religious traditions.[1] The result is that certain religious traditions are ignored. For example, First Nations, Métis, and Inuit traditions do not fit within the standards set out by Western policy makers and scholars (Beaman, 2002).

Dominant ideologies are embedded in language and reinforced through frameworks of power, such as politics, economics, the media, and other authoritative institutions (Hall, 1980). These are supported in a cyclical pattern so that these ideologies can be viewed either as created by the system of power or as created by the culture to which the system of power is responding. As Barnard states, 'knowledge is never benign, and, certainly, apparatuses and institutions of knowledge production will always contextualise any knowledge thus produced' (2004, p. 4).

Jakobsen and Pellegrini ask, 'How did it come to pass that secularism as a "world" discourse was also intertwined with one particular religion?' (2008, p. 1). They argue that the secularism narrative mistakenly posits secularism as a universal trait somehow different from particularised religion when in fact 'secularism remains tied to a particular religion, just as the secular calendar remains tied to Christianity' (2008, p. 3). Jakobsen and Pellegrini critique commonly held assumptions about secularism and secularity as being the binary opposite of religious ideologies:

> Our argument is not that this secularism is really (essentially) religion in disguise, but rather that in its dominant, market-based incarnation it constitutes a specifically Protestant form of secularism. The claim of the

secularization narrative is that the secularism that develops from these European and Christian origins is, in fact, universal and fully separate from Christianity.

*(2008, p. 3)*

What do we therefore focus on when we imagine "religion"? Do we centre our analysis on the official practices and those with authority, such as religious leaders and authorised rituals – or do we focus on everyday and ordinary members who state that they follow a particular religious tradition (which may be in conjunction with other religious traditions)? The turn to lived religion encourages a focus on the latter. Nevertheless, this is not to the exclusion of authorised norms, texts, rituals, and religious leaders, for understanding this dimension is equally crucial in grasping the context for religious engagement and how power dynamics operate in those contexts. But lived religion emphasises a bottom-up approach, which puts the everyday practitioner at centre stage. This also means that we get less hung up on divisions between phenomena such as religion and spirituality, and although much time has been spent delineating these two terms, it becomes more useful to assess why individuals themselves see there to be a difference between the two (McGuire, 2008). Indeed, the social dimension of religiosity – and its sociological significance – needs to be foregrounded. As Beckford argues:

> whatever else religion is, it is a social phenomenon. Regardless of whether religious beliefs and experiences actually relate to supernatural, superempirical or noumenal realities, religion is expressed by means of human ideas, symbols, feelings, practices and organisations.
>
> *(2003, p. 2)*

Individuals themselves are therefore implicated in these broader processes and structures of power relations and may even be impacted even if they are not religious themselves. Rather like sexuality, religion forges its own forms of hierarchy and power differentials, but these formulations are not inevitable or fixed.

So how do we come to conceptualise religion and sexuality together? We have already indicated that we take a "lived" approach to both – but we are not simply interested in individual experiences. Instead, we are keen to understand how general normatives are forged between the two. As Lofton argues, 'the history of sexuality and the history of religion are co-constitutive. Sexual decision making is often connected to religious ideas or practices; religious life is often regulating sexual life' (2016, p. 19). But the relationship between the two should not assume to take standardised understandings, where sexuality comes to be associated with progress, and religion with repression and tradition. As White (2016) argues, such an understanding rests on the assumption that "religion" and "sexuality" can be straightforwardly understood. But this is not clear-cut, and the terms themselves have varied historically. For example, homosexuality, a

**6** Introduction

term coined in the late 19th century, came to have much broader resonance in the 1950s, especially among some Christians. Although "homosexuality" came to be read as something that "Christianity" had always had a perspective on, this was untenable when the term was so new. And older forms of same-sex activity and desire, related to the term "sodomy" – were equally unevenly applied and described. Indeed, it does not make sense to assume something called "religion" is inherently homophobic or anti-woman; there is no singular role for religion to play in society because of its sheer diversity. Contextual and detailed analysis is therefore needed to best understand the complexity at work.

In this book, we bring together our overview of the field, utilising the lens of our own research projects to do so, and cover theoretical and methodological issues, as well as pertinent themes. In this ambitious endeavour, we recognise our own blindspots. We reside in geographical locations where Christian forms of religiosity are more prominent, and it is on Christianity that most socio-logical research on religion and sexuality has been conducted. The influence of Christianity has also been facilitated through the historical dominance of Western regimes and the huge impact wrought by a colonialist empire – the leg-acies of which are still impactful today. As a result, much of our engagement with the topic is through this lens, with an aim of demonstrating the ways that forms of Christian discourse have had an enormous impact on sexuality regulation.

Further, much of the research to date on religion and sexuality has been done by white researchers with high numbers of white respondents. Addressing race and racial differences in the study of religion(s) and sexuality(ies) is critical for sociology and religious studies, but also for academia at large. In acknowledging our blindspots, we also position ourselves by our own identities as white schol-ars, who identify as cis-gendered women. While the research that is available is dominated by Christianity and white perspectives, similarly it focuses largely on gay and lesbian identities, relationships, and positionality. Our goal in producing this volume is to also be able to identify the gaps in the research available, so that future endeavours can begin to encapsulate the differences and similarities across ranges of identities and experiences.

## The projects

This book draws much from our insights on the various religion and sexuality projects we have worked on, especially two key studies that looked at youth, religion, and sexuality. From this empirical work, we will be including data – this will sometimes reference other publications too, and in other cases we will introduce data that has not, as yet, been published elsewhere.[2]

*Religion Youth and Sexuality* (RYS) project: This project was a major investiga-tion into the ways in which religious young adults, aged between 18 and 25 and living in the UK, managed their religious and sexual identities, and was conducted between 2009–2011. Drawing on data from individuals with a variety of religious and sexual identifications, and levels of religiosity, the study comprises the most comprehensive investigation into young adult religion and sexuality in the UK to date. The methods utilised were comprised of questionnaires with 693 individuals, 61 of whom participated in in-depth qualitative interviews, with 24 of those who participated in an interview going on to undertake a video diary. This project generated a vast databank that has been published from extensively (Page, 2014a, 2015, 2016a, b, 2017a, b; Page and Yip, 2012a, b, 2017a, b, 2019, forthcoming; Page et al., 2012; Yip and Page, 2013, 2014, forthcoming; Yip, 2015).[3]

*Religion, Gender and Sexuality among Youth in Canada* (RGSY) project: This mirrored the RYS project, but was conducted in Canada between 2012 and 2014, and also included non-religious individuals. The approaches and methods were the same, with the use of near-identical questionnaires to the RYS project, modified to the Canadian context (i.e. same-sex marriage was legal in Canada at the time of the questionnaire, thus the questions and categories of relationships were adjusted to reflect this). The Canadian project was comprised of 486 questionnaire responses (483 to the English questionnaire and 3 to the French questionnaire), 32 interview participants, and 10 video diaries, and also comprises a large publications bank (Young and Shipley, 2014, 2020, forthcoming; Shipley and Young, 2014, 2017a, b, forthcoming; Shipley, 2015, 2018a, b; Young et al., 2016; Young, 2015, 2019).[4]

The *Abortion Debates in Public Spaces* (ADPS) project was conducted in the UK between 2015 and 2020 with the aim of understanding how abortion was framed in public forms of activism, particularly activism taking place outside of abortion clinics; other campaigns and anti-abortion marches were also mapped. The main methods were comprised of ethnography, involving interviews with participants, and photographing religious objects and signs utilised as part of the campaign. Thus far, 30 sites of activism have been mapped, along with five March for Life events (held in Birmingham or London). The findings from this project are still emerging, with a number of publications forthcoming (Lowe and Hayes, 2019; Lowe and Page, 2019; Lowe and Page, forthcoming).[5]

The *Religion in Intimate Life* (RIL) project investigated how religious individuals from a variety of traditions narrativised their attitudes to abortion, homosexuality, and same-sex marriage. Conducted in England and Wales, the project explored how attitudes were formulated in qualitative contexts, and ascertained what sort of role religion played. In total, 15 in-depth semi-structured interviews were undertaken between 2017 and 2018.[6]

*IICSA Church of England Analysis* – the Independent Inquiry into Child Sexual Abuse (IICSA) was set up in England and Wales in 2014 to investigate institutional contexts where sexual abuse had occurred, such as councils, schools, and churches. The Church of England – England's established church – was one of the religious organisations investigated. Thus far, hearings have been comprised of three parts – a 15-day hearing in March 2018, focused on the Chichester diocese, which was identified as having major safeguarding problems where numerous clergy had been prosecuted through the courts; a five-day hearing in July 2018 focused on Peter Ball, a bishop convicted of abusing 18 young

**8** Introduction

men between the 1970s and 1990s, and a hearing in July 2019, focused on the wider Anglican Church and their response to child sexual abuse. Each day of proceedings roughly generated 200 pages of transcript. A thematic analysis was conducted of the first 15-day hearing.[7]

The *Anglican Clergy Mothers* project was conducted between 2005 and 2009 and focused on in-depth qualitative interviews with clergy who were mothers in the Church of England, a group who had hitherto received little research attention, to ascertain whether or not they were fully incorporated into the contours of the church institution, how gender norms operated, and how motherhood was experienced and conceptualised. A number of publications have emerged from this project (Page, 2011; 2012; 2013; 2014b; 2016c).[8]

*Exploring Religion and Sexuality in Ontario's Education System* was funded by a Jack Shand Small Grant Award, Society for the Scientific Study of Religion, and conducted between 2012 and 2014. It consisted of focus groups and semi-structured one-on-one interviews with high-school students in Ontario to ask about both the experiences of religion and sexuality in school and to consider current media controversies about high school and the impact on their day-to-day lives (Shipley, 2019).

The *Sites of Resistance: Identity Formation in LGBTQI and Allies' Student Life* project was conducted between 2017 and 2018, funded by the Queen's University Faculty Association (Kingston, Ontario). It consisted of one-on-one semi-structured interviews with self-identified LGBTQI students, faculty, and staff and self-identified allies. Trinity Western University is a faith-based university in Langley, British Columbia, Canada, which has been the site of a national debate about religion and sexuality – in particular, responding to their request for a law school and opposition to the request based on their mandatory Community Covenant. The Covenant, now no longer in force for students, required that students agree not to engage in certain activities, among them same-sex relationships (Shipley, forthcoming).

## Chapter synopsis

Chapters 1 to 3 will introduce some of the theoretical insights that have informed the sociological study of religion and sexualities. We start in Chapter 1 with a focus on how we even begin to think about theorising the terrain, understanding that this endeavour is emplaced and embodied. Chapter 2 focuses much more on Foucauldian understandings of the regulation and censure of sexualities, while Chapter 3 is concerned with identity.

Chapter 4 moves onto methodological issues concerning the sociology of religion and sexuality, considering why taking a feminist queer methodological approach is beneficial, while also showcasing how numerous methods have been utilised in this field.

Chapters 5 through 9 will focus on more thematic-based issues. Chapter 5 will start to develop how normative forms of sexuality have been constructed, with Chapter 6 expanding on this to consider how religious spaces have enabled or denied queer bodies to exist. Chapters 7 and 8 will focus on the relationship between gender, religion, and sexuality, considering regulatory forms of sexuality and how this has been embodied and gendered. Meanwhile, Chapter 9 will highlight institutional contexts, and the impact that institutions themselves have in understanding sexuality and religion, focusing on issues such as child sexual abuse and institutional denial. Finally, we will offer a conclusion to emphasise the key themes of the book.

## Notes

1 The prevalence of mainstream Christian (often Protestant) values in social institutions such as law is a point argued very effectively by Beaman (2002) and Sullivan (2009), among others.
2 When our own data is introduced, pseudonyms have been used.
3 The project team was comprised of Professor Andrew Kam-Tuck Yip (Principal Investigator), Dr Michael Keenan (Co-Investigator), and Dr Sarah-Jane Page (Research Fellow). The research team is grateful for the *Religion and Society Programme* funding, as well as the invaluable contribution from the respondents, individuals, and groups who helped with the recruitment of the sample, and the members of the advisory committee. The project was funded by the *Arts and Humanities Research Council* and the *Economic and Social Research Council* under the *Religion and Society* Programme [Award no. AH/G014051/1].
4 The project team was comprised of Principal Investigator, Professor Pamela Dickey Young (Queen's University), Collaborator, Dr Heather Shipley (University of Ottawa), and Research Assistant, Ian Cuthbertson. It was funded by the *Religion and Diversity Project* (2010–2017), a Social Sciences and Humanities Research Council of Canada (SSHRC) Major Collaborative Research Initiative, led by Professor Lori G. Beaman, Project Director, University of Ottawa. The research team is grateful for the incredible support, financial and substantive, from the *Religion and Diversity Project* and the commitment that was made by Lori to ensure this project could be undertaken. All of the participants gave their time and personal narratives generously; this project was enabled by those contributions.
5 The project team was originally comprised of Dr Pam Lowe and Dr Graeme Hayes; Dr Sarah-Jane Page became involved from 2016. The current project team as of 2019 is comprised of Lowe and Page. The project is grateful for support from Aston University, and for those who have participated in the project.
6 Dr Sarah-Jane Page was the sole researcher. She is grateful for the funding provided by the *British Sociological Association's Sociology of Religion Study Group*, the interviewee participants, and those who helped with recruitment.
7 Dr Sarah-Jane Page conducted the thematic analysis in 2019. She hopes to be able to continue the analysis with a focus on further hearings, not just pertaining to the Church of England, but regarding other religious organisations too.
8 Dr Sarah-Jane Page undertook this project with funding provided by the ESRC (Award numbers PTA-031-2004-00290 and PTA-026-27-2911). She is grateful to the clergy who participated in the project, as well as the gatekeepers who assisted with recruitment.

# 1

# SITUATING SEXUALITIES AND RELIGION

## Place, space, and the body

## Introduction

The relationship between social theory and the study of religion and sexuality is a complex one. The sociology of religion has not traditionally focused on sexuality in any explicit way; only in recent years has there been an emerging focus on studies concerned with *both* religion and sexuality. The two are rarely studied as two equally important categories. Other issues have predominated in the sociology of religion, particularly the secularisation debate (Beckford, 2003; McKinnon and Trzebiatowska, 2014). Meanwhile, the study of sexuality within sociology has a much stronger history, thanks to queer and feminist scholarship. Yet the inclusion of religion into these accounts has been minimal; only rarely do edited collections on sexuality reference religion to any great extent (Stella *et al.*'s [2016] edited collection, *Sexuality, Citizenship and Belonging*, is unusual in dedicating a section to religion). There has traditionally been a gap, therefore, between the study of religion on the one hand, and the study of sexuality on the other. This impacts how theory is understood and applied to each of these research areas. In general terms, the sociology of religion has not been very adept at cultivating theoretical terminology to explain the contours of religion and sexuality, a result, to some extent, of the lack of scholarship in this area. Instead, it is the study of sexuality which has done the most leg-work in developing theoretical concepts and ideas that have been utilised by religion and sexuality scholarship. This is despite the fact that there are some concepts solidly developed within the sociology of religion which could be more fruitfully and consistently applied to the study of religion and sexuality (one example we will refer to later is lived religion). This is not an issue peculiar to the study of religion and sexuality. As Beckford (2003) and McKinnon and Trzebiatowska (2014) note, theoretical silos have emerged in broader terms between the discipline of sociology in general, and the sociology of religion specifically. The parameters of this chapter and the two that follow will largely sketch out how we conceptualise the theoretical terrain in relation to religion and sexuality. In this chapter, we specifically focus on place, space, and the body.

This chapter is not arranged by taking specific theorists in turn, nor does it prioritise the classical sociological theory of Marx, Weber, and Durkheim, where one can firmly locate the analysis of religion but find only brief references to gender and sexuality issues (Jackson and Scott, 2002). Readers interested in exploring the relationship between sexuality, religion, and classical theory should read Turner (2008), who has extrapolated their ideas in this regard – namely, examining Marx's understanding of the relationship between modes of production and sexuality regulation, and the relevance of Weber's theories regarding the Protestant ethic, forms of authority and patriarchy for understanding reproductive and bodily control. Also see Mellor and Shilling (2014), who utilise Weber and Durkheim to discuss sacrality in relation to the erotic.

This chapter is organised according to themes, within which theoretical concepts and ideas are discussed. The first section locates the study of religion and sexuality. The notion of time will then be examined more closely, particularly in relation to normative understandings of time and how sexual bodies are seen as fitting in or as displaced from this. Bodies are central to this location-based understanding, and we will articulate the relevance of embodiment to the study of sexuality and religion. We will also utilise scholarship from theology to further embed the importance we give to embodiment within the study of religion.

## Theoretical omissions: Integrating sexuality into the sociology of religion

To theorise is a contextual endeavour, situated in place and time. How we interpret social phenomena is grounded in particular contexts, impacted by places, spaces, and the body. This very book is imagined through our own social locations as researchers in two distinct places – the UK and Canada. These places impact on our ways of knowing, and our dominant understandings of social life. This knowledge is also embodied through our situatedness in terms of gender, ethnicity, age, social class, and (non)religious identity. As Boellstorff (2005) notes, as we undertake research, our very bodies and positionality in social life will impact on who we are able to talk to. This inevitably leads to blind spots, both in terms of the research under investigation and the types of theorisation we deploy. Following a Foucauldian line, Beattie (2004) argues that a feminist study of religion should be mindful of the power–knowledge configurations that structure the assembling of data and theory. She argues that self-reflexivity, and acknowledgement of situatedness, are needed to manage this. Meanwhile, Ahmed (2013) highlights the power dynamics embedded in researcher citation practices and how particular scholarship is represented. Who do we cite? Who gets omitted? And what impact does the erasure of authors' own gendered classed and raced bodies have on understanding knowledge production?

Most sexuality research and theorising has been undertaken through a Western lens. If non-Western contexts are examined, Western theorisation still becomes the default means of theorisation. This is a perpetuating cycle as classical theories of sexuality are reused and reinterpreted, solidifying the assumed importance of Western forms of knowledge, despite the way such theories are often blind to diversity in terms of gender, ethnicity, and class. Historical accounts typically analyse European contexts and the trends that have impacted Western societies. For example, Jackson *et al.*'s (2008) analysis of East Asian sexualities notes the Western hegemony and how other cultures become reified through Western eyes, arguing that recognising diversity is crucial to 'guard against the Western tendency to stereotype and exoticize the East' (2008, p. 3). These forms of exoticisation are rooted in racial hierarchies where certain bodies are coded in terms of their assumed ethnicity. In the process, whiteness comes to be deemed normative and the position from which other bodies are understood. This Western focus can also lead to misinterpretation, such as the way the hijra in India have been read as a "third sex" by scholars, disrupting traditional gendered dualisms, and used as evidence of gender fluidity. But as Marchal (2016) cautions, 'the situation of hijras is richer and more complicated than such a comparison can indicate' (2016, p. 316), and invoking Western notions of gender can undermine the historic and contemporary configurations of hijra identity that relate in complex ways to Hinduism and caste systems.

Similarly, much theorising within the sociology of religion has taken Western contexts (especially North America and Europe) as normative, with these interpretive frames being imposed on other places and spaces that have experienced power relationships very differently. Historical accounts, as well as contemporary studies, tend to prioritise Christianity over other religious identities, and this impacts on how data is theoretically situated. Taking Christianity as the normative object of study also creates theories that are reliant on a singular religious perspective (despite, of course, the diversity of Christian practice).

Theorising specifically within the sociology of religion has been somewhat elitist. McKinnon and Trzebiatowska (2014) note its politically right-leaning tendencies, leading to the exclusion of more marginalised voices and perspectives, such as queer, Black, and women's viewpoints (Woodhead, 2007a). Whereas sexuality scholarship has been reenergised in recent decades by taking feminist and queer theory seriously (though we acknowledge the historic tensions between these approaches – see Jackson and Scott [2010] for more information regarding this) – it is the case that theorisation within the sociology of religion has been far more conservative and reluctant to fully incorporate the experience of marginal voices into its theoretical assumptions. Although there have been a plethora of studies examining the relationship between religion and gender in recent decades, this collective knowledge is often dismissed or ignored when the dominant theoretical perspectives of the field are relayed, deemed 'an optional extra' (Woodhead, 2007a, p. 567). One example relates to secularisation. Secularisation theory has been the undergirding *raison d'être* of the sociology of religion, preoccupying much scholarly time and attention. Any undergraduate textbook on the sociology of religion will have at least one chapter devoted to the subject; often it is prioritised through its proximity to the front of the book. Yet as Aune *et al.* (2008) demonstrate, secularisation theory has been immune to any thorough gendered analysis (see also Woodhead, 2007a). The inclusion of gender is not simply about seeking recognition for women's lives and activities – an 'add women and stir' (Neitz, 2003, p. 292) approach. Rather, to take a gendered perspective alters the underpinning assumptions on which secularisation theory rests. Men's experiences are taken as the normative, so that 'when men leave religion, religion is said to be dying, regardless of its continuity in women's lives' (Vincett *et al.*, 2008, p. 5).

Women's engagement with religion is more complex, given the very different ways they were incorporated into the industrialising project and configured in relation to the public and private spheres (Vincett *et al.*, 2008; Woodhead, 2007a). Therefore, it is significant when, in the wake of 1960s sexual liberation, new forms of femininity – focused on independence and entitlement – emerged (Brown, 2001; Woodhead, 2008). Traditional churches were not dynamic enough to respond to and incorporate newer forms of femininity, and women's interest in such religious spaces waned, therefore leading to an exodus from mainline traditions (Brown, 2001; Joy, 2017; Woodhead, 2008). Yet this is not the full story. At the same time, women who find new gendered imaginings disconcerting seek out religious practices that affirm their more traditionally oriented femininities. Meanwhile, those women who eschew patriarchy as experienced through religious practices seek out alternative forms of spirituality (Woodhead, 2007a, 2008). As Neitz argues, 'For sociologists of religion, adding women is a dislocating act. New questions present themselves. Categories are problematised, and they can't so easily be re-established, generalizations don't hold' (2003, p. 292–3).

Starting from the perspective of gender emphasises important avenues of inquiry. As Woodhead (2007a) argues, power is fundamental to the study of gender, but power itself has been little-explored within the sociology of religion, despite the classical inheritance of Weber. Taking power into account matters when considering religion because religion itself is 'a system of power' (Woodhead, 2007a, p. 568). More work is needed to understand the impact of what Woodhead calls 'sacred power' (2007a, p. 569), and how this impacts the terrain of sexuality and gender. Such considerations have profound implications for understanding the role religion plays in either supporting or challenging traditional gendered and sexual orders. Utilising the work of Nason-Clark, Neitz (2003) highlights the new knowledge generated when domestic violence is situated in relation to religious cultures. Abuse is all at once understood as abhorrent but also challenging the notion of the sacred family, leading to complexity regarding the relationship between women's agency and religious authority. Parallels

**14** Situating sexualities and religion

can be drawn with queer perspectives. To what extent would the parameters of secularisation theory be altered were queer perspectives fully accounted for? For example, the importance accorded to heteronormative assumptions in many religions will potentially require extensive revision, given that not only queer young people but also heterosexual young people of a religious disposition take the issue of queer equality incredibly seriously (Yip and Page, 2013; Young and Shipley, 2020).

In short, this book takes seriously a new way of imagining social theory within the sociology of religion and offers some insights into how this project can be imagined. We will largely prioritise feminist and queer perspectives in this endeavour, thereby situating ourselves somewhat differently from the traditional sociology of religion scholarship. hooks stresses the power imbued through theorising from marginal spaces, in focusing 'on the center as well as on the margin' (2000, p. xvi). This also highlights the importance of an intersectional analysis when understanding the relationship between sexuality and religion. Although we have already emphasised gender, other key axes of identity are also paramount to understanding equalities and inequalities in relation to religion and sexuality, including ethnicity, age, and social class. We will return to the theme of intersectionality in Chapter 3.

## Locating sexuality and religion in time and space

The way in which spaces are constituted are not static but are subject to different flows and mediations. Globalisation is central to these processes, as religious ideas are taken up in new spaces, and people travel with their religious identities. Knott (2005) emphasises religion as the original globaliser, its own transformation apparent as it moves from one location to another. Knott ponders how the old homelands intersect with the new. While some forget their homeland entirely, choosing to focus on their new location, others retain strong ties and links with a homeland. This is akin to Tweed's (2006) idea of dwelling and crossing, where religion all at once resides in certain locations and simultaneously moves through places. Tweed notes how religion is contained in sites such as the home and the body, moving through space as those bodies travel as pilgrims or migrants. Equally, religion is embodied through the lifecourse, taking in the contours of birth and death, hope and despair. Tweed references the Feast Day to Our Lady, practised by Cuban Catholics living in Florida and exiled from their homeland. The Feast Day is an important reference point in remembering the homeland and introducing the next generation to Cuba – who have never even been there – to the history of exile. What these accounts offer is a rich engagement with the complexity of globalising bodies. Too often, there is a tendency to equate globalisation solely with the movement of fundamentalist ideas when referencing religion (Beckford, 2003), but here global flows and change are understood in diverse ways, sometimes engendering positive outcomes, and other times negative ones.

Sexualities too 'are the product of globalising forces' (Boellstorff, 2012, p. 171), "crossing" and "dwelling", just like religion. Boellstorff focuses on language and how sexualities are described is reappropriated and reconfigured due to globalisation. Words and identities circulate so that Western concepts such as "gay" are adopted elsewhere. Meanwhile, in other contexts, new words for similar sexual identities are forged. But Boellstorff is mindful that when the same word is deployed, or indeed when a different word is used, it does not mean that the term is identical to, or different from, its Western version. Language is contextual – the term "gay" does not even carry a singular definition in the West. Although terms such as "gay" and "lesbian" have been given international recognition through the gay liberation movement, they are also terms that invoke hierarchies.

Knott (2005) examines the spatial turn and its relevance to religion. The "secular" and the "religious" have been constructed in contrastive and binary terms. Knott contests this understanding, arguing that the secular and religious are entwined. One must start by analysing how space is constituted in terms of the religious and the secular, and how they are understood in relation to each other. Rather than seeing the religious and the secular in opposed camps – in that a space is *either* religious *or* secular – Knott contends that spaces are fluid and changeable; things and spaces which can be described as secular in one moment may be reinterpreted as religious in another. Knott emphasises 'how the two are entangled in the same *field*' (2005, p. 76, emphasis in original), and it is too simplistic to think that the religious and the secular can be separated. This is pertinent when thinking about sexuality, for seeing the religious and the secular in binary terms has also been the dominant means through which sexuality has been understood in relation to religion. As noted above, at one level, there has been a detachment between the two fields in terms of sociological analysis. The study of sexuality and the study of religion have traditionally been undertaken separately, with both fields largely excluding the other from its scope of analysis, leading to the utilisation of different theoretical frames. In addition, as will be detailed more fully in Chapter 2, religion has been dominantly constructed as a space in which sexuality rights are trampled on; the "secular" is perceived as the best place from which to protect and extend sexuality rights. While there is certainly a case to be made regarding negative religious discourses (indeed we will explore this more fully in Chapters 5 and 6), it is too simplistic to assert that religions are inherently problematic for sexual minorities; it is equally oversimplified to understand the secular as a space where sexuality rights can be guaranteed (Scott [2018] offers a clear case regarding how the construction of the secular has historically infringed the rights of women and sexual minorities). However, the divide that is understood as existing between the sexually negative "religious" and the sexually positive "secular" is analogous to Knott's discussion of the binary divide between the religious and the secular. Following Knott, it is more helpful to understand these fields as embedded in each other, so that how the religious and the sexual are constituted in relation to each other

**16** Situating sexualities and religion

can be examined. This also means being attentive to the relationship to the non-religious too, and how this is constituted in relation to sexuality.

Thus far we have articulated the importance of imagining space and context when understanding religion and sexuality, with recent configurations of religion being especially mindful of globalising forces and influences. But space as a concept is embedded in notions of time; bodies move concurrently through both. The relationship between subjectivity and time is socially constructed. Grosz (2005) notes that theoretical endeavours often implicitly reference concepts of time without fully acknowledging the underpinning temporality that governs their construction. For example, common-sense notions of sexuality often hinge around the idea of a "lifecourse", where the lifecourse pattern follows birth, marriage, reproduction, and death. This temporality would be recognised within many religious traditions, given the way these events are often memorialised and marked through religious ritual. Religions enact longstanding cultural codes and meaning-making, invoking strong frames of reference. But this conceptualisation of time – a notion that underpins many of our Western assumptions regarding the expected direction of our lives – is a construction of time, conceived in linear terms, and follows a heterosexual script, where reproduction is centralised, with each generation succeeding the next. Boellstorff (2007) calls this linear and heteronormative understanding of the lifecourse "straight time". Juxtaposing notions of queer time and straight time, Boellstorff (2007) emphasises the critical endeavour of queer theorists to question "straight time", and the potential of "queer time" to offer a challenge to "straight time", but he argues that political endeavours such as the desire for same-sex marriage can reimpose straight time narratives on queer lives. In other words, the salience of heterosexist patterns of time is so strong that to dismantle their construction and to queer them is difficult. Wilcox (2009) uses Boellstorff's conceptualisation of queer time to analyse how her queer spiritual participants related to time and lifecourse narratives, and the potential for queer life narratives to disrupt the saliency of straight time. For example, even the narrative device of "coming out" can have consequences for how one's life is imagined, potentially invoking more cyclical understandings of time over linear ones. Wilcox notes her participants' refusal to be linear in their accounts, instead moving backwards and forwards around significant events, reinterpreting past events in new ways. Wilcox notes how one participant understood the categories of "Jewish" and "lesbian" as oppositional and could not conceive of how they came together, even as she lived out her identity as a Jewish lesbian. Therefore, in one sense, the straight time narrative erased the possibility of linking together Judaism and lesbianism, while simultaneously a queer time narrative challenged this straight time conceptualisation. Wilcox's participant was living both/and, indicating the multiplicity of time, and how identities invoked in time can operate at numerous concurrent levels. As Grosz argues:

> Time functions "simultaneously" as present and as the past of that present. The future, which has no existence in the present, is generated through the

Situating sexualities and religion **17**

untimely reactivation of the virtuality of the past which has been unactualized in the present.... This double orientation of temporal movement – one force directed to the past, the other to the future – is the splitting of time, the generation of time's divided present, a present that is never fully present.

*(2005, pp. 3–4)*

How identities are oriented in relation to the past, present, and future is important to map when intimate lives are imagined, and how such orientations to time weave through both straight time and queer time narratives (indeed we will consider this in more detail in Chapter 5). Page *et al.* (2012) emphasise how the notion of the imagined future becomes an anchoring mechanism for religious young adults. By imagining their futures, young adults seek out their prospective identities, thereby conventionally adopting notions of linearity in their identity construction. While the notion of the imagined future is often deployed within sociological accounts of youth, it has not been as influential within the sociology of religion. What does it mean to imagine one's future intimate life in relation to religion? Page and Yip (2019) and Page *et al.* (2012) note the routinised futures that young adults are imagining – which often feature marriage and children – thereby reinscribing notions of straight time. Such procreative imperatives are encouraged within many religious traditions, such as Christianity, Judaism, and Islam, but also underpin many secular discourses too. The adopting of this "straight time" account was couched in terms of ambivalence; young women were already imagining anticipated gender inequalities when they embarked on motherhood. The inevitability of becoming mothers therefore structured their future orientations (Page and Yip, 2019). Yet, at the same time, these conventional narratives can be jolted with dramatic changes that are imagined by some participants as occurring at some future point. One Buddhist participant in a same-sex relationship actually envisaged a point in time when he would become a celibate Buddhist monk, thus revoking his existing relationship to enable this to happen (Page *et al.*, 2012). To envisage a change in one's life, especially that of a dramatic nature, is usually easier to contain when it is situated in the far distance, rather than imagining it in the short-term. Yet this research also demonstrated that privileged identities were able to fulfil the expectations to narrate a future-oriented self. Those participants who were currently in risky situations downplayed the future, due to the uncertainties it generated. This was especially the case for queer participants whose sexual identity was not supported within their broader religious community.

While dominant religious traditions such as Christianity encourage linear-based temporalities, other religious and spiritual traditions emphasise different time-based mediations, such as cyclical conceptualisations. Raphael (1999) explains the cyclical form that Goddess spirituality takes, where context and the body are embedded. Goddess spirituality resacralises women's bodies, in a context where many patriarchal traditions have denigrated them. This offers

**18** Situating sexualities and religion

the potential to celebrate bodily processes that are often deemed disdaining or even disgusting within Western formulations, such as menarche and menopause. Goddess spirituality concentrates on the temporal movement between the virgin, mother, and crone, explicitly rejecting hierarchical and patriarchal understandings of gender. In this process theology is displaced with *thealogy*. Whereas theology references a god, *thealogy* puts the goddess at its centre. Because of the challenges that *thealogy* makes to authorised forms of religion, and because it invests in a radically different understanding of the sacred, its relationship to the temporal also rejects the linear formations embedded in other traditions, as Raphael explains:

> thealogy occupies an interesting boundary territory: that of the time between times. It promises a post-patriarchal future that is at the same time something of a return to a pre-patriarchal past.
>
> *(1999, p. 51)*

In envisioning a movement away from patriarchy, thealogy embraces links between the past and the future, in an almost suspension of time itself. It is not wedded to one moment in time and instead links together different epochs. Yet at the same time, in imagining a more positive future, elements of linear temporality remain, in the sense that a narrative of linear progression is being invoked. So although Goddess spirituality and thealogy disrupt the dominant Western formulations of the temporal, it is much harder to fully dislodge its influence.

Ezzy's (2014) study of the Baphomet ritual within a Pagan group also indicates new spiritual–temporal imaginings. Baphomet is a goat-headed deity that many Pagans deem too controversial, especially due to its associations with the devil. However, Ezzy's ethnography maps a group dedicated to the Baphomet ritual, where the erotic is invoked. Although interest in the Baphomet ritual has centred on its sexual components, where some will participate skyclad (naked) and have sex, Ezzy situates the ritual in its broader contours, where followers desire to live a life 'with soul'. This is a meaning-making community-oriented form of ethics, where ritual is utilised for transformative effect. The ritual itself takes place in a remote area of Australian bush; people leave their everyday and ordinary lives behind. Donning special clothing, rejecting their usual schedules (e.g. by staying up all night), and taking up different performative roles creates an environment where time is suspended, 'a time out of time' (2014, p. 49) is created.

These examples emphasise that how time is imagined in religious and spiritual cultures is not inevitable; it also shifts and changes. Similarly, the relationship between sexuality and time is not static. Scientific and biomedical advances disrupt heteronormative forms of reproduction. Braidotti (2011) notes how technologies allowing eggs and embryos to be frozen enables reproductive time to be stalled, dislocating eggs and foetuses from the body from where they came. Sex and reproduction become decoupled, thereby changing notions of reproductive time and space. Certain religious traditions have taken issue with this "meddling", even from religions where fertility and procreation are highly prized, such as the Roman Catholic Church's condemnation of IVF. This undermining of authorised time–space configurations disrupts theologies that are heavily invested and reliant on tradition and unchanging social norms.

Meanwhile, Lowe (2016) demonstrates how the meanings generated when a pregnancy has begun have shifted considerably over time. Women's own bodily observations would have historically been the marker of their pregnancy status, where women themselves would have significant authority in determining their pregnancy. This has now been replaced with pregnancy kits so that women increasingly rely on scientific measures to confirm their pregnancy. The further development of tests that determine pregnancy before menstruation shifts these timescales again, increasing the likelihood that women who previously would have interpreted the onset of menstruation as a heavy period would now experience it as a lost pregnancy. Time–space configurations are therefore not static and are subject to change.

This section has emphasised the importance of mapping how space and time are constituted, recognising that this is never neutral, benign, or inevitable, but is constructed in particular ways. Subsequent chapters will develop these ideas further, especially how spaces are often configured in relation to power, with heterosexual bodies being privileged. Indeed, the next section will examine the notion of embodiment more closely, and the various ways in which certain bodies are excluded.

## Embodiment

We have emphasised the body as the interface between space and time. The concept of the body is at the centre of contemporary sociological thought (Howson, 2005) and sociologists of religion were at the forefront of scholarship that "rediscovered" the body, exemplified in Turner's *The Body and Society*, published in 1984 (here we reference the third edition, published in 2008). Although he focuses his attention on many aspects of bodily concern, a key thread taken up in Turner's book is the control of sexuality (and ultimately women's bodies) and how this relates to systems of religious thinking (although in practice his principal example is Christianity). This is read through the lens of classical sociological theory, Marx and Weber in particular, and Turner's account offers a lens in which to interpret the rather scant material these classical theorists offered on the issue of sexuality and the body. Turner also productively links classical sociological thinking with more contemporary theorists such as Foucault and Goffman.

Turner's core argument for our purposes is that religion has been a key mechanism in ensuring the laws of inheritance, so property passes through the line of sons, enabled through the control of women's bodies, and this has historically been theologically supported (especially in relation to feudalism and early capitalism). In the medieval period, surplus sons and daughters could be deployed

**20** Situating sexualities and religion

in the religious houses of the Roman Catholic Church. However, this type of regulation becomes unnecessary in contemporary formations of capitalism; religious control gives way to other disciplinary regimes, noted by Foucault as being administered through the state. Turner's key contribution in this regard is the consideration of sexuality in relation to secularisation, and how religion loses its function as a mechanism for the social control of women's bodies, as he argues in *Religion and Social Theory*:

> Because the economic system does not depend on concepts of honour, chastity or chivalry to secure the distribution of resources, capitalism is not disrupted by high levels of divorce, filial disobedience or nymphomania. In capitalism, deviance typically assumes a commercialised form which is wholly congruent with the economic patterns of "normal" culture. This is not to say that husbands do not prefer faithful wives, obedient daughters and loyal sons, while they themselves adhere to a double standard of sexuality. It is simply to argue that the capitalist economy is not dislocated when these patrimonial preferences are not realised.
>
> *(1983, p. 201)*

A similar argument is reproduced in *Body and Society* where Turner (2008) optimistically argues that patriarchy is diminished in late capitalism through the new orthodoxy of individualism, which displaces traditional authority based on the patriarch. Although early capitalists were able to accommodate individualism and subordinate women at the same time (through seeing women as appendages to men, they only became classified as individuals through their relationship to men) Turner argues that this becomes untenable in late forms of capital.[1] Indeed, Pateman (1988) gives a more convincing account of the way women are unable to be full citizens in early capitalism, offering a feminist analysis of the gendered components of social contract theory, as will be elucidated in Chapter 7. Turner's argument that patriarchy is undermined in late capitalism downplays the new forms of patriarchal inequality arising when women's financial capital increases. While Scharff's (2012) feminist analysis highlights the normative femininities that emerge (centred upon investment in bodily change, e.g. beauty therapies), Turner's own assessment of gendered embodiment (e.g. anorexia) is understood as economic regulation, without due regard to its patriarchal formations. He also downplays the contemporary forms of religious control of sexual activity, contraception, abortion, and reproduction (expanded upon in Chapter 8). He overplays the role of the economic, and despite his concern with bodies, his account is an overview of the interplay of religious and economic systems and the broad trends this has on gendered lives. In the process, real bodies are lost in his account, despite his attempts to reclaim the body. Given the recognition that it is women's bodies which are frequently impacted here, their real experiences of religious and economic systems are not expanded upon in Turner's account. He also fails to incorporate queer perspectives to any significant extent.

Mellor and Shilling also contribute to the discussion of embodiment within the sociology of religion. In various publications, Mellor and Shilling – individually and together – have utilised the body as a theoretical starting point, taking religion seriously in their analysis. Their theoretical approach is more closely tied to embodiment than Turner's, with a focus on the changing significance of the body in late modern, individualising, and secularising society. They note the rising obligations to our bodies, in order to extend their life, and avoid ill health, giving particular attention to the problem of death in a society where religious meaning systems wane (Shilling, 1993). *Re-forming the Body* (Mellor and Shilling, 1997) resonates with Turner's *Body and Society*, but whereas Turner's underpinning analysis is an economic one, and the changes brought about by differing means of production, Mellor and Shilling's offers a contrast between different religious forms and their embodied impact, namely the difference between Catholicism and Protestantism. They tread familiar ground to Turner, for our purposes, explaining the negative perception of women's bodies as forms of sin and temptation, with women's behaviour needing scrutiny lest they sully the family lines of inheritance through bearing illegitimate children. But they are more specific regarding the changes brought about within Protestantism, where the rule of the priest is displaced by the rule of the authoritarian father, who was invested to control the domestic sphere. This entailed a greater emphasis on childrearing, given the prevailing thinking that children were bearers of original sin, and needed to be disciplined to curtail their assumed inherent willful and evil nature. Meanwhile, Protestantism retained and re-emphasised women's role in reproduction, with Luther arguing that wives should be pregnant as much as possible. There were fewer spaces outside of married motherhood for women to occupy within Protestantism, given the closure of Catholic convents. Women desiring this were constructed as opposed to the essence of Christianity itself, through rejecting God's plan for them as child bearers. Their analysis also considers contemporary formulations of the body, termed the *baroque modern body*, and hinged around an attempted rejection of a Christian concern with sin to an adoption of new sensual forms, but these attempts to overcome the Protestant inheritance lead to new bodily anxieties and insecurities. Relationships become more transient and disposable; social contracts are more individuated and are more easily revoked, evidenced through rising rates of divorce. Although on the one hand this is advantageous to women, who can reject traditional gender roles, on the other hand, there are many choices to make and much more negotiation to do. Giddens' (1992) notion of the pure relationship, where intimate partnership is premised on choice and reciprocal consent so long as the relationship remains satisfying, is understood by Mellor and Shilling as the epitome of fractured sociality, given the fragile nature of such bonds. But their criticism emerges from the emphasis within the pure relationship on maintaining intimacy through talk and discursively disclosing one's desires and secrets rather than focusing on the physicality of sex. This removes the body from view and does not cohere with how real

**22** Situating sexualities and religion

bodies – and real relationships – operate. They end with a consideration of Bataille and the erotic, and the potentiality for our eroticism to reconnect our bodies with the sacred, in a way that the pure relationship – with its focus on talk – can never achieve. The implications of all of this – and how the broader contours of sexuality are reconfigured in the process – remains largely unclear; for example, similar to Turner, there is little analysis here regarding the part played by heterosexuality in the contemporary ordering system and what the implications are for erotic sensibilities, either in terms of gender or queer identity. One clue rests at the end of the book, where they discuss the morality of the contemporary city, and how relationships are fractured and shallow, but the outcome of this is an 'overriding moral expectation... that people will be left alone to live their lives as they want to' (1997, p. 199). This at least creates the possibility for the permissibility of various sexual relationships and configurations without moral censure and control, and also opens the door to wider acceptance of non-normative relationships. But it gives little indication regarding the relationship between real bodies having sex in an ethically considered environment. In Jung et al.'s (2005, n.p.) words, to what extent is 'good sex' prioritised, thereby overcoming the gender inequalities historically embedded in sexual relationships?

Mellor and Shilling's later work, *Sociology of the Sacred* (2014), does start to address these issues, in their analysis of both Weber's and Bataille's writings on eroticism and the sacred. Here their configuration rests on the concept of "the sacred" rather than religion. The underpinning idea conveyed is that the sacred cannot be contained within the religious, and instead can take non-religious formations. They create four ideal types of sacred modalities, which interact to either enhance or undermine religion. Indeed, this is a broader project in analysing forms of religious decline and resurgence. Specifically, on the issue of the erotic, they follow Weber, who theorised the erotic as a reaction against the iron cage of bureaucracy. They therefore emphasise that the erotic can take either a this-worldly or an other-worldly form. The former is depicted through its immanence and this-worldly groundedness, and the latter is understood as transcendent, such as erotic experiences garnered through highly charged religious experiences; St Teresa of Avila would be a good example. In terms of this-worldly eroticism, they recognise its gendered implications, in that it is women's bodies who suffer as a result of contemporary erotic formations – both in terms of intimate relationships and how consumer culture is sexualised. Meanwhile, they examine other-worldly eroticism principally in terms of the fetish, and how an intensity of feeling surrounding a given object can collectively create an erotic charge:

> religious images, icons and objects can be used to enhance the 'collective "orchestration" of the habitus' of religious groups. In seeking a common focus – whether this be using prayer mats to facilitate common prayer, a particular version of translation of the holy book, or a particular holy

image – individuals and groups can stimulate religious presence and maintain religious identities that possess a particular content and direction in relation to this-worldly and other-worldly matters.

*(Mellor and Shilling, 2014, p. 128)*

Their argument allows for conflicts between this-worldly and other-worldly forms of the erotic sacred to be examined, citing the example of the vilification of pornography by some Christian groups. Understanding the contours of the different forms of eroticism and their relationship to the sacred – of both secular and religious kinds – therefore offers a potentially strong theoretical framework for projects on sexuality and religion.

The notion of the sacred (invoking both religious and secular) is significant in gendered and queer terms, for the sacred has disavowed certain bodies. For example, Raphael has argued that patriarchal religion 'has owned women's bodies but disowned the sacrality of those bodies' (1996, p. 20). She details how religious spheres have constructed women's bodies as dangerous, defiling, and profaning, with menstruation being an archetypical illustration regarding how women's bodies are viewed. Women's seeming profanity has been used against them in taking up positions of religious authority, such as presiding as a priest at communion (Furlong, 1988; Page, 2011). She demonstrates how goddess spiritualities have done much to reappraise women's bodies, so that blood and birthing are sacredly reconfigured, and bodily encounters such as menstruation and menopause are positively reappraised (see also Raphael, 1999). It is therefore not inevitable that religious spaces denigrate women's bodies. But associating women's bodies with the profane run deep. Her argument is that although menstrual blood is reconfigured to some extent within secular cultures – it is no longer seen as dangerous in literal terms, for example – it is still bound up with feelings of shame and embarrassment, so that menstruation is heavily concealed by women and the sight or smell of menstrual blood continues to invite opprobrium.

Meanwhile, Jung (2005) interrogates embodied meanings of sexual activity, asking the provocative question: how many women in heterosexual relationships are having good sex? She notes the impact that religious sexual regulation – in this case Christianity – has had not only regarding how sexuality is broadly organised, but the intimate experience of sexual activity, where vaginal sex has been esteemed over other forms of sex such as masturbation and oral sex, saying 'The absence of sexual joy in so many women's lives is in part a consequence of the way good sex has been constructed in Christian moral traditions' (Jung, 2005, p. 83). She argues that a religious ethic surrounding sex should be premised on good sex and mutual forms of pleasure, instead of cultural scripts that privilege male pleasure only.

Isherwood and Stuart (1998) have examined the positioning of bodies that are deemed not to fit the sacred normative. Positioning their work within Christian theology, they argue that dualisms operating within Christianity – between

**24** Situating sexualities and religion

the sacred mind and the profaning body – have been extremely damaging, as men have been dominantly considered spiritual and women as bodily. This is despite the fact that the generosity of a woman's body – Mary's agreement to birth Christ – underpins the Christian story. They outline the struggle that women have had to convey their spirituality – citing Bynum, they note that the medieval women mystics would engage in extreme fasting to demonstrate their piety, given there was little else that women had control over. In a later work, Isherwood (2007) also reflects on Christian embodiment at a moment when women obtain more rights and access to the public sphere. As women's bodies occupy more spaces in society, new means of control are operationalised, so that women's bodies are contained. Repulsion to fatness – and the association of fatness with sinfulness – is one element to this. Given Christianity's aversion to the sensual woman and excessive sexuality, food is equally constructed as taking a sensual form and deemed in need of restriction, so that 'the female body will... shrink publicly' (2007, p. 20). Isherwood highlights the market within Christian diet cultures and fitness regimes encouraging women to "Slim for Him" – thereby adding a spiritual directive to be thin for Jesus. Isherwood successfully maps how trends noticeable in the broader secular culture interact in religious contexts to produce religiously driven outcomes that are not that far removed from secular narratives.

Isherwood and Stuart (1998) examine how these constructions have ongoing embodied legacies, such as the heavy regulation of sexual acts, even those that take place within marriage. For example, while early Protestants encouraged prayer before intercourse, contemporary Christian women are taught to be submissive in the bedroom, with a husband's pleasure prioritised (see also Jung *et al.*, 2005). This highlights the regulation of heterosexuality, which also has implications for queer bodies. Isherwood and Stuart argue that queer bodies need to be given space to speak their embodied experiences, given how they have been devalued. They examine this in relation to emotionality and Pride parades – within Christian discourse, pride has been deemed a sin, but this is recast to be a positive thing as queer people celebrate their bodies and seek justice through reclaiming the public space as their own, making visible their identities in a heteronormative environment.

Braidotti (2011) sees embodiment as challenging dualistic modes. Bodies are deemed complex; a multiplicity of features interrelate in diverse ways, in what she calls the nomadic body:

> Complexity is the key to understanding the multiple affective layers, complex temporal variables, and internally contradictory time and memory lines that frame our embodied existence. In contrast to the oppositions created by a dualistic mode of social constructivism, a nomadic body is a threshold of transformations. It is the complex interplay of the highly constructed social and symbolic forces. The body is a surface of intensities and an affective field in interaction with others. In other words, feminist

emphasis on embodiment goes hand in hand with a radical rejection of essentialism.

*(Braidotti, 2011, p. 25)*

Braidotti captures the movement and stasis of bodies, their deployment in space, place, and time, thereby reconnecting to some of the themes we emphasised earlier – indeed, the notion of the nomadic body correlates well with Tweed's notion of religion as crossing and dwelling. Here, bodies are understood in terms of emplacement and displacement, margins and centres, insides and outsides. She explains how bodies are branded through place – coming from a particular location will engender a certain set of meanings; bodies from the "wrong" place can be negatively branded. She references her own migratory history, and how her Italian roots were never "white" enough when she migrated to Australia. This is similar to Puwar's (2004) work on bodies out of place, with some bodies made to feel like they belong – others are constructed as space invaders. This is pertinent to religious spaces, where certain bodies – queer bodies, Black bodies, women's bodies – have been constructed as not belonging. But equally, it is also reminiscent of how religious bodies have also been denied validation, such as queer Muslim bodies denied access at border control, or hijab-wearing Muslim women banned from the public sphere in some European countries.

Braidotti's is an anti-essentialist embodiment underscored through sexual difference. Although poststructuralist feminists have deemed sexual difference to be hugely problematic, Braidotti resituates it in an anti-essentialist terrain so that politics can be achieved. Both the material and the post-structural are incorporated in the process. This is very much a political project to challenge injustice. In order to do this, she understands sexual difference in a highly complex way, consisting of three dimensions. Firstly, a mapping of the varying subjectivities of men and women and how women may desire to enact a different kind of selfhood to men; secondly, the different subjectivities that emerge *between* women, and their differing experiences and identities; and finally, the embodied subject as signified in discourse and lived embodied experience, encapsulating the fluidity and variability of a singular identity. In this way, she is able to account for bodies as multiply positioned, subject to change, and embedded in networks and processes of power, and how this leads to marginalisation and exclusion. The reason for retaining the notion of sexual difference is to politically embed her embodied project:

> The nomadic subject I am proposing is a figuration that emphasizes the need for action both at the level of identity, of subjectivity, and of differences among women. These different requirements correspond to different moments, that is to say, different locations in space, that is to say, different practices. This multiplicity is contained in a temporal sequence whereby discontinuities and even contradictions can find a place.
>
> *(Braidotti, 2011, p. 164)*

**26** Situating sexualities and religion

In terms of religion, Braidotti considers the role of a religious subjectivity within political mobilisation, understanding this in terms of a "post-secular" sensibility. While traditionally feminists have understood religion in terms of oppression, with no consideration for its potentiality as a site for emancipation, Braidotti instead argues that forms of religious piety can cultivate new modes of political action, centred upon an 'ethics of becoming' (2008, p. 19), where spiritualities allow and enable individuals to imagine and seek out alternative futures. Faith is at the heart of this subjectivity; she notes that even secular politics is underscored by faith *in something*. While religious systems can indeed be oppressive – indeed, continuing with Braidotti later in the chapter, we will discuss the implications of religious interventions into reproductive technologies – they can also cultivate subjectivities motivated to achieve ethical forms of action, something that feminists specialising in gender and religion have understood for a long time. In conceptualising religion and sexuality, this offers a framework for examining what political subjectivities are produced within religious modes to cultivate emancipatory forms of action – indeed, it is the nomads – those at the margins, who move between spaces and encounter feelings of insecurity – who are best-placed to understand flux and imagine new futures (hooks, 2000). At the same time, Braidotti does not privilege sexuality as a basis for identity-formation and critiques the heightened emphasis on heteronormativity as a key determinant of power-based inequality; her Foucauldian approach to understanding power means that, in her view, such a construction solidifies power relations in one location, when she understands power more fluidly and network-like.

Although the body has been a longstanding site for analysis by sociologists of religion, the significance in terms of sexuality is only starting to be fully articulated, especially through feminist and queer scholarship. At the same time, studies of embodiment and religion have tended to prioritise gendered embodiment with sexuality being referenced in relation to the gendered implications of sexual inequalities. This means that women have typically been the focus of embodied accounts, particularly in relation to how reproductive technologies impact them, but this can overshadow the ways in which men too are embodied.

More recently, Brintnall's (2016) exposition of religion and embodiment foregrounds sexuality. Taking embodiment as the starting point, Brintnall firmly links religious embodiment with desire. As religious bodies desire connection to the transcendent, in whatever form that takes, the body's relationship to desire will be cultivated through religious norms – this may be where food is restricted or consumed, where special clothes or no clothes are worn, and where sexual desires are encouraged or denied. Therefore, Brintnall opens up the broader possibilities of imagining an embodied understanding of religion. This firmly rejects accounts of religion which have in the past ignored the body, or ignored sexuality. This also enables a more holistic understanding, for the starting point is the religious body, thereby implicitly recognising the varying ways in which embodiment and religion are linked together. As Knott articulates:

In the West, individuals are normally marked as "either/or", rather than an amalgam of both. They are either male or female, destined for heaven or hell, religious or secular/non-religious. It is only with the development of critical discourses of androgyny, bi-sexuality, the hyphenation of identity, hybridity, third-space, and post-secular religiosity that we begin to see the creative exploration of the embodied engagement of differences... The question remains, however, whether such explorations constitute the opening up of a new third option or alterative space, a "space of representation". Which is more than just the sum of two parts or a critique of two former positions or poles.

*(2005, p. 199)*

Therefore, embodied approaches offer a broader perspective to understanding subjectivity, and open up, rather than close down, potentiality. As Knott notes in the above quotation, taking an embodied approach enables binary oppositions such as male/female and religious/secular to be undermined; if the starting point is the experience of the body, it means that long-standing categories such as the "religious" may become untenable or unintelligible. Taking embodied experience as a starting point is closely linked with the concept of lived religion, which we will return to in Chapter 3. One of the key architects of the concept of lived religion, McGuire, was an early advocate for taking embodiment seriously in the study of religion (McGuire, 1990), emphasising that religion is experienced through real material bodies, and our perception of the world is imagined from an embodied perspective. This understanding underpins a radical re-examination of how we conceptualise religion itself, for if we focus on embodiment and 'personal religious experience and expression' instead of viewing religion through the lens of institutions, religion becomes 'an ever-changing, multifaceted, often messy – even contradictory – amalgam of beliefs and practices that are not necessarily those religious institutions consider important' (McGuire, 2008, p. 4).

## Summary

This chapter has demonstrated the need for closer attention to the theorisation of religion and sexuality. We have noted the disjunctures that have arisen between the study of religion and the study of sexuality, and the way that theoretically, there can be a lack of connection between the two. We have noted the importance of theorising in relation to time and space and recognising the way these are socially constructed. We have also examined the way embodiment is a particularly important and significant lens through which to understand context and how theories are lived out in bodies. Embodiment also challenges certain dualisms that have emerged in relation to religion and sexuality, such as the mind/body dualism and the sacred/secular dualism, and helps to complicate identities to recognise multiplicity and complexity. Bodies are constituted in a multiplicity

## 28 Situating sexualities and religion

of ways connected to the religious, the sexual, gender, ethnicity, and class among others. These bodies are also embedded in socially constructed time and space locations, with context – and its configuration – having a significant impact on how bodies encounter the spaces in which they are located. We have noted that the sacred cannot be located solely with the religious and that identities are cultivated in both sacred and secular spaces. The next chapter will focus on the relationship between bodies and regulation, and how sexual and gendered religious bodies come to be regulated within social life.

## Note

1 It must also be acknowledged that there are forms of authority that are not represented in Turner's work, not only in terms of male property ownership, but also the bodily autonomy denied to slaves brought to North America, and treaties which "guaranteed" land ownership and rights to Indigenous communities that were routinely violated.

# 2

# UNDERSTANDING SEXUALITIES AND RELIGION THROUGH CENSURE AND CONTROL

## Introduction

Religion is commonly understood as a mechanism for the control of sexuality, with the decreasing influence of religion (in particular Christianity) in many Western societies deemed a good thing in relation to sexual and reproductive rights. However, the association of religion with regulation, and conversely secularity with freedom, is oversimplified, especially given the role other societal institutions play in the regulation of sexuality. This chapter comprises three themes in considering the relationship between sexuality and religion, and the notion of censure and control. Firstly, we will examine the dominance of the notion of *Secularisation* to the sociology of religion. We will not rehearse all of the debates pertaining to secularisation here; our aim is to specifically tease out the role sexuality has played in the construction of the concept. In the next theme, *Surveillance and Biopower*, we will examine Foucault as a key architect of the theorisation of the displacement of Christianity in the regulation of sexuality, and how new secular techniques of power take hold in disciplining the body. But this displacement of religion will be questioned through examining Mishtal's (2015) empirical investigation of sexuality in Poland. The final theme, *Organising Normatives*, will examine the concepts of heteronormativity, homonormativity, and homonationalism in order to understand the contemporary configurations of religion, sexuality, and control in more detail, ending with Puar's work on the global significance of dominant discourses which reify both religion and sexuality in various ways.

## Secularisation

As previously highlighted in Chapter 1, the theory of secularisation has typically not incorporated the issue of sexuality. Standard overview accounts of

**30** Censure and control

secularisation typically reflect on the ways in which the classical sociological theories of Marx, Weber, and Durkheim mapped the declining significance of religion (read: Christianity) in modernity, include a definition of secularisation and the contestations around this, and an analysis of what is happening in contemporary society, with varying interpretations offered. The overarching trends are then typically mapped, for example, the relationship of religion to the state may be examined, or the extent to which contemporary forms of choice in religious belonging are consumerist in nature, or whether religious identities are being successfully "passed on" to the next generation. Sexuality itself is of tangential concern, a footnote rather than a major driver of secularisation processes.

This format was challenged with the publication of Brown's (2001) book, *The Death of Christian Britain*. Brown's historical analysis emphasised a causal link between the death of Christianity and women's opting out of the churches in the 1960s, when Christianity starts to dramatically decline. Up to this point, Brown demonstrates how women not only bolstered, but pretty much maintained, the cogency of the churches, through the free labour they provided, even though ordained leadership was typically denied them. This was cultivated through how feminine piety had been envisioned throughout the Victorian period, where middle-class women became the guardians of Christian faithfulness. Women opted into this; their role in the private sphere was limited, and charity work enabled a much greater role than that offered in their "ordained" domestic roles. Indeed, this feminine piety was connected with respectability, and sexual purity was crucial to its enactment. Single unmarried women were to be chaste and wholesome; married women were to be dependable mothers and wives, faithful to their husbands and devoted to their children. It was this sexual propriety and good moral standing that gave certain women (white, middle-class) access to esteemed social roles in the church; sexuality and gender were therefore entwined. Meanwhile, respectable masculinity was not similarly dependent on Christian belonging. Men could therefore legitimately opt out of the churches earlier. Brown's argument is that traditional secularisation theory has mapped only the exit of men from the churches. It was only when respectable forms of femininity too did not depend on Christian piety, and they also became uncoupled from Christian belonging, that women also deserted the churches, with secularisation becoming inevitable. As soon as women's labour was withdrawn from churches, the churches faced immediate decline. While criticisms have been made of Brown's work (e.g. he exclusively focuses on Protestantism – Geiringer, 2019), Brown does challenge long-held assumptions that have dismissed the role of sexuality and gender.

Vincett *et al.* (2008) develop some of Brown's ideas, emphasising that the history of secularisation has been the history of men – not queer people or women – offering a contemporary analysis regarding how religion, gender, and secularisation can be understood in the modern world. Their approach emphasises the importance of moving beyond Christianity to understand how other religious identities mirror or contest secularising processes. The assumption that a woman entering the workplace will lose their religious identity to some extent may be assuming a Christianised perspective, which may not follow for other religious groups, such as for Muslim women, especially given the importance for Muslim women in displaying their religious identity publicly. Indeed, many of the chapters within their edited collection focus on the complex negotiation of religion in contemporary society, contesting the idea that all women have ceased being religious, and questioning the extent to which Christianity no longer enacts a disciplining force on women's sexuality. Sharma's (2008) research on young Christian women in the UK and Canada examines how the notions of "good" and "bad" still regulate women's behaviour, where chastity and marriage are upheld as ideals. At the same time, Sharma notes that those participants who could not succeed in enacting a pious femininity that accorded with the values of their churches simply left Christianity – leaving was therefore a viable option. This corresponds with Heelas and Woodhead's (2005) notion of the subjective turn, where people draw on subjective experiences, such as their own feelings and their desires in their religious choices, and become less bound to tradition and religious institutions.

Whereas Sharma mapped the impact on institutional disaffiliation for heterosexual young women who can no longer subscribe to the strict sexual codes of their churches, Yip has done the same in relation to lesbian, gay, and bisexual (LGB) Christians, arguing similarly that 'the self plays a far greater role than church authority as the basis of the respondents' Christian faith' (2003, p. 136), where one's personal experience triumphs over tradition or doctrine. Yip articulates that distancing oneself from the institution can become a necessity for self-preservation and self-acceptance for LGB Christians, so that spirituality is instead cultivated outside of institutional contexts. The fact that Sharma's and Yip's participants can successfully leave without reputational repercussions is an important one; as Brown (2001) notes, historically, this would not have been possible in Britain, especially for "respectable" women to eschew a pious Christian identity. Zuckerman (2012) emphasises the pivotal role sexual activity can have for religious practitioners reassessing their priorities, so that religion is fully rejected. In one stark assessment, one participant 'lost his virginity, along with his faith' (2012, p. 81). Meanwhile, in other social contexts, the regulatory mechanism of belonging to a religious institution remains strong. Amakor's (2019) investigation of unmarried Christian mothers in Nigeria highlights how the option to leave church – even in the face of much judgement and condemnation from fellow parishioners due to their "sinful" actions – is rarely an option and can further denigrate one's social status.

Such studies point to the potentiality of successfully rejecting dominant religious discourses and using one's own subjectivity and desires as the basis for this. As Woodhead argues, this '"turn to the self" has been a major factor in secularization' (2007b, p. 239). Increasing dissatisfaction with institutional Christian discourses about sex was a key impetus for disaffiliation following the sexual revolution of the 1960s. Woodhead (2007b) notes how women in particular

## 32 Censure and control

were more likely to challenge how their sexuality was silenced by dominant church discourses, with the Roman Catholic encyclical, *Humanae Vitae* of 1968, epitomising the limiting choice church authorities were willing to give Catholic women in their own sexual lives, leading many to question why they should be subservient to this authority (see also Geiringer, 2019). Meanwhile, Woodhead (2007b) notes that since the 1960s some churches have entrenched their messages about sexual conservatism ever-further, bolstering numbers through appealing to a minority opposed to liberalising sexual values.

Thus far we have largely presented the question of secularisation from the perspective of individuals, and the choices made regarding whether belonging to a religion offers coherence to one's identity. This is one key strand of secularisation theory — the extent to which individuals belonging to religions is diminishing. While traditional forms of religiosity have managed to bolster individual respectability, especially for women (Woodhead, 2007b), this has altered significantly since the 1960s, and in many Western liberal contexts, religious belonging becomes optional. However, another means through which secularisation can be considered is the role that religions play in relation to the public sphere, and especially state processes. An assumption embedded within secularisation theory is that religion starts to lose its public sphere influence and authority. But this is a notion that has been contested by theorists such as Casanova (1994), who argues that in the latter half of the 20th century, religion was deprivatised and started to take on a significant role in the public sphere. For example, Vaggione (2002) notes the lobbying role that the Roman Catholic Church plays in many societies in promoting conservative sexual values, which are explicitly contrary to feminist endeavours and queer rights. While individuals may choose not to be personally religious, they may still be implicated in religious norms through the way in which religion helps to regulate sexuality at a state level.

Jakobsen and Pellegrini (2004), for example, analyse the US context — despite the official separation of church and state, their argument, through an analysis of case law, is that Protestant Christianity continues to regulate the management of sex. This is through the "family values" narratives that are espoused at a state level, which epitomise the so-called "good life", where monogamy, heterosexuality, and reproduction in marriage is privileged. These values are not recognised as religious in nature; they are so historically ingrained that they come to be viewed as religiously neutral. They discuss the ways in which certain sexual practices — in particular homosexuality — come to be seen as immoral, in a discourse that often fails to recognise the religious basis of the morality being espoused, so that the secular state uses religious ideas, even if they are not labelled as such. Jakobsen and Pellegrini examine the heteronormative assumptions underpinning the case of *Bowers v. Hardwick* (1986). This was a Supreme Court case to determine whether the anti-sodomy statute in the state of Georgia was constitutional. As they wryly note, 'Apparently some sex acts are so far from being moral that even privacy and consent do not insulate them from government interference' (2004, p. 23). The defendant in the case, a gay man, had been arrested in his own bedroom. As a Supreme Court ruling, their judgement had resonance for all the other states that at the time upheld similar laws (it has since been overturned) but the argument to uphold the statute was based on the idea that "sodomy" (meaning here oral and/or anal sex of either a heterosexual or homosexual nature) was an unquestionable affront to morality. Reference was made to the 'weight of moral tradition' (2004, p. 29) against sodomy, but this treatment of sodomy corresponds with a Christian legacy, and how some Christian traditions have historically interpreted sodomy. To confirm this point, one justice in the case even invoked the 'Judaeo-Christian moral and ethical standards' (2004, p. 30) on which the judgement should rest, even at the same time enacting a judgement in a context of church-state separation, giving no account of the complexities inherent within both Jewish and Christian traditions, and instead collapsing both religious traditions together. Lest this could be deemed an egalitarian judgement, the unevenness with which the statute applied was laid bare when a heterosexual couple argued their own potential culpability in breaking the law, but this was dismissed. It was homosexual sexual acts, and not heterosexual ones, which were on trial, and an embedded conservative religious morality was being deployed to secure its prohibition.

One of the values that Jakobsen and Pellegrini (2004) interrogate is the notion of tolerance. This is esteemed as a great liberal ideal, seemingly offering inclusivity to those with diverse identities. Yet at the outset, the concept of tolerance marks out those who are to be tolerant, and those who are to be tolerated, creating an unequal power relationship. The "tolerant" are constructed as normative, but this normative is defined through 'maleness, heterosexuality, whiteness, or Christianness' and these 'are so taken for granted and naturalized in the United States that they function as the very measure of the human' (2004, p. 118–9). Tolerance as a liberal value therefore needs to be questioned:

> It is sometimes difficult to see what's wrong with tolerance because tolerance is so often invoked as the best response to discrimination and hatred... However, tolerance doesn't really fight the problem of hatred; it maintains the very structures of hierarchy and discrimination on which hatred is based... tolerance establishes a hierarchical relation between a dominant center and its margins.
>
> *(Jakobsen and Pellegrini, 2004, p. 50)*

They note how this played out in the 1996 Supreme Court case of *Romer v. Evans*, where Colorado's attempt to enshrine sexual orientation discrimination was overturned. Although on the surface this can be seen in positive terms, Jakobsen and Pellegrini analyse how this created a legal contradiction; the *Hardwick* ruling prohibited oral and anal sexual acts, but *Romer* protected homosexual identity – in other words, we will tolerate your sexual orientation but we will not tolerate your sexual preferences. In this way, homosexuals were tolerated only to a given extent and were not deemed equal citizens.

**34** Censure and control

Jakobsen and Pellegrini's analysis of recent US history emphasises the continuing legacy of religious normatives that can have a bearing even in contexts that claim to be secular. Next we turn to a similar but at the same time different example, France. France also claims its identity as a secular state, enshrined in the concept of *laïcité*, which consolidates the separation of church and state. However, the basis for secularity in the US and France differ markedly. Whereas in the US, the individual is theoretically protected from religious interference, in France, it is the state which is protected. This has meant particular sexual regulations for certain religious bodies in the French context – namely Muslims. Davie (2007) emphasises the ways in which the French context is hugely ambivalent and even hostile to religious minorities. The institution of *laïcité* in 1905 was a clear rebuttal to the Roman Catholic Church and an entrenching of its subordinate status to the state. Embedded in the concept of *laïcité* is 'a widespread and very French belief that religion... might be a threat to freedom' (2007, p. 162), and those religions that are not "like" Christianity – such as New Religious Movements and Islam – are singled out for particular concern. This is compounded within Islam, given the way religious practice is not easily subsumed into the private sphere. Davie notes how this contestation came to a head in the *l'affaire du foulard* – the headscarves affair of 1989 – where three girls were sent home from school for wearing the hijab. Indeed, the French understanding of *laïcité* is such that one should be a neutrally perceived French citizen in the public sphere – this is deemed a successful marker of integration – and any notion of a religious identity on display in the public sphere is deemed a threat to this. To be French is therefore to be secular; wearing a headscarf puts into question one's citizenship status as French. Fernando (2017) examines the impact this has in relation to the state regulation of Muslim sexuality in France, noting that Muslim women have to "prove" their normative sexuality to satisfy the demands of the French state. Therefore, in the French case, both sexuality *and* religion are under surveillance when one's religious identity is deemed subject to suspicion. Examples Fernando cites are regarding the way the veil is constructed as all at once hiding and revealing sexuality; secular dress is constructed in terms of making the female body visible (short skirts; shoulders on display) and the veil is constructed as obstructing that gaze, but in the process sets up other sexualised gazes. Scott makes a similar point, arguing that 'an entire vision of national identity is said to rest on the visual availability to men of women's sexualized bodies' (2018, p. 181). Meanwhile, Selby (2014) examines the Parisian riots of 2005 that occurred in Muslim-majority areas, this time emphasising not only the intersection of gender and religion, but social class too. The electrocution of three young men who believed they were being pursued by police in an area where racial profiling was rife incited negative comments from government officials about the victims, which led to riots. But the media focus that followed centred on the issue of polygamy – the idea that the Muslim families in the riot locations had lost control of their children because, was the inference, they had too many; this was buttressed with the claim that many families were polygamous in nature. This shifted the blame from a lack of resources and racist policing practices to be the fault of the sexual practices of a poor religious minority.

Thus far we have examined various components of secularisation, both in terms of people individually opting out of religion, and the role that secular states play in regulating both religion and sexuality. We have already noted that in terms of religion, it is particular minority religious groups – specifically Muslims – who are singled out for scrutiny at a state-sanctioned level. We now turn to the work of Scott, whose concept is not secularisation per se, which she takes to be the academic study of religious decline in the wake of state control of religion in Western Europe, but secular*ism*. She treats secularism as a dominant discourse that has operated since the Enlightenment, but it takes on new meanings in contemporary society:

> In the eighteenth and nineteenth centuries, secularism was deemed the progressive alternative to religion – the sign of the advance of civilization. In our current context it is portrayed as a practice threatened by the return of religion, specifically Islam.
>
> *(Scott, 2018, p. 9)*

In this discourse, all religions are deemed problematic, but in the contemporary period, Islam in particular is emphasised – 'In this discourse secularism guarantees freedom and gender equality while Islam is synonymous with oppression' (Scott, 2018, p. 1). The basis for this discourse is that secularism is the best position from which to articulate rights and freedoms; that the inherent nature of secularism would ensure that equality norms prevail. It is regarding gender equality and sexuality where the terrain is fought – these are singled out as being liberated in contexts of secularism, and oppressed in contexts of religion. Indeed, certain strands of secular feminism take up this cause with gusto, for example, interpreting forms of Islamic veiling in wholly oppressive terms without fully accounting for context, and uncritically endorsing the perception that Islam is inherently patriarchal (see also Mahmood, 2011).

Scott (2018) comes to the same conclusion as Jakobsen and Pellegrini (2004) regarding the way Christianity becomes embedded in notions of Western democracy so as to be neutralised. This means that privileges are accorded Christian practices that are not given to other religious groups, such as the way crucifixes in some European countries become equated with the "culture" of the country in question and thereby become reified in terms of the secular. Meanwhile, Islam is singled out in particular as being oppressive to women and sexual minorities. The premise of Scott's argument is to challenge the basis of this discourse, and to argue that the roots of secularism do not invoke gender and sexual equality at all. Instead, the Enlightenment processes where church and state were separated were in fact premised on gender and sexual *in*equality. For example, Scott (2018) notes how new investigative techniques premised on scientific inquiry were utilised to determine the biological differences between men and women,

**36** Censure and control

thereby confirming the perception that men were naturally born to lead and dominate. Meanwhile, discourses of biology and nature supported the institution of marriage, seeing it as naturally inevitable and a marker of civilisation. Religious discourse was therefore displaced with biological determinism; the inferiority of women and the condemnation of homosexuality were not just perpetuated within this new discourse – they were enshrined and deemed fundamental, further evidenced in the long struggle women had to obtain the vote within Western democracies.

A key benefit of Scott's (2018) approach is to specify exactly what discourses are at work regarding secularism, and what alliances are being made when "the secular" is invoked as the only means through which liberation can be achieved. Such discourses have a powerful part to play in denigrating or denying the subjectivities of certain religious bodies.

In summary, secularisation has been premised on two dimensions – the declining significance of religion in the public sphere and its relocation to the private sphere – and the declining numbers of individuals who are privately religious. This public/private juxtaposition has undergirded the parameters of secularisation theory. While sexuality has not been an integral aspect to standard theorising in relation to secularisation, we have here sketched out the implications in Western societies.

Firstly, the individual rejection of sexual morality as supported by many Christian churches (e.g. opposition to sex before marriage, divorce, same-sex relationships), and a desire for sexual ethics to be individually negotiated instead of being inscribed through church authority. Sexual matters become one reason for disaffiliation. Although this may compromise the vitality of certain churches, it is actually the mainline churches that lose the most footfall (Woodhead, 2007b). Sexually conservative churches paradoxically bolster their numbers, as those who reject the liberalising sexual values of society at large seek out a like-minded space where conservative values are endorsed. Meanwhile, individuals who leave churches on the basis of sexuality do not necessarily reject religion – just its organised formations. Instead they may seek out alternative ways of being religious. Women critical of patriarchal forms of religion may turn to goddess spirituality (Vincett, 2008). Queer people may formulate new kinds of religiosity that are cultivated through their own resources instead of institutionally, or they may join spaces that are explicitly inclusive of their sexuality, such as the Metropolitan Community Church, originally set up by a gay man in order to cater to queer Christians (Taylor and Snowdon, 2014a; Wilcox, 2009; Yip, 2005). In addition, the theory of secularisation has privileged Christianity and the extent to which Christian belonging in Western societies is waning. Migration into Western societies of other religious groups who retain stronger affiliations to their respective religious traditions, along with buoyant levels of commitment to religion in many societies outside of the West, complicates any easy understanding of the relationship between individualism and religious identity. And even those professing a queer identity may still choose to remain within the institutional religious context (Wilcox, 2009; Yip, 2005; Yip and Page, 2013).

Secondly, the prevailing assumption is that religion loses its function and influence in the public sphere, and this enables gender and sexual rights to be secured, as traditional forms of religiosity are privatised and have no longstanding public influence. Individuals may choose to belong to a conservative religious tradition but this does not influence the public sphere in any significant way. Yet this assumption – of the privatisation of religion and its loss of public function – has been questioned, and instead, authors such as Casanova (1994) have persuasively argued that religion's role has been recalibrated in the public sphere to potentially be more influential, rather than less. The continuing influence of religion in public life has been met with alarm by individuals who see religion as indiscriminately opposed to sexual and gender equalities. Here we have examined the secular states of the USA and France to explore that the way the secular state is imagined has an enormous impact in the way individuals themselves are regulated by religion and/or the state, noting that religious influence can have far-reaching implications for the regulation of sexuality in seemingly secular contexts, and the way that religious and sexual minorities can be implicated in these forms of regulation. Importantly, the binary enacted between the secular and the religious becomes untenable; neither the secular nor the religious can lay claim to being the space from which sexuality and gender rights can be secured. It is more accurate to say that rights are articulated in complex ways in relation to both secular and religious mediations. And as Scott's work indicates, it also begs the question of why is it at this particular moment in time that sexual and gender rights become the focus of attention, generating much international currency. Indeed, the way nation states imagine themselves in relation to gender and sexual equalities are not undertaken in a vacuum but operate on a larger world stage, subject to its own rationales that may actually have little to do with a real desire for gender and sexuality rights. The rest of the chapter will examine this more closely, starting with Foucault's theorisation of sexuality and biopower.

## Surveillance and biopower

As Chapter 1 highlighted, the body has been implicated in many religious traditions, particularly within Christianity, as a site of surveillance, with individuals themselves becoming responsible for ensuring their body falls in line with particular bodily expectations (Harvey, 2013). Foucault's poststructural insights have been influential in this regard. This internalisation of embodied practices often references his concepts such as technologies of the self and biopower. Although we recognise Foucault's shortcomings, given his narrow – even elitist – focus and, crucially, his exclusion of a gendered analysis, his theories do offer much purchase to analyse systems of power that can be fruitfully applied to other areas (Butler, 1990; Ramazanoglu, 1993).

**38** Censure and control

Foucault focuses on the various discourses at play within a given society, starting his *The History of Sexuality Part I* by debunking the idea that the Victorians were non-vocal on matters of sex. He argues that instead of sexual matters being silenced, there emerged 'a steady proliferation of discourses concerned with sex' (1976, p. 18), with various fields of institutional power setting themselves up as sexual authorities. Foucault examines how the church itself was the original authorised institution to determine licit from illicit sex, with the confession acting as a powerful tool in regulating the sins of the flesh and metering out suitable penance. He discusses the detail that confessionals went into regarding the type and manner of sexual activity – the positions, what was touched, what generated pleasure – so that language itself was the method of regulation. The individual was compelled to comply and disclose all, lest they jeopardise salvation itself. The precedent achieved in the Roman Catholic Church was later extended when new forms of governance took hold; the classification of sexuality that fitted into new rational systems of thought. The notion of population comes into parlance, 'with its specific phenomena and its peculiar variables: birth and death rates, life expectancy, fertility, state of health, frequency of illnesses, patterns of diet and habitation' (1976, p. 25). Sexuality became subject to scientifically rational means, endorsed through counting and measurement. Although sexual morality – and what was deemed a sexual sin or not – was no longer the principal motivation, the underlying desire to determine what was deemed "normal" and "abnormal" sexual activity remained, given the focus on procreative forms of sexual activity and the extent to which births taking place were "legitimate" or not. It was other institutions – such as the medical professions and new fields of inquiry such as psychiatry – which became the key institutional regulators. Those deemed "abnormal" in the eyes of these new professionals could be prodded, poked, examined, and even locked away in an asylum if they were deemed to fit the new categories of mental illness that had been devised by such "experts". The basis of this – like the confession – was talk. The patient needed to explain themselves, just like the confessions of old. Same-sex desires came under ever-greater scrutiny. In line with the desire to classify and catalogue, the concept of the "homosexual" came into being for the first time. Whereas '[t]he sodomite had been a temporary aberration; the homosexual was now a species' (1976, p. 43).

Accompanying the changing discourses and power–knowledge configurations are new regimes of surveillance. The law historically metered out punishment in the form of violence against the body by an external force – capital punishment for example – with the sovereign having control over who lived or died. But in Foucault's argument, new technologies of power emerged, displacing this emphasis on death, or at least giving control back to the individual over their own life and death (suicide, for example, ceases to be a crime). This new focus on life complemented the emergence of capitalism, given the necessities of capitalism to be underpinned by machine-like disciplined bodies. Processes of control determined their health status and life expectancy, through bureaucratic and rational means. Demography and population control entered the lexicon, this new regime being named by Foucault as the era of biopower. Social institutions such as schools, prisons, and hospitals cultivated this new power–knowledge nexus, and biopower was internalised, operationalised through new technologies of the self, where the individual took responsibility for complying with the requirements of biopower. Regulation is individualised and opted into for one's own good. But Foucault's conceptualisation of power is not viewed in terms of repression. Rather, because power is not shored up in various institutions but instead 'comes from everywhere' (1976, p. 93), he sees power in productive terms; formations of power embed modes of resistance. This notion of resistance has been much-utilised when analysing the complex relationship between religion and sexuality.

Surveillance and biopower offer useful theoretical tools to tease out the implications of religion, sexuality, embodiment, and regulation in various social contexts, and Foucault has been much-deployed to understand the ongoing power–knowledge nexuses that certain religious discourses continue to play. Mishtal's (2015) study of abortion and the Roman Catholic Church in Poland, for example, demonstrates the surveillance by Catholic priests in the reproductive choices of women. She utilises Foucauldian notions to situate the Church as 'a regime of disciplinary power' (2015, p. 13), examining how regulatory forms are internalised by women when they respond to questions by Catholic officials about their reproductive lives. Whereas Foucault's notion of biopower mapped the emergence of secular forms of state-sanctioned power–knowledge claims in contexts where religion had been displaced, Mishtal notes how in the context of Poland, religion instead becomes integral to national identity in a post-Soviet era, cementing itself to forms of sexual governance and regulation. Various and extensive strategies are deployed; for example, the Kolęda involves the priest annually visiting everyone's home, whether householders typically attend church or not, in the process enquiring about their religious commitments (have all the Catholic sacraments following birth, marriage, and death been followed, for example), and intrusive questions such as the numbers of children couples are planning to have. Married couples with no children or one child only are singled out, especially given the likelihood that they are using forms of contraception forbidden by the Church. Despite this all-encompassing regulatory system (it is difficult to opt out as this would identify you as an unbeliever, meaning that there are huge pressures to conform to the ritual), Mishtal notes the various strategies that women deployed in subverting priestly authority. For example, obtaining prior knowledge from friends who had already been visited by a priest, so that they could prepare in advance and manage the questions they were likely to face. Polish women therefore do not simply accept Church authority but, following Foucault, they instead cultivate forms of resistance.

## Organising normatives

Sexuality studies have used the notion of regulation, sometimes following Foucault, to powerful effect, in examining how sexuality is controlled in

**40** Censure and control

contemporary societies. Here we follow Richardson's (2018) pattern regarding how regulation can be divided between heteronormativity, homonormativity, and homonationalism.

Heteronormativity can be understood as the means through which heterosexuality becomes the standard against which normative sexuality is measured. As Richardson asserts, heteronormativity

> refers to the process whereby the normative status of heterosexuality is institutionalized and legitimated through social institutions and cultural norms and practices that naturalize and privilege particular forms of (gendered) heterosexuality as normative ways of living as well as normative sexuality... The analytic focus, in other words, is how the heteronormative ordering of the social is (re)produced through everyday practices, norms, subjectivities, identities, bodies and relationships... heteronormativity regulates the lives of heterosexual as well as non-heterosexual identified people.
>
> *(2018, p. 16)*

In sociological accounts of sexuality, religion is typically understood as promoting a heterosexual normative where heterosexuality is privileged (Plummer, 2003; Weeks, 2014). In the recent past, homophobia has been used to explain the marginalisation of queer people, but this term has been critiqued (Yip, 2011). For example, Fone (2000) argues homo*phobia* is aligned with a psychological fear towards homosexuals. Not only does this displace the discriminations other queer people face, such as lesbians, it also presupposes a psychological reaction – a phobia towards homosexuals – that is often not accurate. Indeed, others have started to use the term homonegativity to expand the forms that negative reactions to homosexuals can take, though this still does not offer a means of exploring other objections and negative attitudes to queer people (O'Donohue and Caselles, 1993). In light of these criticisms, the term heteronormativity has become a better means of capturing the marginalisation and silencing of queer sexualities, through its relationship to heterosexuality, also accounting for social structures. Heteronormativity indicates how heterosexuality itself is also subject to various hierarchies, with certain formulations of heterosexuality falling short of the normative of "married with children" (Jackson, 2006). Indeed, it is important to note that heteronormativity is not heterosexuality per se; one can be heterosexual and still not fit the required standards of heteronormativity (e.g. single parents, children born outside of marriage). As later chapters will illustrate, studies have demonstrated how religions typically sustain heterosexual systems through both the control of queer sexualities and women. Indeed, many religious traditions have formulated norms of compulsory heterosexuality, cultivated through strict gender norms and policed in various ways.

However, as Weeks (2014) suggests, heteronormativity as a concept suggests itself as a determining influence or invisible force that does not account for agency or change. In a similar way to how patriarchy has been critiqued for being understood as an all-encompassing system, heteronormativity can be interpreted as a very structured account. This has implications for religion, as religion as a concept often gets implicated as an inevitable heteronormative force. Care must be taken not to oversimplify the case and assume all religions in all times and spaces will be heteronormative. Secular institutions have a long history in equally endorsing heteronormativity, with secular states much invested in maintaining heterosexuality.

Homonormativity is a term coined by Duggan (2003), who explores the role that neoliberal systems have played in relation to inequality, and what new configurations of power emerge. Neoliberalism can be understood as a system of governance emerging from the 1970s, recognised in terms of market deregulation, greater levels of competition, privatisation, and the rolling back of provisions made by the welfare state, thus reducing any sense of a safety net. In other words, the neoliberal environment makes the workplace more precarious (e.g. the proliferation of zero-hours contracts) and it is at this very moment that there is less social support if things go wrong. In order to justify the removal of welfare support, success and failure are individualised, so doing well becomes the sole responsibility of the individual, and they are deemed at fault if they do not succeed. Neoliberalism has been presented as a neutral, rational process that goes beyond any specific political allegiance. The inequalities generated, and the exacerbation of the gap between rich and poor, is 'framed as due to performance rather than design, reflecting the greater merit of those reaping larger rewards' (Duggan, 2003, p. xiv).

Duggan explores what the implications are for the regulation of sexuality, alongside other social inequalities, arguing that:

> Neoliberalism, a late twentieth-century incarnation of Liberalism, organizes material and political life *in terms of* race, gender, and sexuality as well as economic class and nationality, or ethnicity and religion. But the categories through which Liberalism (and thus also neoliberalism) classifies human activity and relationships *actively obscure* the connections among these organizing terms.
>
> *(2003, p. 3, emphasis in original)*

As markets are deregulated and receive less scrutiny, other parts of life come under greater levels of surveillance, for example, sexuality – especially the sexual lives of those who are economically precarious, exacerbated by neoliberal economics. Although Duggan's principal context is the US, her understandings can be extrapolated to other contexts such as the UK. McKenzie (2015) highlights the increased welfare surveillance of unmarried mothers living on a council estate in the UK. As welfare is further reduced, the conditions of access become ever-harder, with mothers often being the ones tasked with "getting by" and providing for their children. McKenzie analyses the surveillance metered out by

**42** Censure and control

welfare officials, with women being creative regarding '"what to say" and how to answer a question – answering a question "wrongly" can have steep penalties' (2015, p. 48). Given how welfare for single mothers in the UK is structured around obtaining funds from "absent fathers", welfare recipients will routinely be asked intrusive questions regarding the father of their child(ren), and if one fails to comply, and disclose the information, benefits will be curtailed or even stopped completely, even if this puts the welfare of the children and the mother at risk (e.g. in contexts of domestic violence). Inequalities therefore intersect; those bearing the brunt of reduced welfare are poor women.

As certain sexualities are being ever-further regulated, Duggan notes that other sexualities are being co-opted into neoliberal forms, emphasising how prominent US-based gay rights groups incorporate neoliberal ideals into their structure and approach to securing greater equalities. Therefore, queer rights come to be representative only to those who constitute part of a queer elite – thereby privileging the experiences of middle-class white gay men, and largely excluding other minority sexualities. Duggan calls this homonormativity –

> it is a politics that does not contest dominant heteronormative assumptions and institutions, but upholds and sustains them, while promising the possibility of a demobilized gay constituency and a privatized, depoliticized gay culture anchored in domesticity and consumption.
>
> *(2003, p. 50)*

Identities are cultivated through processes of consumption and the commodification of gay-friendly leisure spaces, with barriers of access to those who comply with the elitist form. As Duggan highlights, homonormativity is configured not as a threat to heteronormativity, but as a complement and extension of it. This is epitomised through the creation of new hierarchies of acceptable sexual behaviour from non-heterosexuals – e.g. those willing to participate in cultures of monogamy, forms of commitment such as same-sex marriage, and spending money in newly created gay-friendly markets. Richardson (2018) calls this being a "good" sexual citizen, noting how the parameters of good sexual citizenship have extended to incorporate some lesbian and gay identities, especially in the growing creation of same-sex marriage legislation in many Western contexts. She also notes how this supports neoliberal goals in the face of reduced welfare spending – if lesbians and gay men form committed partnerships, this offers a network of care which in turn reduces the burdens of responsibility on the state, especially in countries with ageing populations. In other words, what on the surface can be seen as extending equal rights to sexual minorities can actually be seen more cynically in terms of supporting neoliberalism, especially given that few can fit the requirements of this "good" citizenship in the first place.

Such barriers of access have a religious component. Shah's (forthcoming) study of British queer Muslims includes the example of participants attempting to gain entry to a nightclub in the heart of Manchester's gay scene, but they are stopped by the club bouncer, who appears to be incredulous that these visibly

Muslim young men should seek access to this space, thereby discounting the idea that one can be Muslim and gay. He asks lots of questions regarding whether they knew what was happening inside the club, and in order to gain entry, one of Shah's participants has to justify his presence by giving explicit details. In this way, the queer club comes to be colonised as secular, with the entry of Muslim bodies being understood in securitised terms.

Puar (2007) builds on some of the ideas embedded in Duggan's analysis in her coining of the term homonationalism. She starts by examining how various countries are scrutinised differently regarding their human rights abuses, in that the torture and hanging of two gay men in Iran in 2006, which rightly provoked international condemnation, is not accompanied by similar outrage towards US practices of homophobic torture of prisoners at Abu Ghraib. She reads this through the powerful rhetoric of Islamophobia, dominating the world stage since 9/11 and the "war on terror" in particular. In short, homonationalism comes to represent the way gay people are selectively incorporated into US citizenship – in a way they have never been allowed to before – as a means of constructing certain regimes as intolerant and illiberal (Iran), and other regimes as exemplars of tolerance and equality-bearing (the US). Whereas Duggan has emphasised how homonormativity plays out in the domestic sphere in supporting neoliberal forms of governance, Puar examines this internationally, and how forms of homonormativity come to impact the contours of power between states and in the remit of homonationalism. Support for LGBT rights therefore becomes a strategy in justifying Islamophobia and intervening in states where support for LGBT rights is wanting. Yet this fails to recognise the very short history of LGBT support in so-called liberal democracies, the ongoing perpetuations of abuse against LGBT people in those democracies, and the selective means through which rights are accorded to LGBT people, which often excludes trans people, bisexuals, religious sexual minorities, and working class lesbians and gay men (Richardson and Monro, 2012). Puar notes that until recently gay people in the US were deemed 'traitors to the nation, figures of espionage and double agents... brought... death through the AIDS pandemic... and gay couples [constructed] as "domestic terrorists"' (2007, p. xxiii). But in new global configurations, it is the Muslim who takes on this "terrorist" identity and who becomes the threat to liberal democracies, evidenced in the widespread concerns over immigration in Europe. Meanwhile, national identity is reworked to incorporate (some) queer citizens, so long as they comply with the hierarchies of good citizenship mentioned earlier (Richardson, 2018). And this recognition remains partial, given the ongoing discriminations and inequalities against queer people (e.g. Barton, 2012). Puar notes the role that LGBT groups have played in furthering the demonisation of Muslim communities who are deemed a specific threat to LGBT people. Therefore, not only is Islam codified in anti-LGBT terms, but Muslims are constructed as fuelling homophobia in their everyday lives. Within this construction, there emerges little space for the subjectivity of the queer Muslim, who is erased from view. As Shah's (forthcoming) research indicates, this construction has ramifications, with visibly Muslim queer people

**44** Censure and control

having to justify access to gay-friendly spaces in the night time economy, with their identifies being seen as incompatible and incongruous.

Puar's contribution is important given the way religion is implicated in her analysis. Islam becomes the *bête noire*, a troublesome religion that seemingly perpetuates sexual minority injustice. Islam is reified in the process, its complexity and multiplicity going unrecognised, with there being little reflection on how Muslims on the ground manage sexual diversity – there is merely an assumption that all Muslims are homophobic, also foreclosing the possibility that some Muslims themselves will be queer. This also ignores and displaces the significant role hegemonic forms of Christianity have played in perpetuating homonegative discourses and behaviour (Barton, 2012; Jordan, 1997), and the global impact this has had (e.g. the influence the teachings of the Roman Catholic Church has had at a global level). Indeed, any argument utilising a sacred component is a useful justification for making it seem more compelling, hence why all religions have been used in sacred claims-making in this debate. Puar's analysis also emphasises the contemporary forms of regulatory regimes and discourses, threading through the insights of Foucault as articulated at the beginning of this section. As Puar argues:

> Debates regarding which communities, countries, cultures, or religions are more, less, equally, similarly, or differently homophobic miss a more critical assessment regarding the conditions of its possibility and impossibility, conditions revolving around economic incentives, state policies on welfare and immigration, and racial hierarchy, rather than some abstracted or disengaged notion of culture per se. Gay marriage, for example, is not simply a demand for equality with heterosexual norms, but more importantly a demand for reinstatement of white privileges and rights – rights of property and inheritance in particular – while for others, gay marriage and domestic partnership are driven by dire needs for health care.
>
> *(2007, p. 29–30)*

Heteronormativity, homonormativity, and homonationalism are important frames through which religion and sexuality can be interpreted. All can be considered a form of discourse, which Foucault describes as a frame of reference which limits how we can comprehend elements of social life. In other words, dominant discourses construct and define how we understand social life, determining what is deemed intelligible and unintelligible. The discourses of heteronormativity, homonormativity, and homonationalism all point to the importance of examining the relationship between religious regimes with other institutional processes such as the state. Such an examination reveals that the common perception that religions act as repositories of gender and sexuality inequality fail to acknowledge the ongoing state-level queer and gender injustices in occurrence, and also hide the pernicious ways that secular states construct themselves as absolved of any gender and sexuality-based inequalities.

## Summary

This chapter has highlighted that regulation is a key lens through which religion and sexuality can be interpreted. Firstly, religion has historically been understood as a form of regulation (Turner, 2008), with Foucault's confession the exemplar mechanism for bodily conformity. But secularising narratives (and Foucault can be included here) have assumed that religion ceases to exert much significance. Secondly, secularisation theory has not incorporated gendered and sexuality accounts to any great extent. When secularisation is analysed from these perspectives, it can change the very assumptions of secularisation theory, as evidenced by the ways men's and women's secularisation stories are vastly different. Thirdly, dominant narratives insist that secularity is the best place in which to argue for sexuality rights. But as Foucault emphasises, secular spaces are equally regulatory, and it is hard to tease out a firm line between the religious and the secular, given how each influences the other. The current positioning of religion as anti-queer and anti-woman needs to be understood in relation to the broader contours and what other effects are being achieved. As the discourse of homonationalism makes clear, certain religious communities are demonised within these wider nationalistic endeavours. Indeed, following Foucault, discourse can be understood as a key means through which regulation occurs. Religion's role in regulation is therefore reified, flattening complexity in the process.

Religion is all at once invoked as being significant and insignificant. We want to pave a middle way between these positions, taking a nuanced approach, emphasising how the role religion plays as a means of regulation is contextual. Religion no longer has the power in many Western contexts to determine how sexuality is lived – the vote in Ireland on same-sex marriage and the right to access abortion put the whole population at odds with the teachings of the Roman Catholic Church. Equally in other contexts, such as Poland and Nigeria, religions continue to have an impactful influence, significantly curtailing queer people and women's rights. It is important to recognise the contextual experience, and the extent to which conservative statements impact directly on one's life. For the Pope to speak against contraception can easily be dismissed in countries where contraceptives are freely available and accessible but will result in real inequalities and medical injustice in contexts where Catholic organisations control the healthcare system (Miller, 2014). We recognise that the various operating discourses such as heteronormativity and homonationalism have an ongoing impact on how people make sense of their sexual lives. But at the same time, religious conservatism is but one approach, and representing religion as inherently sexually conservative overshadows the liberatory role religion can play in such matters, such as in relation to the religious communities who are fighting for same-sex marriage equality or who are supportive of reproductive rights. Religions have been powerful censures of non-normative sexualities. But so have other institutions such as the state, media, and the education system. In the contemporary climate, it is religion, more so than the other institutions, which is upheld as being sexuality-negative and unaffirming. In some cases, this analysis is rightly justified, such as the way religious adherents petition abortion clinics, or stage protests at gay pride events. But often the inclusive spaces that religions cultivate are not on the general radar. News media is polemical in presenting these issues, with a religious leader opposed to same-sex marriage or abortion will invariably be called upon to speak for, and to represent, "religion". Meanwhile, a religious actor is rarely called upon to represent a pro-same-sex marriage or pro-choice stance (Brintnall, 2016). In the next chapter, we will be taking a more agency-driven approach to understanding how individuals themselves make sense of their religious and sexual lives, deploying the concept of identity.

# 3

# IDENTITY, SEXUALITIES, AND RELIGION

## Introduction

This chapter engages with the concept of identity and how it has been varyingly applied by scholars of religion and sexuality. Giddens (1991) has been influential in theorising the implications for selfhood in a context of declining traditional significance. His reflexive projects of the self are reliant on choice-based opportunities to enable individuals to construct their identity in a coherent manner. Negotiation is central to this, where individuals are no longer bound by traditional anchorages and ties, but instead follow out pure relationships where a sexual relationship is sustained only for as long as both parties remain satisfied. Despite the feminist critique of Giddens for overplaying the role of choice, especially the inequalities women in heterosexual relationships continue to face (e.g. Jamieson, 2002), this reflexive project of the self and the navigation of identity in a context of choice has been influential. The demise of tradition-bearing forms of religiosity, replaced with greater choices, as we noted in the last chapter, also create the potential for reflexive religious and sexual identities. Yet this is still undertaken in contexts of constraint and power imbalances. This chapter will begin by focusing on the notion of identity and how identity-work is achieved, followed by four ways we note that it has been deployed in religion and sexuality research. This comprises narrating identity, performing piety, stigma, and commodified identities. The chapter will then focus on three theoretical frames which recognise the significance of identity, including lived religion, intersectionality, and queer theory.

## Identity

Identity has been a fundamental concept in the study of religious and sexual identities, but its importance has increased in recent years (Greil and Davidman, 2007).

**48** Identity, sexualities, and religion

Many studies profess to examine Jewish identities or Catholic identities or Muslim identities. Likewise, scholarship has focused on lesbian identities, trans identities, gay identities, and so forth. And more recently, studies have brought religious and sexual identities together and focused on the identities of lesbian Muslims or bisexual Christians or gay Jews (Schnoor, 2003; Shannahan, 2009; Toft, 2014). The concept of identity can be used unconsciously and unthinkingly; a project focused on, say, gay Muslim identities, may be deemed self-evident. Indeed, the notion of identity is frequently invoked outside of academia too, especially the idea that everyone has a "real" identity to be unearthed (Lawler, 2008). But theoretical claims are being made by utilising the term of identity; not all branches of social thought are positive towards its usage (e.g. Braidotti, 2011). It is therefore helpful to return to sociological perspectives on identity and the diversity in evidence in how sociologists conceptualise identity.

## *Identity-work and the achieving of an identity*

There are both sociological and common-sense understandings of identity. One populist idea is that everyone has a core identity that remains unchanged and embedded deep within the individual – a real "self" that can be revealed once the outer layers are removed. However, this idea is challenged within sociological thinking (Lawler, 2008). Sociological perspectives tend to emphasise the way in which identity is socially constructed, thereby critiquing the idea of a core self. Sociologists examine the work individuals undertake in cultivating and achieving their identity; in other words, sociologists explore exactly how identity-work is undertaken.

Of sociological interest is also how one's identity connects with, or disconnects from, various groups we become associated with as a result of our identity (e.g. if I identify as a Liberal Jew this gives me a connection to other Liberal Jews). This is very pertinent in studies of religion and sexuality as one may find inclusion on the basis of one element of one's identity but exclusion on the part of another. For example, a gay Christian attending a conservative church may need to conceal their sexual orientation within their church but conceal their Christian identity in their workplace (Yip and Page, 2013). The identity tensions that are perceived to underpin queer and religious individuals' experiences are often the very reasons why these identities become the focus of scholarly attention and broader public interest in the first place. As Gray and Thumma argue in relation to the US context, 'it seems that the nation's press and the public's attention are captivated by accounts of conflict between religious entities and gay men, lesbians, bisexual, and transgender individuals' (2005a, p. xi), and there is less focus on cases where there is compatibility between religious and sexual identities. Indeed, in order for tensions between identities to emerge, this needs to be created – the tension is not inherently there but is instead made to appear natural, through emphasising small differences between groups and magnifying them (Lawler, 2008). In this way, being a heterosexual Christian is naturalised so that to be anything other than heterosexual is deemed unnatural or at least non-normative in many Christian contexts.

There are various sociological understandings of identity; here we focus on four that have been pertinent to the study of religion and sexuality – narrative accounts of identity-work, identity as a performance with a particular focus on performing piety, identity as a stigma, and commercialised forms of sexual identities.

### Narrating identity

This approach understands identity as mediated through the stories we tell about our lives. In order for the narrative to be intelligible, it needs to use recognisable cultural meanings, through emplotment, where the stories are assembled through a coherent plot:

> Through process of emplotment, social actors constitute a life, and in the process, constitute an identity... Emplotment configures a self which appears as the inevitable outcome and actualization of the episodes which constitute a life. The self is understood as unfolding through episodes which both express and constitute that self.
>
> *(Lawler, 2002, p. 249–50)*

This involves memory work, where episodes are remembered and retold. But because memory is unreliable, this involves interpretation of past events – indeed, certain levels of fabrication, exaggeration, or minimisation may occur in the process. Access to an unmediated "truth" is not possible. Narrative identity work is a social process, where those around you can validate or deny your story. This is hugely significant in cases of sexual violence where survivors' narratives have not been believed; their narratives have therefore not been socially validated. The narrative approach is also significant in relation to queer identity, extensively conveyed in Plummer's (1995) *Telling Sexual Stories*. He argues that accounting for one's sexual life has become ever-more prevalent. He discusses the public appetite for sexual stories, where the coaxing priest in Foucault's confessional is replaced by the talk show host, and guests are encouraged to "tell all" in a public environment. Plummer maps the trajectory of the "coming out" story, its history and emergence from the 1960s onwards, emphasising that the salience and primacy given to the "coming out" account is not inevitable, but is dependent on a coherent and recognizable narrative that an audience is willing to validate: 'for narratives to flourish there must be a community to hear... for communities to hear, there must be stories which weave together their history, their identity, their politics' (1995, p. 87). The "coming out" account conveys itself in terms of truth – my true identity is being revealed by my affirmation of being gay/lesbian/bisexual/trans/queer – so it presupposes that one's identity has been hidden away and concealed. This is seen as positive and affirming; one's previous "confused" understandings of oneself can be set aside, and a new coherent identity can be articulated. "Coming out" disrupts the taken-for-granted heterosexual script but the burden is on the person coming out to articulate a different identity to that which is assumed. This identity-generation does not occur in a vacuum. The terminology attached to same-sex attraction such as "homosexual", "gay", "lesbian" have emerged only recently, and being able to "come out" is dependent on a set of social understandings connected to the meanings of these terms. To declare one's homosexual identity would have been impossible before the end of the 19th century – for such an identity did not exist, even though same-sex desire did. Therefore, the coming out narrative becomes intelligible only in an environment where the terms one aligns with are readily available. It is oft noted that heterosexuals do not need to come out; this proves the normativity of heterosexuality, to which everyone is assumed to belong until proven otherwise (Jackson, 2006). Heterosexuals rarely define themselves through their sexuality – when Yip and Page (2013) asked heterosexuals about their sexual identity, a good number could not comprehend the question; they had never had to ponder this before and found it challenging to answer, in a way that those identifying as queer did not – indeed, queer people are expected to account for, reflect on, and *narrate* their sexual identity.

"Coming out" can be understood as a form of liberation and identity-affirmation. But scholars of religion have noted that it can cause significant harms. Barton's (2012) study of queer people living in the US Bible Belt highlights that revealing one's sexual identity can put one's livelihood and job in jeopardy, also noting this is a community that may not recognise a queer status and therefore will not accept the coming out account. When one participant in her study, Kimberley, tried to tell her mother about her sexual identity, 'her mother repeatedly responded by making homosexuality unmentionable' (2012, p. 99). Her identity was therefore silenced. Revealing one's sexual identity also put Barton's participants at risk of being forced to participate in ex-gay ministries, which aim to reorient queer people to heterosexuality. This is an environment where the storytelling narrative is unwilling to be heard, or when it is, the narrative is not received in an affirming way, thereby putting the storyteller at risk. For religious individuals in particular, coming out is a process; one may conceal their sexuality in certain contexts, e.g. to a religious community, yet be "out" to those in one's immediate family. As Keenan argues, '"coming out" is not a singular event but rather a story that requires constant retelling' (2006, p. 169).

## *Performativity and identity*

A second key way in which identity has been sociologically understood is as performativity. Lawler (2008) uses Goffman and Butler to examine the relationship between a perceived inner and outer self. This notion of there being a "real" inner self pervades popular culture – Lawler gives the example of Cinderella who becomes her "real" self through being transformed – stylistically – into a princess. There is a common perception that the inner and the outer elements of our identities may not match up – Cinderella's shabby clothes and status as a cleaner did not indicate her "true" nobility; this is only made manifest when the interior and exterior reflect each other. Goffman argues that our identities are constructed through everyday interaction between the frontstage and backstage regions of our lives, with the frontstage constituting the place where we are visibly on show – our appearance is carefully crafted and we monitor our behaviour. The front stage will include a setting, including props to assist the performance, such as the way a doctor is legitimated through being surrounded by medical equipment. This interacts with the personal effects of the individual in the role, such as donning a white coat, giving an authentic, believable, and convincing performance (Goffman, 1959). Meanwhile in the backstage one can let off steam and relax. This is not necessarily premised on a public/private split. Performances in the public sphere can be both of a backstage or a frontstage nature; the frontstage can become the backstage and vice versa. While some argue that Goffman is upholding an inner/outer distinction, with one's authentic self being located backstage, thereby displaying an interplay of true and false selves, Lawler critiques this interpretation, arguing that personhood is dependent on playing out a role whether in the backstage or the frontstage – 'To be a person... is to perform being a person' (2008, p. 106). Indeed, 'the person, for Goffman, is not *behind* the mask; rather, it *is* the mask' (2008, p. 108, emphasis in original). This dramaturgical analogy has been very useful when considering sexual and religious identities, such as Keenan's (2006; 2009) study of gay Anglican priests. Being a priest engages much frontstage work; the priest is always on call, with parishioners readily available as an audience to the performance. Priests are therefore already a heavily scrutinised group (Page, 2016c). But when a priest is gay, the impression management needed is intensified, especially given the censure of same-sex sexual relationships among Church of England clergy. Therefore, participants often had to conceal their sexual identity, and those who were living in open relationships had to present this as a model relationship. This visibility also increased their vulnerability, feeling they had to be nice to parishioners at all times. Following Lawler, Keenan (2009) too understands this as a form of identity work which does not inherently produce a false self. Although the backstage may be hidden, it actually cultivates and supports the impression management in the frontstage. Keenan uses the analogy of an embroidered picture with the neat stitches on the front, contrasted with the messy threads on the back. Therefore, both backstage and frontstage coexist; different parts of the same thing and constitute the presentation of self.

Lawler brings Goffman and Butler into conversation with each other, arguing that 'Both... highlight the ways in which anxieties about "authenticity" continue to haunt notions of identity', but whereas Goffman understands 'social order as always fragile, as always potentially disintegrating, and as needing to be continually repaired' (2008, p. 121), Butler is more concerned with challenging the social order per se, and emphasising what gets subjugated in the process. Even

**52** Identity, sexualities, and religion

though Butler does not reference Goffman, they are addressing similar issues, especially in Butler's notion of performativity. Butler (1993) draws on Derrida's idea of iterable practice to understand not only how subjects are formed, but how they are *reformed* over again, through everyday performativity. When we repeat language/bodily actions, it creates a sense of stability, but this stability is twinned with its own instability. As we constantly repeat and reconfigure our identities in a never-ending pattern of performativity, this means that we may fail – thus change and resignification can occur. Butler's ideas challenge the assumption that the biological precedes the social – the material body cannot exist outside of its entry to language. There can thus be no meaningful distinction between sex and gender. Although some, such as Howson (2005), argue that by discursively situating the body, real, material bodies are written out in Butler's account, Lawler disagrees and interprets Butler as offering a conceptualisation of identity that is produced through the body. Gender only seems stable by the repeated actions of the body, so that gender identity – and heterosexual relations – are naturalised. Performativity is not performance – these are not roles one can adopt and discard at will. Rather, discourses will impact on what identities are and are not possible.

### *Performing piety*

The notion of identity as performativity has been explicitly utilised in the study of religion and gender. Mahmood (2005) utilises Butler in her theorisation of piety amongst Muslim women in the Egyptian mosque movement. Like Butler, Mahmood situates her project within poststructuralism and, following Foucault, considers how subjectivity is produced through discursive power relations.

Mahmood has been fundamental in demonstrating the complexity of the relationship between gender and religion, especially in a context where feminists have treated religion simplistically and in wholly negative terms as a repressive force, especially in relation to Islam. Indeed, Muslim women have been charged with being falsely conscious regarding their religious identities, even from feminists who would in other circumstances critique such notions of false consciousness. As she outlines:

> The pious subjects of the mosque movement occupy an uncomfortable place in feminist scholarship because they pursue practices and ideals embedded within a tradition that has historically accorded women a subordinate status. Movements such as these have come to be associated with terms such as fundamentalism, the subjugation of women, social conservatism, reactionary atavism, cultural backwardness, and so on.
>
> *(2005, p. 4–5)*

Mahmood's insights came at a crucial moment in moving beyond assumptions from secular feminists that religion inevitably oppresses women and religion scholars who argued that even patriarchal traditions inevitably accorded women

Identity, sexualities, and religion **53**

agency and freedom. Instead, she argued that agency was broader than what is recognisable when one is challenging authority – in other words, agency was more than resistance. She asks scholars to consider more closely how power operates in all its manifestations, and not solely from one angle. While poststructuralist feminists have done much to critique the notion of the rational subject, they have located politics in terms of freedom, and therefore look at ways of enhancing and expanding women's scope for freedom. But this is one construction of politics. For Mahmood's participants, piety, not freedom, was the motivating action underpinning their agency.

The women in the mosque movement were religiously diverse. But they shared a desire to resist the idea that Islam was mere culture, to instead cultivate a distinguishable Muslim piety oriented around religious duty and Islamic values over custom. Given Mahmood's thoughts on agency, she does not emphasise forms of behaviour that seemingly resist gender and sexuality norms; instead she captures other forms of agency that are lived out. One example is Amal, a participant who is confident and outgoing but who wants to cultivate shyness, which is deemed more modest and pious. Many feminists would understand this as a form of coercion to conform to masculinist norms of feminine behaviour, with women's bodies and identities being repressed in the process. Instead, Mahmood returns to Butler's notion that performativity engenders agency, with performativity itself being vulnerable as it is not necessarily flawless and consistent:

> The model of ethical formation followed by the mosque participants emphasizes the sedimented and cumulative character of reiterated performatives, where each performative builds on prior ones, and a carefully calibrated system exists by which differences between reiterations are judged in terms of how successfully (or not) the performance has taken root in the body and mind. Thus the mosque participants – no matter how pious they were – exercised great vigilance in scrutinizing themselves to gauge how well (or poorly) their performances had actually taken root in their dispositions.
>
> *(2005, p. 163–4)*

Mahmood goes beyond Butler, however, in arguing that failed performatives do not necessarily disrupt the system of gender or heteronormativity; in the case of the mosque participants, failure at piety can affirm the system through encouraging participants to thereby reach bodily piety. This is because it is through the body that pious identity is achieved – and not through, as Butler would assume, the body being *a sign* of pious identity. For change to occur, it is not enough to destabilise the sign – instead, the whole body has to be retrained (here Mahmood draws upon theories of habitus). A feminist challenge that offers a different symbolism therefore simply will not work. Mahmood notes why feminists would find the cultural normatives structuring gender and sexuality in Egyptian society problematic. One participant highlights the social stigma that is attached

**54** Identity, sexualities, and religion

to a woman's single status, which is absent for men. The custom of men asking women for their hand in marriage means a man's unmarried status indicates an unwillingness to get married; for women, it indicates being unwanted. Instead of rejecting this embedded understanding of singleness, her piety cultivated a form of forbearance and perseverance (*sabr*). Some explicitly interpreted this action as a form of passivity. But it was through cultivating *sabr* that she was ultimately able to lay claim to that higher goal of piety, given that *sabr* constituted piety.

### *Identity as a stigma*

Goffman (1963) focuses on the mundane interactions we routinely engage with in our everyday lives, and the social rules that are enforced through face-to-face communication. On meeting new people, we make an immediate impression of them, and we essentially classify them. Goffman's concern in his book, *Stigma: Notes on the Management of Spoiled Identity*, is with those who are deemed not qualified to be accorded full societal recognition and acceptance – those who are stigmatised in some way. He makes reference to three types of stigma:

> First there are abominations of the body – the various physical deformities, next there are blemishes of individual character perceived as weak will, domineering or unnatural passions, treacherous and rigid beliefs, and dishonesty, these being inferred from a known record of, for example, mental disorder, imprisonment, addiction, alcoholism, homosexuality, unemployment, suicidal attempts, and radical political behaviour. Finally there are the tribal stigma of race, nation, and religion, these being stigma that can be transmitted through lineages and equally contaminate all members of a family.
>
> *(1963, p. 14)*

The concept of stigma therefore has a wide scope, with homosexuality and religion both identified as potentially invoking a stigmatised identity. Goffman then goes on to explain the various strategies through which stigmas are managed, such as concealment, or campaigning for the stigma to be no longer stigmatised, as has occurred with claims for queer equality and recognition. Indeed, the increased queer equalities that have emerged in recent years in a number of Western countries, buttressed through legislation, emphasises that the situation of "the homosexual" is rather different from when Goffman was writing. Yet contemporary religion and sexuality scholars continue to locate theoretical mileage in the concept of stigma, especially in contexts of continuing religious constraint on sexual identities. For example, Yip (1997) notes the hostile environment that gay Christians often encounter from their churches. Yip explores the various strategies gay Christians utilise to manage their stigmatisation, such as attacking the stigma itself, through challenging the Biblical verses that are usually utilised to condemn homosexuality, as well as attacking the stigmatiser –

i.e. the church. This strategy involves seeing the church in suspect terms in its treatment of homosexuality, with its prejudices being likened to slavery. Indeed, Yip's participants often emphasised how their gay relationships followed codes of ethics that chimed with Christian principles. One powerful means of combatting the stigmatised identity was through the ontogeneric argument – i.e. that god made me this way, and one's sexual identity should be celebrated as part of god's creation (see also Thumma, 1991). Invoking the transcendental sacred is a powerful means of consolidating and affirming one's sexual identity, but also implies that one has a core identity that is unchanging. As previously critiqued by Lawler (2008), this does not correspond with most sociological accounts of identity. Despite its appeal in validating identity, this notion of a core self is contested within poststructural thought such as Butler's aforementioned notion of performativity, and queer theory more broadly, which we will analyse later.

Meanwhile, Barton (2012) utilises Goffman in her study of Bible Belt gays. Because of the broader community censure that strongly condemns same-sex desire, those who identify as queer are immediately recognised as being stigmatised. Barton also emphasises that this stigma is broader than the queer individual, and utilises Goffman's notion of the sticky stigma to convey that 'One need not be gay oneself to experience the stigma of homosexuality. One may only need to be associated with a gay person by blood, marriage or friendship to suffer homophobia' (2012, p. 57). The ongoing salience of stigma is also located in Amakor's (2019) research with unmarried Christian mothers in Nigeria, emphasising how these women are stigmatised within their religious communities due to their status as sexual sinners. In punishment, the women in some churches are publicly shamed by being "backbenched" – they are forced to sit at the back of the church, and are stripped of any church roles they hold. Similar to Barton's utilisation of sticky stigma, Amakor notes that this bodily discipline extends to the mothers of the unmarried pregnant woman, and they too are stripped of their church roles and are forced to sit at the back of the church. Meanwhile, men experience no such censure, whether that be the men who got the women pregnant or the fathers of the pregnant women. Instead, mothers are deemed responsible for their daughters' actions and are punished accordingly.

### Commercialised and commodified sexual identities

Sex is now far more visible in Western culture, especially in the context of the internet and the easier access to pornography (Attwood, 2009). Porn stars are accorded celebrity status, and porn has infiltrated everyday media such as music videos, advertisements, film, and TV. As Attwood argues, sex has gone from the 'sleazy backstreets' (2009, p. xiv) to the main high street. Women have been reconstructed as consumers of sex, emphasised through the popularity of sex toys such as the Rampant Rabbit, the increased numbers of lingerie shops, pole dancing classes, and burlesque nights. This marketisation of sex has an impact on identity-formation. Following Giddens, Attwood frames this as utilising sex

**56** Identity, sexualities, and religion

for the purposes of fulfilment; sex becomes for pleasure and fun rather than reproduction.

The sociology of religion has assessed the commodification of religious forms, and how spiritualities are marketised (particularly in corporate contexts) so that they can be bought and sold (Carrette and King, 2005). These marketisation techniques are seen as damaging due to the way they are co-opted into neo-liberal regimes, disabling religions from taking up a critical role of the current economic system and the inequalities generated. Others have focused on the ways religions market themselves as a product, through, for example, advertising. Heelas and Woodhead (2005) have examined the increased popularity of spiritual wellbeing and mind-body-spirit endeavours, such as yoga and aromatherapy. In a context of religious institutional decline, individuals experiment with new forms of religiosity that take individualised and subjectivised forms. Sociological questions have arisen regarding to what extent this type of engagement is a form of consumer practice, as religious or spiritual practices are chosen in a "pic-n-mix" fashion.

There are far fewer studies which link these spheres together and which analyse sexuality and religion from the perspective of commercialisation, commodification, or marketisation. For those that do address this in some way (though not all actually frame their findings in terms of commodification and commercialisation), there can be ascertained at least three approaches. Firstly, there are those more conservative forms of marketisation that explicitly endorse traditional religious messages about sex, but use new commodified forms to make these traditional messages more appealing and "on trend". Moultrie's (2017) work on the Black ministries that are marketed to Black single women in the US is an example where it is clear that a product is being created and cultivated, and sold *en masse*, and is dependent on a carefully crafted stage management of the stars at the heart of these popular ministries. Merchandise such as DVDs, books, and bracelets become marketable commodities to this particular demographic, enabled through social media platforms, conferences, and live events. And it is incredibly profitable. Meanwhile, White (2012) has emphasised the ways in which purity culture is marketised to young people; virginity is popularised by the selling of slogan t-shirts and jewellery. Similarly, in the ADPS project, Lowe and Page (forthcoming) have detected the ways in which anti-abortion contingents in the UK capitalise on youthful commodifications in an attempt to present a more palatable and "youthful" message. This is exemplified at the March for Life event, which takes place annually. A professional stage is created, featuring live music, where the lyrics of popular songs are altered to feature an anti-abortion message. This is accompanied by stands selling merchandise with anti-abortion messages. A festival-like atmosphere is attempted, where entrants to the event are given blue festival-style wrist-bands with the message, "Life at Conception; No Exception".

Secondly, there are forms of commodification that embrace certain sexualised formations. In these examples, religious cultures (including conservative ones) embrace commodified forms of sexuality such as sex toys and sex manuals, but typically reaffirm traditional notions of sexuality, in that the commodified practices are legitimated within heterosexual marriage only. In this sense, marketised forms of sexuality that initially seem deviant actually uphold long-standing sexual norms. Burke's (2016) study is an excellent example of this, where Christians participate in an online community where sex is discussed in frank and detailed terms. This is not just about confessing their sexual experiences, desires, and problems in a Foucauldian sense, but co-constructs their religious identity. Some of the sexual practices that her married heterosexual participants engage with – such as cross-dressing or female masturbation – would be negatively perceived within the broader contours of conservative Evangelicalism, yet through online mechanisms, her participants situate their practices as godly and sacredly endorsed. This is enabled through the debating mechanisms the online spaces allow, which makes the individual responsible for their own sexual ethic. At the same time, all practices are understood in a broader conservative normative where strict gender codes are adhered to, and where sexual activity is restricted to those in heterosexual marriages. In this way, participants understand their sexual engagement in godly terms, and as fulfilling God's intentions for them, and therefore within a Christian framework, but these decisions about permissible and impermissible acts are individually negotiated within marriage itself. Burke also highlights the role played by online sellers of sexual products to religious individuals, such as sex toys, and whether religious consumers are willing to pay the marked-up price for a product that has been carefully screened and selected for that audience. In a similar vein, DeRogatis (2015) has highlighted the booming sales of Evangelical sex manuals, where careful marketing decisions are made regarding what diagrams, if any, are depicted, and how graphic the images utilised should be. Again, the selling of sex manuals to a Christian audience is not deemed deviant, so long as the "sex-within-heterosexual-marriage" normative is maintained.

More work is needed to theoretically situate such examples within the context of marketisation more generally. Given that religious communities have often protested the use of sexuality as a means to sell products, what are the ramifications when religious identities are entwined with marketised forms of sexuality? In the case of White's (2012) and Lowe and Page's (forthcoming) research, a particular view on sexuality is being promoted through commodified means, which correspond with youthful interests to make them more popular, so it is not about using sex to sell a product, but using products to sell a certain idea about sexuality. Meanwhile, in Burke's example, the sellers are trying to promote a product that does not become associated with the trappings of "worldly" sexuality, but presents sex toys as part of a wholesome and godly heterosexual marriage. Products are carefully selected for the website so that this ideal is adhered to. But what about examples where it is some form of sexuality itself that is being commodified? We now turn to our third example of sexual–religious commodification.

**58** Identity, sexualities, and religion

Wilson (2017) examines how the Buddhist concept of mindfulness has been commodified for various audiences. Although mindfulness has been constructed as a therapeutic practice in health and wellbeing terms per se, Wilson specifically focuses on the promotion of "mindful sex", in various guises. He identifies three terrains where mindful sex is conveyed to non-Buddhist audiences: the medical terrain, where mindful sex is deemed a means of overcoming sexual problems, particularly gynaecological ones; the self-help and therapy culture which addresses more populist audiences to promote better sex, again often with a particular focus on women; and spiritually engaged practices oriented around Buddhist ideas, which aim to enhance one's sex life, such as Orgasmic Meditation (see also Pilcher, forthcoming). This is where practitioners stroke each other intimately, promoting sexual satisfaction. This sits uneasily with traditional Buddhist interpretations of mindfulness and sex, especially given that mindfulness in Buddhist monastic traditions was utilised as a means of dampening sexual desires, rather than heightening them. Wilson argues that the appropriation of Buddhist concepts in secular therapeutic culture demonstrates the fluidity between the secular and religious, the scientific and spiritual, especially given that this-worldly forms of Buddhism – effecting change in one's immediate life – have always existed. Wilson's analysis also highlights the reproduction of gendered stereotypes and assumptions, given that women are often the focus of mindful sex – while men's sexual problems are constructed as being solved through Viagra pills with a very material focus, women's sexual problems are instead understood in terms of mental constraint, even in contexts involving major surgery such as a hysterectomy. Women in particular are therefore understood as being able to particularly benefit from mindful sex. This points to the complex interweaving of spiritual and secular narratives in re-emphasising traditional gendered understandings of sexuality.

Within these three approaches, the kind of commodification in relation to religion and sexuality varies. But what ties together these three formulations is the typical promotion of heterosexual and gendered forms of sexuality.

## Creating identity through lived religion

Lived religion has recently become an important conceptual framework within the sociology of religion. Initiated by scholars such as McGuire (2008), Orsi (2007), and Ammerman (2014), lived religion focuses on the diverse ways individuals negotiate their religious lives. It contests the idea that individuals absorb religious edicts and rules to be simplistically implemented in their lives. Instead, lived religion focuses on the messiness of belief, action, and belonging, and how individuals meld and mesh together different frames of reference in making sense of their lives, prioritising what is meaningful to them in a given moment. It should therefore not be surprising when individuals adopt more than one religious framework, or choose some elements and not others of a religious tradition, or go against "authorised" forms of religion. It also leaves room for individuals

Identity, sexualities, and religion **59**

who identify with spirituality but may not see themselves in religious terms. It therefore focuses on people's lived experience of the sacred. It also prioritises an embodied approach:

> Lived religion is, for many people, immediately connected with the well-being of their bodies and minds, because they do not experience their spiritual lives as separate from their physical and mental/emotional lives.
>
> *(McGuire, 2008, p. 137)*

Lived religion has a great potential to theoretically situate and understand intimate life issues, yet it has not been fully developed in this regard (Page, 2017a). Stories of sexuality are more incidental in accounts such as Ammerman's and McGuire's, and although neither purposefully excludes sexuality from their object of analysis, sexuality is not the main focus. Both instead give significant attention to other areas of embodied life, such as health and illness. There are glimpses of incorporating sexuality in Ammerman's accounts, such as the way one Catholic participant navigated her faith after she had sex before marriage, and another who debated the permissibility or not of birth control. Meanwhile, McGuire recounts the story of Bernie, a middle-class African American woman whose relationship has ended. Lived religion is practised in relation to the long conversations she has with friends around the kitchen table, where relationship issues are discussed. Bernie discloses that she is missing sex, but is also feeling more sexual without a partner as she has recently become more comfortable with her body. Such examples indicate the compatibility that a lived religion perspective has in relation to understanding sexual lives. In their respective books, Ammerman and McGuire set up the conditions for a more encompassing analysis of the relationship between lived religion and sexuality. But this has not been undertaken to its full potential. Meanwhile, Orsi's lived religion perspective underpins his analysis of a Catholic community in Harlem, including his own autobiographical reflections. He explores how church-based forms of religious practice are threaded through populist practices such as devotion to the Catholic saints. He recalls the life of his uncle Sal, a Catholic living with cerebral palsy, and how his disability was understood in relation to Catholic narratives about pain:

> This was a darkly erotic aesthetic of pain, one expression of the wider romanticism of American Catholicism in this period. But for all this culture's fascination with physical distress, the sensual pleasure it took in feverish descriptions of suffering, it was also deeply resentful and suspicious of sick persons. A nasty edge of retribution and revenge is evident in these accounts.
>
> *(Orsi, 2007, p. 23)*

Orsi's complex exploration of how illness and pain were constructed in Catholic discourses examines 20th century Catholic literature, and how those in pain

**60** Identity, sexualities, and religion

were considered closer to the suffering saints; at the same time, illness was problematised as a divine punishment from God. Sal finds comfort in connecting with certain saints and devotional practices. Orsi manages to convey the competing frames of reference in which Sal experienced his life, as well as the complex emotions involved, not only of his uncle, but also the reaction of others to him – how he is infantilised and sexualised. Orsi details the idle talk of care home staff, and how the sexuality of patients becomes the butt of jokes; speculation about the size of disabled people's genitalia, as well as the sexual acts patients engaged in. One story circulated that men wheeled themselves in the middle of the night to women patients to be fellated, something that was logistically impossible. When interacting with patients, they would ask the patients to comment on good-looking women and what they would do with them sexually. This was constructed as banter rather than harm:

> the discourse of the holy cripple turned people like Sal, Jimmy, and Joey into inhuman others whose inner lives were radically unlike everyone else's, and ultimately unrecognizable... It denied them the full range of human desires and hopes, including those for love, mastery, and independence. It hid their dismay at the condescension and the good intentions of the volunteers who spoke to them in loud voices and simple words.
>
> *(Orsi, 2007, p. 43)*

Such detailed accounts offered by lived religion scholars such as Orsi, McGuire, and Ammerman, which take account of emotionality, sensory experiences, and embodied encounters, offers a significant opportunity to theoretically frame the study of religion and sexuality. Such accounts enable a careful analysis of identity formation, the context for this, and the complex mediations that occur in relation to religious and spiritual experiences. Lived religion expands the scope of what is considered meaningful for sociologists of religion to consider, with McGuire in particular asking scholars to ask different questions and explore lives from different angles.

This approach also allows for ambiguities and transgressive experiences to be accounted for. While a focus on personal spiritual life promotes forms of lived religion that cultivate bodily wellbeing, such as the spiritual benefits of gardening, this is embedded in darker personal stories, as previously highlighted in Orsi's account, as well as McGuire's (2008) description of a participant who was finding ritual mechanisms to cope with childhood sexual abuse. But while these examples highlight forms of lived religion that address pain and anguish, and how this is managed through various devotional means, they also reference those forms of lived religion that are more ambivalent and potentially invoke harm for others. As McGuire argues:

> We need to allow for the very real possibility that just as there are creative spiritualities, there may also be destructive spiritualities. Just as some

Identity, sexualities, and religion **61**

people may seek spiritual practices that bring their lives into a greater sense of harmony, beauty, peace, and compassion, others may engage in practices that develop a purer hatred of the Other and that literally, as well as figuratively, embody violence and aggression.

*(2008, p. 117)*

Both Orsi and Ammerman include photographs in their respective books of anti-abortion activism; this too is not necessarily officially endorsed by religious authorities (see Lowe and Page, forthcoming), but religious practices are deployed by activists to deter women from seeking an abortion. Such activities are an attempt to curtail women's reproductive rights and cause much controversy (Lowe and Page, forthcoming). Munson (2002) examines their motivations and religious identities. In line with a lived religion approach, traditional forms of religion – i.e. religion as a set of beliefs – is limited in explaining his participants' commitments. The relationship the activists have to religion is complex, and some were often very negative about their religious institutions for not opposing abortion loudly or clearly enough. For these Christian activists, prayer – both of a collective and individual nature – was crucial to living out their anti-abortion activism. While these individuals frame their activism with an underlying religious vocabulary, the contours and nature of those prayers are individually and collectively created, outside of the dominant structures of religious institutions. The controversial nature of this activism is captured in Lowe and Page's (forthcoming) ADPS (Abortion Debates in Public Spaces) research, which emphasises the role of counter-demonstrations to anti-abortion activism. Much of the counter-demonstration activism takes an anti-religion framing; religion is ridiculed or dismissed. But some pro-choice participants utilise religious resources to counter the claims of the anti-abortion activists. One participant displayed her Bible featuring a love-heart post-it note, on which she had written "The Way of Love – Love is Patient, Love is Kind" (1 Corinthians 13). This disrupted the sacred monopoly being claimed by the anti-abortion activists and contested the idea that religion always equates to reproductive conservatism.

## Intersecting identities

Intersectionality started as an intervention in feminist debates, which emerged from Black women's experiences of exclusion from a white-centric feminist movement and sexist civil rights activism. While Crenshaw (1989) is widely credited with coining the term, its history goes back much further, to, for example, among others, the Combahee River Collective's (1977) *A Black Feminist Statement*, which focused specifically on the interlocking oppressions that Black women experienced (Collins and Bilge, 2016). The roots of intersectionality can also be located in Truth's (1851) famous declaration, "Ain't I a Woman". Collins and Bilge (2016) chart those contributors to the concept who have been forgotten, and critically reflect on why their scholarship has been marginalised, and

**62** Identity, sexualities, and religion

why the term comes to be embedded with the work of Crenshaw, a legal scholar. While not dismissing Crenshaw's contribution, they argue that Crenshaw's badging of the term fitted with an academy ready to adopt and incorporate this idea, which the academy could then go on to utilise for its own purposes. Instead of recognising the concept as one that had been collectively derived through decades of previous work by Black women, it was more convenient to connect it with an individual scholar, evidencing the citation issues we referenced in Chapter 1. Although intersectionality is now far more widely appropriated, and beyond academic discussion, these roots need to be recognised to highlight the exclusions and inclusions that occur in academic scholarship, and the power dynamics that are forged in the creation of a term which ultimately aims to critically interrogate those same power-infused inequalities.

Intersectionality is a means of analysis which emphasises complexity over simplification. At its heart is a desire to comprehend more fully how social inequalities are perpetuated through examining various facets and angles, and not singular issues. It moves beyond a class-only, gender-only, or ethnicity-only analysis to recognise how these factors are mutually constitutive. Intersectionality therefore critiques additive models of identity (Taylor, 2016). Typically, intersectionality has focused on how race, class, and gender intersect, with a particular emphasis on those who experience multiple disadvantages in relation to these axes, but more recent work has started to unpack how privilege and disadvantage intersect, as well as focusing on other social divisions such as sexuality. For example, Taylor's (2011) study of lesbian and gay parents explored how their experiences were refracted through a classed lens. Geographical insights have also been important in this regard (e.g. Valentine, 2007), in highlighting that the spaces individuals navigate may prioritise certain elements of one's identity over others, therefore producing differential outcomes. For example, Valentine uses the case study of Jeanette – a white middle aged woman who was deaf. She found her Deaf club supportive in relation to her disability, especially in a broader environment hostile to accommodating her disability. But she experienced abuse from the same community when she entered a same-sex relationship. Valentine highlights that differential spaces will alter the terms of inclusion and exclusion. Intersectional experiences are not fixed and immutable but are under constant flux.

Intersectionality is more than a theory of identity (Collins and Bilge, 2016). A key aim of intersectionality is to explore and explain the perpetuation of intersectional inequalities while also recognising differences between individuals with seemingly similar profiles. Therefore, intersectionality is concerned with examining power dynamics and how inequalities become embedded through time and across spaces. Religion has not hitherto been an overt subject for intersectional analysis (Page and Yip, forthcoming), but is implicitly positioned in two different ways in intersectional investigation – firstly, as a form of identity that could be experienced marginally (e.g. the experience of Muslims living in Western countries with policies that are ultimately hostile to them – see Shah, forthcoming), and secondly, as constitutive of forms of power that may intersect and interlock with other systems of power, for example, in collaboration with the state (e.g. the way in which church and state in Nigeria intersect in their interests to curtail unmarried women's access to contraception – see Amakor, forthcoming).

Intersectionality has a fruitful and rich role to play in the study of religion and sexualities, and although arguably, any project focusing on religion and sexuality is intersectional in design, the explicit deployment of intersectional theorisation is rare, although work is currently being undertaken to explore these implications (Page and Yip, forthcoming; Taylor, 2016). Taylor (2016) embeds an intersectional analysis into her study of young queer Christians, referencing the important part space plays in this navigation. She notes how the concepts of "youth", "religious", and "queer" may at first appear jarring and dislocated from each other, but a careful reading of young queer religious lives emphasises complex patterns of inclusion, exclusion, and (de)legitimation. For example, lesbians may experience church exclusion on the basis of their gender alongside their sexuality, given the prioritisation of male leadership in many church spaces. Equally, Taylor reflects on the middle-classedness of her sample, and how this impacts on processes of privilege and disadvantage when intersectional identities are comprised of various complex strands.

While on the one hand, intersectionality can be utilised analytically to explore individuals with varying sexual orientations and religious identities, there is also the potential to explore how intersectionality has been framed in larger-scale conversations relevant to religion. For example, Barrett-Fox and Yip (forthcoming) have undertaken a crucial analysis of the way intersectionality has been mainstreamed in US culture, to be varyingly interpreted by religious groups. Their analysis specifically focuses on how conservative Christian commentators have used the message of intersectionality to critique it and to argue that intersectionality is a dangerous attack on Christianity itself. Indeed, the way intersectionality has been vilified in various quarters has been documented elsewhere. Collins and Bilge (2016) highlight how some white middle-class cyberfeminists deem intersectionality elitist due to its alleged inaccessible language style. But they dig deeper to analyse what sits behind this critique. For Collins and Bilge, the cyberfeminist attack on intersectionality re-centres and prioritises the concerns of white middle-class women, denying a space for other women's voices, therefore upending the origins of the term itself and once again challenging the research endeavours of Black feminists. Meanwhile, for Barrett-Fox and Yip, conservative Christian churches' rejection of intersectionality allows them to legitimate sexist, racist, classist, and homophobic narratives, in the process arguing that they do so in the name of Christianity.

## Queering religious identities

Queer theory decentres the normativity of heterosexuality, epitomised in Butler's (1993) aforementioned notion of performativity, where the socially constructed

**64** Identity, sexualities, and religion

parameters of sex and gender are emphasised. Queer theory challenges and critiques normative assumptions about social life which are assumed to revolve around a heterosexist imperative. It therefore corresponds with the concept of heteronormativity, which we discussed in the last chapter, where heterosexuality is deemed normative and anything else is perceived as a deviance. Instead, queer theory relocates heterosexuality to the margins and its dominant assumptions are challenged. As Richardson argues:

> Queer theory sought to deconstruct contemporary sexual and gender categories, challenging the idea of identity as fixed and stable and instead emphasizing fluidity, openness and fragmentation.
>
> *(2018, p. 15)*

This has been powerfully utilised in relation to religion, particularly in queer theology, which reimagines sacred texts (in particular, the Bible) through new queer frames (Althaus-Reid, 2003; D'Costa, 2007; Loughlin, 2007). It also has sociological implications. As Daniels (2016) indicates, two main intellectual stimuli for queer theory include Freud and Foucault, both of whom foregrounded the idea that sexual identity is not anchored and immobile. Foucault, using his genealogical method, emphasised how sexual identity is *historically* produced, through the nexus of power-knowledge. Queer theory utilises these ideas to critique normative assumptions about religions. For example, Jordan (1997) questions dominant assumptions about the historical use of the term sodomy within Christianity. Using a queer lens, Jordan challenges our current knowledge frames regarding how we imagine past Christian communities as having understood sodomy and homosexuality (with this historicising having an important impact in how homosexuality is perceived in contemporary Christian communities), to instead offer a new perspective. The tight connection between sodomy and homosexual practice simply did not exist historically. Instead, sodomy related to all manner of practices, of both a sexual and non-sexual nature, and varied in context and over time. The slipperiness and unstable nature of the term indicates how sodomy was invented at different moments, influenced by the particular power-knowledge nexus operating in that given context. This has radical implications for how current Christian communities understand the interpellation of homosexuality historically, in that using a historical path indicating opposition to homosexuality is erroneous. As White (2016) cautions, history treats religion and sexuality in fixed and immovable terms, even though both have been variously experienced and understood over time. In addition, the current Christian preoccupation with homosexuality is recent; 'the Christian teachings about homosexuality produced after 1950 actually do not represent millennia-long tradition. They represent something distinctly new' (White, 2016, p. 212). This is why queer accounts are important in challenging dominant assumptions, categorisations, and terminology, especially when claims are made about a historical past, even when this past is constructed and invented through contemporary frames.

Empirical investigations have emphasised the role that queering plays in religious lives. For example, Yip's (2005) study of British LGBT Christians and Muslims emphasised how dominant interpretations of religious texts were revised and reformulated in relation to queer knowledge. This is undertaken in a context of constraint, given the esteem that sacred texts receive, not only within religious communities themselves, but also outside of them, for 'Even opponents with scarce theological knowledge often use clichés such as "The Bible says so" or "The Qur'an says it is wrong", to justify their stance against homosexuality' (2005, p. 49). But in recent years, queer Christian theology has become well-established; meanwhile, Islam has a much more minor, but emerging, field of queer scholarship. Yip examines the strategies that are employed when LGBT Muslims and Christians queer a religious text. This can involve critiquing traditional interpretations, critiquing the authority of theologians, or re-casting religious texts, with the effect that the religious text becomes more aligned with one's experience and are less likely to be considered in anti-LGBT terms:

> Queering religious texts… has a de-stabilizing effect, through the transgression and de-construction of naturalized and normalized hermeneutics, which reinforces heteronormativity… queering exposes the socio-cultural embeddedness and temporal specificity of the texts, as well as the ideological framework of the authority that constructs such hermeneutic.
>
> *(Yip, 2005, p. 51)*

Others have focused on the cultivation of queer spiritual spaces (e.g. Browne *et al.*, 2010). Browne (2010) notes how spaces can constitute repair as well as harm. This contests the idea that religious spaces will always be hostile to queer bodies, while also recognising the spatial harms religions have created, especially in religious spaces that remain unwelcoming. This corresponds with Cuthbert and Taylor's (2018) analysis of the Metropolitan Community Church (MCC), and how this was constructed as a "home" and "family" for many participants, significant in contexts where their identities had been rejected within other religious spaces. Where family had rejected them because of their queer identity, the MCC literally became their new home. Meanwhile, Fielder and Ezzy's (2018) study of LGBT Christians in Australia emphasises that queering enables their participants to live what they call 'authentic lives' (2018, p. 1) that correspond both with their religious and sexual identity. This identity-work is challenging, given the emotional and psychological negativity they have often encountered during their upbringing. The queering of space enables MCC churches in Australia to be a haven for queer Christians, offering affirming theologies and supportive environments, where orthodox belief systems are displaced and queered. But they question the extent to which the MCC churches enable a full queering to take place, noting the embedded heteronormative and homonormative assumptions that arise, especially in relation to gender. While a relational spirituality offers the potential for queering to take place, a failure to emplace

**66** Identity, sexualities, and religion

one in another person's shoes means that prejudices remain, particularly in relation to bisexual and trans community members. Bisexuals, for example, were often aligned with promiscuity and immaturity:

> The essentialist understanding of an authentic sexuality leads to bisexuality being viewed as an "immature" state. Ambiguity disturbs individuals. Ambiguity threatens the safe spaces that are created in the MCC. Individuals feel safe in spaces that are unsurprising and in some sense "normative". The queering of religious space occurs insofar as the individual and group needs are met in the desire to live an authentic life... Despite challenging heteronormative mainstream Christianity, the MCC creates its own "homonormative" space.
>
> *(Fielder and Ezzy, 2018, p. 158)*

Wilcox (2018a) meanwhile has undertaken an ethnography of queer nuns belonging to the Sisters of Perpetual Indulgence. While the Order started in the US, branches can now be located throughout the world. The Sisters parody the religious orders of the Roman Catholic Church, utilising drag artistry and performance as a form of activism to highlight church hypocrisy and injustice. Practices engaged with vary, but include safe-sex programmes such as distributing condoms, publicly challenging ex-gay ministry drives, and die-in performances, which emphasise how the Roman Catholic Church's policy on condoms is deadly.

This is an act of queering in the sense that the nun is resignified within the Sisters of Perpetual Indulgence, in a form which Wilcox terms 'serious parody':

> Serious parody... is a form of cultural protest in which a disempowered group parodies an oppressive cultural institution while simultaneously claiming for itself what it believes to be an equally good or superior enactment of one or more culturally respected aspects of the same institution. In the case of the Sisters, this means enacting parodies of Roman Catholic rituals and figures such as nuns and priests while also claiming in all seriousness to be nuns.
>
> *(2018a, p. 70)*

This queering of religion and gender is emphasised in Wilcox's concepts of genderfuck and religionfuck. While 'genderfuck challenges and even undermines cultural assumptions about the way genders, bodies and desires cohere, then religionfuck might be said to challenge and undermine cultural assumptions about the ways religious identities, roles, practices, beliefs, and appearances cohere' (2018a, p. 86). On the one hand, genderfuck challenges the normatives regarding who can claim to be a nun; those with penises and beards adopt the insignia of a nun's order, while on the other hand religionfuck challenges the contours regarding how religion is constituted. Their focus on challenging sexual injustice in relation to the Church can be considered antagonistic and opposed to religion. But their performativity as nuns is more than a confrontation with religion; theirs also offers a ministering role to those in the LGBT community; they will hear confession and will give blessings. In this way, Wilcox explores the complex enactment of queering in relation to religion, and the way queer bodies are resacralised in the process.

## Summary

Research on religion and sexuality has often privileged identity-based theoretical frames to analyse their findings and situate their analysis. The appeal rests on research questions which are keen to explore how religious and sexual identities can be reconciled, especially in contexts where sexual identities are not sanctioned in religious spaces. This also relates to late-modern concerns regarding how individuals reflexively create their selves in relation to the choices available to them. A focus on identity risks becoming idiosyncratic and subjective; concentrating on choices can mean that power dynamics are ignored. But many of the studies utilising this framework are exploring complexity, nuance, and the interworkings of choice and power. While queer approaches have been popular in studying religious and sexual identity, perhaps because of the way queer approaches have not only been adopted in mainstream sociological research but have also been captured in many theological accounts, other approaches have not as yet developed their full potential. Lived religion, for example, is only starting to be utilised as a theoretical approach to studying religion and sexuality (Page, 2017a) and is currently limited by its over-focus on Christian contexts. Intersectionality, despite its popularity within the sociological mainstream, also has much more to offer (Page and Yip, forthcoming). For example, what findings would emerge from a study of working-class religious queers? What if disability was fully incorporated into a religion and sexuality analysis? The theoretical mileage of these concepts is endless.

# 4

# METHODOLOGICAL INSIGHTS

## Researching religion and sexualities

### Introduction

This chapter focuses on the challenges and opportunities accorded researchers studying religion and sexualities. Our own experience of conducting two substantially sized mixed methods projects enables much reflection on methodological approaches and our attempts at conducting ethical research. We argue for research that is mindful of power dynamics and research hierarchies, and critically interrogates how knowledge is formulated from the types of methods selected and how they are deployed. We will argue the merits of taking a queer feminist approach to research, as both are concerned with privilege and marginalisation and seek to challenge normatives and the taken-for-granted. We will showcase specific methods deployed in religion and sexuality research, and while this chapter is not intended to provide an overview of all sociological methods, it does capture many of the standard approaches to the study of religion and sexualities.

### Queer and feminist approaches: Redrawing methodological boundaries

Historically, sociological research has prioritised the accounts and worldviews of privileged individuals, whether that be in terms of geography, ethnicity, social class, gender, sexuality, age, or dis/ability (Hammers and Brown, 2004; Letherby, 2003). Religiously too, there has been greater focus on those belonging to dominant religious traditions such as Christianity. Those who align with religion in certain ways (e.g. attending a place of worship) are also more likely to be accounted for in research terms (Wilcox, 2009). Certain groups have therefore been omitted from the research story, their accounts silenced. Wilcox (2009) raises this issue in relation to locating queer women, who may not necessarily be found in queer-affirming places of worship. For example, Wilcox notes the male dominated structure of the Metropolitan Community Church within the district she was researching, which put off women from attending. While the Church was queer-affirming, it was not deemed woman-affirming. She therefore deployed different tactics to find queer spiritual women beyond congregations. Since the 1980s, feminists have emphasised the importance of accounting for religious women's perspectives, and how this radically shifts our understanding of social reality (Brasher, 1997; Davidman, 1991; Griffith, 1997; Neitz, 2003; Woodhead, 2001). More recently, specific attention has been focused on women's sexualities within religious contexts (Gaddini, forthcoming; Moultrie, 2017; Sharma, 2008, 2011). In the last 15 years or so, accounts have been produced specifying the challenges that queer religious individuals face (Barton, 2012; Hunt and Yip, 2012; Shipley, 2014; Thumma and Gray, 2005; Yip, 2005). Because these research endeavours have emphasised the lived realities of those often marginalised due to their sexuality, these voices have traditionally been omitted from research accounts. The question that emerges, then, is firstly what methodological approaches are best able to map accounts where power differentials are embedded, in order to account for marginalised voices, and secondly, what developments need to take place to critically interrogate more privileged identities (e.g. middle-class Christian men's sexualities, heterosexuals) and analyse how their power is sustained.

We argue that feminist and queer methodological perspectives are crucial to this endeavour; both critique taken-for-granted accounts that privilege certain formulations of masculinity and heterosexuality, and both stress the importance of power differentials in the research encounter (Browne and Nash, 2016; Finch, 1993; Macke, 2014; Oakley, 1981; Slee *et al.*, 2018). Tensions have been highlighted between queer and feminist perspectives, due to, for example, feminists prioritising gender, and queer theorists prioritising sexuality, as well as some strands of feminism advocating an essential gender identity fitting uneasily with the fluidity emphasised in queer accounts (McLaughlin *et al.*, 2006). But following Pilcher (2016), we argue that they can be mutually supporting:

> the crux of what a feminist and queer analysis can do is to expose the ways in which gender and sexualities, in their processes of being constructed and articulated, are *mutually constituting* one another, in different ways and in different times and moments... a queer feminist approach can bring to the fore how both gender and sexuality are constructed in ways that centre them within hierarchical social divisions, recognising that the power of normalising discourses in particular contribute to reproducing structural inequalities.
>
> *(2016, p. 19, emphasis in original)*

A queer feminist approach therefore offers a much richer conceptual framework than either a queer or feminist approach can offer in isolation. And as

## 70 Methodological insights

McLaughlin *et al.* (2006) argue, a queer feminist approach is closely connected with intersectionality. As we outlined in the previous chapter, intersectional analysis originally focused on the multiple disadvantages experienced by Black women. Crenshaw (1989), and other Black feminist scholars, highlighted the additional barriers that Black women face, where law narrows issues into single categories of identity, to instead consider how identity is multiply constituted. Intersectionality is also important in mapping the relationship between researcher and participant, and how power, privilege, and marginalisation operate on many different axes (Browne and Nash, 2016; Taylor, 2016). Intersectionality has often focused on the so-called "big three" of class, gender, and ethnicity; religion has often been excluded from intersectional analyses (Page and Yip, forthcoming), as has sexuality (Taylor *et al.*, 2011). A focus on religion and sexuality emphasises intersections that have not been captured extensively in research terms, such as how religion and sexuality intersect with ethnicity, social class, age, and gender, among others. While both feminist and queer approaches have rightly focused on those traditionally marginalised in the research account, there is also the potential to explore how certain identities have come to be privileged and made normative, therefore offering much scope for analysing masculinity and hetero-sexuality in new ways.

This chapter will chart what it means to pursue a queer feminist episte-mology, starting with a focus on the underlying principles that we identify as being important to this endeavour – namely, critiquing the taken-for-granted and accounting for power (Browne and Nash, 2016). We will then focus on various methods that can be utilised, emphasising those that may enable greater innovation in pushing boundaries. In effect, we explore how knowl-edge is created through research decisions and methodological choices, as well as focusing on the crux of the methods themselves while recognising that there is a clear difference between methods and methodologies. As Browne and Nash argue:

> Research "methods" can be conceptualised as what is "done", that is, the techniques of collecting data (interviews, questionnaires, focus groups, photographs, videos, observation, *inter alia*). By contrast, methodologies are those sets of rules and procedures that guide the design of research to investigate phenomenon or situations.
>
> *(2016, p. 10–11)*

We will draw on reflections from our own research experiences, elements of research that we see as fundamental to good research practice such as reflex-ivity and the importance of aligning research principles with our own ethical commitments. This will also consider the personal impact of undertaking sensi-tive research, in research encounters where participants are not only potentially revealing very personal information but also abuses that have happened to them, such as experiencing sexual violence.

## Power, hierarchy, and researcher reflexivity

As indicated in Chapters 1 to 3, context, power, and identity are crucial in understanding sexuality and religion. Firstly, contexts differ – as Shah (2018) notes, while gay Muslims are problematised in Britain because of their religious identities, they are conversely maligned in Malaysia because of their sexuality. Secondly, the contextual will relate to power differentials and which discourses become dominant – e.g. the "Muslim terrorist" trope in the UK (Mirza, 2013). Thirdly, identities are embedded in these constellations; individuals are trying to live out their religious and sexual lives within these broader power-infused discourses. With increased interest in conducting research among groups negatively impacted by such discourses, there is correspondingly increased analysis as to the social construction of vulnerability and the power relations created between people with variable amounts of power (Pells, 2012; Tisdall and Punch, 2012). In order to address the power relations in research with those who have been marginalised, some researchers endorse participant-led engagements (von Benzon and van Blerk, 2017). Qualitative research often encourages participation (but not always) and attempts to address research power imbalances (Aldridge, 2014; Cahill, 2007).

Undertaking research with marginalised populations assumes that access is possible – indeed, some researchers have reflected that access to queer religious individuals is not as difficult to achieve as one might initially assume (Yip, 2008). However, it is worth reflecting on who still gets excluded. Research ethics committees can be deeply unhappy about sexuality research conducted with those under the age of 18, and these considerations certainly shaped the design of the *Religion Youth and Sexuality* (RYS) and *Religion, Gender, and Sexuality among Youth in Canada* (RGSY) projects; the young people in our research were all adults. In Canada, to conduct research among individuals under the legal age of consent requires parental permission, thereby creating barriers of access for young people who have important contributions to make. In a study among high school students in Ontario considering the implications of a cancelled sex education curriculum promoting diversity, Shipley (2019) encountered students who did not want to obtain parental consent because their families did not support their queer identities. This therefore raised questions over the risks of research participation for some groups, and also meant that certain groups were silenced from sharing their views and experiences.

Critical reflection on how power and privilege become part of what is being analysed is also crucial to a queer feminist research endeavour. While much religion and sexuality research has done cogent work on exploring how marginalised groups have fared in challenging religious contexts, equally we need to engage with how normative forms of sexuality and gender are reproduced (Butler, 1993). This involves a critical interrogation of more privileged identities, such as heterosexuality. Heterosexuality is often so normative it is not even named (Moultrie, 2017; Weeks, 2011). Asking heterosexuals about their sexuality

**72** Methodological insights

in the RYS project could produce a bemused response – that there was nothing to reflect on. This emphasises the deep-seated ways in which heterosexuality has been made normative, but it is only through analysing how it comes to such prominence that we can understand the power dynamics at work (Yip and Page, 2014). Understanding power needs a considered and nuanced approach. Power dynamics are more complicated than zero-sum configurations; at the level of the individual, it is usually not the case that individuals are either wholly privileged or wholly disadvantaged. Intersectional approaches emphasise how identities are configured in complex ways, with individuals potentially aligning both with advantaged and disadvantaged positions, offering a more nuanced understanding of privilege and marginalisation (Page and Yip, forthcoming).

Once access is possible, deep reflections are required regarding the power dynamics between the researcher and participants; obtaining ethical approval through signed consent forms is not enough; ethical issues run through the research process, both before and after any consent form is signed (Shipley, 2019; Taylor and Snowdon, 2014b). The researcher influences the way data is produced. Whether we are "insiders" or "outsiders", our stance and perceived objectivity (or lack thereof) impacts the design of the project, its implementation, and the response from participants. Researchers are not free from the dominant norms and scripts that permeate our social, legal, and familial contexts, impacting on which research questions are deemed important (indeed this is also impacted upon by the types of research that are seen to be worth funding). The language of normativity impacts how we learn about non-normative experiences. The way in which we learn about diverse sexual experiences becomes centrally important and requires reflexivity.

Researcher privilege is tied to insider and outsider distinctions (Chinwuba, 2014; Siraj, 2012; Taylor and Snowdon, 2013). At the same time, it is often not clear-cut in determining our "insider" or "outsider" status, and as researchers, we occupy both positions concurrently (Gorman-Murray *et al.*, 2016). Indeed, the insider–outsider relationship is unstable; connections with others are formed and reformulated continually through the research process (Nash, 2016). Researchers are often (although not always) accorded authority in the field, which will shape their negotiations, how they are perceived and received, and what access they are given. But this will be shaped by other factors too, such as age, gender, ethnicity, sexuality, and class dynamics. Without reflexivity and self-awareness, analysis of the results will importantly miss the complex dynamics at play in the spaces (literal and figurative) that are created to conduct the research and gather responses from participants. The following sections will examine specific methods, and how they correspond with these issues.

### *Surveying religion and sexuality*

Surveys are forms of data collection at a single moment in time, usually involving a large number of cases (Bryman, 2004). The data collection method varies but

Methodological insights **73**

typically involves either structured interviews or questionnaires. Religion and sexuality research has not typically adopted survey approaches, instead focusing on qualitative approaches, such as semi-structured interviews and ethnographies. This is no coincidence for projects taking a feminist and/or queer starting point; feminist and queer scholars have had an uneasy relationship regarding utilising quantitative approaches. Many have noted how quantitative approaches have actually enabled the erasure of women's and queer bodies from the research endeavour, through systematically ignoring those experiences, also including historical assumptions where research on heterosexual men can be generalised to everyone else, as well as failing to ask questions pertinent to gender and sexuality issues (Millman and Kanter, 1987). Quantitative research is often based on certain epistemological assumptions such as esteem for research that is measurable, value-free, and neutral (Mies, 1993). This encourages an environment where well-defined and clear categories are established, which in turn are understood as generating facts (Denzin and Lincoln, 2011). But this does not enable a critical interrogation of how those categories emerge in the first place or what assumptions are being made. The fluidity and movement of such categories is instead given over to 'static facts' (Day and Lee, 2014, p. 347). In sexuality research, for example, the homosexual/heterosexual binary has loomed large, and been a core binary for queer studies to deconstruct, but this in no way accurately represents how people actually perceive or live out their sexual lives (Browne, 2016; Sedgwick, 2008). Given the centrality of categories and variables to the quantitative endeavour, it becomes hard to move beyond this, and any such cultivation of category lists is a political endeavour (Browne, 2016). Wilmot's (2007) research regarding how sexuality should be asked about in Office for National Statistics surveys highlights diversity in how categories are labelled. Ticking a box such as "prefer not to say" gives no clear idea regarding the motivation for selecting that category and does not necessarily mean that the individual would prefer to select a queer-identifying label that is not available to them. Indeed, this also throws into question the whole notion of reducing identities to categories and whether this is even possible or desirable in fluid and complex social lives – can sexual identities really be reduced to lesbian/gay, bisexual, and straight/heterosexual as many questionnaires assume (Nash, 2016)? Yet, giving individuals the option to insert whatever label they choose risks having such diversity that the categories cease to be measurable (Browne, 2016).

This issue was directly encountered at the questionnaire stage in both the RYS and RGSY projects. On the RYS project, the question, "How would you define your sexuality?" (Lesbian, Gay, Homosexual, Heterosexual, Bisexual, I do not define my sexuality, Other – please state) produced much disquiet. A minority of participants were unclear of the differences, particularly between the category of "homosexual" and "heterosexual", such as Isma, a heterosexual Muslim woman who said in the interview 'I always confuse homosexual and heterosexual'. But more pertinently, religious young adults often disliked the very act of labelling (Young and Shipley, 2020), and a significant proportion

**74** Methodological insights

of questionnaire respondents chose 'I do not define my sexuality', while others defined in an alternative way, creating new categories such as "bicurious", "asexual", and "heteroflexible" (see Yip and Page, 2013). The option to self-disclose on the questionnaire thereby emphasised that there were other potentialities beyond the categories presented. As Heckert (2016) has argued, the heterosexual, homosexual, and bisexual divide simply does not relate to reality and how people experience their lives. Participants move between categories over time, and in interviews could adopt alternative ways of defining their identities. And many – indicated by the proportion of RYS participants who chose to not define their sexuality – were reluctant to view their identity through the lens of sexuality, lest this became a master label. Joshua, a gay Christian man within the RYS project, said that 'Long before I would define myself as gay, I would define myself as Joshua… I am who I am because I am the sum of my parts, not because [of] one aspect of my life (e.g. my sexuality)'. The categories themselves also take on new meanings and understandings; at conferences, some have questioned the inclusion of the term "homosexual", this being a contentious term with a problematic history, utilised by those opposed to homosexuality, and in the language of conversion therapies of both a medicalised and religious nature.

Meanwhile, in the RGSY dataset, conducted a few years after the RYS project, the sticking point for participants was binarised forms of gender identity, with participants contesting the dividing of identity between male and female, choosing instead other less rigid gender configurations (Young and Shipley, 2020). A number of participants resisted seeing themselves in 100% male or 100% female terms. In the qualitative interviews, it was clear that the young adults were not only questioning the gender categories themselves, but all the associated meanings tied up with those categories, such as the stereotypes attached to each gender, which could lead to an explicit cultivation of an ambiguous gendered subjectivity, through dress and other forms of embodiment. The questioning of gender was less common in the RYS research, perhaps indicative of its earlier timeframe when gender binaries were less likely to be questioned. But there were similar indicators, such as Emma, a Buddhist who strongly objected to binary forms of gender, saying 'I don't care what gender I am. I would rather [endorse] genderless instead arguing for a genderless completely. [Gender binary] is a game I don't want to play'. Emma instead adopted the label "trans" as a challenge to the binarised system (see Page and Yip, 2017b). This coheres with Nash's research, whose participants were locating themselves as trans in a 'political sense of refusing a legible gendered, embodied, sexualised identity, opting instead to be "read" as largely unintelligible to others with normative gendered, embodied and sexualised frameworks in all spaces' (Nash, 2016, p. 140). Research with young people demonstrates the negotiated, thoughtful, and deconstructed ways they experience their identities and how these contest category-focused identity formulations.

There are few large-scale representative surveys specifically designed to answer research questions about religion and sexuality, given the expense required (though we will go on to talk about some momentarily). Instead, researchers often try to work with national surveys (often focused on social attitudes) which are not specifically designed with their research questions in mind. For example, questionnaires asking attitudinal questions to issues such as same-sex marriage and abortion can be analysed in relation to religious identification – so long as religious identification was something that was asked about. Yet there has been much controversy regarding how questionnaires ask about religious identification and whether the way the question is asked creates misleading results, especially in social contexts where surveys are accorded much power and authority (Day and Lee, 2014). For example, Day (2011) questions how the 2001 Census in England and Wales asks about people's religious identification. The question, "What is your religion?" assumes that everyone has a religion. Day's qualitative examination of people's response to the Census question enabled her to demonstrate why so many non-religious people had identified as Christian, which were aligned with national and ethnic identity (see also Day and Lee, 2014). When such surveys have been produced at a national level, the individual researcher has little input into how such categories are defined and operationalised, therefore questioning the reliability of the data. Equally, the ways in which inferences are drawn from single measures on questionnaires can be problematic – for example, if an attitudinal question on same-sex marriage is used as an indicator of negativity towards homosexuality, this could be quite distorting – firstly, many in the queer community have themselves opposed same-sex marriage for requiring queer people to opt into heteronormative forms of relationships that make same-sex sexuality socially acceptable (see Duggan, 2002; Hooghe *et al.*, 2010). And secondly, opposition to same-sex marriage may be accompanied by strong support for the right to identify as queer, and therefore does not successfully represent wholesale negativity per se. As Yip (2011) has found through focus groups with heterosexuals from traditionally more conservative demographics, individuals can be opposed to some equality-bearing mechanisms such as same-sex parenting, while they support the right to same-sex marriage. He identified a continuum amongst his participants; while the recriminalisation of homosexuality was not supported at all, and there was little support for unequal treatment towards LGBT+ people in employment, for example, there was more consternation regarding support for same-sex marriage, with most conservatism reserved for the issue of LGBT+ parenting. Therefore, there were many differing elements and facets to the opinions he gathered, so that opposition to LGBT+ equalities was actually multi-layered and contextual. This example demonstrates the dangers of using a singular measure to operationalise a concept that goes far beyond the original measure, such as the way in which same-sex marriage does not equate to "homosexuality"; a questionnaire question on attitudes to same-sex marriage gives only an indicator of a person's perspective to "homosexuality", and cannot be used on its own as a measure of tolerance or otherwise to homosexuality per se (Hooghe and Meusen, 2013; Shipley, 2014). But equally, researchers will be limited by the original questions that have been posed within national surveys.

**76** Methodological insights

With these caveats in mind, some have deployed national surveys to useful effect. Clements (2015) focuses on Britain, utilising various existing data sets (including the nationally representative British Social Attitudes Survey, British Election Study, European Values Study, European Social Survey, and Eurobarometer) to ascertain the relationship between religion and public opinion, thereby conducting secondary data analysis. While the topics considered are wide-ranging, his focus on homosexuality and abortion are most relevant. Clements' study highlights the specific challenges when focusing on survey data not specifically designed for one's research questions; for example, not all of these survey sets had questions on religious beliefs, with religion sometimes being more narrowly defined in terms of belonging and behaviours (e.g. attendance at a place of worship). Meanwhile, categories and meanings could change over time. And because Clements was mapping attitudes across time, this meant it was hard to gather data on those belonging to minority religions, so the analysis focuses far more on Christianity. In addition, Clements was not able to access all the data breakdowns (e.g. differences between religious affiliations), particularly from surveys from decades ago. But combining various data sets across time allows Clements to 'provide as robust and detailed an account of trends in public opinion in recent decades as possible' (2015, p. 128). Regarding abortion, Clements is able to tease out the differences between Christian groups (with Roman Catholics most opposed – but with significant variation amongst Catholics) as well as indicating what exactly is being opposed, focusing on differences between "abortion on demand" versus abortion in very specific circumstances. He also examines attitudes to the legal position and what religious individuals feel regarding the availability of abortion. Clements tracks these changes over time, thereby pulling together the various surveys to convey common trends, indicating that all religious groups, generally speaking, have liberalised their attitudes, and even amongst Catholics, those totally opposed to abortion comprise a very small number of Catholics as a whole. Meanwhile, on homosexuality too, views amongst religious individuals have liberalised, and, like abortion, those who attend religious services more frequently are more likely to be opposed.

While Clements utilised existing data sets, Woodhead (2013) commissioned a nationally representative survey in Britain on ethical opinion and religion, covering a number of sexuality issues such as abortion and same-sex marriage. It was administered by YouGov, a company specialising in obtaining data on public opinion, and surveyed 4,437 adults. Because of its specialist design and focus on religion (also over-sampling certain smaller religious traditions to ensure good representation), this survey offers revealing insights into the levels of religious conservatism and the extent to which there is a correlation between having a religious identity and being conservative on issues of abortion and same-sex marriage. The key finding was that being religious was only impactful if one belonged to the 8.5% of the sample who Woodhead describes as a "moral minority". Therefore, religion per se was not found to invoke traditional views, unless belonging to the moral minority, a category containing a significant number of highly religious individuals, and more likely to be comprised of Muslims, Baptists, and Roman Catholics. It was this group that was more likely to be opposed to abortion and same-sex marriage.

Regnerus (2007) probably represents one of the largest-scale surveys specifically designed to map issues relating to religion and sexuality in significant detail, focusing on 13–17-year-olds, as well as parents of teenagers. This project drew on a nationally representative survey of 3,370 teenagers across America (the National Survey of Youth and Religion, which Regnerus helped devise), obtaining a large amount of information regarding sexual attitudes and practices, such as the use of contraception, pornography use, premarital sex, and masturbation. As a mixed methods project, this was followed up with interviews with 267 teens. Regnerus also used supporting data from the National Longitudinal Study of Adolescent Health dataset. The advantage of also obtaining interview data enables a much fuller exploration of the issues, enabling Regnerus to convey a complex and revealing picture regarding the attitudes and experiences of American teens.

Attitudes-based research at a global level can be very insightful in mapping trends. The Pew Research Centre's *Global Attitudes & Trends* project reports on a series of global public opinion surveys. In 2013, this included a survey distributed across 40 countries asking 40,117 respondents their views on "moral issues". The response scale was (1) morally acceptable; (2) morally unacceptable, or (3) not a moral issue (Pew Research Center, 2014). The majority believed that extramarital affairs (78%), homosexuality (59%), and abortion (56%) were unacceptable. The unacceptability of premarital sex (46%), divorce (24%), and contraception (14%), meanwhile, were deemed unacceptable by a minority.

According to this survey, the majority global attitude towards homosexuality is that homosexuality is morally unacceptable. Factoring qualifiers such as variations in state and religious influence on social attitudes, a majority of the 40 countries (22 of 40) where the survey was distributed held negative attitudes toward homosexuality. Across the globe, sexual diversity policies have increased in recent decades; the trend in Western societies towards legalising same-sex marriage has steadily increased – a significant amount of policy change has occurred in a relatively brief period of time (Green, 2010). But the policy changes do not necessarily reflect predominant attitudes within a particular nation. In some European nations, equality-bearing policies were the result of entry into the European Union, not as a result of changing public opinion or advocacy (Stan and Turcescu, 2011). In Romania, anti-homosexual attitudes have remained unchanged, regardless of the adoption of national policies on sexual orientation and marriage equality. In 2018, the leader of the Social Democrat Party, Liviu Dragnea, along with other influential religious groups, successfully campaigned to hold a referendum on a national ban against same-sex marriage (Mutler, 2019).

Where citizens do not accept policy or legislative changes, the mismatch between policy and public opinion can lead to legitimacy problems. The role

**78** Methodological insights

religion plays on the influence of attitudes towards homosexuality varied; assessing the data related to four religious organisations, Gerhards states:

> We expect support for homosexuality by religious orientation to go as follows: people with no religious affiliation will show higher levels of support towards homosexuality than will members of religious communities; Protestants will show moderate levels of support, and Muslims, Orthodox Christians and Catholics will show the least support.
>
> *(2010, p. 17)*

Attitudes towards homosexuality also serve as a barometer for other kinds of national statements on values; in the Netherlands, acceptance of homosexuality within the public and political spheres has served to further us/them divides regarding new immigrants, especially Muslim immigrants (Dudink, 2016). Policies about multiculturalism and immigration have been targeted as generating discord within Dutch society, where 'non-negotiable moral principles' about the equal treatment of homosexuality are deployed against Muslim immigrants whose own (assumed in some cases) anti-homosexual values are cited as the 'reason' for their failure to integrate (Dudink, 2016, p. 3).

Surveys such as Pew are important in mapping global trends, and they have the ability to reach a wide range of individuals. What is gained by collecting mass data is the ability to conduct statistical analysis, often utilised for predictive modelling analyses. However, questionnaires and surveys deployed on a large scale are also the subject of criticism because of what they do not capture by the nature of their scale; nuance and context can be lost in the deployment of a questionnaire or survey because of the inability to flesh out either the questions or the answers. The "blunt instrument" (Day and Lee, 2014) of the survey allows for particular types of data gathering, but also inhibits the more nuanced qualitative data that is made possible through qualitative methods such as interviews and ethnographies.

The RYS and RGSY projects both deployed questionnaires as part of datagathering. Beyond the demographic questions, many questions were attitudes-based and sought a Likert-scale response, ranging from "strongly agree" to "strongly disagree". We asked participants to convey their views on religion (e.g. 'I make decisions in my everyday life with reference to my religion'), sexuality (e.g. 'Heterosexuality and homosexuality should be treated equally'), sexual practices (e.g. 'Ideally sex should take place only within the context of marriage'), gender roles (e.g. 'Religious authority figures [e.g. clergy] should be male'), perceptions of their religious tradition in relation to sexuality (e.g. 'My religion is against any form of sexuality other than heterosexuality'), factors of influence (e.g. participants were asked to rank the factors that they think influence their sexual values and attitudes, with the list comprised of religious factors, family, friends, and media sources), as well as questions around being religious in a secular society (e.g. 'I believe people from my religious tradition are portrayed negatively in the media'). This mixture therefore aimed to obtain a broader understanding of how their religious and sexual identity was experienced, but much of the focus was on participant attitudes (for a full list of questions see Yip and Page, 2013; and Young and Shipley, 2020). Some of the negatives of surveys acting as "blunt instruments" were mitigated by including open-ended questions, such as 'What does your religion mean to you?' and 'What does your sexuality mean to you?' Such "open text" responses could be as long as the participant desired. Some wrote lengthy responses, while others gave one-word answers. However, participants still disliked the bounded categories. One participant on the RYS project reflected, 'I could have written an essay on some of the questions and for many others my ideas didn't fit into any of the categories provided'. Another participant wanted greater opportunities to expand qualitatively to every attitude conveyed, in order to demonstrate the nuance of their opinion. Similarly, in the RGSY project, participants used the reflection spaces to share their challenges with fitting themselves into the questions they were asked. Both projects went on to conduct in-depth interviews with a sample of participants who had completed the questionnaire, so this allowed the complexity and nuance of attitude formation to be explored. But this emphasises the limitations of projects which solely utilise questionnaires, and the frustrations those completing these questionnaires often feel.

These examples demonstrate the complexity of engaging questionnaires when undertaking religion and sexuality research. Both are considered sensitive topics, and participants can be alienated from the moment demographic questions such as religion or sexual identification are asked. In addition, such approaches can include bias and distortion. As most surveys are conducted on a volunteer basis, and increasingly administered online, the results tend to be skewed towards individuals who are willing and able to complete them. Even with targeted recruitment strategies, it can be very difficult to obtain a representative sample. And even in unusual cases where the questionnaire is nationally representative, one can still experience distortion in the responses themselves – one cannot test for honesty through a survey, or determine that the respondent definitely fits the eligibility criteria (especially for online surveys). While this does not render survey research unusable, it is important for researchers to acknowledge these limitations.

Ensuring that the recruitment strategies focus on multiple, diverse venues of access (religious, non-religious, spiritual, queer-affirming, inclusive organisations) offers possible vehicles for accessing wide-ranging populations. However, conflicts and tensions that arise relate to certain religious perspectives and sexual diversity can also dissuade potential participants in any of these above-mentioned spaces from wanting to be involved in such a study – persistent feelings of hostility and anxiety can make the study itself seem a component of that negative experience, rather than an opportunity to communicate and explore it. Some of the RYS participants felt very uncomfortable and unwilling to answer some of the questionnaire questions, deeming the matters too private for broader

**80** Methodological insights

disclosure. One participant said that 'I would not be comfortable encouraging friends to participate due to some of the content of the questionnaire'.

The format of an online questionnaire or survey can also pose distinct advantages – especially when researching religion and sexuality. The space of anonymity that can be provided allows for the possibility of a more honest, at times raw, series of responses. To date, however, survey research has focused on youth and one of the two aspects of identity (religion or sexuality) with a paucity overall in research bringing the two together, though this issue is not restricted to questionnaires.

## *Ethnography*

Ethnography engages in the study of beliefs, social interactions, and behaviours, especially in group settings. Ethnography primarily involves participant-observation (Berry, 2004; Denzin and Lincoln, 2011; Reeves *et al.*, 2008). Data collected by participant-observation is typically recorded in field notes (Denzin and Lincoln, 2011). Ethnography developed as a way to capture the way humans behave in more natural settings. In its earliest form, ethnography made no attempt at representing the point of view of the people being observed; rather it reported on the actions of those under observation. The shift in ethnography came when researchers such as Malinowski began introducing the points of view of those being studied through the immersion of the researcher into the culture under study (Elliott and Jankel-Elliott, 2003). This shift provided the capacity for 'thick' ethnography to develop (Berry, 2004; Geertz, 1993).

Ethnographies have been frequently used in the study of religion and sexuality. These methods enable the examination of dynamics within, for example, a queer religious congregation (Wilcox, 2009) or at a non-traditional gathering, such as Gray and Thumma's (2005b) study of "Gospel Hour", a drag show in Atlanta that mixes Evangelical gospel music with drag performances. Observational methods provide access without imposition. When considering the dynamics of lived religion and lived sexuality, ethnographic methods provide the additional space of reflection on practice and dynamic engagement in a lived, experiential forum, but this can also create ethical and positional research dilemmas.

Winder (2015) studied responses to anti-gay religious teachings among young Black gay men, using both semi-structured interviews and ethnographic observation data, to consider the role non-religious youth organisations have in the negotiation of religious and sexual identities among participants. Winder's inclusion of 18 months of ethnographic observations, attendance at weekly gatherings and social events, intentionally sought to illuminate 'community building and collective negotiations of religious teachings' (2015, p. 375). Winder wanted to consider both how these non-religious, youth organisations helped young Black gay men understand and navigate authoritative messages on religious teachings and to work towards reclaiming these messages.

Winder's participation in the weekly gatherings and at social events over the 18-month period worked to dispel the initial hesitation many had felt about having a researcher "use" them for their own interests. Further, Winder's own identity as a young, gay Black man helped build trust among the group. Combining interviews and observation data, Winder was able to unpack the nuance of the experiences of his participants.

Shah (2018) investigated the particular lifeworlds of gay Muslims and how they managed the dominant discourses that either positioned them as victims of an oppressive religion or as religious deviants. This contextual focus encouraged Shah to adopt an ethnographic approach, effectively "hanging around" with his gay Muslim participants in both Malaysia and Britain, accompanying them in their leisure and religious spaces. In Britain, Shah specifically focused on a prominent Muslim LGBT support group, regularly attending gatherings and even adopting a volunteer role within the organisation. His reflexivity on his own positionality as a gay middle-class Muslim emphasised the complexities regarding interpretation and how to convey these lived realities in a research account. One key issue for Shah in both contexts of study is Shah's interrogation of his classed assumptions; his attempts to understand the lives and experiences of working-class LGBT Muslims made Shah question his understanding of himself as having "insider" status simply by being LGBT himself.

While Winder (2015) and Shah (2018) could identify points of commonality between them and their participants, other researchers have accessed fieldwork spaces in which they are fundamentally opposed and are not necessarily welcome. Maguire *et al.* (2018) undertook research at conferences, rallies, and conventions arranged by Christian organisations opposed to LGBT people. As all members of the research team were LGBT themselves or were LGBT allies, this posed enormous emotional burdens on them as they navigated spaces where their "lifestyles" were not welcome, and where their very existence was delegitimised, joked about, and constructed in extremely negative ways. As Maguire *et al.* (2018) portrayed themselves outwardly as aligned with the values of the anti-LGBT organisations, the performativity required to collect the data was profoundly challenging. While not wanting to lie, they would convey certain facts about themselves that were read in particular ways – for example, having children would be "read" as being heterosexual. Meanwhile, Lowe and Page's (forthcoming) ethnography of religiously derived anti-abortion activism across the UK (ADPS project) equally carried emotional burdens, given that both unequivocally support access to abortion. The challenges in engaging with participants while being honest about one's own positionality created tensions in the research encounter, with some refusing to engage in the project at all. As Detamore argues, research with others always produces 'ethical entanglements' (2016, p. 168), where our own values and those of research participants have to be navigated and negotiated. In order to understand why anti-abortion activists participated in clinic vigils required access to their stories so that a more nuanced understanding – rather than a mere caricature of their position – could

**82** Methodological insights

be produced. Without their input, the research, limited to observation only, would have missed the layers of meaning that anti-abortion activists subscribed to their practice. Gaining access to these stories required careful negotiation, and much emotional investment. But at the same time as the researchers sought to understand activists' motivations, they were unable to identify with their positionality, and indeed witnessed the harmful effects of their actions, such as the detrimental impact on women trying to access abortion services.

Ethnographies require large commitments of time and energy. They also cultivate deep questions about one's positionality and emotional wellbeing when research is sustained over a long period. But ethnographies do provide much greater information on the contexts of people's lives, and how social worlds are constructed. The notion of "hanging around" gives the researcher access to the mundane and small details of participants' lives, offering good opportunities to explore facets of lived religion (see Chapter 3). But unequivocal access may never be possible. Much researcher-involved ethnography focused on religion and sexuality issues has concentrated on public and semi-public spaces. Hanging around a religious meeting is one thing. Hanging around a private home is quite another.

### *Interviews and focus groups: Spatial and identity dynamics*

In-depth interviews are often one of the most standard forms of data gathering in religion and sexuality research. While structured interviews come under the badge of the survey (where questions are standardised with the aim of producing comparable responses), here we are concerned with semi-structured interviews, which are more flexible, and while the researcher may start with a series of set questions, narrative space is provided to allow for expansive discussion on specific topics, themes, and in response to the questions – it is exploratory in a way that a survey is not. Its focus on how meanings are generated is also insightful – interviews allow participants not only to recount their experiences, but to elaborate and explain their perspectives.

Interviews are excellent for exploring sensitive topics such as religion and sexuality, and enable participants to convey a more rounded response on a given issue. Semi-structured formats allow participants to convey their lived realities on their own terms, with participants often already pre-empting before the interview the story they want to share (Hesse-Biber, 2007). Because interviews are very much underscored by the personalities of those involved, this makes reflexivity a key recommendation. How an interview is formatted, where it is held, and the ways in which comfort or discomfort is invoked will have a profound impact on the data obtained. The researcher's own embodiment of space, (dis)comfort, and approach to the questions also influence the dynamic of the interview and the resulting information gathered. This is crucial to consider when the topic area is sexuality and religion.

Both the RYS and RGSY projects included in-depth semi-structured interviews. Care was needed regarding the location for interviews; many young adults

Methodological insights **83**

still living at home with their parents wanted to talk to us elsewhere. But this created its own dilemmas. Are cafes and other public locations suitable places to talk about intimate matters, where participants may recall their first sexual experience or even instances of sexual abuse, and where passers-by may overhear? Where possible (and because of budgetary resource), the UK team were able to hire meeting rooms to ensure interviews were conducted with appropriate privacy. Within the Canadian context, rooms on university campuses were utilised. The remaining interviews were conducted via telephone or Skype for those located across Canada in cities the research team were unable to travel to. Yet, even when participants had arranged to be home alone, interviews could still be disturbed by the unexpected arrival of parents, flatmates, and friends, leading to an abrupt end to conversations. Furthermore, the researcher had to be comfortable in asking quite personal questions. As all interviewees had participated in the questionnaire already, there were no surprises per se, and the questionnaire enabled the expectation for intimate topics to be discussed. But the interviewer had to make a judgement regarding how much to probe. For example, given broader youth discourses focusing on women's sexual empowerment, the RYS team were keen to explore issues of power in intimate heterosexual relationships, asking how much emphasis participants placed on women's orgasm, but this could be delicate to broach, particularly in situations where participants were not yet sexually active. Nevertheless, such questions were often generously acknowledged, perhaps because of Sarah-Jane's own positionality (who conducted most of the interviews) as a woman, and who at the time of the data collection, was not that much older than many of the participants. Levels of disclosure could be quite high, with participants discussing everything from smear tests and oral sex to BDSM (bondage and discipline, sadism and masochism). At the same time, interviews could open up old wounds – a question such as 'have you lost your virginity?' could result in a complex recollection of a sexual encounter that had occurred against the participant's will. Interviewers had to be prepared to hear incredibly distressing stories of childhood sexual abuse, rape, and domestic violence. The embodying of the empathetic listening ear was absolutely crucial in being able to give space to the participant to disclose what they felt able to. As researchers, we would constantly question whether we had got the balance "right" or whether the questions we were asking were too intimate in nature. The participants who went on to create video diaries differed in their levels of disclosure. Without the researcher being present, some participants actually disclosed more intimate details than had been conveyed in interviews (e.g. how orgasm was experienced spiritually) while others tried to avoid talking about sexuality issues altogether.

Siraj's research with minority ethnic gay men and lesbians in England and Scotland uncovered multiple levels of reflection for her; her own sexual identity (as a heterosexual) and religious identity (as a hijabi Muslim) and the influence of these aspects of her identity in interviews were a source of methodological complexity. The positions of privilege she occupies as a heterosexual, as well as

**84** Methodological insights

the potentially authoritarian presence represented by her hijab, meant she had to 'continually reflect upon (her) location in terms of sexual orientation and religion, in order to avoid reducing the experiences of (her) participants solely on their sexual orientation' (2012, p. 62).

Taylor and Snowdon's (2014b) research among queer religious youth in the UK led them to reflect on the researcher-researched positionality and the ways researchers may perform normativity and how this might influence the results of the study. Visibly pregnant, how would participants view Snowdon's heterosexually enforcing pregnant body? Her worry was that she was physically embodying a particular sexual hierarchy, but in fact, her pregnancy became an ice breaker which eased participants into the interviews.

Power's (2014) analysis of interviews about same-sex marriage in Canada considered the power dynamics of the interviewer–interviewee in an interview setting, since the interviewee needed to determine their own sense of ease to express their attitudes, particularly when expressing unpopular views – i.e. anti-same-sex marriage attitudes in a social climate predominantly supportive of it. Power argues that the complexity of the interviewer–interviewee relationship, which relies on creating a space where the interviewee feels comfortable to share, but where the interviewer remains objective, can be influenced by this particular tension; when an interviewee invites the interviewer into their views and values, the role of the interviewer to remain impartial can be challenged. "Us" and "them" dynamics can be reinforced through the interview process when conducting research on controversial issues. Either the interviewee feels as though their values are being invalidated by the research itself, or they can seek to evoke empathy and understanding of their values through the research process; both of these situations can influence the results that are produced and require the interviewer to negotiate tensions and complexities in the moment, regardless of one's own personal view.

Research environments are similarly important to the research itself. Van Klinken's (2015) research among gay men in Zambia included interviews conducted in the house of the convener of a local gay support group. In the midst of the dominant discourse of anti-gay religiosity in Zambia, the house offered safety for group members, allowing them to explore their own narrative identity formation without fear of being overheard. Allowing space for participants to respond to his questions, creating narratives about their identities in contrast to popular assumptions about religion and sexuality, Van Klinken's methods prioritised spatial safety for research participants, especially important given that the environment surrounding them was already hostile.

Focus groups can either alleviate or exacerbate power dynamics. Focus groups allow space for groups to discuss and reflect on issues together, clarifying their views and utilising multiple perspectives. Different forms of communication within a group setting enables day-to-day interaction, from jokes to disagreements, to be explored. Focus groups can also encourage participation from individuals who might find a formal interview intimidating and elicit responses from

Methodological insights **85**

people who would not want to be the focus of the discussion, but who become more comfortable contributing in a group conversation (Kitzinger, 1995).

But they can also enforce a group dynamic that provides unequal space for dominant voices. Amakor (2019) undertook interviews with unmarried mothers in Nigeria, alongside focus groups with church members and leaders. The focus groups tended to cultivate a consensus regarding the "poor morals" of the women who got pregnant, along with a narrative that their own particular church offered these women unconditional support. The women themselves, however, disclosed rather different reasons for their pregnancy (rape in some cases) and narrated a contrasting account which revealed the negative treatment they had received from their church. Such projects demonstrate the way focus groups can do much to forge group identities, bound around a common narrative, so that the data reveals much more about how those group dynamics are configured than it does about what focus group participants really think.

## *Visual methods*

Visual methods, such as self-portraits, photo journals, relational maps, timelines, and video diaries, have increasingly been seen as valuable complements to other qualitative methods, especially interviews. The use of artistic tools within an interview is seen to open up the participant's interpretation and reflections on a question, integrating creativity in the process of discussing meaning and associations (Bagnoli, 2009; Taylor and Snowdon, 2014b; Yip and Page, 2013), and offer new ways of understanding social and cultural experiences by encouraging out-of-the-box thinking and representation.

Overreliance on interviews and questionnaires privileges particular forms of cerebral knowledge production and knowing, including over-emphasising spoken accounts, and has the tendency to ignore the reality that not all knowledge is verbal (Eisner, 2008), thereby missing experiences that are sensory, visual, and experiential that cannot readily be captured through verbal or textual means (Greenough, 2018). Visual and artistic methods are frequently used to engage with young people and children, whose verbal capacities are often more restricted than adults; however, use of non-verbal methods have shown to be illuminating across age groups, and among marginalised populations allows expression for that which is felt rather than said (Greenough, 2018; Taylor and Snowdon, 2013).

Taylor and Snowdon (2014b) detail the use of visual methodology in their study of queer-identifying religious youth. Drawing on multiple qualitative techniques (interviews, maps, and diaries), Taylor and Snowdon explored the everyday lives, practices, and identities of young people, arguing that 'showing the world' through visual methodologies produced by research participants 'is more agentic than [the] traditional format of "telling a world" through interview' (2014b, p. 296). The use of drawing can also provide a vehicle to inspire memory associations, capture the unsaid, and concretise the conversation (Bagnoli, 2009; Morrow, 1998). The deployment of mind-maps in Taylor

**86** Methodological insights

and Snowdon's study asked participants to reflect on 'the ways their identities change across these spaces and times' (2014b, p. 296). The result of the creative and open-ended mapping exercise is represented in diverse and colourful visual data that ranges from pictures and graphs to Mandalas. Taylor and Snowdon's methods sought to destabilise the power imbalance between the researcher and researched as it also intended multiple means of communication and reflection for the participants, where narrative "telling" is one part of the larger frame of how young people experience and capture their religious and sexual identities. This approach proved effective for underrepresented participants who might not feel comfortable in more traditional research environments. Their incorporation of visual mapping methods enabled participants to convey difficult experiences (Taylor and Snowdon, 2013). Where participants had felt the need to make light of their experiences in interviews with the researchers, deeper significance was expressed in visual methods and their journals, evoking a more complicated and, at times, troubling narrative. As stated by Taylor and Snowdon (2013, p. 21), 'Arguably, "showing a world" is more agentic than the more traditional format of "telling a world" through interview...' Exploring meaning-making through these visual representations allows for space to explore emotions that might not be easily expressed through words, including painful experiences (Guillemin, 2004).

Video diaries were utilised in both the RYS (see Page, 2017b; Yip and Page, 2013) and RGSY (Young and Shipley, 2020) projects, as one of three methods for gathering data from young people in the UK and Canada. These were participant-led; diaries were conducted over the course of seven days, and were undertaken at the participants' own preferred time and location, offering flexibility and a more comfortable setting for their contributions. This accessed a different kind of data, enabling participants to focus their discussions around in-the-moment experiences, such as reflections on what books they were reading and conversations they were having. At the same time, video diaries created their own research dilemmas; while we had assumed participants would relish the opportunity to speak to the camera given the youthful popularity of YouTube-style direct camera interactions, the levels of comfort differed (Page, 2017b). Firstly, and as already indicated, despite already having participated in an online questionnaire and a face-to-face in-depth interview on the topic of religion and sexuality, some participants chose not to discuss sexuality any further in their video diary contributions, instead focusing solely on religion. This raises issues regarding the way the researcher becomes a coaxer (Plummer, 1995) in other research encounters (e.g. by penning questionnaire questions or by asking certain interview questions), which pushes participants into realms of discussion they would ordinarily eschew. Meanwhile, other participants chose to disclose greater personal information than had been discussed in the interview, such as intimate experiences of menstruation. Secondly, some participants demonstrated higher levels of proficiency and comfort with the video diary method compared with others. Those with more privileged biographies – e.g. in terms of class,

Methodological insights **87**

gender, and ethnicity – tended to relish the task and had greater amounts of confidence in putting forward a video camera "performance". Meanwhile, others were more hesitant and cautious, and avoided looking at the camera or utilised notes as an aide. Page (2017b) has reflected whether video diary methods, while offering everyone the chance to speak, may cultivate certain barriers to access, extending the voices of the already-privileged, and failing therefore to dislodge existing inequalities. Video diaries are still underpinned by very cerebral forms of participation, with potential additional burdens to "perform" to the camera. Careful reflection is therefore needed to ensure visual methods – which are often badged as being inherently participatory (Brown *et al.*, 2010) – actually do enable full participation.

The use of visual methods in religion research is pertinently linked to lived religion approaches. Ammerman and Williams (2012, p. 117) argue that the changing forms of religiosity as understood in the sociology of religion necessitates that 'finding religion requires asking different kinds of questions in different ways'. Visual methods can enable researchers to capture lived religion and lived sexuality in their dynamic contexts; shifting trends in the practice of religiosity demonstrate that textual, doctrinal, or authoritative religious teaching are only one part of the larger experience of "being religious". As the experience of both religiosity and sexuality become represented through intersectional lenses, the means of capturing this through a sociological method must also become more dynamic and multi-pronged. Therefore, visual methods become a key facet through which these aims can be realised.

## *Multiple/mixed methods*

Incorporating multiple methodological approaches offers the ability to negate limitations of one approach by deploying data gathering tools to accommodate for the potential gaps of the other; where an online questionnaire might be limited in its contextual interaction with the participant, a follow up interview can explore the nuance of the participant's responses and allow for in-depth complexity to be portrayed.

While multiple methods relates to any form of method combination, mixed methods approaches specifically relate to the incorporation of both qualitative and quantitative data, with the aim of enhancing the validity and reliability of the research, and cancelling out many of the limitations of singular methodological approaches. Mixed methods also allow for a broader range of research questions and more precision in the data that is gathered. Trends can be made more visible through the use of text and narrative, complementing quantitative and predictive analytics, and the production of various data enables the development of deeper understanding of the subject itself. Mixed methods projects are, however, often more costly and time consuming, requiring sophistication to ensure that the methods complement each other, and data is coherently analysed.

**88** Methodological insights

Muhammad *et al.* (2017) combined a self-administered survey at 12 randomly selected colleges in Malaysia with face-to-face interviews to explore the role of religion on sexual activity among college students. The interviews provided space to explore related factors and other influences in the decision-making process, beyond the more rigid survey formula, and this highlighted similarities in male and female attitudes not emphasised in the questionnaire data. When responding to the survey questions themselves, participants were providing simple answers to the questions; it was only during interviews that the gender similarities were uncovered.

The RYS and RGSY projects were both designed as mixed-methods projects (Young and Shipley, 2020, 2016, 2014; Yip and Page, 2013). Each project utilised an online questionnaire, semi-structured interview, and video diary, and provided differentiated spaces for reflection and expansion from the participants to speak to their identities – in written form, in response to questions and in an open-ended video capture. While questionnaires were formulated around opinion elicitation with only minimal opportunities to relay their personal stories, the in-depth semi-structured interviews enabled participants to tell their life story, recalling significant moments in their biography, in relation to their religious and sexual journeys. Meanwhile, the video diaries captured the everyday mundane moments – the TV shows they watched and the food they ate. These capture variations provided the researchers with space to reflect on the responses, including gaps in the initial questions, and an opportunity to revisit areas of key concern through the stages of data gathering. Each of the methods deployed had limitations. However, the combination of methods allowed for richness in the results and an opportunity for researchers to flesh out the more static responses produced from a questionnaire to narrate the construction and negotiation of identities (Shipley and Young, 2014).

### Analysing text and media

Determining the dominant discourses in a given context encourages the analysis of text and media sources, such as novels, self-help books, online blogs, newspapers, and official statements from religious organisations. This can offer important insights into how the discursive realm is constructed and conveyed, and how individuals interpret it (e.g. the huge potentiality offered through the internet, allowing people to express their opinion and debate particular issues). Research into sexuality and religion has readily embraced such approaches for a variety of reasons. In sensitive research areas, it can be challenging to obtain access to individuals to engage in face-to-face research. Some groups remain particularly underrepresented in religion and sexuality research, and utilising text and media analysis can offer one way of enabling greater access. The analysis of text offers relative ease of access into social worlds, even as this prompts certain questions such as the ethical basis for utilising material in semi-public spaces (e.g. Facebook posts) for the purposes of research analysis (see Berry, 2004; Bryman, 2012;

Hookway, 2008 for a fuller discussion on the ethical implications of utilising the internet as a source of research).

Jordan (1997, 2000, 2011) has undertaken an extensive genealogical investigation of sexuality discourses in relation to Christianity, offering a historical lens through which to understand sexuality not as inevitable or fixed, but permeable, changeable, and repeatedly reconstructed and reassembled. In *The Invention of Sodomy in Christian Theology*, Jordan examines numerous texts and artefacts penned by artists, playwrights, and theologians to examine the variable characteristics of sodomy. *Homosexuality in Modern Catholicism* focuses on Roman Catholic teaching – past and present – on something now called "homosexuality", and the intersection between Church authority and power and the control of clerical bodies, while *Recruiting Young Love* highlights 20th-century Christian preoccupations with male homosexuality, and the various discursive strategies that have been deployed. Influenced by Foucault (see also Jordan, 2015), Jordan (2011) interrogates the role of power in how certain terms and ideas come to have salience and influence, calling into question any sense of inevitability regarding how Christianity manages same-sex desires and sexual practices.

Davie and Starkey (2019) analysed the letters received by the Diocese of Lincoln in England following the announcement by the Anglican Bishop of Grantham that he was in a same-sex relationship, after he was threatened with being "outed" by a Sunday newspaper. Given that the letters in the main declared support for the Bishop and expressed a desire for the Church to be sexuality-inclusive, Davie and Starkey utilise this as an opportunity to analyse changing values in the Church of England and society at large, and the relationship between the two.

DeRogatis (2015) analysed an array of Christian Evangelical sex manuals and guides, as well as web-based material, to determine the dominant discourses surrounding contemporary American Evangelical sexuality. DeRogatis argued that Evangelicals are not anti-sex as is so often assumed, but actively engage in secular sexual cultures, often adopting the tropes of sexual empowerment and liberation. This allowed her to show the complexity of Evangelical sexuality, its various sources of influence, but how sexuality remains firmly understood in relation to Biblical interpretations.

Burke's (2016) focus is similar, but the online space is her particular focus. She analysed 36 Christian Evangelical websites focusing on sexuality, examining the role this plays in enabling conservative Evangelicals to interpret their sexual lives within a particular theological framework. As digital technologies have transformed discursive engagement, such websites offer new platforms for intimate matters to be openly discussed, but with relative anonymity. With candid online discussions between Evangelicals regarding "acceptable" sexual practices and what "good godly sex" looks like, Burke is able to demonstrate the ways in which internet spaces have become key arenas for people to construct their sexual practices within a framework of Conservative Christian values alongside liberalising attitudes towards sex more broadly.

**90** Methodological insights

Shannahan (2009) considers the internet and the online spaces that are created by Muslims navigating the complex issue of Islamic authority in relation to sexuality issues. Grappling with traditional scholarship, Qur'anic interpretations, jurisprudence, and various hadiths, competing claims are made to authoritatively interpret Islam's approach to sexuality. Shannahan's study, focusing specifically on LGBT Muslims who are often displaced in traditional interpretations, outlines how sexual and religious identities are negotiated using online self-help discussion boards.

Many authors cited here have not undertaken text analysis in isolation but have combined this with other methods. Lalich and McLaren (2010) conducted a content analysis of online narratives among 24 gay and lesbian Jehovah's Witnesses who had left the movement, based on pre-existing personal narratives posted online. They also conducted a semi-structured interview with a former Jehovah's Witness, founder of the support group for gay ex-Witnesses, A Common Bond, where they also conducted participation at its conference and had informal conversations with active and former Jehovah's Witnesses (homosexual and heterosexual). Using these triangulated methods, they considered the stigma experienced by gay and lesbian Witnesses, concluding that even Witnesses who manage the tension externally are still burdened internally by their perception of a 'sinful inner state' (2010, p. 1314). While all 24 online narratives were written by ex-Witnesses, their relationships to their religion, expressed and analysed in line with participant observation of ex-Witnesses at the Common Bond conference, provided the researchers with the ability to reflect on the online narratives in line with teachings, observable behaviour, and relationship management.

In short, the analysis of narrative in its various guises offers a valuable contribution to our understandings of religion and sexuality. What "text" means and how it is analysed can vary widely, and certain decisions will be made depending upon its public accessibility. For example, Davie and Starkey (2019) were given access to the Lincoln Letters by invitation of the diocese. Other researchers have noted the inaccessibility of some texts, such as records pertaining to the Magdalen laundries (Gott, 2018), which remain under the control of the Irish Catholic Church.

## Summary

This chapter has provided a critical overview of the methodological approaches commonly deployed in religion and sexuality research, including those that have been utilised by the authors, in order to think more deeply about the particular challenges and opportunities that arise. While giving a broad sketch of the types of methods that have been deployed in the field, we have also indicated our own preferences for a methodological approach that is inclusive and reflexive, mindful of the power dynamics embedded in research processes, and advocating approaches that are contextually informed, that reveal research complexity and nuance. To that end, we are strong advocates of a queer feminist approach to research.

Queer and feminist approaches to research critique the very basis regarding how knowledge has been created, and what assumptions underpin the research endeavour (Browne and Nash, 2016; Hammers and Brown, 2004; Ramazanoglu and Holland, 2002). Both have been concerned with power dynamics and who gets to speak, and what happens when certain privileged forms of knowledge are centred upon heteronormative and/or male dominated assumptions. Both disrupt the starting points for research (e.g. the male and/or heterosexuality as the normative), often giving voice to those who have been marginalised in research terms. Tensions have been noted between queer and feminist approaches, for example, feminist approaches rooted in essentialist understandings of gender as opposed to forms of feminism and queer approaches which endorse the idea of the fluid subject, where identities are never fixed in place but are always in flux (Pilcher, 2016). But many argue for a refocusing on the synergies and connections between the perspectives (Hammers and Brown, 2004; Macke, 2014). A queer feminist approach is also an intersectional endeavour that does not come to forge its own hierarchies, or privilege certain perspectives over others (Taylor *et al.*, 2011). This is more than being inclusive; this demands a radical questioning of how knowledge comes to be forged, and what assumptions are being made. As part of this process, methodological approaches and the choices of specific methods needs to be critically interrogated. We have noted how quantitative approaches are oriented around charting the stable subject (Browne and Nash, 2016), and in this chapter we have highlighted the problems that occur when research agendas are fixed upon given categories of identity, and the limitations this has caused in our own research, especially when participants navigate labels that they do not fully identify with. Having facilitated mixed-methods projects, we are firmly of the view that while quantitative approaches should not be dismissed outright (Letherby, 2003), they should be deployed with care, and, wherever possible, combined with qualitative approaches, so that the complex ways social realities and identities emerge can be explored. This also fits in with our commitment to lived religion as a theoretical lens in which to study religious lives and contexts, which is concerned not with neatness and standardised categories, but with complexity and identities in flux (see Chapter 3). At the same time, qualitative approaches do not offer a "quick fix" to solve issues of depicting social reality more "truthfully" or "accurately". Research encounters are mediated affairs, imbued with hierarchies and power relationships, impacting on the type of data being generated, and the knowledge that is cultivated. We have recognised the challenges in our own projects when interviewing young people about sexuality, and how to navigate the types of questions asked. Our own positionality – for example, in terms of age, gender, social class, and ethnicity – impacted on this negotiation, and how comfortable participants were in disclosing details about their lives. At the same time, this creates its own dilemmas when one is the "coaxer" (Plummer, 1995) of the story, and whether cultivating a comfortable interview encounter encourages participants to over-disclose and reveal more than they intended (Finch, 1993). Reflexive engagement with the research process thus becomes crucial in interrogating those dynamics, and on what basis the knowledge created from our research findings is being forged. It is also the case that Christianity has been privileged in research terms, dominating much of the research field regarding sexuality. More critical engagement is needed on the absences and silences, and what elements of this topic have not been studied. There is woeful attention to certain religious traditions, contexts, and identities. And we would also argue that there needs to be greater critical interrogation of power and privilege to understand how certain types of religiosity and sexual identity comes to be deemed normative and unremarkable.

# 5

# CONCEPTUALISING THE "NORMATIVE"

## The straight time model

### Introduction

A queer feminist analysis highlights that, whether focusing on "religious" or "secular" cultures, sexualities and gender are subject to various social normatives. Despite greater equalities forged for sexual minorities across the Western world, heteronormativity (taking heterosexuality as the norm) features strongly in many contexts, even in those that are positive towards sexual and gender diversity (Jackson, 2006; Jackson and Scott, 2010). Dominant gender and sexuality norms have imposed and regulated experiences across geographies and time. In this chapter, we will explore the construction and maintenance of heteronormativity and its subsequent relationship to the intersection of religion and sexualities. These theoretical frameworks offer contextualisation regarding the way research on religion and sexualities are conducted, the assumptions that inform the questions that are asked, and the intent and purposes of research on religion and sexualities. As such, understanding the implicit and explicit stereotypes embedded in contemporary notions about sexual and religious normativity facilitate greater capacity for reflecting critically on existing research and methodologies.

The chapter will emphasise the ongoing dominance of heterosexuality, through emphasising the prominence of the lifecourse model. This has been particularly salient in furthering the reach of heteronormative assumptions, which has traditionally endorsed a linear development starting with maintaining virginity, then getting married and having children, underpinned by an assumed heterosexual identity. This "straight time" account (Wilcox, 2009) is often maintained in religious contexts. Its impact, however, can be felt among heterosexuals and queer individuals alike. For many heterosexual religious people, maintaining virginity until marriage is difficult (Yip and Page, 2013). Not every married heterosexual couple wants to procreate (Llewellyn, 2016). For queer individuals,

**94** Conceptualising the "normative"

the notion of "coming out" disrupts the straight time model, as does the acquisition of legal rights for (monogamous) queer couples to marry. This chapter will focus on the complex dynamics of understanding how normative sexuality is constituted in religious contexts and the implications for heterosexual and queer religious individuals.

## Constructing the heterosexual/homosexual binary

While the terms "heterosexual" and "homosexual" were formulated in the late 19th century, their medicalised framing became more commonplace during the 20th century. Heterosexuality became described as natural and inherent, and focused on reproduction, reinforced through the idea of homosexuality as deviancy (Fumia, 2007; Gleason, 1999), as older laws punishing sodomy intermingled with new medical interventions to "cure" the homosexual (Fone, 2000). The more negative connotations ascribed to homosexuality arose intensely in a post-World War II climate where gender roles were reinforced and as women were compelled to return to domestic labour. Rigid associations of gender roles and sexual orientation are therefore linked to supposed natural and biological characteristics of sexuality. While many successful attempts were made to challenge sodomy laws in the latter half of the 20th century, they often only succeeded in removing the most punitive elements – e.g. the changing of seeing homosexuality as a criminal activity to one deemed a disorder. Queer rights activists spent decades trying to overcome this negative framing. It was only at the start of the 21st century that increased equality-bearing legislation started to emerge in Western contexts, but often not without contestation.

## Heteronormativity

While the term "heterosexual" is of relatively recent vintage, its underpinning assumptions go back much further; as we argued in Chapter 1, historically, there has been investment in reproductive control and the promotion of heterosexual formations, especially connected with inheritance rights of males. But with the coining of new terminology and the creation of the binary divide between the "homosexual" and "heterosexual", each term became dependent on the other for its existence. While heterosexuality was promoted, homosexuality was denigrated. If "natural" (i.e. "morally good") sex is defined by heterosexual, monogamous pairings, then all other sexualities are implicitly and explicitly framed more negatively, varyingly perceived as immoral, unnatural, or less-than-ideal. Rich (1980) has called the salience given to heterosexuality "compulsory heterosexuality", a term denoting the way heterosexuality structures sexual pleasure around the needs of (heterosexual) men. While compulsory heterosexuality impacts everyone, it particularly negatively impacts queer communities and heterosexual women. Meanwhile, as described in Chapter 2, another way of conceptualising this is in terms of heteronormativity. Heteronormativity as a meta-narrative assumes distinct gender binaries, male and female, which are defined both as "natural" and as having prescribed roles in life. Heterosexuality is seen as the normative sexual orientation; all other sexual orientations are categorised as deviations from this "norm".

A heterosexual orientation on its own, however, is not enough to comply fully with the norms of heterosexuality. Rubin (1993) specifies a heteronormative hierarchy which places monogamous, reproductive sex between married heterosexual couples as receiving the highest esteem. Situated further down the heterosexual hierarchy are cohabiting couples with or without children, heterosexual marrieds without children, single people, and single parent families (Richardson, 2018). How various family configurations are perceived is subject to context and does change; indeed, in many Western contexts, greater heterosexual diversity is deemed acceptable and there has been a broadening out of family types deemed respectable (Plummer, 2003). However, those following the most "authorised" versions of heterosexuality are significantly less likely to experience scrutiny of their behaviour.

Prescribed gender roles are therefore constructed and reinforced, connected to notions of gender complementarity, which form the basis of the assumption of heterosexual normativity and a subsequent sex "hierarchy" delineating "good sex" as that which conforms to these norms (Rubin, 1993). This is regulated through social, legal, and institutional policies, practices, and performances of normative (acceptable) and non-normative (unacceptable) identities and their corresponding engagements. Within the strictest forms of heteronormative frameworks, sexual relationships and marriages are only recognised as legitimate if they consist of individuals of the opposite sex. In such contexts, same-sex relationships are not authorised, and no status is accorded them. Across the world, such heteronormative formations continue to dominate.

Heteronormativity relies on gender binaries and stereotypical gender roles; it similarly imposes a particular "heterosexual time" (Cavanagh, 2007) in which the expected stages of life accomplishment are built around marriage and childbearing. This straight time account (Wilcox, 2009) frames our culture. Significant investment is made in marking out these life moments, epitomised in the way the "white wedding" pervades Western culture, and is structured in consumerist terms (Cokely, 2005; Ingraham, 1999). Rigid notions about gender, where "male" and "female" are conceived as being two separate, distinct, and complementary categories "naturally" inclined to mutual attraction, are the foundation for the institution of heteronormativity. Gendered binaries and their corresponding assumptions ignore and exclude trans, nonbinary, fluid, and genderqueer experiences and identities.

Yet even in countries where rights have been accorded to queer people, the public presentation of normative relationships is built from heterosexual standards and expectations (Duggan, 2002; Valverde, 2006). Even in contexts where queer people have achieved significant gains, they are still subject to heteronormative control (Richardson, 2018). In other words, heteronormativity does

**96** Conceptualising the "normative"

not just evaporate when sexuality rights are delivered. Heterosexuality is often assumed in everyday encounters. Queer individuals are expected to "come out"; heterosexuals are not expected to publicly declare their sexuality. In everyday language, heterosexuality is emphasised; such as the conversational assumptions that someone's partner will be of the opposite gender. Meanwhile, the representation of sexual diversity in popular culture has been framed within particular scripted boundaries (McLelland, 2005) and relegated primarily to gay or lesbian "best friends" whose identities as gay and lesbian are known but not "visible". Any portrayal of same-sex sexual activity can provoke indignation and even outrage. While films such as *Brokeback Mountain* (2005) have a more receptive audience than they might have had even 10 years ago, it can be argued that one of the main characters in the homosexual relationship had to die in the film because a contemporary audience would not accept a homosexual couple "living happily ever after". [1]

In cultures with greater sexual diversity, queer people are often expected to abide by the norms of heterosexuality, in what Mariana Valverde (2006) terms "the respectable same-sex couple" (RSSC) – an urban, consumerist, monogamous, and sexless representation of the kind of same-sex couple that one would find in popular culture. The RSSC is removed from the gay sexuality receiving most condemnation – promiscuity, HIV/AIDS, club culture, and so on. Instead, this new visualisation of homosexuality focuses on complementing wedding dresses and matching tuxedos – 'drag queens seem to have vanished from view' (Valverde, 2006, p. 158).

These narrowed representations of "acceptable" sexual diversity, limited in scope to particular constructions of "harmless" sexual diversities which most closely resemble acceptable heterosexuality, repeat the message that homosexuality as a category functions on a symbolic level as oppositional to heterosexuality (Halperin, 1995; Namaste, 1994).The acceptance of sexual difference and diversity occurs only when homosexuality can be packaged as a form of acceptable heterosexuality. All non-normative forms of sexuality subsequently continue to be precariously located outside the bounds of social acceptance and continue to be obliged to fight for recognition.

Critics of heteronormativity point to the discriminatory and oppressive mechanisms it overtly and covertly imposes. As indicated in Chapter 2, Foucault (1976) identified the mechanisms of discipline and punishment to regulate the population. Sexuality as a core element in power relations became a central object in need of regulation, surveillance, and discipline, as evidenced by the policy regulation of contraception. The emphasis on monogamous pairings insists that sexuality is validated through a particular family construction. Asexuality, bisexuality, polyamory, and plural relationships all fall outside the scope of mainstream or normative sexuality.

Heterosexual privilege is acutely noted in relation to queer sexuality and sexual relationships. Social, legal, and political norms continue to be developed and sustained by heterosexual normativity; from legal definitions of marriage, to access of healthcare benefits based on normative definitions of family, to policies requiring marital status in order to adopt, thus denying same-sex couples access to adoption in places where same-sex marriage is not legal, the repercussions of heteronormativity are widespread (Cossman, 2007; Cossman and Ryder, 2001; Jakobsen and Pellegrini, 2004; Kinsman, 1996). These norms are embedded in multiple spheres, including policy and legislation, media, education, and popular culture.

It is vital to assess the role non-religious or secular ideologies play in boundary setting, discrimination, and disadvantage. Frequently in relation to the development of policy and legislation, the separation of church and state in Christian-oriented contexts becomes framed as the "rationale" to explain inclusive versus exclusive policy framework (MacDougall and Short, 2010; Scott, 2018). Nation states that define themselves as being inclusive (progressive) often also claim to have separated church and state, thus explicitly tying exclusive (conservative) policies to religion and religious ideologies.

From both feminist and queer critical lenses, secular states have enacted and permitted ongoing negative experiences for women and queer individuals and communities (Aune *et al.*, 2008; Jakobsen and Pellegrini, 2004; McGarry, 2008; Scott, 2018). Scott (2018) argues that the separation of church and state was built on the inequality of the sexes, where masculinised dominance in political and economic spaces was maintained. While religion is often a regulating force, it is by no means the only one. The embedded ideologies in secular discourse continue to validate normative sexuality. In contexts where same-sex marriage is legal and sexual orientation rights are protected, the acceptance of sexual difference within a "secular" framework is often achieved through discursive interventions which constitute a "new" normalised sexual subject. In other words, homosexuality becomes an accepted category of identity when it can be framed as something similar to heterosexuality. The result of this reframing is that access to rights becomes possible only for "normalised" gay and lesbian individuals and couples.

## Religion and heteronormativity

Religious ideologies too have played a dominant role in the construction of normative sexuality, such as the denial of same-sex marriage within religious organisations and the influence of those ideologies in shaping legal and political history. For example, within the Canadian context, Canadian law derives first from the British Common Law system, both of which are immediately and overtly tied to Christian (primarily Protestant) ideologies (Menendez, 1996). The state's role in the regulation of sexuality and sexual behaviour derives from Protestant Christian ideologies regarding sexual normativity; the initial framing of marriage within Canadian law as a singular heterosexual relationship responded to concerns about plural marriages within Mormonism, not same-sex relations (Carter, 2008). That narrow definition became the foundation for

## 98 Conceptualising the "normative"

denial of same-sex marriages until the *Civil Marriage Act* (2005) with arguments in defence of heterosexual marriage relying on "religion" as the justification (Young, 2012). This framing of marriage as "inherently" heterosexual, however, ignored the religious individuals who identified as both religious and lesbian or gay as well as the religious organisations who argued that their inability to perform same-sex marriages was a restriction on their religious freedom (Halpern *et al.*, 2003).

Diversity within and across religious traditions challenges the construction of "normative religiosity" (Beyer, 2008; Shah, 2018; Taylor and Snowdon, 2013; Yip and Page, 2013; Young, 2012; Young and Shipley, 2020). This research challenges the idea that the religious values of a group are always in unity with one another and also challenges static representations of the relationship of religion to sexual diversity (see Shipley and Young, 2014; Taylor and Snowdon, 2014b; Yip and Page, 2013). There is not one singular religious view regarding homosexuality but still the notion that religious values inherently oppose same-sex relationships is often left uncontested. There is a wide body of literature highlighting the discrepancies between religious texts and lived religion (Beyer, 2008; Jordan, 2000; McGuire, 2008; Orsi, 2007 among others). It has become increasingly evident in public discourse that there is not one unified understanding of what "being religious" means.

The first usage of the term homosexual in the Bible (Revised Standard Version) occurred in 1946, and its introduction was connected directly with sinfulness (White, 2015). White's historical analysis of the way sodomy and homosexuality became integrated in subsequent Christian teaching demonstrates that until the explicit framing of homosexuality in this way, the Bible had been largely silent about homosexuality. Kinsey's research demonstrated that his participants usually knew little about what the Church thought about same-sex activities. They were much clearer about diktats on masturbation and premarital sex:

> Most chroniclers of the history of religion and homosexuality… have taken the Bible's new meanings as age-old testimony. As a consequence, stock narratives about the emergence of a gay identity movement assume an oppositional tug between the conservative forces of religious condemnation and the progressive momentum of modern change. What we hear, as a result, is about a transition "from abomination to disease", by which the therapeutic sciences superseded centuries-old religious prohibitions. We hear about how an emerging identity movement gradually emancipated itself from the vestiges of an anti-homosexual religious past. We hear of progress forestalled by a religious backlash that resurrected ancient strictures.
>
> *(White, 2015, p. 4)*

Relatedly, defining marriage as a historically religious institution is a common argument promoted by religious interest groups who seek to preserve the heterosexual institution of marriage. This religious definition ignores the history of the institution of marriage and seeks to create a binary division between the religious/heterosexual and the non-religious (read: immoral/homosexual). This is problematic for it presupposes that one cannot be both religious and queer. Meanwhile, there are more instances of biblical condemnation of hypocrites than passages condemning homosexuality, and yet queer discrimination far outweighs what the Bible seemed to emphasise (Boswell, 1980). In the Roman world, same-sex marriage existed *de facto* until 342 C.E. (Boswell, 1980), and it was not until the 'middle of the eleven hundreds [that]... Peter Cantor campaigned for the condemnation of gay love affairs among the clergy' (Helminiak, 2000, p. 23).

Religious prescriptions regarding sexual normativity have significantly contributed to the heteronormative organising described in the previous section. Marriage as a lifecourse ritual embedded within both religious and social norms is underpinned by gendered stereotypes and places limitations on sexually diverse individuals. Legal provisions for same-sex marriage are not static nor are they guaranteed. In the United States, the Supreme Court ruled in favour of same-sex marriage at a national level in 2015 in *Obergefell v. Hodges*. But in 2018, Kansas and Oklahoma passed legislation that allows state-licensed welfare agencies to deny adoption placements in LGBT homes, citing religious beliefs (AP News, 2018). Other cases have tested the *Obergefell* ruling, including refusing to put married same-sex parents on birth certificates and denying benefits to same-sex spouses. These cases have been overturned by the Supreme Court, but they demonstrate same-sex equality resistance, even in the face of a Supreme Court decision.

It would be inaccurate to locate the sole cause of heteronormativity with religion; religion is far more complex than this, and as previously discussed, we must question what purposes are served when it is religion on its own which comes to absorb all the negativities associated with heteronormativity. Yet at the same time, religion has had a significant role to play in the regulation of sexuality, especially the way particular hierarchies and standards of sexuality have been based on religious ideologies. Religion's role in the regulation of gender norms forms the foundation for the prescriptive regulations regarding sexual norms. This binarised and complementary understanding of gender – rooted particularly in the Abrahamic religious traditions – has huge repercussions for how sexuality is organised. This gender ordering prioritises marriage and procreation, emphasising particular obligations of heterosexual pairings. Broadly speaking, Christianity's dominant script prioritising heterosexual marriage and procreation overshadows the greater number of theological sexual scripts available, such as singleness (Aune, 2002; Llewellyn, 2016). And even in Christian traditions which outrightly condemn homosexuality, such as Roman Catholicism, cultures have been cultivated where queer aesthetics are celebrated (Jordan, 2000; Stringer, 2000). This is also challenged by affirming congregations, and through the lived religious experiences of Christians whose values and identities do not

**100** Conceptualising the "normative"

conform to those dominant scripts (Helminiak, 2000; Young, 2012). While Islam's sexual prescriptions acknowledge sexual pleasure, traditional Islamic practice has tended to restrict this to heterosexuality (Dialmy, 2010; Hunt, 2010). The strength of the prevailing understanding that "the Qur'an says" that homosexuality is forbidden, even by those who have never read the text, means that queer Muslims invariably face incredulity that their sexual and religious identity can co-exist (Yip, 2004b, 2005). Judaism, too, emphasises sexual pleasure within marriage, but similarly typically privileges heterosexuality (Hunt, 2010). But many wings of Judaism accept and include queer individuals (Schnoor, 2003). Non-Abrahamic traditions have been more accepting of gender and sexual diversity, as the impact of gender complementarity derived from the Genesis legacy of Adam and Eve has not been embedded, but given that Christianity was at the heart of many colonial endeavours, this has meant that strict gender binaries have been impactful.

## *Religion as lived: Living out sexuality and religion*

While religion is lived in various ways, with individuals selecting the aspects of a tradition that conform best with their own values and ethics (Beyer and Ramji, 2013; Yip and Page, 2013; Young and Shipley, 2020, among others), it is also true that individual perceptions about "what religion teaches" regarding sexual diversity can be felt as inherently negative, regardless of the lived fluidity of religious expression. When asked 'What does your religion mean to you?' in both Canadian and UK contexts, young people responded by pushing back on the question itself; did we mean "their" religion (how they interpret and practice) or did we mean "the" religion (as it is written and taught)?

These projects also asked the question, 'What does your sexuality mean to you?', which demonstrated how heteronormative scripts were absorbed, rejected, and revised. In the RYS project, heterosexual participants were far more likely not to have reflected on their sexuality, typified by Megan, a Christian woman, who said her sexuality meant 'nothing. I've never thought about it' (Yip and Page, 2014). This indicated the taken-for-grantedness of their heterosexual identity, so that it was normatively assumed (Weeks, 2011). Meanwhile, because queer people continually have to explain and even defend their sexuality, such lack of reflection was rare, with some queer participants creating essay-length responses to the question. This taken-for-grantedness meant that heterosexuals had often absorbed the inevitability of the straight time account and were reworking this into how they imagined their futures. They imagined religion in their future lives as being a place where they would participate in rituals (such as marriage), and where they would bring their children for religious and spiritual education, resulting in a meshing together of their imagined sexuality and religion. Because of the key role religion played in marking out significant moments of the straight time account (e.g. birth and marriage), religious heterosexuals inevitably saw these spheres as intertwined. Such interconnectedness could not be assumed for queer participants, whose futures were more likely to be fraught with anxiety. These future projections of religious practice were also found in the Canadian study, where young people's identities were comprised of multiple, complex nuances that included (non)religion and spirituality, but where most felt the regular practice of religion would be a part of their older adult lives (Young and Shipley, 2020).

The influence of religious norms regarding sexuality is wide reaching. Religious teachings might be contextualised by individual adherents, but the impact of normative expectations and the casting of morality based on heterosexual identities has significant impact. Self-harm, suicide ideation, and suicide attempts are reported at higher levels in queer youth than in heterosexual youth (Remafedi *et al.*, 1991); bullying based on real or perceived sexual diversity is a regular experience for high school students in Canada, and in some cases perpetrated by teachers (Friedman *et al.*, 2011; Taylor and Peter, 2011); and queer young adults report higher rates of mental illness than their heterosexual peers (King *et al.*, 2008; Mustanski, *et al.*, 2010). These experiences of queer people are not relegated to religious spaces or institutions, however, the ideological impositions embedded on "morally good" sexualities and subsequently "immoral" sexualities cannot be ignored.

## Challenging the dominance of the lifecourse model

The lifecourse model is frequently deployed as a justification for heteronormative expectations and articulations. Within this model, particular trajectories of life stages (birth, puberty, marriage, procreation, death) are seen not just as potential paths, but as a desired route to secure personal and social fulfilment. This sequence of events and roles are not inherent or natural, but rather socially defined. However, within the heteronormative framework, this expected pattern becomes framed as "natural" and "morally good". Through heterosexual marriage and the production of children, binary gender roles are reinforced and the cycle of normative gender and sexual expectations, along with the reproduction of what constitutes "acceptable" family, is perpetuated. Same-sex marriage equality has pushed back at these dominant framings to some extent but has also served to feed into the RSSC model, Valverde (2006) articulates, where standardised expectations emerge for both heterosexuals and queer people.

### *Virginity*

Lifecourse experiences are influenced, and respond to, a number of external factors – including the adoption and rejection of sexual scripts (Carpenter, 2010). In Western contexts, the expectation to remain a virgin until marriage has altered considerably over the last 50 years (Carpenter, 2005; Weeks, 2014). Even for women, retaining a virginity status for too long can be deemed stigmatising (Carpenter, 2005). If individuals do put a major emphasis on retaining their

**102** Conceptualising the "normative"

virginity until marriage, it is usually for religious reasons (Adamczyk and Felson, 2006; Page and Yip, 2012a). The popularity of virginity pledges is premised on its youthful appeal (Bearman and Brückner, 2001). Adolescents who pledge are less likely to have intercourse than adolescents who do not pledge; however, age has an influence on the efficacy of the pledge as does "pledge identity" (Bearman and Brückner, 2001). Pledges are most effective when there are not too many or too few other pledgers in the social context, indicating that the effect is largely contextual (Bearman and Brückner, 2001).

Religious discourses can have a significant impact on how individuals navigate sexual activity, particularly in contexts where sex before marriage is deemed wrong. In the RGSY project, Teresa (queer, spiritual but not religious [SBNR], woman) reflected on the relationship between religious values and sexual values as being connected to social scripts and external expectations, stating that her concern is that it is determined by 'other people… who are you supposed to marry or how are you supposed to feel, how are you supposed to act'. Lauren's (Christian, "probably straight", woman) attitude towards sex and sexuality has been separated from her religious values, 'I think I have a really healthy sex life and that my religion has nothing to do with it. Because I think if I were taking my religious tradition into account I wouldn't have a healthy sex life because I wouldn't be having sex'. Lauren's anxiety about sex was connected to the taboo of premarital sex; she was unmarried at the time of the interview and said that it had taken her months to have sex with her live-in boyfriend, because the religious teachings about premarital sex had been so deeply ingrained.

The notion of virginity is tied up with particular gendered and heteronormative understandings. Penetration of the vagina is what virginity loss is typically understood to mean (Carpenter, 2005), as terminology such as the "technical virgin" attests – where sexual activity occurs, but not vaginal penetration (Regnerus, 2007). Therefore, queer religious youth feel disconnected by this language of virginity given its heteronormative overtones. Within the RYS project, queer youth put far lower emphasis on the notion of virginity than heterosexual youth (Yip and Page, 2013), and in the RGSY project, neither group gave virginity heightened significance. For example, Jacob, a gay Jewish man in the RYS project, actually saw his virginity status in stigmatising terms (Carpenter, 2005) when he said '[My virginity status] does play on my mind… it is… a slightly strange stigma, because it is… invisible'. But for a minority of queer youth, the heteronormative emphasis placed on virginity within their religious tradition loomed large. Stephen, a gay Christian man, transferred his understanding of virginity to his same-sex relationship, thereby replicating the importance given to virginity loss:

> It bugged me a little bit in the way that I wasn't his first [sexual partner], but now it would bug me if I dated someone and ended up having a relationship with them and I was their first… I wouldn't be able to give

## Conceptualising the "normative" **103**

[virginity] to them... I would certainly want them to have experienced something other than me just so that I'm not taking something from them.

*(Stephen, gay Christian man)*

Stephen saw his virginity in terms of loss; he had already had sex so would be unable to "gift" his virginity to someone else (Carpenter, 2005). Virginity was deemed so meaningful that he did not want the responsibility of "taking" someone else's virginity. Other queer RYS participants took this further, to insist that sex could only be of a heterosexual nature, thereby arguing that "true" virginity loss could only happen in a heterosexual relationship. This had repercussions regarding how they navigated their own sexual activity, such as Ryan, a gay Christian, who was envisaging what he termed a "godly celibate relationship" with a same-sex partner; while they would share a bed, no sexual activity would take place:

> God's purpose for sex is sex within marriage [between a] male and [a] female and I think that is clear in the scripture... So that means the sex stuff that I desire, although it is a part of me, it is not how things were meant to be... my sexual identity is part of what God has created me to be... [T]he Bible says that homosexual sex is not right... Therefore as a Christian who is gay and feels the way I do, it means it is not appropriate for me to go looking for sexual fulfilment in homosexual sex... This whole idea of a godly celibate relationship... [indicates] it is a possibility to live with someone and have close emotional intimacy without it having to be sinful in terms of the sexual side of things... I am thinking of it as an alternative for people who are gay... something that isn't marriage but is still a place where you can share an intimacy in different ways.

As Ryan's and Stephen's experiences attest, lifecourse patterns are modelled on heterosexual expectations, which queer religious individuals have to navigate. The extent to which salience was given to virginity by queer youth was contextually dependent, with more significance given in religious contexts where high esteem was accorded to heterosexual virginity loss, and where this was associated with sex-within-marriage-only. Given that same-sex marriage has legally only been possible in a minority of places relatively recently, this adds further complications regarding virginity within marriage being a marker of significance for queer youth, who instead form other kinds of meaning-making in their sexual lives. Given that in general terms, even those expressing a desire to remain a virgin until marriage often do not meet this expectation (Page and Yip, 2012a), the availability of same-sex marriage to queer people is highly unlikely to raise the significance of virginity, apart from a minority of cases.

## Marriage

Exceptions of "date, sex, mate" sequencing typically are connected to strong religious convictions, with pressure to conform to a particular milestone by a certain age. In the RYS project, while more young people in the UK are entering higher education, once education was finished, families often expected the search for a suitable marriage partner to commence in earnest (Page *et al.*, 2012; Yip and Page, 2013). Isma, a heterosexual Muslim woman, had been raised in a home where there was a strong expectation for early marriage. She was the first in her family to attend university, and used this as leverage to stall the expectations placed on her to marry, but as her time at university was coming to an end, she had to contemplate these pressures once more:

> [The pressure to get married] has left me sleepless on quite a lot of occasions. When you get into your 20s and your parents are like, 'Oh, do you think about getting married?... But personally... I think that after I get my [postgraduate qualification], I will be 25, 26. That is a suitable time to possibly get married but... I find the whole marriage system scary really.

Isma was able to utilise further study as a means of resisting the expectations placed on her, but she realised she could only use education for so long as a delaying tactic. Meanwhile, the pressures of the straight time account could be acute for queer youth. Yasmin, a Muslim woman, did not define her sexuality but had previously been in a relationship with another woman. Her family assumed that she was heterosexual:

> I live in constant denial all the time... I've just turned 22, which means that I am way, way late by sort of marriage age terms... Every single time I go back home, mum's like, "What kind of guy do you like?"... [W]hat is this? like I have a deadline of some sort.

Meanwhile, Navreet, a lesbian Sikh, said:

> My dad is always saying, "Navreet, you're 24 now and your sister got married when she was 23"... So I just say I want to concentrate on my career... It's very difficult... I'm next in line to get married on both sides; there is a lot of pressure on me at the moment and it's just a case of me joking it off.

In such instances, queer people are compelled to navigate broader heteronormative scripts where marriage – of a heterosexual nature – is expected. Delaying tactics of educational achievement and career success could only work for so long, until suspicions arose regarding queer youth's commitment to the straight time narrative. Until then, for these individuals who were concealing their sexual identity, visible singleness was the only option. To bring home a partner of the same sex would have been anathema.

Hinging equality rights for queer individuals and groups on marriage reinforces normative expectations about lifecourse models, as one that necessarily includes marriage (with one other person) and continues to perpetuate disadvantage for individuals whose sexual identities still remain unprotected by these legal changes. Non-normative sexualities, such as polygamy and bisexuality, are left out of the equality framework when rights are based on monogamous marriage. For individuals whose sexual identity does not "fit" within the traditional, monogamous marital framework, the repercussions of these limitations are both immediate and long-lasting.

Young people are also socially encouraged to opt in to the straight time narrative. Aune's (2002) research with Evangelical Christians showed the discrimination that single people experienced in churches. Church activities typically focused on couples and families, thereby excluding single congregants, and sermons rarely considered the issues faced by single people. Similarly, Imtoual and Hussein (2009) noted that being single within many Muslim communities is highly undesirable. Gendered differences add further layers to how singleness is viewed; Muslim women were expected to perform 'the myth of the happy celibate' (Imtoual and Hussein, 2009, p. 25), with men having no such expectation. Celibacy is understood as a temporary placeholder in the lifecourse, preceding marriage, and also a long-term commitment (Cornwall, 2013). And while many religions promote certain forms of sexual abstinence, such as condemning pre-marital sex, the expected trajectory is monogamous, marital pairings, rather than life-long celibacy.

The religious exemptions created for religious groups opposed to same-sex marriage has often curtailed the rights of queer religious people to obtain a marriage within their own religious tradition. For example, despite legislation in England, Wales, and Scotland allowing same-sex marriage, the established Church of England is not legally allowed to perform them; those who dissent face a potential prison term. Same-sex marriage is a highly contested issue within the Church, given the broader disputes over homosexuality (Brittain and McKinnon, 2011), and legally barring the Church from offering same-sex weddings let the church off the hook. A quirk of the legislation has allowed Anglicans living in Scotland to have a same-sex wedding, if the priest agrees. In the UK, provision for same-sex weddings in religious contexts is low (Johnson *et al.*, 2017). While some groups such as the Quakers and Liberal Jews campaigned for same-sex marriage, and there are places where same-sex couples can obtain a religiously endorsed wedding, there remain barriers to access. A place of worship may in theory allow same-sex weddings, but one may need to be a regular member to benefit. Those without a place of worship offering same-sex weddings in close proximity are at a significant disadvantage.

For many queer religious people, same-sex marriage has not been a priority; merely obtaining acceptance within their religious space has been their overriding concern (we will discuss this more fully in Chapter 6). At the same time, younger populations of queer youth are imagining the possibility of being able to have a same-sex wedding (Gahan, 2016; Page, forthcoming). Gahan's (2016)

**106** Conceptualising the "normative"

study of young Australian religious LGBT people demonstrated their imagining of a life where they would be married with children, especially in the context of more liberal interpretations of religious texts by queer theologians, along with greater secular acceptance of same-sex relationships. In the RYS project, Stephen, a gay Anglican, recognised the importance of marriage within his religious tradition and the lengths his friends would go to, to experience a religiously blessed wedding ceremony:

> There is something special... about getting a union recognised before God... [My friends], a gay couple [are] having their civil partnership[2], and then they're going round to... an ordained priest who is going to bless their union... Within the church it's about making your promises before God. This couple are... going to exchange vows before God... there's something powerful about [that]... there's this divine bit which stands outside of any form of social construct where for me it's between two people, two people who love one another and that for me is extraordinary, two people who out of all the world... have managed to meet, fallen in love, and decided to pledge themselves to one another in complete fidelity, and out of love, that's extraordinary and I think whether it's between people of indeterminate genders, people of the same gender, or opposite gender, that is something to be treasured and to be celebrated.

Despite the legal restrictions placed on Anglicans obtaining a same-sex wedding within the Church (and civil partnerships before that), Stephen describes the fundamental importance of having a partnership religiously endorsed. Stephen is asking to be included in marriage, which upholds particular sacred norms for him, and which he believes same-sex couples should have unrestricted access to. Stephen is not asking for fundamental change; he is ultimately requesting access to the straight time account; his same-sex relationship should not be a barrier to access.

## *Reproduction*

The issue of reproduction has raised much disquiet regarding same-sex relationships, with assumed harms coming to children who are raised in queer families (Yip, 2011). Kilmer (2014) highlights the highly negative reaction of conservative churches to gay adoption, specifically noting the staunchly opposing views of Pope Francis, who argues same-sex adoption discriminates against children. In his rhetoric, the traditional family of mother, father, and children is invoked, with the explicit idea that same-sex adoption puts the "family" at risk; at no point is a family headed by a same-sex couple considered legitimately. As the previous section indicated, queer religious people do desire the straight time markers of getting married and having children, but often religious contexts makes this very challenging to achieve. Even in contexts where same-sex marriage has been legalised, there remain significant constraints on obtaining access to religiously endorsed services. Meanwhile, acceptance for queer families with children in religious contexts can be incredibly difficult, especially in situations where even same-sex marriage is contested and negatively perceived. This means that imagining a scenario where one can be given legitimacy as a queer person with children in a religious context may simply be unimaginable. At the same time, some religious traditions have made attempts to welcome same-sex families, such as churches which baptise children with same-sex parents (Kilmer, 2014). But given the opprobrium towards queer families with children emerging from spaces beyond religion, these factors can severely curtail the available options for queer people. In the RYS project, Jacob was part of Liberal Judaism, a religious tradition which has strongly supported queer people and same-sex marriage. Despite this, Jacob expressed huge anxiety and concern about his desire to have children in a hostile secular context:

> I think I would like children… but I think it is a very difficult decision at the moment… would [I] adopt a child if I was in a gay relationship, basically because of the societal stigma against that child… when your child is… in the playground [and] is bullied and beaten up because they've got two dads. I think that brings them to stark relieve that it's very difficult.

Jacob therefore imagined encountering hostility in the education setting, and although he did not envisage any negativities emerging from his religious tradition, he still felt constrained in how he imagined his future. Indeed, more scholarship is needed regarding how queer families with children navigate religious cultures; not enough research of this nature has been done, understandably, given that a key concern of religion and sexuality research has focused on acceptance issues per se.

## *Older generations*

Lifecourse patterns shift over the course of one's life and also bear differing outcomes and results for members of the same generational cohort (O'Rand, 1996). The experiences of lifecourse expectations will be different for individuals who are involved in the paid labour force continuously throughout their life than for those who have unsteady employment. Under-employment of trans individuals, related to problems with identification discrepancies, the process of transitioning while maintaining employment, as well as discrimination in the workplace (Mizock and Mueser, 2014; Rundall and Vecchietti, 2010) significantly impact financial security, home ownership, and subsequently retirement and pension access. An intersectional approach, where an account is given to how sexuality intersects with other identity categories such as social class and gender, are important in understanding the variability in how social life is mediated within a single cohort. These barriers necessarily impact how older age is experienced, depending upon what resources one has available.

## 108 Conceptualising the "normative"

In addition to the variability that exists within a cohort, there are also varying experiences across generations. Expectations for young people today are not the same as the expectations that would have been experienced by individuals now aged over 50. Social expectations and social norms have shifted significantly in the last several decades in many Western contexts. Queer youth today are growing up in environments where legal and policy changes are framed within a discourse of human and equality rights. Older queer individuals did not have access to such legal mechanisms in response to discrimination. While the experiences of harm, bullying, discrimination, and violence towards queer communities are still very much present (Taylor and Peter, 2011), these legal mechanisms were long fought for by previous generations of feminist and queer activists and the resulting environment for identity exploration is markedly different (Cossman, 2007; Short, 2013; Smith, 1999). Research among queer elders demonstrates how heteronormativity has been used for personal survival for individuals and groups whose sexual identities needed to be hidden – living in times and places where individualism and same-sex rights were a long way from being possible (Rosenfeld, 2009). These experiences mean that queer adults and seniors experience yet still different norms and expectations about their identities, demonstrated by fears of being "outed" in their senior residences or refusing to disclose their sexual identity to healthcare providers (Harley *et al.*, 2016; Orel, 2014). These experiences are additionally complicated when considering the role of religion or spirituality in queer elders' lives, both historically and currently (Harley, 2016). Thus far, most religion research has focused on younger populations and we simply do not know enough regarding the intersection between sexuality and older age. What we do know from more general studies is that queer seniors also report discrimination and bullying in senior residences and long-term care (Ibbitson, 2018). In the US, SAGE (Services and Advocacy for GLBT Elders) released a report in 2014 identifying the increased harm for GLBT seniors whose vulnerability is experienced across the intersections of age and sexual diversity. LGBT seniors report higher levels of isolation, with smaller support networks, higher levels of fear, and experiences of discrimination related to their sexual orientation, and many report that their primary healthcare providers do not know about their sexual orientations, a subject they are reluctant to discuss for fear of being judged or receiving inferior care particularly among transgender seniors. The survey, however, did not ask any questions about religion, neither as potentially problematic nor as a possible source of comfort. King's (2016a; 2016b) research uncovers the ways older LGBTQI+ people experience challenges in housing and policy, excavating the inequalities lived across the LGBQTI+ lifecourse. Correspondingly, there is little data to disaggregate trans, asexual, polyamorous, bisexual, lesbian, and gay results to the studies that have been conducted thus far (King, 2016a, 2016b). We simply do not yet have the data to unpack and understand better the realities of non-heterosexual or non-gender-conforming experiences among older adults and seniors, let alone in relation to their religious or spiritual identities.

## Summary

Normative prescriptions about sexuality rely on sexual behaviours which are typically connected to the straight time account (Wilcox, 2009) – they represent the reproductive futurity of a group or culture and require rigid boundaries as defence mechanisms for deviations (Cavanagh, 2007). A queer feminist analysis highlights that this is a constraining mechanism for both heterosexuals and queer people. Straight time has dominated both religious and secular cultures, and while religious contexts have often upheld straight time normatives more rigidly, religious resources have also been the source of a means of challenging the straight time account. The straight time narrative does not stay static, but changes over time, such as the way that pre-marital sex has latterly become a concern only for those in more religiously conservative contexts. Meanwhile, the opening up of queer equalities such as same-sex marriage has all at once fostered greater inclusions, but also reified straight time normatives, as queer people are included – but only on the terms dictated to them by heterosexuals. Some religious traditions campaigned for same-sex marriage, this being seen as a logical marker in the lifecourse that should be equally accessible to queer people, where love and commitment become sacredly endorsed values. But religious spaces have formed powerful contestations to same-sex marriage, putting huge barriers in place for queer religious practitioners. In many cases, queer religious individuals do not want to be revolutionary, but simply want to be included into the straight time account. While some have viewed such goals as a greater entrenchment of the straight time model, for religious practitioners, marriage is often understood in sacred terms. At the same time, it is now time to reflect more broadly on the redefinition of what constitutes a "typical" lifecourse model. While heterosexual time and lifecourse models predict heteronormative, monogamous, gender-stereotypical, and pre-determined actions and expectations regarding sexual behaviours, marriage, and reproduction, the increasing diversity of relationship and family models demonstrate a growing body of family "types" that cannot be contained within the normative understanding of straight time.

## Notes

1 *Brokeback Mountain* (2005) depicts a love story between two men, though both maintain public heterosexual relationships (both are married to women and have children). One of the two men, Jack, is subsequently killed for being "queer", and Ennis ends up alone, having left his wife. While the plot is not unrealistic, it can be argued that the widespread public is not yet ready for a homosexual couple to live "happily ever after". *Casablanca* (1942) provides an earlier example of cultural standards influencing film. Director Michael Curitz originally intended to have Humphrey Bogart's character walk off into the sunset with Ingrid Bergman, however, it was thought to be too racy to have the movie end with a marriage breaking up (Bergman's character is married to another man).

2 At the time of the RYS study, same-sex marriage was not legally possible; instead same-sex partnerships were recognised through the *Civil Partnership Act* (2004).

## 110 Conceptualising the "normative"

While the Church of England is legally barred from offering same-sex marriage, the Church also refused to offer civil partnerships, although it did allow clergy to obtain a civil partnership (clergy are not allowed to enter a same-sex marriage). At the time of Stephen's interview, priests were under the instruction that they could not offer a same-sex service or perform a blessing, even though, unofficially, such services were taking place. Therefore, the example Stephen gives here is of a priest operating at the very boundaries of possibility within the rules of the Church at the time. Once same-sex marriage came into force, the Church advised that while informal prayer was allowed, the blessing of a same-sex marriage was forbidden, but some priests have started offering thanksgiving services which are seemingly deemed to comply with the policy. The guidelines can therefore be considered confused and muddled (see Bethmont, 2019).

# 6

# NAVIGATING THE "NORMATIVE"

## Constituting safe and unsafe space

### Introduction

The last chapter analysed how "normative" sexuality is constituted, using a queer feminist analysis. This chapter continues with our queer feminist framing to focus on the experience of this, and the extent to which the concept of heteronormativity has salience in everyday lived religious practice. The last chapter emphasised that the "straight time" model (Wilcox, 2009) infuses culture and has an impact on sexual practice in religious contexts for both heterosexuals and queer people. Here we are taking those arguments further to demonstrate how straight time has been experienced by queer people in various spaces.

Social norms and expectations develop from explicit and implicit norms, translated through religious, familial, and institutional practices (McGuire, 2008). Various spaces therefore become fundamental regarding how straight time is experienced, and the extent to which straight time can be contested. Factors that influence individual attitudes towards sexuality, marriage, and sexual behaviour frequently intertwine religion, familial, and social teachings including received gender and sexual disciplining for any deviations (Taylor and Peter, 2011; Young and Shipley, 2020).

We will start by emphasising the saliency of space when considering heteronormativity and will go on to specifically examine the extent to which queer people have been included or not in places of worship, home, and school. We will then focus more specifically on identities which have been marginalised under the "queer" banner such as trans identities and bisexual identities. In this endeavour, we will draw significantly from the RYS and RGSY projects.

### Constituting space

As explored in Chapter 1, space is important in relation to experiencing social life. Rather than understanding space as something that simply exists, we argue

**112** Navigating the "normative"

that spaces are created and co-constituted; they are dynamic, fluid, and constantly changing (Munt, 2010). It is often assumed that queer religious people will encounter spaces negative to their identities, but it is not necessarily as simple as this. Taylor and Snowdon's (2013) research on queer religious youth in the UK showed that these youth were actively creating spaces in response to the difficult experiences they had navigating the two identities (queer and religious), which outsiders frequently viewed as incompatible. Further, participants in their study challenged the framing of their sexuality within LGBT boundaries (Taylor and Snowdon, 2014a). What is demonstrated through this research is that young people's framing of their identities when they are "outside" the normative script necessitates the creation of new spaces where safety, understanding, and belonging are sought.

This may necessitate opting out of one's religious tradition. Kolysh (2017)'s research on non-religion in the lives of Black LGBTQ people highlights the influence of their Christian upbringing, reinforced through school and church. In this context, being LGBTQ was seen as un-Christian and sometimes associated with whiteness. For Kolysh's participants, 'some neighborhoods were constructed as Christian, connected to one's childhood and hostile to LGBTQ people, while others were LGBTQ-friendly, albeit largely white and gentrified' (2017, p. 1). Because of the negativities they experienced, the majority of Kolysh's participants ultimately left Christianity, embracing a non-religious identity.

These reflections by Kolysh's participants mirror the experiences of sexually diverse, two-spirit, and queer members of Indigenous, Métis, and Inuit communities in Canada (Monture-Angus, 1995). Two-spirit people are often caught between their racial identities and their gender and sexual identities, where instances of homophobia within Indigenous communities are seen to have emanated from the influence of colonisation and settler colonial violence (Brotman and Ryan, 2004). Further, lack of awareness of the history and tradition of two-spirit identities within Indigenous communities complicates whether and how individuals associate themselves. The impact of these influences and negative perceptions about being two-spirit means that they 'struggle to achieve safety through a variety of means, not least of which is choosing to leave their community' (Brotman and Ryan, 2004, p. 61).

For queer people, finding a safe space may mean moving out of the family home, moving between religious institutions, or moving schools (Browne *et al.*, 2010; Rasmussen, 2004; Wilcox, 2003). Although we have not got the space to comment on all the potential spaces that queer religious people navigate, here we include some key ones: places of worship, home, and school.

## *Places of worship*

Places of worship are experienced variably by queer people. Some spaces have been hostile, injurious, and highly damaging. Other religious spaces have prioritised queer experiences, not just in terms of welcoming queer individuals, but

Navigating the "normative"  **113**

using their experiences as the starting point for inclusion. And in between these two examples are a wide variety of experiences.

How religious spaces can cause significant harm to queer people is aptly mapped in Barton's (2012) coverage of the Bible Belt in the United States. Here, the influence of religious negativity towards queer people not only pervades church sermons, but is referenced frequently in broader society, with Barton herself being told in her own garden that her sexuality was an "abomination". Some of her participants had experienced being questioned in a hostile manner by other churchgoers to determine whether they should be excommunicated because of their sexuality. Barton charts the highly negative consequences of this environment for queer people, including being disowned by churches and family members, mental health crises, and attempted and actual violence. In such an environment, the way the space is constituted makes a difference:

> In rural areas, with few public places to gather, church communities serve as both social support and entertainment… A Bible Belt gay… who has been kicked out of a parish, loses not only her social network, but the whole community – including of course her family – witnesses the public shame; some family members may even share the disgrace.
>
> *(Barton, 2012, p. 30)*

Barton explores ex-gay ministries, which aim to turn the queer person straight, through various "therapies". Such approaches do not validate the idea that god made someone queer; instead, one's queer identity is seen as rectifiable. Such conversion attempts typically do not work, and despite psychological language used to describe the "therapies", these are usually professionally discredited. Indeed one prominent organisation, Exodus, closed down in 2013 and apologised for the harm they had caused to lesbian and gay people (Creek, 2014). But in religiously conservative families with a queer child, parents often turn to conversion therapy as a means of solving the "problem". Yet even in such negative environments, individuals were able to challenge the spaces as they were dominantly determined. For example, at one ex-gay conference, Barton (2012) noted that it was used as an opportunity for people to engage in hook-up sex, unbeknown to the conference organisers.

Such constraining cultures can have an enormous impact on young religious people who are trying to work out their identity. Within our own projects, queer young adults had only just begun to grapple with the navigation of spaces, and to manage potentially hostile situations. One 18-year-old Anglican lesbian RGSY participant said, 'My sexuality has been a constant struggle for me, particularly as I feel it clashes with my religion. I have finally begun to accept it and myself, but still find it can be difficult to do so'. Meanwhile, as one Roman Catholic lesbian participant said, 'It's a source of stress because it's something I can't control, something that is contrary to my faith'. Such young people were trying hard to navigate the negative spaces of their various Christian traditions.

**114** Navigating the "normative"

Some religious environments are so negative towards queer individuals that groups specifically catering for them are set up to offer support and succour. The Roman Catholic Church's disavowal of homosexuality (Jordan, 2000) has led to the development of Dignity, though this group has experienced negative repercussions from the Church, such as priests who have been sacked for allowing Dignity services to take place in their churches (Jordan, 2000; Miller, 2014). Other groups include A Common Bond, which offers support for Jehovah's Witnesses (Wilcox, 2003), or Imaan, set up to support gay Muslims (Shah, 2018).

While the Bible Belt that Barton (2012) studied constitutes a wide geographical space where negativity towards queer people is cultivated, other geographical areas are differently constituted. Wilcox (2009) examines how Los Angeles is crafted as a welcoming place for queer people, offering a fertile environment for the growth of queer-affirming religious places. Therefore, at the other end of the spectrum, religious spaces have operated from a queer-inclusive starting point. For example, the Metropolitan Community Church (MCC) was initiated by Troy Perry in the USA in 1968 and ahead of the Stonewall riots. Perry had been forced to relinquish being a church preacher for being gay, so he started his own queer-inclusive church, which quickly became popular (Warner, 2002). A queer-inclusive theology was forged, attracting Christians from all manner of backgrounds. This could cause tension, especially because of the diversity in Christian practice. As Warner describes, 'MCC services have come to feel like an eclectic mix of Catholic, Episcopal, and Lutheran liturgical forms with the preaching style, gospel hymns, and democratic prayer circle of twentieth-century charismatic fellowships' (2002, p. 285). Thumma's (1991) research emphasises the tensions some of his participants felt regarding this eclecticism, with some feeling that 'they were putting gay before God' (1991, p. 337). Theological commitment could therefore override the positive impact of engaging with a queer-friendly space. Wilcox (2003) argues that MCC offers much to support the Christian who has just come out, but once they have developed a strong integration of their religious and sexual identity, they often move on to religious spaces they find more spiritually fulfilling.

While queer-affirming spaces can offer queer people much-needed support, they can be built on other exclusions, such as gender, ethnicity, or class. Wilcox (2009) maps how some LGBT churches can be racist. She also notes the gendered tensions within the MCC, and how gay men have tended to dominate the authority structures to the extent that women have sought out religious experiences elsewhere. For example, Warner (2002) has noted some resistance to feminist theology in some MCC spaces. Some gay and lesbian affirming spaces can exclude other sexualities such as bisexuals. Daniels recalls that while not encountering explicitly overt discrimination, she was subtly told in her MCC to seek out her 'true identity' (2012, p. 14), with an implicit undertone that she needed to decide whether she was "really" a heterosexual or lesbian. Meanwhile other religious spaces try to cultivate intersectional inclusion, exemplified by

Gleig's (2012) analysis of a queer Buddhist Sangha which explicitly fosters ethnic diversity.

This highlights the complexities regarding how religious spaces are constituted, and the grounds on which queer people are included are excluded, such as whether having a queer religious leader is enough, to the types of theologies that are conveyed. How this is communicated is fundamental, especially for young people. For example, in the RYS project, Abby, a lesbian, belonged to Liberal Judaism but was very clear that queer people were affirmed, through the theologies she had encountered as well as the religious practices she had engaged with:

> Liberal Judaism, it's not a problem at all. Like I went to the most liberal wedding you could go to. It was an inter-faith lesbian wedding. It was just like, I was like this is getting ridiculous now [laugh]. I've actually got this leaflet because all the Liberals in the synagogues all do leaflets on everything you can imagine. And I got this one on sexuality and it was like, it says that maybe, it basically just shows you a different way of interpreting the laws.

On the basis of the high levels of comfort she had experienced within Liberal Judaism, Abby wanted to become a rabbi. Taylor and Snowdon's (2014a) Christian lesbian participants deemed gender inclusivity – and the right of women to be in religious leadership – as fundamental to their belonging, with them seriously questioning their commitment to any church which denied a place for women at the leadership table. Some of their participants were training in Christian ministry, highlighting the changing landscape going forward as more worship spaces include lesbians in positions of authority, and the impact this has for both gender and sexuality inclusivity.

## *Home*

Home is often constructed as a place of safety; it is often the underpinning reference point within people's lives (Thomson, 2011). But homes can be volatile and even dangerous spaces for queer people. Barton's (2012) aforementioned study of people living in the Bible Belt notes the heightened hostility families could demonstrate towards queer family members, invoking injurious speech as well as physical violence; in 'interview after interview, subjects shared similar tales of rejection, abuse, and violence' (2012, p. 46). One mother told her son that it would have been easier had he been a murderer rather than gay. Even once participants were able to successfully navigate an exit from their families of origin, it did not mean that the pain abated, as they felt tremendous loss given that their families often disowned them. The stark consequences of individuals living in very conservative religious homes can indicate why coming out is not a choice taken lightly; indeed, religious individuals may well decide to hide their sexual identity by remaining single, or even through entering a heterosexual

**116** Navigating the "normative"

partnership. Jaspal (2012) conveys not only the acute sense of rejection his gay Muslim participants felt from their families when they disclosed their sexuality; much angst was also generated simply by *imagining* the familial reaction and the anticipated disowning that would follow. These issues can be compounded by the heightened significance given to familial ties in South Asian families with a history of migration, with familial interdependence a core strategy in managing the racism and negativity experienced by wider society and resulting in numerous kin-based obligations (Yip, 2004a). The support offered by families can be significant, having an impact regarding the extent to which one can disclose one's sexuality. Yip's (2004b) research focused on non-heterosexual Muslims, examining how this could lead to compartmentalised lives, as individuals wanted to authentically live both the religious and sexual elements of their identity. To be honest to themselves meant their queer identity could not simply be relinquished or extinguished. Despite these challenges, 50% of Yip's participants had come out to their parents, with higher numbers disclosing to a sibling (Yip, 2004a). Parents often accepted their child's sexual identity but continued to pressurise them into a heterosexual marriage. In a minority of cases, participants were punished and asked to leave the family home, leading to deteriorating mental health and even suicide attempts. Some experienced physical violence at the hands of their families. The reception within religious families to a queer identity can be wide-ranging and context-dependent. Although conservative religious traditions increase the likelihood of a negative and injurious reaction, this is not the whole story. In some cases, families can personally accept the queer-identifying individual, so long as it does not become public knowledge. They are therefore motivated more by community censure rather than inherent negativity towards queer identity (see Page and Yip, 2012a). Indeed, in the RGSY project, some non-religious participants – while having a positive experience coming out to their families, also noted ambivalences. As a gay man, Michael did not welcome 'being associated too much with being like flamboyant or… the stereotypes of being gay', and worried about how his family would react if he wore 'sparkly [women's] jeans… something like that, then they'll notice… and might make fun of it'. Therefore, non-religious families too can demonstrate tensions in unconditional acceptance of queer identities.

## *School*

Children's bodies have been societal markers for the morality of society (Weeks, 2014), bound up with notions of their innocence, vulnerability, and need for protection – especially protection from sexual influence (Jackson and Scott, 2013). But this is a relatively recent understanding of childhood, cemented through Locke and Rousseau's philosophy, who understood children as blank slates, thereby overriding the prevailing notion that children were inherently sinful and demonically influenced (Forna, 1998). Children were increasingly understood in de-sexualised and sexually unblemished terms, demonstrated in Britain with the raising of the age of consensual sex for girls to 16 in 1882 (Jackson and Scott, 2013; Weeks, 2014). As the sentimental idea of the bourgeois and innocent childhood gained strength, their participation in paid work was questioned; instead, schools became the context within which children were to be cultivated and harnessed into productive and good citizens (Jackson and Scott, 2013). Religions have been crucial to this endeavour, with their longstanding role in providing education and other care services.

Education is therefore a critical space to consider, where ideologies are performed and enforced and where sexual and gender identities are implicitly and explicitly taught. Education about religion, gender, and sexuality are hotly contested across multiple nation states and, at present, are not taught either consistently or systematically. In a number of Western countries, as more rights are accorded to sexual minorities, sexual diversity education within schools often becomes a controversial issue (Heyes, 2019; Rasmussen and Leahy, 2018; Shipley, 2019). Homosexuality has been constructed as a risk to children, with homosexuals often understood as being predatory and likely to corrupt children's innocence (Barton, 2012; Klesse, 2007). In Canada, the Premier of Ontario, Doug Ford, sought to overturn the updated sex education curriculum of 2015 in the province because it contained "controversial" content – such as teaching about gender identity, sexual diversity, and consent. This backlash comprised of removing curricula, opening an online portal for concerns, and suggested the creation of a "snitch line" for any teacher caught teaching this curriculum. The Ontario Human Rights Commission and the Canadian Civil Liberties Association both filed lawsuits against the provincial government alleging discrimination and violation of *Charter* rights. This controversy is tied to numerous related controversies in the province regarding religion, gender, and sexuality in high schools (see Shipley, 2019). Meanwhile, the Australia Safe Schools programme, aimed at cultivating inclusive schools for queer youth, has been accused of being a recruiting tool for the lesbian and gay movement, with teaching materials aimed at assisting queer youth in working out their identities sensationalised in the press (Rasmussen and Leahy, 2018). In Birmingham, UK, an inclusive curriculum has invoked protests outside a small number of Muslim-majority primary schools. The protests quickly escalated beyond the school community to involve agitators with broader conservative agendas, and a court order placed an exclusion zone around one of the schools (Parveen, 2019).

In 1988, in England, Wales, and Scotland, the government imposed legislation called Section 28. It barred local authorities, and the schools within their jurisdiction, from "promoting" homosexuality, and what Margaret Thatcher called "pretend family relationships" (Weeks, 2014). At the heart of these debates was a double concern: that queer lifestyles were becoming too visible and public, and in turn, that "family life" was therefore under grave threat (Weeks, 2014). Specifically, this was legislation that targeted schoolchildren, deemed most at risk of being "corrupted" by "homosexual values". In the wake of AIDS and increased hostility towards queer people (Weeks, 2014), this had a devastating

**118** Navigating the "normative"

impact regarding how queer issues were effectively silenced in school contexts, thereby cultivating high levels of homophobic abuse (Epstein *et al.*, 2003). The legislation was repealed in 2003, but there was a whole generation of children educated under its guise. This impacted on queer participants in the RYS project, who experienced bullying and other negative actions as a result of this environment where queer identities were silenced.

Many older RYS participants were impacted by its legacy, particularly those who identified as queer. In the school setting, their experiences can be divided between those encountered within the "formal" curriculum – typically school spaces under the direct control of teachers, such as the syllabus delivered in the classroom, and the "informal" curriculum – the peer-controlled elements of school life, such as encounters in the corridor, on the sports field, and in the classroom away from the watchful eye of the teacher (Page and Yip, 2012b; Warwick *et al.*, 2001). For the RYS participants, homophobia and homonegativity were most acutely experienced in the informal contexts, where name-calling was routinised, leading to violence and social isolation in some cases, as depicted in the following quotes:

> My school was so aggressive and so racist and stuff, I used to have a friend who was bisexual, and she got beaten up so many times.
>
> *(Fahima, heterosexual Muslim woman)*

> I was outed at school as being bisexual when I was 15… which went down pretty badly. And I was kind of bullied quite a lot because of that… My group of friends pretty much ditched me because I was outed as being bisexual. And I was viewed as an outsider by them from that point on. They stopped inviting me to stuff and stopped hanging around with me so much at school.
>
> *(Stuart, bisexual Christian man)*

Because Section 28 led to the curtailment of even mentioning homosexuality, this left teachers ill-equipped to manage the discrimination queer students faced (Epstein *et al.*, 2003). Meanwhile, given the constraints around Section 28, participants recalled only learning about heterosexuality – and the normative nature of this – in the formal setting of the classroom:

> [In] RE [Religious Education] lessons, I don't remember gay people ever being brought into it whatsoever; it was always about 'don't commit adultery, do not fornicate' and it was always about a man and a woman.
>
> *(Stephen, gay Christian man)*

It was participants' experiences in some of the conservative religious schools where the formal curriculum encultured explicitly homophobic sentiments. Erica, a 20-year-old Jew attending an Orthodox school, discussed the competing narratives she encountered. She did challenge some of the heteronormative thinking, describing herself as someone who would 'make the Rabbis feel awkward'. Tensions arose over any discussion of homosexuality within the formal curriculum, noting that such topics would be 'left until the end of term' because of the controversies surrounding it. Erica's experience of school coincided with broader sexuality equalities being debated and normalised, including the repeal of Section 28. This, therefore, left the school staff needing to convey an orthodox position on the impermissibility of homosexuality, within the framework of a broader equalities narrative. (Similarly, Hanemann [2016] discusses these tensions regarding how homosexuality is discussed in a liberal Catholic school.) Erica experienced some peer negativity, but she felt protected because of her close-knit group of friends, who supported her. But the most injurious moment came in a Religious Education class where the teacher aligned homosexuality with bestiality (Page and Yip, 2012b). Such associations align homosexuality with the unnatural and the less-than-civilised, positioning homosexuality as excluded from legitimate citizenship, deemed different, less than worthy, and "other" (Richardson, 2018). Erica, however, did not experience this as a totalising culture in a Goffmanesque sense, given that she had other resources, such as the support of her friends, to draw upon. But notable in all instances of homonegativity experienced in school settings by the RYS participants was the lack of positive intervention by staff, and little censuring of staff with homonegative views. Indeed, participants in such school environments found such behaviour as routine, it was not deemed worthy of even reporting it, because the homonegative culture pervaded the whole institutional setting.

Meanwhile, participants in the RGSY project highlight the confusion and social disciplining that exists within high school environments in particular; Colin (male, polyamorous/bisexual, spiritual but not religious [SBNR]) attended a public high school in Ontario and stated:

> Well the first influence that my peer group had on me sexually was in high school. Growing up in public school, you really didn't want to be gay and I still kind of struggle with this whole bisexual thing, like I mean I don't, I don't identify as gay, I identify as MSM, if you'd like, man who has sex with men, or bisexual, and I think that, and I still have a lot of discomfort, it takes a long time for me to warm up to a sexual partner who is male and I do really strongly associate that with... the sort of homophobic environment that maybe still exists in high school but it certainly did when I was going through, especially for men.

Colin's current concerns about his own sexual self-expression are heavily influenced by the peer environment in high school, where males identifying as gay were derided and discriminated against. Although Colin is no longer in that environment, the effects remain. The experiences of sexuality being disciplined from a secular (non-religious) perspective inform how Colin describes

**120** Navigating the "normative"

himself and how he interacts; religion has not been the source of these impositions for him. As Colin indicates above, experiences in high school have long-lasting impacts on personal identity and his willingness to identify outside the "accepted" boundaries of his high school classmates. In the broader contestations around school curricula and how sexual inclusivity is taught, what is often lost is the voices of queer youth themselves, and how such debates impact negatively on their school experiences – with these often having long-lasting effects.

## Finding safe spaces beyond 'L' and 'G'

Thus far we have mapped how various spaces are constituted in relation to queer people, highlighting a variety of experiences. Religions can commence from queer inclusivity or queer rejection; many traditions are situated somewhere between the two. While young people have been impacted by how these discourses get debated and played out, much focus has been placed on the impact on gay and lesbian people. Far less emphasis has been put on other sexualities, and here we focus on the specific exclusions felt by bisexuals, trans people, asexual, celibate, and polyamorous people. In all these cases, these groups are more likely to face greater scrutiny and censure from secular as well as religious spaces, though religious discourses can be used to cultivate a congruent identity.

### *Bisexuality*

While there has been a growth of research in the areas of sexuality and religion, particularly focused on lesbian and gay experiences, bisexuality and its relationship to religion continues to be understudied, though scholarship is increasing (Diamond, 2003; Monro, 2015; Shepherd, 2019; Young and Shipley, 2020; Toft, 2012, 2014; Toft and Yip, 2018). Perceptions about bisexuality, at times negatively framed as a "confused" sexuality rather than a defined one, continue to influence experiences of exclusion, including within queer communities (Carillo and Hoffman, 2018; Toft, 2012, 2014). When paired with religious identity, there is a clear gap between understanding and recognition.

Of the respondents to the RGSY survey, 12.1% identified as bisexual. Of those who claimed bisexual identities and who also answered the questions about sex/gender identification, 87.5% identified as female, 15% as male, and 5% as trans.[1] Meanwhile, in the RYS project, bisexuals comprised 7.9% of the sample, with 63.6% identifying as female and 36.4% as male. In both studies, the majority of bisexuals identified as Christian (45% in RGSY and 67.8% in RYS).

In the RGSY project, bisexual respondents felt strongly that their religious tradition understood the issues queer individuals faced. Given the personalised ways bisexual respondents describe and negotiate their religious identities, this might reflect the (non)religious identity they experience rather than reflections on doctrinal or traditional religious views (Shipley and Young, forthcoming). However, bisexual respondents were clear that tensions exist in their daily lives related to their sexual identity, most frequently occurring in their interactions with others. Participants stated that their sexuality is often perceived as a lack of commitment to either homosexuality or heterosexuality, which can impact their ability to have sustained romantic or sexual relationships (see also Anderson and McCormack, 2016; Carillo and Hoffman, 2018). While some participants acknowledged that bisexuality may be a "safer" designation in some contexts than lesbian, gay, or queer, they stated it can also bring with it questions about a lack of self-awareness and more persistent negative treatment (Shipley and Young, forthcoming).

Meanwhile, in the RYS project, only 30.6% of bisexuals either agreed or strongly agreed that their religion understands the issues lesbian, gay, and bisexual people face.[2] A number of bisexual RYS participants in religious environments where their sexual identity was not welcomed felt fears around disclosure. Some prioritised relationships with the opposite sex or were remaining single (see Yip and Page, forthcoming). James, a Christian bisexual, explained the tensions that ensued in that if he dated a woman this would be welcomed by his Evangelical church, but would be seen negatively in his queer secular friendship circles, saying:

> My gay and lesbian friends, a lot of them give the impression that they would be happier if I was just going out with a guy and could treat me as gay, rather than embarrassingly turning up to a gay club with a girl, too much straightness there.

Compared with his church, James was able to disclose his sexuality more openly within his queer networks, but exclusions remained. He was not fully accepted as bisexual, because it led to the possibility of him being in a cross-sex relationship. Full acceptance in his queer network was therefore dependent on him being in a same-sex relationship. In order to satisfy the demands of his church and his queer friendship network, James had opted to remain single. Other bisexuals found the religious spaces they belonged to more welcoming, such as Lily, a Buddhist, who argued that she

> couldn't be part of a religion that didn't accept me, me being I suppose in a sexual sense bisexual... it's so safe that I haven't even thought about it, it hasn't even crossed my mind that that's not acceptable in Buddhism, until you kind of asked that question. So I suppose they're very interlinked, otherwise I just wouldn't be a Buddhist.

Lily's unconditional acceptance into her Buddhist community was deeply affirming; her bisexuality was never questioned nor problematised (see Yip and Page, forthcoming).

**122** Navigating the "normative"

Bisexuality continues to be disputed in both religious and secular spaces, because bisexuality unseats the dominance of monosexism, a deeply entrenched ideology, which Toft and Yip describe as

> a cultural ideology, a set of institutional practices and individual attitudes that demand a person's self-identification firmly and exclusively with one sexual identity. Monosexism operates on, and perpetuates, the hegemony of the hetero/homo dichotomy. Consequently, "heterosexual" is a normative thus often unproblematized identity – and "lesbian" and "gay" are increasingly accepted identities – but this system of identification and stratification insists on an individual's attraction to either members of the same sex or opposite sex. This concretizes the exclusive occupation of one side of the hetero/homo and opposite-sex/same-sex taxonomy.
>
> *(2018, p. 234)*

In this way, even in contexts where lesbian and gay relationships are accepted, bisexual identities may not necessarily be welcomed. The prevailing dominance of monosexism has led some to argue that bisexuality is a confused sexuality, with bisexuals needing to decide which side of the fence they sit. In addition, the ideology of monosexism has also led to accusations that bisexuals are inherently unfaithful (thereby disrupting another esteemed value – monogamy – that cross-cuts both religious and secular cultures). While such discourses can be located in secular spaces too, religious spaces have also articulated strong monosexist overtones. One such document which aptly demonstrated deep bi-phobia, in holding a deep-seated monosexist view, was the publication of the Church of England's *Issues in Human Sexuality* (1991), which argued that bisexuals are incapable of faithfulness, and because they are assumed to have a "choice" regarding their sexual identity, they should exclusively embrace heterosexuality. As Shepherd (2019) argues, this document demonstrated a lack of compassion towards bisexual people, and the unprecedented status given to the document meant that Shepherd had interviewed trainee priests in the Church who had had to sign up to this viewpoint, even though they fundamentally disagreed with it.

### *Trans identities*

Similar to bisexuality, trans identities have been silenced within many religious communities. As Daniels (2012) articulates, trans people in many religious traditions are not even "on the page". But as the idea of gender as fixed and immutable continues to be undermined, this has unleashed a backlash in some quarters. The recent *Male and Female He Created Them* (2019), penned by the Vatican Congregation for Catholic Education, strongly reasserts and reaffirms gender dualism, while Blyth (2018) has noted the forms of symbolic violence Conservative Christian groups have conveyed against trans people, with their very existence being denied. When trans identity is associated with the Christian concept of sinfulness, trans people have been told they must repent and relinquish their trans identity, and conform to their assigned gender at birth. If they do not, the message is that there is no room for them. Some religious traditions are therefore threatened by what they see as an attack on a god-ordained gendered order (Bernhardt-House [2012] notes how some trans people are therefore accused of playing god through changing their gender), but in the process this denies the very humanity of trans people within those communities. This can cause enormous hardships in a trans person's spiritual life, as they are othered by and denied a space within their religious communities. In her research with trans and genderqueer individuals, Wilcox (2018b) explores the enormous struggles and personal challenges they face. One way of managing the broader negativity experienced by religious communities is through an affirmation that they were made trans and are loved as trans people by their religious, spiritual, and sacred creators (Wilcox, 2018b). Meanwhile, Hall (forthcoming) has explored trans identities in Poland, where the Roman Catholic Church has an influential presence and where gender dualism is promoted. She notes how trans people are often socially excluded from church and other settings. Furthermore, a desire to "pass" as gender normative means that trans people in Poland are underrepresented in queer support networks, putting them at greater risk of potential isolation. More steps need to be taken to listen and hear the narratives of genderqueer and trans individuals and communities, especially from a religious perspective (see also Levy and Lo, 2013).

Other religious traditions have made attempts to create more welcoming and inclusive spaces. Daniels (2012) highlights the greater number of resources in MCC congregations which educate cis-gender individuals about trans experiences. Some religious traditions have embraced new rituals, such as marking gender transition. The Church of England has written guidelines for a baptism service to welcome into the Church those who have changed their identity. Small acts of recognition can be fundamental; Beardsley (2015) highlights the high levels of spirituality among her trans participants, who simply wanted acceptance from religious institutions. She notes how priests actively supporting trans individuals can go some way to address the damage caused by churches. More broadly, religious institutions can also have a lot of resources to support gender diversity. Zachs (2015) notes how Judaism is replete with resources to affirm gender diverse identities, and has the ritual emphasis to enact that recognition through modifying ritual. Meanwhile, Cornwall (2019) notes the key supporting and pastoral role chaplaincy can offer when trans individuals are seeking out medical services.

Those expressing a nonbinary identity do not view themselves in exclusively male or female terms; younger people in particular are embracing broader and more inclusive definitions of gender (Young and Shipley, forthcoming). For example, in the RGSY project, Priya defined herself as a genderqueer femme. Priya resisted the normative pressure in relation to both her sexuality and gender

**124** Navigating the "normative"

performativity, identifying her tomboyishness as evidence that she wasn't 'playing a good role heteronormatively'. She thought that this disconnect from normative gender identity meant that she was also a lesbian. Realising that the two categories did not rely on one another took time, and while she has grown to understand herself and these identities more fully, she feels society requires a certain suppression of masculinity within heterosexual women. This left her feeling like an 'awkward gender inbetweener', as she tried to conceptualise her gender and sexual identity in a social environment where binary gender was endorsed. At the same time, she was able to utilise religious resources to challenge this. She drew on various stories of gender diversity from her Hindu background, including characters who changed gender, to help resist the dominant social normatives which dictated very narrow forms of gender identity. In many religious traditions, there are the resources to be inclusive of trans and gender nonbinary individuals, but the monopoly of conservative voices impacts on the cultivation of such alternative interpretations.

## Asexuality and celibacy

The huge emphasis on sexual lives in contemporary culture can marginalise those whose identities are not focused on sexual activity, whether in the present moment or at some future point. As Terry argues, 'Sex has, to a large degree, become seen as an imperative to the basic function of a mature individual's identity, without which a person is deemed incomplete' (2012, p. 872). Such prioritisation of sexuality and sexual identity ignores those identities where sexuality is understood differently. Scott and Dawson describe asexuality as 'a lack of sexual desire and/or attraction, but this does not necessarily mean a lack of interest in intimacy or its component factors (love, sociability, emotional depth) that help build close relationships' (2015, p. 3; see also Scherrer, 2008). Asexuality is both under-recognised and little-understood, and far more research is needed in this area (Stuart, 2015). Even though some religious cultures have promoted forms of behaviour which may be deemed to be asexual, such as celibacy, it is important that these are not conflated. As Terry (2012) argues, celibacy denotes a more deliberate choice not to engage in sexual activity, rather than denoting a lack of interest in sex per se. But both celibacy and asexuality sit uneasily with contemporary cultures focused on the idea that one can only be fulfilled through engaging in a sexual relationship. Some participants in the RYS project displayed their disdain towards celibacy, deeming it unnatural. Others felt that celibacy involved repression and held a high personal cost (Page, 2016a). However, for queer people, celibacy is often expected of them by their religious institutions, as one homosexual Evangelical male RGSY participant explained: 'I feel that because of my attractions I should stay celibate, or marry without physical attraction necessarily being there' and 'I am expected to either stay celibate or marry one woman for life'. These feelings of either expected celibacy or engagement in relationships with opposite-sex partners in order to attain acceptance reinforce the participants' feelings of shame and disconnection between their identity and the expectations placed on them.

Both celibacy and asexuality disrupt the straight time account, where it is assumed that at some future point one will sexually engage in order to subscribe to reproductive imperatives. Giving greater legitimacy to asexual identities may disrupt and challenge such normative understandings. As Richardson argues, 'asexual activism could encourage a much more fundamental kind of "decoupling" that would be productive of new meanings of (sexual)/citizenship and, perhaps, lead towards a de-sexualization, as distinct from merely a de-heterosexualization, of citizenship' (2018, p. 89–90).

In the RYS project, Alex, a Buddhist, identified as asexual and aptly demonstrated the issues he faced regarding his identity not being properly understood. In a context where peers were defining themselves as either gay or straight, Alex could not make sense of his own identity until he came across a website about asexuality, which he found more affirming and running closer to his own understanding of himself than the other labels available to him. His experience problematised the impetus to label one's sexuality in concrete terms. But like the aforementioned definition of asexuality by Scott and Dawson, Alex too did not equate being asexual with not having any physical contact with others, and he welcomed the opportunity to be tactile with others (e.g. through hugging) but he was concerned about how this would be perceived in a culture that reads such activity through a sexual lens:

> It's part of the sexual world we live in because I can hardly hug someone or say something without making them think of what I want [sexually] with them. So if I was completely celibate and I practise celibacy then it would put this barrier or wall between physical contact with people.

For Alex, the idea of being celibate did not accurately describe his identity because he saw this as an identity which ruled out physical contact. But he felt he was constantly at risk of being misunderstood by those around him, who would inevitably interpret his actions only in sexual terms. Alex found in his Buddhist community a greater acceptance of his sexual identity, and this was where he felt at home. Not only were gay and lesbian identities welcomed and incorporated, his community cultivated a broader inclusivity, as he explains:

> [In] the Buddhist community... we are very, very open... giving me the opportunity and the freedom to think that I can relate with people in lots of different ways and not just in a sexual way... So yeah definitely something in Buddhism I feel more free to just explore.

Alex therefore found congruence between his asexual identity and his Buddhist community, where he was accepted for who he was, and was not defined through any predetermined labels. The frame of reference, unlike his broader youth culture, was not dominantly influenced by sexuality, and instead other issues were prioritised. He found this very freeing.

## *Non-monogamy and polyamory*

Non-monogamy as a sexual or relationship practice continues to be viewed negatively in secular culture more broadly (Page, 2016a). Certain religious traditions have been dominantly coded as perpetuating non-monogamy, and these have been cast in a negative cultural light. For example, Islam has been linked with polygamy as has the Church of the Latter-Day Saints (Mormons), although a variation in practice exists with both of those traditions – the Church of the Latter-Day Saints outlawed polygamy in 1890, but breakaway groups continue to practise it (Campbell, 2014; Selby, 2014). Non-monogamy has been framed as inherently harmful, particularly to women and children, and much public controversy about polygamous practices have been played out in US and Canadian courts (Calder, 2014). Associating some religious traditions with non-monogamy ignores the reality of the practice and further casts those relationships as inherently harmful. Given the hostility towards polygamy, very few communities are willing to participate in research. Campbell (2014) conducted one of the few studies of a breakaway fundamentalist Mormon community in Bountiful, B.C., which offered insights into the ways Mormon women see their roles, relationships, and choices beyond the outsider imposition. Research has suggested that it is not polygamy itself which is exclusively harmful, that in fact many of the harms expected of polygamy can also be found in monogamous relationships (Calder, 2014).

Meanwhile, young people who engage with polyamory (described by Sheff (2006, p. 621) as those who 'openly engage in romantic, sexual, and/or affective relationships with multiple people simultaneously') deem it as ethical, thoughtful, and respectful (Young and Shipley, 2020). But they are very aware of its negative social perceptions, which requires them to downplay or deny this sexual identity:

> I experience the restriction of coupledom – I am a polyamorist person, who practices open relationships and has more than one lover. I wish that I could find acceptance of my "free love" expression. My congregation mostly accepts my lifestyle, but Unitarian Universalism does not, to my knowledge, provide administrative support for me. For example, I would love to feel free to commit myself through religious marriage to more than one person at a time, but I cannot.
>
> *(queer Unitarian Universalist woman)*

Similar findings were noted in the RYS project, with those practising polyamory facing much opprobrium. This negativity could emerge as much as in secular spaces as in religious ones; indeed, one Quaker-Buddhist-Pagan participant

Navigating the "normative" **127**

(Ellie) was called a "whore" from a friend of one of her sexual partners, while her religious communities were more supportive. Indeed, Ellie grounded her polyamorous practices within the ethics of her religious groups; it was how Ellie rooted the ideas of honesty and agency theologically which provided the ethical grounds for her sexual practices (Page, 2016a). The way young people experimented with sexual scripts demonstrates how the landscape of sexual normativity is shifting. However, the lines are being redrawn continually by excluding those who do not fit within the current, acceptable standard of normativity, demonstrated also through the way young people challenge specific sexual identity categories. In the RGSY project, Colin (male, bisexual, polyamorous, and non-religious) struggled to conceptualise his polyamorous lifestyle, especially in relation to the term "gay".

## Summary

As demonstrated throughout this chapter, the boundaries of normativity continue to permit and deny access based on religious and sexuality indicators. The ways that these boundaries are navigated shift and change over time but what remains constant is the insistence on particular designations of normativity, ascribed to ideological standards currently connected to lifecourse trajectories. As a result, the terminology itself needs to be analysed and critiqued – the construction of heterosexuality and homosexuality as identity categories and further the ways in which both of these categories become embedded with other subjective concepts about what constitutes "natural" sexuality. The consequences of these categorisations and the correlating punishment for deviations have been responsible for problematic, harmful, and at times violent responses to the range of ways individuals live out their gendered and sexual lives.

As more equality rights are granted to sexually diverse individuals and groups, those who remain outside the boundaries of what is reconstituted as normative continue to be disadvantaged and also must continue to challenge the boundaries of normativity to access rights and recognition. Even within lesbian and gay communities, there are ongoing challenges when legal provisions provide for access to marriage equality but hinge health benefits and adoption to marriage. The relationship of religion to these public, governmental, and legal policies are both historical and contemporary. Legislative and governmental codes have a direct relationship with the majority religions in a given country; even where a country declares the separation of church and state, the embedded ideologies and normative prescriptions remain reconstituted through discourses of "natural" behaviours.

While we use the term "queer" throughout this book, the reality of equality rights and access to spaces of inclusion and acceptance are quite different for individuals who are lesbian, gay, trans, two-spirit, queer, and intersex, in addition to those questioning and in transition. Same-sex marriage as a disruption of normativity has become enveloped within what has been called the homonormative

**128** Navigating the "normative"

frame (Duggan, 2002; Valverde, 2006). Marriage equality provides access to certain rights for some types of monogamous couples; it does not transcend barriers to provide acceptance, recognition, or inclusion to trans, bisexual, polyamorous, or non-conforming individuals or relationships. Much more work is necessary to comprehensively attend to the challenges, experiences of harm, and possibilities for recognition, especially for sexual minorities such as bisexuals and asexuals.

## Notes

1 Participants were able to select more than one category for their responses.
2 Total number of valid responses: 49.

# 7

# GENDERING SEXUALITY AND RELIGION

## Introduction

To understand the gendering of sexuality within religious contexts, one must start with the body. Embodiment connects together religion, sexuality, and gender, and underpins our queer feminist approach. Women's bodies – in historical and contemporary discourse – have been considered inferior in various ways. While how gender is constituted has varied over time and space, dominant Western understandings, separating gender into two distinct categories, have had much impact on how sexuality is perceived, helping to make heterosexuality normative. Where gender is conceptualised in terms of male and female, there is an accompanying tendency to see these genders as distinct, with differing characteristics.

Heteronormativity is based on the assumption that "female" and "male" constitute the standard form of sexual attraction. From this, assumptions have been made that women's proper sexual role is in terms of the private sphere – childbearing and childrearing. Religious discourses have done much to support and embed these constructions. This chapter will start by giving a brief overview of the ways in which dominant constructions of gender have historically emerged, with a specific focus on the importance given to separate spheres and gender differentiation from the Enlightenment onwards, and the role that religion played in this construction. The chapter will then move on to look at specific examples of this demarcation, and how notions of sexual difference and gendered normatives were consolidated through the prizing of women's virginity and modesty. At the same time, in order for male bodies to retain their normative and authoritative status, women's bodies were further demarcated in terms of impurity. The chapter will end by arguing that an embodied understanding of gender, sexuality, and religion is needed to fully understand their relationship.

## Separate spheres, Christianity, and a colonial inheritance

Societies read bodies through a gendered lens, and typically, religious discourses play a role in sustaining particular understandings of the gendered body. In the Western world, much emphasis has been placed on a binary gendered logic, where the individual is firmly defined as either male or female. This boundary between male and female has historically been policed by various institutions such as medicine (operating on bodies that do not "fit" the normative gendered schema), schools (defining academic subjects as either "for boys" or "for girls"), and the workplace (defining certain jobs as being "for men" or "for women"). Such categorisations have been accompanied by stereotypes and assumptions about what gendered bodies *do* and what sort of body is "best" for certain tasks and activities. Historically, middle-class women were seen as too fragile to participate in certain jobs; they were seen as unsuited to academic tasks as these were seen as a threat to their fertility (Robinson, 2009). And they were deemed too weak to undertake manual labour, despite working-class and Black women's long-standing participation in back-breaking work (McClintock, 1995). This was facilitated through separate spheres ideology, a product of the Enlightenment, where women became associated with private sphere activity and men became associated with the public sphere.

Pateman (1988) offers a powerful account of the development of separate spheres ideology and the intertwining ways in which political and religious systems intersected to ensure women were structurally under the authority of men in Western societies. Up to the 17th century, power was firmly located in the father as head of the family, buttressed through scripture and sermons from the pulpit. The pervasive logic was that the patriarchal family formed the origins of society and civilisation itself. Fathers ruled sons as well as mothers and daughters. Yet in the 17th century, this mode of thinking was displaced by another political construction, where each individual is considered autonomous and free to make social contracts with other autonomous individuals. The rule of the father was therefore dislodged, theoretically allowing women to be perceived as autonomous persons. However, women were ultimately excluded from this contract-making personhood. The view of the social contract theorists was that only men can enter into contracts with each other. In this sense, patriarchy becomes fraternal instead of paternal. Pateman calls it the difference between the social contract and the sexual contract. It was at this moment that the separation of public (cultural; male) and private (natural; female) spheres cemented sexual difference. Women were denied access to the public sphere, whereas men were freely allowed to move between the public and the private sphere, and rights to make contracts in the public sphere. The only contract women were legitimately allowed to participate in was the marriage contract, which cemented a husband's rights over his wife in terms of sexual access and property rights. On this separation of social life into the public and private spheres, women were firmly located in the private sphere.

# Gendering sexuality and religion **131**

Women's supreme vocation was therefore situated in the domestic sphere, as wives and mothers, and not as paid workers. This construction of separate sphere was not only gendered; it was also classed and raced. Indeed, separate spheres ideology was crystallised through Western colonial expansion projects, especially the British, perpetuating inequalities where racism, classism, and sexism intersected. Colonial expansion was constructed as an inalienable good, a means of promoting these "civilised" political and social values to other territories and lands deemed "uncivilised" and in need of cultivation. As McClintock (1995) argues, women's placement in the private sphere, their role principally understood through childbearing, underpinned ideas about colonialism and imperialism, for it was men who were to conquer this "virgin territory"; indeed, the colonised lands themselves were gendered and seen as ripe for white men to explore and exploit. White middle-class women's bodies came to denote the domesticity and civility craved for by the colonists; these women were responsible for reproducing the white nation, and their bodies were therefore heavily controlled, accompanied by a Victorian preoccupation with sexual purity. White middle-class women were to remain bounded to the private sphere and were not to cross sexual borders, lest it be "contaminating". Whereas white middle-class women became the focus of passive reproductive sexuality, Black women's bodies became associated with active pleasurable sexuality, their bodies understood in excessively sexualised ways (Jantzen, 2005). Racial hierarchies were devised by the Victorians, where bodies were mapped – skulls were measured, and clitorises examined. These borders – between public and private, "civilised" and "uncivilised" – were heavily policed. Because both Black women and working-class women did not epitomise idealised domestic femininity and were not representatives of sexual purity, they were considered suitable for back-breaking work. These contradictory understandings of femininity were highlighted through the example of the Wigan pit women who worked at the coalface in the Lancashire coal mines:

> The Wigan women epitomized the contradictions in Victorian attitudes to women's work and threw into stark relief the conflict between the image of the idle, ornamental woman and the actuality of female manual labor. Yet much of the outrage vented at the spectacle of trousered women wielding picks and shovels was hypocritical, for their work was often less gruelling and less injurious than other occupations. A young maid-of-all-work, for example, could work longer and more exhausting hours carrying buckets of water or scuttles of coal up many flights of stairs, emptying stinking slop pails, scrubbing, cleaning and polishing – all the while isolated from family or community, pitifully paid; and frequently emotionally and physically at the mercy of the men of the household. But domestic work, if often more difficult and more debilitating, was domestic work, hidden in kitchen and scullery – a less visible affront to the emerging ideology of female idleness.

## 132  Gendering sexuality and religion

> And since it was not a field of competition with men, there were no outcries on these women's behalf.
>
> *(McClintock, 1995, p. 114)*

Religious discourses had an important part to play in upholding separate spheres and its raced, classed, and gendered dimensions. The domesticated, privatised white middle-class femininity that was cultivated was predicated on Christian piety – indeed femininity became entwined with piety. In the British context, such ideas were exported through colonial expansion, and the racial hierarchies that developed in colonies such as Australia and Canada. As Brown (2001) argues, between 1800 and 1950 in Britain, Christian piety, premised on the popularity of Evangelicalism, enjoyed unrivalled success and this piety was constructed as feminine in nature – women were considered to be equal to men at a spiritual level. But this came with the expectation to raise respectable, morally upstanding Christian citizens. White, middle-class women were understood as epitomising the Christian virtues of sobriety and sexual morality, cemented in the Victorian ideal of the "Angel of the House". This, however, was privatised authority, for 'Women had become divine, but an angel now confined to the house' (Brown, 2001, p. 58). Women failing in their duty (e.g. by raising "morally suspect" citizens) were vilified. But this status as the guardians of Christian morality enabled middle-class women to carve out certain roles that were deemed commensurate with their feminine piety. For example, their engagement with charitable and volunteer work was deemed a suitable pastime. But this had the consequence of middle-class women enacting forms of surveillance towards working-class lives, in relation to children's education, sobriety campaigns, and prostitution (Brown, 2001; Gill, 1994; Weeks, 2014). This also extended to a role in missionary work in colonised countries, for 'Wives and mothers were regarded as potent vectors of culture and belief' (Semple, 2010, p. 118), thereby cementing the classed and raced hierarchies of respectable femininity. Christianity itself was understood as a civilising project in "uncivilised" countries. Indeed, it was Western definitions of welfare which determined the activities and focus of the women missionaries, thereby emphasising the power white, middle-class women could garner over and above not only working-class women in their own countries but also women living under colonial rule.

Religions can be powerfully effective in supporting the status quo, especially due to the way the notion of tradition can be invoked, cementing a particular way of doing things. In addition, traditions, as rooted in sacred-bearing texts and practices, are often given special status by followers. Feminists have been rightly suspicious of religions for upholding traditional ways of thinking and hindering or even blocking women's agency. Many religious traditions have readily endorsed separate spheres ideology, in the process curtailing the public roles women have in public life, for example, as religious leaders. Instead, women's piety has been constructed in terms of domesticity and childrearing; women's respectability and middle-class femininity were seen as threatened were they to step outside of these clear roles and become preachers, for example – especially as this was disruptive of their assumed non-relationship to the public sphere (Peart, 2008). Religious traditions have also had a role to play in the bodily control of women. As Turner (2011, p. 22–3) argues, 'Patriarchy has specific and important connections with religion as a principle of reproductive legitimacy. The rites and rituals that surround birth and rebirth are fundamental to all religions, and the notion of regeneration has been crucial to ancient cosmologies'. Because paternity cannot be assured, systems have historically been implemented to assure men that the child they are raising – and the sons that will inherit their wealth – are biologically theirs (O'Brien, 1981). While not inevitable, control of women is one way of achieving this. For O'Brien, the separation of the public and private is a result of the need to separate women from other men, in order to secure paternity for the man she is married to. A whole buttress of laws and ideologies – including religious ones – are created in order to support this system.

It is also the case that religion has historically given women access to certain opportunities to contest their social situation and to carve out different forms of femininity. For example, while through contemporary eyes, the Enlightenment construction of women as pious and godly may be deemed limiting, it could engender the right for some women to challenge the status quo. Apetrei (2010) documents how early Enlightenment women could productively utilise their associations with Christian piety to develop roles for themselves in religious leadership. Instead of the Bible being a text supporting existing understandings of gender, scripture was utilised to articulate women's equal status, for example, refusing to obey one's husband during the marriage vows, for there was no biblical basis for it. By the 19th century, religion continued to frame the discussion regarding women's emancipation, with the Bible forming the critical backdrop to discussions over gender equality (Schwartz, 2010a).

The relationship between the gendered body and religion is highly complex, fluid, and variable. First-wave feminists, influenced by Evangelical Christianity, were keen to portray a respectable femininity and were dissuaded from campaigning on sexuality issues (Schwartz, 2010b; Weeks, 2014). They located the problems women experienced in the excessive sexualities of men, and the illogic of the sexual double standard, which punished women for sexual misdemeanours rather than men. The response to this, however, as Weeks (2014) highlights, is as equally likely to be a conservative one (e.g. promoting chastity and sexual restraint for all sexes) as much as what today would be considered emancipatory. In this sense, conservative elements of a religious tradition (in this case, Christianity) could be utilised with the intention of enabling greater agency for women.

In summary, the heuristic device of separating the public sphere associated with culture and the private sphere associated with nature was gendered. Women were firmly located within the private sphere, meaning that their attempts to access public sphere tasks – e.g. to be educated or to be in paid work – was a challenging one. We have focused here on Christianity specifically because of

**134** Gendering sexuality and religion

the enormous influence Christianity had through colonialist forms of empire-building, where control of countries across the globe was seized by a handful of Western nations. Because separate spheres ideology was fundamental to the logic of the colonialists, this ideology therefore had a significant part to play in imperialist expansion across the world, with ideas about gender being relocated to colonised spaces. Christianity, as the religion of the colonists, shaped these gendered understandings, with Christianity constructed as a means of promoting "civilised" morals and values, and Christianity itself being upheld as superior to any other religious traditions encountered. It was on the back of this sense of Christian superiority that some women – namely, white middle-class women – were able to achieve forms of authority, but this was predicated on a sense that their Christian piety surpassed that of other women.

## Gendered bodies: Sexual demarcation and regulation

The gendered dualism, where women's and men's bodies were understood as being fundamentally different, had repercussions for how the gendered body was perceived. In order for gender dualism to be maintained, sexual difference needed to be emphasised. And women's and men's bodies became sexually marked in different ways. This was epitomised in the dominant constructions of femininity and masculinity that pervaded the Victorian imagination, emphasising the sexual propriety and purity of women's bodies, as evidenced through the regulation of clothing and virginity. Although these gendered constructions have altered over time, in the contemporary period we can witness the legacy of these pervading understandings. This section will therefore start with an examination of virginity and clothing expectations to demonstrate how sexual demarcation fed into constructions of pious femininity. Meanwhile, although women's bodies were demarcated as representing the purity and the goodness and boundaries of one's very community, this could not undermine the dominance of the male body as normative. Therefore, various means were deployed to relegate women's bodies to a differential status, through, for example, the exclusion of their bodies from professions in the public sphere, and their denial of sacredly endorsed roles as religious leaders. But many of the reasons for this exclusion were rooted in dominant understandings of women's bodies and the way a woman's body was deemed unfit for these tasks. Menstruation was utilised as a mechanism for this exclusion, having repercussions to this day.

## *Virginity*

Virginity has been highly prized in many religious traditions, though not universally so. Virginity does not have a singular meaning, though it is typically understood as someone who has not had sex. But given that "sex" itself is culturally contingent, meanings of virginity often rest on dominant understandings of what "sex" is. Therefore, typically, the revoking of one's virginity is understood

Gendering sexuality and religion **135**

as where the vagina is penetrated by the penis. This therefore relies on heteronormative and gendered assumptions (Carpenter, 2005; Rahman and Jackson, 2010). The meanings surrounding virginity are not, however, dependent on having sex per se. Historically, religious meanings of virginity have altered; in early Christianity, one's virginity was at risk of being revoked if one had lustful thoughts. Likewise, those who had been raped remained spiritual virgins in the eyes of the early Christian community (Carpenter, 2005). Later, Calvinist forms of Protestantism attempted to sever the link between virginity and sacrality, as virginity was seen as embodying Catholicism, and therefore to be rejected (Carpenter, 2005; Isherwood and Stuart, 1998). There is also a difference between virginity and chastity. While many religions have traditionally upheld beliefs in virginity until marriage, chastity – the eschewing of sexual relationships indefinitely – has not gained as much support due to the way this potentially disrupts procreative sexuality (Cornwall, 2013). For example, in Judaism and Islam, while virginity before marriage is often esteemed, celibacy is not (Hunt, 2010). Meanwhile, in contemporary culture, much discussion has been generated regarding the notion of "technical virginity" – are those who participate in oral, anal, or masturbatory sex with another person still deemed a virgin (Carpenter, 2005; Dialmy, 2010; Sharma, 2011; Uecker *et al.*, 2008)? In religious communities where sex before marriage is condemned, such strategies have been utilised as a means of managing intimate relationships, especially in contexts where the time between sexual maturity and marriage is lengthening. What counts as virginity is therefore contingent and dependent on context. Virginity is not a biological fact, but socially determined (Hastrup, 1993).

Virginity has typically been more than about sex per se, and says something meaningful about one's identity or community. Hastrup (1993) argued that the meanings and wider relevance of virginity will vary, in that in some societies, one's virginity is one's own concern, whereas in other contexts it is the concern of one's immediate family or even the wider society. Identifying someone as a virgin is meaningful in contexts where that virginity status is esteemed and recognised and can therefore enable group identities to be forged on the back of that reverence. Early Christians made a point of emphasising their commitment to virginity (and chastity more broadly) as a means of distinguishing them against other social groups (Ahmed, 1992). In contemporary culture, Savage *et al.* (2006) note how North American Evangelical purity cultures are not about virginity per se, but about defining oneself as a Christian and marking out one's identity in a youth culture where virginity status is no longer prized or emphasised. In other contexts, even amongst religious cohorts, virginity does not feature as strongly. In the RGSY project, only 19.3% agreed or strongly agreed with the statement, 'It is important that I am a virgin when I get married', and even fewer (13.3%) thought that 'It is important that my partner is a virgin when I get married'. Meanwhile, in the RYS project, these rates were double – with 41.9% affirming the first statement, and 27.5% the second. The RYS participants certainly endorsed virginity more than their Canadian counterparts, but this was still not

**136** Gendering sexuality and religion

a majority affirmation (for further discussion on virginity and the gendered and religious analysis of this, see Yip and Page, 2013).

Douglas (1966) argued that societies operate in terms of borders, with bodies representing boundary systems. This is especially pertinent in contexts where the group in question has a minority status. Virginity therefore is often about boundary-marking, with the focus typically resting on women's bodies, with the hymen representing the sacred boundary (Hastrup, 1993). This is why there was reluctance in the 20th century to issue tampons to unmarried women, lest it somehow interfered with their virginity status (Delaney *et al.*, 1988). While many communities have dismissed the significance of the hymen along with the importance of virginity per se, in some religious contexts the significance of the hymen remains. Within the RYS project, young religious adults highlighted how the woman's body was at the centre of importance for some religious communities, particularly Muslim communities. Whereas virginity was largely inconsequential for male Muslim participants, it was of paramount importance for female Muslim participants. Iqbal, a Muslim man, said on the difference between a woman's and a man's virginity that 'There is no way of telling with me but I can with her'. Sabrina articulated that for a woman in her Pakistani Muslim community to lose her virginity:

> Would be very bad, somehow people will find out and it will be very bad, people gossiping and it will cause a lot of problems in that family... He may not be a virgin... that wouldn't be an issue at all... But if she wasn't then it would cause a lot of uproar in the family... It's obvious when a girl's a virgin and you can't tell whether a guy's a virgin or not... the task is really easy for them, whereas the girl will bleed.

Therefore, the repercussions were far greater for women within the Pakistani Muslim community within which Sabrina belonged, with a sense in which women were somehow marked and identifiable through their virginity loss – Sabrina's narrative highlights not only the community investment in a woman's virginity status but also the idea that something fundamentally would change for women in a way it did not change for men, and the hymen breaking was at the forefront of this. Douglas's (1966) work on bodies representing borders, especially for minority and marginalised communities, may help explain why the hymen was significant for only some religious populations in Yip and Page's (2013) research. Others have highlighted the significance accorded the hymen in Muslim communities, where, despite understandings that hymens routinely break while participating in non-sexual activities, blood on one's wedding night is expected (Dialmy, 2010; Imtoual and Hussein, 2009; Shalhoub-Kevorkian, 2008). Some women therefore go to extreme lengths to ensure that the hymen is intact, in medically reconstructing the hymen through a hymenoplasty. This hymen-focused understanding of virginity is not, however, unique to some Muslim communities. Carpenter (2005) outlines the narrative of a Christian woman who was accused of not being a virgin when she did not bleed after her first sexual encounter.

Indeed, the extent to which religious traditions with a commitment to virginity before marriage police this is subject to variation and is subject to classed and raced variations. For example, the practice of bundling was historically common in rural working-class communities, where an engaged couple would spend the night together while fully clothed. Any unmarried pregnancy occurring as a result of bundling was managed within the community through the couple in question getting married (Carpenter, 2005; Weeks, 2014).

In the early 20th century in Western contexts, virginity was still assumed (Weeks, 2014). But over time, a lessening of social control occurred. By the mid-20th century, a woman who had had sex with her intended marriage partner was not necessarily chastised in all contexts (however, Chapter 9 will examine Magdalene Laundries and the part they played in punishing women for unmarried sex in 20th century Ireland). The connection between virginity on marriage was further undermined by the greater availability of contraception, especially the Pill (Weeks, 2014). For Jantzen, 'Once sex is unlinked from reproduction, it becomes much less obvious why it should be restricted to marriage... Good sex thus becomes pleasurable sex that is fully consensual' (2005, p. 10). The sexual revolution of the 1960s had enormous repercussions for the configuration of gendered sexualities and religions had to make sense of where they fitted in. When hopes in the wake of Vatican II that the Roman Catholic Church would allow certain forms of contraception for married couples were dashed, many questioned their faith and some ultimately left Catholicism for good (Guest *et al.*, 2012; Helmick, 2014).

While religious and secular understandings of modesty, purity, and virginity were once aligned, increasingly, they came under rupture. The most recent reconfiguration of women's sexuality in Western contexts has emphasised newer forms of femininity, with modesty and piety being replaced with expectations for sexiness (Harvey and Gill, 2011). As Harvey and Gill articulate, 'in the postfeminist, post-Cosmopolitan West, heroines must no longer embody virginity but are required to be skilled in a variety of sexual behaviours and practices, and the performance of confident sexual agency is central to this technology of the self' (2011, p. 56). These trends, part of the so-called sexualisation of society, have resulted in various strategies by religious traditions regarding their own negotiation. Within the RYS project, some religious groups were far less concerned with virginity, in particular, liberal Christians and Buddhists. For example, fewer than 10% of the Buddhists argued that 'It is important that I am a virgin when I get married'. For these religiously identifying young people, virginity was not something that generated significant meaning (Page and Yip, 2017b).

While the relationship between religious cultures and commitment to virginity is mixed, those abstaining from sex before marriage often cite religious reasons (Abbott and Dalla, 2008; Adamczyk and Felson, 2006). Yet research

**138** Gendering sexuality and religion

indicates that it is more likely to occur in a communal context, where social bonds facilitate a pledging culture, rather than religious edicts or opinions about virginity motivating actions per se (Bearman and Brückner, 2001; Carpenter, 2005). Close dense religious networks where sex before marriage is frowned upon inhibits early sexual experience (Adamczyk and Felson, 2006). The creation of a moral community committed to virginity forges a particular identity (Bearman and Brückner, 2001), enabling those belonging to these networks to embrace being an "uncool" Christian, and eschewing expectations such as for women to wear sexualised clothing (Wilkins, 2008).

The purity movement in the USA was energised in the early 1990s by the creation of True Love Waits, an organisation encouraging teenagers to pledge their commitment to virginity until marriage, and was quickly supported by various conservative Christian churches, also feeding into a broader sex education initiative that eschewed content about safe sex and contraceptive advice to instead focus on abstinence (White, 2012). Although on the one hand, this can be considered counter-cultural, where sexuality as something that is sacred and pure is reclaimed, the virginity pledge message is cleverly packaged in discourses of women's empowerment and choice, as well as through the embracing of youth culture elements such as t-shirts and jewellery (DeRogatis, 2015; White, 2012). Yet it is clear that traditional gendered scripts are being reinscribed in these narratives (DeRogatis, 2015; Lowe, 2016). For example, DeRogatis considers the role that purity balls play in American Evangelicalism, whereby a father accompanies his daughter to a ball where she pledges her virginity until marriage. Virginity is given esteemed and sacred status, and the rituals invoked around purity balls give fathers the power in this "exchange" so that traditional notions of the bride price and parental choice in a woman's partner are invoked. As DeRogatis argues, 'female sexuality is viewed both as sacred and dangerous, not simply because of unwanted pregnancy, disease, or emotional distress, but because sexual desire could compromise a young woman's value as a virgin prior to marriage' (2015, p. 13). Such is their controversy that even some Evangelicals are critical of purity balls for the messages they invoke (DeRogatis, 2015). This notion of virginity as sacred, and a gift to be given on marriage, pervades Evangelical cultures (Freitas, 2008). But it is usually women's virginity that is understood as the gift, rather than men's. As Carpenter argues, men do not typically describe their virginity in terms of a gift: 'The belief that women's virginity is a gift, which informs the classic double standard for sexuality, can probably be traced back to women's historic status as property transferred from fathers to husbands' (2005, p. 60). And this is not unique to Christianity. Hall (2002) emphasises that similar discourses of gift-giving can be found in the Sikh community, where family honour is epitomised using women's bodies, with women's virginity being bestowed as a gift in marriage. While pledging cultures have little resonance in the UK context, the RYS project highlighted the increased levels of surveillance of women's bodies within religiously framed ethnic minority communities (see Page and Yip, 2012a). While for some participants – particularly for Pakistani Muslim young

Gendering sexuality and religion **139**

women – this led to a focus on the hymen as epitomising virginity – for others, the key issue was that the religious community did not find out about any sexual activity. Pregnancy, rather than virginity loss, was to be avoided, as this would be an embodied marker of sexual transgression. Shalini, a Hindu woman who had engaged in premarital sex, emphatically said that for her to get pregnant before marriage 'probably would be the worst thing that I could do'.

Therefore, virginity is typically understood as marking out women's, rather than men's bodies, and in cultures where virginity is expected, it is a woman's transgression that is emphasised. As this can cultivate feelings of familial and community embarrassment and shame, this means that it is women's movements and actions that are under greater curtailment and scrutiny. One area that this manifests itself is regarding clothing, and it is to this issue we now turn.

## *Clothing*

Given how women's bodies come to represent religious communities, they are therefore subject to greater levels of scrutiny in terms of sexual purity. This goes beyond whether a woman has actually had sex or not. Indeed, in religious contexts where women's bodies represent the boundaries of her religious community (Douglas, 1966), it is her broader conduct and behaviour that will be monitored. Clothing comes to have paramount importance regarding how women are perceived in their religious communities. In many contexts, women have borne the responsibility to convey a pure and pious body, especially through the clothing they wear (Moultrie, 2017; Sharma, 2011). Women's bodies, and how they are adorned, is therefore subject to scrutiny in many religious communities in order to ensure that they are depicting all that is sacred as opposed to all that is profane. This positioning yet again asserts the dominant dichotomy where the sexual and the spiritual are deemed on oppositional poles. Sharma (2011) notes how young Christian women actively monitor their bodies to ensure that modesty prevails; her participants were mortified if a concealed bra strap became exposed. Meanwhile, Moultrie (2017) observes how the policing of attire takes on deeper resonance for Black women, who are further chastised for keeping their modesty in check, due to prevailing stereotypes regarding the "hypersexual" Black woman's body. For her participants, church officials would distribute modesty cloths to be put over skirts that were deemed too short. Exceptions do occur. Within the conservative Mennonite tradition, young single women are allowed greater freedom in their clothing; allowance is made for the fit of their dress to be tighter, enabling women to position themselves as sexually desirable to a potential marriage partner. On marriage, however, women are expected to return to the strict modesty rules (Graybill and Arthur, 1999). This emphasises how dress is regulated to the extent that it does not interfere with the forming of heterosexual marriages. Men's bodies in the Mennonite community do not carry the same connotations, as their bodies are not representative of the piety of the whole community. But clothing comes to be a proxy not only for one's sexual morality

**140** Gendering sexuality and religion

but for one's religious piety. As Graybill and Arthur assert, 'While a woman's level of religious piety cannot be objectively perceived, symbols such as clothing are used as evidence that she is on the "right and true path". Consequently, appearance is constantly scrutinized' (1999, p. 10). In the RGSY project, female participants noted both the scrutiny and oversight of their bodies and choices within religious communities and also as imposed from society in general. In the RYS project, similar findings were encountered amongst Muslim women, who experienced scrutiny of their bodies not only from within their religious communities but also outside of it. Many Muslim women articulated that clothing was important for displaying their piety and their belonging to Islam. But they were critical when others interpreted what that should entail. Adala was frequently asked why she did not cover her hair as a Muslim woman, but she argued that modesty was not dependent on any sort of veiling practice, but was about her broader approach to her clothing choices:

> a lot of people have asked me that question – would you ever wear [the hijab] – and I'd say I'd never, ever wear it because I know that I'm modest in other ways… I see a lot of girls wearing the hijab but they're wearing jeans where you can see their entire figure. So I don't see how that's modest with the scarf on your head. Or if you're wearing a lot of makeup. I don't understand how that can be modest.

Adala was therefore emphasising the importance of modesty but she did not innately connect this to any form of veiling practice. Meanwhile, Layla, who did wear a hijab, was critical of the way that veiling had been misunderstood, and argued that:

> a verse in the Qur'an that actually says that the women should veil themselves and when it means veil it's not actually talking about the hair veiled; it's more about the whole outlook… there are certain restrictions with the way the men dress [too].

Layla argued that men's bodies were also subject to modesty codes within the Qur'anic verses, but these were rarely enforced. Indeed, Muslim women's clothing choices – in particular veiling practices – have come to generate broader meanings and even concern beyond their religious communities, drawing veiling practices into broader debates regarding whether Muslim women are oppressed, even among those who have shown little concern for women's oppression before (Duits and Van Zoonen, 2006; Mahmood, 2011). This has specifically fed into juxtaposed debates between clothing items that seemingly represent sexual liberation (e.g. bikinis and mini-skirts) and religious dress deemed oppressive (Pedwell, 2011). In reality, such oppositional contrasts are unhelpful – as Pedwell asserts, they do not leave room for those who may embrace both, such as wearing a G-string alongside religious attire. Indeed, Muslim women themselves

Gendering sexuality and religion **141**

invest their clothing with varying meanings, and often utilise them as a form of identity-generation, embedded in cultures of religion and fashion (Lewis, 2015). As Duits and Van Zoonen argue, although 'Girls' bodies have become the metonymic location for many of the social and cultural struggles in Western European immigration societies', we rarely hear 'The voices of girls themselves' (2006, p. 114).

This is the crux of the matter regarding both virginity cultures and clothing cultures – the extent to which women and men themselves have a voice in their choices and whether their choices are supported or not. For many women, going against the rules of their religious community has serious repercussions, and can cost one access to that community. Therefore, choices are always made within contexts of constraint.

## *Menstruation*

In many religious traditions, menstruation is either perceived in terms of the magical – and therefore potentially threatening – or the repulsive (Delaney *et al.*, 1988; O'Brien, 1981). It is rarely invoked in terms of mundanity or ordinariness, and instead is seen in powerful terms. As Archer (1990) explains, in the Jewish tradition, a blood taboo emerged, dividing women from men. Women came to be defined as unclean during menstruation, with this status all at once cultivating both a defiled and a powerful status, for this became 'a source of female power by virtue of the fact that anything that threatens also wields power' (1990, p. 31). However, Archer (1990) goes on to explain that women's structural positioning within Judaism in general terms became secondary, associated with nature rather than culture, with this having a negative impact on their involvement in the public sphere. Whereas the male rite of circumcision came to be understood as the culturally controlled emission of blood that connected participants to god, women's involuntary period blood was seen as ritually polluting, and needing intense management and control. Meanwhile, within the Roman Catholic Church, Davies (2011) pinpoints the traditional exclusion of women from the sanctuary around the altar as connected to menstrual taboos. Because priests within Catholicism are exclusively male, and celibate at that, this embeds a sexless and genderless emotional symbolism, given the way that women, rather than men, are constructed as representing both sex and gender (Furlong, 1988), with menstruation being a key symbol of this (Furlong, 1984). This is further complicated by the explicit place blood has in Christian sacred rites, in that Christ's blood is deemed within the Eucharist to represent life. Menstrual blood is constructed as diametrically opposed to this blood symbolism, given that it is associated with death rather than life (Isherwood and Stuart, 1998), and therefore creates a symbolic incompatibility, resulting in women's exclusion from offices such as priesthood (Furlong, 1984, 1988). Page's (2010) research with clergy mothers in the Anglican Church indicated the way menstruation was negatively perceived, particularly by male priests. Jill, who was

**142** Gendering sexuality and religion

ordained in the first cohort of women priests in 1994, was told by fellow male priests that women should not be allowed to preside at the Eucharist 'because it is profaning the holy'; similarly, Kate, who was ordained the same year, had been told by a male vicar that 'women couldn't be priests because they shed their own blood, whereas a priest obviously has to shed Christ's blood. Obviously somehow, we might get it mixed up' (Page, 2010). Menstrual blood was therefore used as a strategy in associating women with the profane and was an attempt to position women as having no legitimate right to access sacred space. These narratives were heard at a contentious moment in time, when there was a protracted debate in the late 1980s and early 1990s regarding whether it was permissible for the Church of England to allow women to be priests. But such narratives can be located in other contexts too. In the process of RYS interviews and asking Muslim women about their understandings of religious leadership, a small number cited menstruation as a reason as to why women could not be imams. This was typified by Yasmin's response:

> Your period blood basically is apparently meant to be sort of like impure… which kind of makes sense because there's this lining that's been there for like ages… so it's not exactly something that's like really pure… And the only reason women can't be imams is basically just that, like when you're on your periods, you know, you're considered like impure… It makes sense to me, like fair enough, it's not that women aren't as good as men; it's just that little clause, physiological clause that you can't do really anything about.

Therefore, Yasmin had internalised an understanding of her bodily processes as impure, thereby ruling out women from positions of religious authority (see Yip and Page, 2013). Yet the relationship between menstruation and impurity is by no means assured within religious discourses. For Orthodox Jewish women, whether one is menstruating or not is of great significance, enacting different codes of conduct, as dictated through *niddah*. These Jewish laws regulate menstrual behaviour, for example, 'physical contact between spouses are prohibited' (Avishai, 2012, p. 276), meaning that couples cannot share a bed, and objects cannot be directly passed between each spouse. The public nature of some of these activities also means that one's menstrual status can be determined by outsiders. On the one hand, this can be considered highly constraining, and also by default views women's bodies as ritually impure. But Avishai (2008, 2012) contests this – women are still allowed to participate fully in Jewish religious ritual – and crucially, among her interviewees, none of the women understood their *niddah* status in terms of impurity. Although these rules were experienced as a burden – especially in contexts where bleeding went on for a prolonged period, thereby extending the timeframe for *niddah* (e.g. in cases of birth or miscarriage), it also enabled women to cultivate their religious piety and commitment to orthodoxy. It was these practices that made them Jewish. Avishai is keen to

Gendering sexuality and religion **143**

contest accounts where women's belonging to conservative religious traditions is (a) ultimately a form of liberation as it allows them to carve out new roles/ sentiments, (b) women resist the official scripts, and (c) women use religion strategically for other ends. For in all of these understandings, religion itself is taken out of the equation as a reasonable reason for participation – in other words, conservative participation *inevitably* has to be about something else. Instead. Avishai argues that women are "doing" their gender in a religious context, with an aim to cultivate an orthodox identity.

Meanwhile, other religious traditions have explicitly embraced the magical instead of the dangerous in terms of menstrual blood (Delaney *et al.*, 1988). Goddess spirituality elevates menstruation to the status of the sacred through linking it with the power of nature and magic. Bowie (2000) discusses goddess narratives where the goddess is understood as the originator of life and fertility. In this construction, the body becomes sacred – and there is no room for any part of the body to be perceived in profaning terms. Instead, menstruation is embraced. Indeed, Vincett's (2008) interviews with goddess feminists emphasised how some participants envisaged god as a menstruating woman. Therefore, the connotations and meanings are fully switched, and menstruation is still being invoked in terms of the magical rather than the mundane (Raphael, 1996). The importance of positive messages about menstruation cannot be underestimated. A Christian woman in the RYS project emphasised how she had come to understand her periods in a positive framework, and specifically utilised goddess understandings in this endeavour. In a context where women's fertility was seen as a burden and a cost to society, she instead invoked an understanding of women's power being rooted in her fertility:

> I do sense that it is sort of an unmentionable. And yet at the same time, you know, nearly every woman on the planet has it so that's at least half of the world's population has a period. And it is quite a big event every month; yeah, it certainly is for me. It can be a deeply spiritual experience... I started reading a book suggesting... priestess religions came before the patriarchal ones... The book suggests that before humans realised that sex led to pregnancy, pregnancy was this kind of magical thing that a woman did so she was all very powerful and worshipped. It makes me think how different it is now. Quite a few women are pregnant at work in various stages of being pregnant and being on maternity leave and having had a baby, and just work is very accepting and encouraging of that. My boss joked that none of the rest of us were allowed to get pregnant because they wouldn't be able to afford it.

Indeed, secular cultures too have problematised issues around women's fertility and menstruation in particular, adopting versions of the menstrual taboo (Raphael, 1996). This is particularly evident in the feminine hygiene market, which often creates anxieties around cleanliness and the smell of one's body.

**144** Gendering sexuality and religion

Advertisers frequently deploy images of women on their period enacting freedom-embracing activities, such as running down a beach in white trousers, but blood itself is tabooed. Any hint of menstruation is to be hidden at all costs. This was emphasised in the case of the London Marathon runner, Kiran Gandhi (2015). The use of sanitary products would impede her run, and she was visibly showing signs of her period through her clothing, creating uproar. Comments on her opinion piece described her actions as 'disgusting and very unhygienic' (Gandhi, 2015, n.p.). This indicates that there is still a high expectation for menstruating bodies to be carefully controlled and managed, leading to a silencing of the menstruating body.

Douglas (1966) notes how it is the symbolism of blood that matters; menstrual blood is not inherently unclean but it is symbolically classified as such. For Douglas, fluids connected with sexuality become broader metaphors for society as a whole, indicating danger and disorder. Purity rules emerge as an attempt to exert control on something that is considered disorderly. But this is written on and through women's bodies, and has a powerful part to play in upholding gendered hierarchies, for while women may be able to garner power through being constructed as virginal, chaste, and pious, when their bodies are also considered unruly, unclean, and problematic, their status as secondary is affirmed (Raphael, 1996).

## Summary

This chapter has demonstrated the relationship between religion and separate spheres ideology, arguing that religion has played a regulating role in the control of women's bodies. Indeed, bodies are at the heart of this engagement, emphasising how an embodied focus is crucial (Brintnall, 2016). Women's bodies come to represent boundaries and crossing points, the emblems and tokens of nation and culture, and heterosexuality is prioritised and made normative. This is a multifaceted and uneven engagement, with different bodies being policed in different moments, but where the white middle-class body is held up as the ideal. For example, the expansion of white middle-class women's leadership capacities in the Victorian era was enabled through their role of increasing surveillance of working-class and Black women's bodies. Hierarchies are therefore embodied, and although the charity work undertaken by middle-class white women enabled them to express forms of feminine piety from which they generated much credit and identity-solidification, this was at the expense of other groups of women. This recognises how although women in general may be disadvantaged by symbolically charged hierarchical orderings, the lived realities of women's lives differ, determined by other social divisions such as social class and ethnicity. This contextual intersectional analysis is crucial in mapping the nuance and complexity of social life. Meanwhile, religious discourses do not simply reproduce repression and regulation. Religious resources also enable women the tools to contest pervasive understandings of gendered sexuality, but the resource-base to undertake such work is uneven; those with greater resources and privilege are better equipped to do so. The chapter has also demonstrated the rather complex interplay between religious and secular cultures, with the example of menstruation, for example, highlighting that both are mutually supporting in creating a culture of impurity and shame. This again indicates that it is too simplistic to see secular cultures as outlets for freedom and gendered emancipation. Far less work has been undertaken in understanding how men's bodies are implicated in religious regulation, and a focus on men's embodiment is important to further unpack the ways in which certain ideals of masculinity underscore heteronormativity. Focusing on men in this regard would allow the specific nuance and multi-layered contours of these relationships to be teased out, and the vulnerabilities and tensions apparent in upholding certain versions of hegemonic masculinity within religious cultures.

# 8

# GENDERED BODIES

## Reproductive and sexual control

## Introduction

The previous chapter explored how bodies are gendered; in other words, bodies are differentially perceived and demarcated, with the burdens of this demarcation falling more heavily on women rather than men. In short, women are subject to greater sexuality regulation. This chapter will analyse further the levels of control women and men have experienced over their sexual bodies, starting with a focus on contraception and abortion. While technological advances have increased control of fertility choices, this is not uniform and depends in large part on the extent to which states are willing to fund reproductive healthcare. As indicated by cases such as *Hobby Lobby* in the United States, access to contraception and abortion is uneven, with religious narratives having a powerful influence in shaping the discourse about their status. Feminists have long advocated for greater sexual rights, including protection from sexual violence and rape, and rights to sexual pleasure and orgasm. Religions have had a complex role in these endeavours. While usually condemning of sexual violence, some religious traditions have nevertheless fostered conditions for the continuation of sexual violence, for example, in intimate relationships. While the connections between religious organisations and various sexual abuse scandals will be separately considered in Chapter 9, here we focus on the complicity of religious traditions in the perpetuation of sexual violence in the home. We will also analyse religion and sexual pleasure. The broader secular focus on sexual pleasure, particularly for women, in the late 20th and early 21st century, has led some religious traditions to respond through producing their own sex manuals and advice streams. Continuing with our queer feminist emphasis, the chapter will then return to the concept of heteronormativity, and how heteronormativity is solidified through the valorisation of heterosexual marriage as opposed to singleness, and how reproductive sexuality, leading to parenthood, is supported through dominant religious norms.

## Contraception

Contraception is a mechanism to prevent pregnancy, whereas abortion is typically understood as ending an existing pregnancy. Yet some view certain kinds of contraception – such as the intrauterine device (IUD), which works by not allowing an embryo to implant – as forms of abortion (Lowe, 2016). Access to contraception remains uneven, with social class having a significant bearing on access. Historically, knowledge regarding methods of fertility control was determined by social class; at the end of the 19th-century literature was widely circulated on aspects of contraception, but this information was less available to working-class women, who were more likely to rely on traditional wisdom (Weeks, 2014). Contraception historically had negative connotations, associated with upper-class sexual excess, meaning that even when information was available, it was not necessarily acted upon. Abortion has been utilised as a form of contraception (Hornsby-Smith, 1987; Weeks, 2014), but at the beginning of the 20th century, doctors started to make a clearer distinction between abortion and contraception (Lowe, 2016). There was much social anxiety about the use of contraception, lest it interferes with women's desire and commitment to motherhood. In England, the original Marie Stopes family planning clinics, set up in the 1920s, were intended for married women who already had children; contraceptive access was dependent on first demonstrating their duty as mothers (Lowe, 2016). During this time, religious organisations remained 'a follower rather than a pioneer of sexual change' (Delap and Morgan, 2013, p. 22), and throughout the 19th century, most churches agreed in condemning it (Thornton, 1988). Yet matters came to a head in 1930, when the Church of England and the Roman Catholic Church diverged in their approach. The Church of England – who at this point in history had a huge amount of power and influence across the world – cautiously accepted contraception in a limited number of situations, a ruling which fellow Protestant churches duly followed (Miller, 2014). In response, the papal encyclical *Casti Connubii* denounced contraception. However, it was not until 1958 that the Church of England's Lambeth Conference *positively* endorsed contraception (within marriage only), and this gave its use respectable status (Gill, 1994; Miller, 2014; Weeks, 2014).

The invention of the Pill was momentous, as Weeks explains:

> What made the Pill so attractive was that it was not only a female birth control device – there had been various others – but that it was easy to use without embarrassment of the earlier devices, and without fundamentally challenging the gendered order. It did not require complex negotiations, was less likely to provoke male shame or resistance, nor did it challenge the existing sexual practices of men or women.
>
> *(2007, p. 70)*

**148** Gendered bodies

Invented by a Roman Catholic, John Rock, he believed it would be considered a natural form of contraception, and would therefore obtain Vatican approval. Although the *Casti Connubii* ruling deemed contraception a violation of God's law, the encyclical also tacitly encouraged monitoring a woman's natural cycle as a form of managing fertility. The Vatican approved the "rhythm method" in 1951, after much deliberation. Rock saw the creation of the contraceptive pill as an extension of this already-approved natural-focused fertility planning (Miller, 2014). In this context, and with endorsement from a number of theologians, once the Pill started to be approved in places like the US and UK, Catholic women started to use it and did not wait for Vatican approval; indeed, the logic was that if the rhythm method was approved because it was deemed as not hampering the principle of intercourse, likewise, 'many proponents of the Pill argued that it was acceptable because it didn't physically interfere with intercourse like other contraceptives' (Miller, 2014, p. 19). Another reason that Catholics were widely expecting the Vatican to immanently approve the Pill was due to the conclusions drawn of an expert-led commission, the Papal Commission for Birth Control, set up in 1963 by Pope John XXIII. This Commission was comprised not only of theologians but also doctors, sociologists, psychologists, and a small number of married women (Geiringer, 2019; Helmick, 2014). As Geiringer (2019) argues, the Commission drew from the dominant secular intellectual traditions of the day regarding sexuality. The fact that the Church was willing to discuss sexuality in this way was a change in its own epistemology – instead of sexuality being proscribed by unchanging Natural Law, the setting up of this Commission implied that sexuality could be understood in other ways, and even contemplated questions such as women's sexual pleasure while using Natural Family Planning (NFP) methods – and this was pushing the research agendas of the secular social sciences as such questions had not been investigated before (Geiringer, 2019). But it was a product of its time. The data, e.g. on women's sexual pleasure, was interpreted by men, and qualitative accounts of women's own sexual experiences were lacking (Geiringer, 2019). The Commission argued that the Roman Catholic Church should support artificial means of contraception. However, these conclusions were superseded by the subsequent actions of the Pope:

> Despite the commission's years of work and theologically unassailable conclusion that the church's teaching on birth control was neither infallible nor irreversible, Pope Paul stunned the world on July 29, 1968, when he reaffirmed the church's ban on modern contraceptives in *Humanae Vitae*.
>
> *(Miller, 2014, p. 25)*

This was a significant blow to Catholics in a number of countries where the Pill had become available, and who had already started using it. The debate over artificial forms of contraception also raised questions about the authority of the Pope – whether previous "infallible" encyclicals could be overturned, and whether the Pope had the right to ignore the Commission's ruling (Geiringer,

2019; Miller, 2014). This also prompted a crisis in faith for many Catholics, as Catholics questioned what gave the Pope the authority to rule on birth control in this way. Due to Vatican II, changes in practice had been plentiful in Catholicism in the years preceding *Humanae Vitae*, for example, the Mass could now be said in the vernacular instead of Latin, giving the impression that 'the church was perfectly willing to evolve doctrine – except when it affected women' (Miller, 2014, p. 26). Miller argues that allowing artificial forms of contraception was so problematic for the Catholic hierarchy because it severed the link between sex and procreation, and this understanding of sexuality was crucial for their hierarchical understanding of gendered sexual relationships.

The outcry in response to *Humanae Vitae* was profound, and its consequences continue to this day. Soon after its publication, 600 theologians signed a letter condemning *Humanae Vitae* (Miller, 2014). Many Catholics deserted their faith (Guest *et al.*, 2012; Helmick, 2014), and for those women who stayed, a significant number started, or continued to, use artificial contraception (Geiringer, 2019; Hogan, 2015). Geiringer's life history testimonies with women who experienced these changes reveal the relative ease with which a number of Catholic women went against the encyclical – some even encountered Catholic priests encouraging them to use the Pill. Even though they might have harboured notions that contraception was sinful, many came to the conclusion – sometimes after much prayer and theological reflection – that using contraception was the right thing to do. What was also clear within Geiringer's testimonies was the huge problems that were caused by following Natural Family Planning – the responsibility to follow NFP was primarily women's who were not only responsible for taking their temperature daily, filling in all the necessary data charts, there were also challenges in managing sexual desire on one's fertile days. Many women experienced significant problems in their marriages by following NFP, to the extent that it was still difficult for some women to talk about.

In the British context, the educated middle classes were liberalising on their views, and this was supported by the Protestant churches, such as the liberal theology emerging from some quarters of the Church of England, as well as the Quaker's 1963 publication of *Towards a Quaker View of Sex* emphasising love, rather than tradition, to determine morality (McLeod, 2007; Weeks, 2014). In many Western liberal contexts, contraception became a private matter – even for Catholics – and contraceptive use became normalised and routinised. Goddard (2015) notes that for Evangelicals, contraception was not considered a significant issue, given that there were few Biblical resources to work with. Some Protestants also endorsed contraception on the basis that it opposed the Catholic approach. Yet there is also evidence of some Evangelicals understanding scripture as not endorsing contraception, often rooted in the basis of a Genesis verse to "be fruitful and multiply". For example, the Quiverfull movement, who explicitly encourage large families, see contraception as a weapon of Satan (DeRogatis, 2015).

Meanwhile, other religious traditions have expressed different understandings of contraception in different contexts. Hidayatullah (2003) notes that

**150 Gendered bodies**

contraception is acceptable within Islam, with the view that God allows all souls to exist, and Allah himself determines life – nothing will stop him from doing so. And Ahmed (1992) notes that historically, medieval Islam took a very liberal view towards contraception. But how this is mediated differs enormously depending on context. Dialmy (2010) notes that some Islamic countries allow free contraception and abortion. But some Islamic sects, such as Wahhabism, supported by oil-rich Arab countries, are more restrictive. In the RYS project, we encountered examples where young Muslims were confused about how to interpret Islamic thought regarding contraception. For example, Yasmin attended an Islamic Saturday School and had been told by her tutor that 'contraception is forbidden in Islam and that was pretty much it; there was no explanation as to why it was forbidden' (Yip and Page, 2013). Page's (2018) follow-up RIL project research on attitudes to contraception also noted the high levels of confusion among young Muslims regarding the permissibility of contraception, especially in an environment where such issues were not broadly discussed. For example, Shereen, a 21-year-old Muslim, said that:

> I spoke to my friend about it and she's a lot more religious than I am… I said something like, "When you get married are you going to have kids straight away?" and she was like, "There's that thing about whether it's even allowed in our religion, whether you should use contraception"… I don't know about what I believe… [I spoke to someone who] studied Islam and she said that you're… allowed to use preventative measures [e.g. condom]… but you can't use the morning after pill because that would be killing the sperm. So you can stop the sperm from coming in but you can't then go and kill it because that would be like having an abortion… I understand that part of it but I don't understand the whether it's allowed or not allowed part of it. I'm sort of on the fence with that one.

Shereen deferred to the knowledge of her friends who had undertaken a greater amount of Islamic study but had subsequently received different accounts. She therefore responded by articulating that it was her decision to interpret how she felt about it. Safia, a Muslim woman in her 30s, was much clearer about a divide between contraceptive forms that were viewed as an abortifacient, which were not acceptable to her, and those which stopped an egg fertilising in the first place, which for her, were acceptable:

> For me, religiously speaking, there is a distinction that I need to make between those contraceptives that are considered to cause an early abortion, and perhaps the egg has been fertilized, in which case those, religiously speaking, for me would be unacceptable… if you're a non-religious person, or you don't affiliate with the same beliefs that I do, then any form is acceptable for you.

Safia, therefore, made a clear distinction that her perspectives applied to her alone, and she did not make any judgements regarding the contraceptive choices of others. Meanwhile, older Muslim women in the project who had experience using numerous methods of contraception, articulated their broader support for various forms of contraception, with their perspective coming from the more practical dimensions of contraceptive use, rather than theology. For example, Husna was a 60-year-old Muslim who agreed with all forms of contraception, even those where an embryo could potentially be formed (e.g. the IUD). Her discontent over certain forms of contraception was more in terms of methods that were less reliable, rather than utilising theological arguments.

More critical interrogation of the relationship between contraceptive choice, use, and lived experiences in religious contexts is needed. Wiering's (2017a,b) research is one example of such a project; he critically interrogates the condom and its materiality in the context of religion in the Netherlands. The condom is widely perceived as a "secular" object by his participants, especially because of its presence in health-based safe-sex campaigns. The condom has therefore come to be understood as a cold, impersonal object that does not represent fulfilling or sacred sex. The condom was therefore ambivalently perceived by his research participants, and although the condom fronted safe-sex messages, because of its connotations with health, rather than sexual enchantment, it was routinely disliked. Meanwhile, in Page's (2018) research it was sterilisation that created a similar negative response, and even those participants who were supportive of many other forms of contraception were hesitant to endorse sterilisation. For example, when Adrian, a 36-year-old Anglican, was asked about his thoughts on sterilisation, he took a sharp intake of breath and immediately said, 'don't agree with it'. This strong reaction seemed to surprise him; he further reflected on his 'visceral response to the word'. His objection boiled down to the idea that 'it sounds so final'. This resonated with other participants' perspectives who also were opposed to the idea of stopping the potentiality for fertility, unless there was a strong medical rationale. This highlights the deep-seated ideas that healthy bodies *should* have procreative potential, even if individuals themselves decide otherwise.

## *Abortion*

Abortion is more widely contested within religious traditions. While there is often a clear distinction made between contraception and abortion in Western discourse (Lowe, 2016), as we have seen, some religious traditions treat devices that are commonly understood as contraceptives (e.g. the IUD) as abortifacients. Being religious is often seen as having a bearing on one's attitudes toward abortion. Recent Pew data from America indicates most adherents of some religious traditions wish to see abortion made illegal, particularly Jehovah's Witnesses, Mormons, and some Evangelical churches (Masci, 2018). The visibility of prayer

**152** Gendered bodies

vigils at abortion clinics also emphasises the religious impetus behind campaigns against abortion (Lowe and Page, 2019; Munson, 2002).

While the visible opposition to abortion is often religiously framed, what is forgotten is that religious traditions have not necessarily always been opposed to abortion, but either remain ambivalent or supportive. For example, in the lead up to the passing of the 1967 Abortion Act in England and Wales, many religious leaders from the Protestant churches spoke in favour, especially given that many were familiar with the consequences of not having access to safe and legal abortion, and the number of deaths and medical complications emerging from the so-called backstreet abortion (McLeod, 2007). The context for access to abortion varies enormously and is subject to various discourses, with different decades prioritising different elements. As Lowe articulates:

> Within both UK and US legal histories, there are a number of different frames of reference. First is the extent to which abortion is a health or medical issue, second is whether or not women should have control over their reproductive bodies, and last is the status of the foetus.
>
> *(2016, p. 63)*

One recent change has been the greater emphasis placed on the foetus, and how the foetus is interpellated and made far more visible (Lupton, 2013). Technological advances, such as ultrasound scans and foetal surgery, have encouraged the visible separation of the woman's body from the foetus; for example, scans are interpreted in terms of assigning independent personhood to the foetus, so that the maternal body is minimised or even disappears (Lowe, 2016; Lupton, 2013). This visibility of the foetus has given leverage to religious opponents of abortion to assert the rights of the foetus. This is achieved through the centrality given to images of the foetus in their campaigning literature, pavement signs, and use of foetus dolls (Lowe and Page, 2019).

While research suggests that certain religious groups are more conservative towards abortion due to particular theologies (e.g. Begun and Walls, 2015), Woodhead argues that in the UK context, 'Most religious people are liberal – in the sense that they believe that individuals should be free to make decisions about the things which deeply affect their own life' (2013, p. 5). Only a minority in Woodhead's survey (fewer than 10%) were conservative on the issue of abortion and they were more likely to be embedded strongly within their religious traditions. In other words, for Woodhead, religion only makes a difference to attitudes when one is intensively religious; for everyone else who identifies religiously, they are more in line with the non-religious population. Page's (2018) research in England and Wales corresponds to some extent with Woodhead's findings. Page assessed abortion attitudes through qualitative interviews, enabling exploration of the complex meanings and rationales of participants. Although most participants remained supportive of abortion in the legal sense, they overwhelmingly argued that there needed to be a "good reason" for abortion. Religious individuals therefore remain deeply ambivalent about abortion. Hierarchies emerged between "good" and "bad" reasons (Weingarten, 2012; Weitz, 2010) – when things were deemed outside of a woman's control, such as in cases of rape, this was seen as a "good reason". But if a woman could have used contraception, then abortion was deemed less valid. Ultimately, women were hypothetically blamed for not managing their fertility properly (Lowe, 2016). Participants did not explicitly draw on religion as a reference point for their views, questioning the extent to which their religious belonging impacted on their decision-making; there was no suggestion that a non-religious sample would articulate their views any differently.

Meanwhile, in contexts where conservative religious traditions have much political influence, the consequences for access to abortion services can be detrimental, such as Poland (Mishtal, 2017). As De Zordo *et al.* argue:

> In a number of post-communist nations abortion rights have been restricted or nearly eliminated due to the political revitalisation of religious institutions, in particular the Catholic Church, and the general 'remasculinisation' of the region manifest in a backlash against the gender equality ideology presumably imposed by communism.
>
> *(2017, p. 6)*

Mishtal (2017) details the restrictions imposed on abortion rights in Poland under the Catholic-nationalist government which came to power in 1989. As Catholicism became part of the state apparatus, and the lynchpin of national identity, moves were swiftly made to remove sex education from schools, and by 1993, major restrictions were placed on access to legal abortion. The current law – allowing abortion only in cases of rape or incest, where the woman's life is at risk, and where there is a major foetal abnormality – is at risk of further restrictions under the Law and Justice Party, elected in 2015. But their desire for abortion to be made fully illegal have currently been thwarted by strong opposition, spearheaded through women-led protest marches. While Church authority applies pressure at the level of governance, this does not stop Catholic women from seeking out abortions, albeit clandestinely (Koralewska, 2018). The Polish case indicates the strong connection between the imagining of nations and how women's reproduction comes to be controlled in this endeavour, with conservative religious ideologies deployed to enable this. Similarly, Whitaker and Horgan (2017) specify how opposition to abortion became the issue that cemented the fractious political groups following the Troubles in Northern Ireland. The deep political divides between Unionists and Nationalists were ameliorated through all main parties' religiously generated opposition to abortion, but this fragile attempt at nation-building comes at the expense of women's reproductive rights. Therefore, abortion control relates to wider political concerns and rationales, and the relationship enacted between religion and state systems is complex. This is not necessarily about a

**154** Gendered bodies

divide between the "secular" and the "religious", but how these interweave in oppressive systems, with religion being utilised as a legitimiser for larger projects of nationhood. This is an ongoing situation in the US context; at the time of writing, the state of Alabama had approved the removal of abortion in pretty much all circumstances, and in direct challenge to *Roe v. Wade*.

## Sexual violence

Sexual violence is embedded in many societal contexts, with religion having a significant part to play in its normalisation (Blyth *et al.*, 2018a, 2018b, and 2018c; Nason-Clark *et al.*, 2018). In a pioneering collection of three volumes, Blyth *et al.* (2018a, 2018b, 2018c) have collated chapters from across the world detailing the role that religions have played in either explicitly justifying sexual violence or complicity in supporting gendered ideologies that enable forms of violence to flourish. Many of the case studies relate to conservative Christian contexts where male headship and wifely submission is endorsed, with chapters examining the repercussions of this ideology. For example, Colgan's (2018) work demonstrates how populist Evangelical marital advice texts infuse notions of romance with male dominance and aggression, where biblical narratives indicating marital rape are reinterpreted as forms of romance. Colgan specifies how this creates a dangerous discourse where intimate partner violence and rape are condoned. Meanwhile, Hobbs' (2018) analysis of online Christian sermons on divorce emphasise the way in which the experience of marital violence is rarely sanctioned as a "good enough" reason for divorce, prompting an environment where Christian wives are encouraged to stay with their violent husbands. Although the use of religious resources is frequently contested, they remain persuasive and normalised within the context of that community. This is seen most clearly in Schoeffel *et al.*'s (2018) work focusing on a campaign to end violence against women and girls in Samoa. Schoeffel *et al.* (2018) reflect on the community reactions to an educational film detailing the causes and consequences of gender violence. In the discussion following the film, participants blamed women and girls themselves for the violence, with the behaviour of mothers in particular being singled out for criticism. Mothers were seen as neglecting their children, with sexual abuse of children by fathers being seemingly caused by mothers failing to satisfy the sexual demands of their husbands. Others saw the problem as rooted in a failure to read the Bible assiduously enough. Meanwhile, men's behaviours – and an assessment of the forms of masculinity where strength and force are valorised – were not scrutinised or held to account (see also Shalhoub-Kevorkian, 2008). Despite church leaders speaking out against gender violence, few Samoan women experiencing gender violence see the church as a source of support.

In other contexts, religion is used as a resource in managing sexual trauma. Fallon (2018) explores the horrific case of the Rwandan genocide where, over the course of 100 days in 1994, it is estimated that between 200–300,000 women were raped. Rapes were often especially violent, featuring gang rapes, multiple

Gendered bodies **155**

rapes, and bodily mutilation. Many women contracted AIDS as a result of being raped. To add further trauma, many women were rejected by their religious communities, being seen as tainted and contaminated:

> the women and girls who survived sexual violence within the Rwandan genocidal context often became constant reminders to their communities of individual and communal trauma at the hands of the enemy; many were subsequently expelled from their communities due to their perceived "pollution".
>
> *(Fallon, 2018, n.p.)*

A small number felt abandoned by god and saw little hope in living. Meanwhile, others drew strength and hope from their religious beliefs. When justice fell short, some felt that god would deliver justice against the perpetrators. Meanwhile, when abandoned by everyone around them, some women were firm in the belief that god had not forsaken them. Others did find support within their religious communities. Overall, it was religious faith that was a key factor in building resilience; those without a religious identity found it far harder to come to terms with the traumas experienced.

Although the participants in the RYS data were young and few were in long-term relationships, some had experienced first-hand the way that relationships could be violent. Shallini was a Hindu woman whose father domestically abused her mother; consequently, they had to secretly leave the family home and she spent six months living in a women's refuge:

> my father is abusive, so there was no way my mum could stay in that situation, but she will never get divorced because... if God has given you a husband... you try and make the best of it... We lived in a safe house in like some refuge centre... [my mother] was so clever, for about a month on end she'd say I'm going to take the bins down, so she'd take the bins down and she'd take one bag of our clothes and toys and things that were mine, and then a bin bag, and her friend would come and pick up the other bag, so she did that over a period of time.

Despite the abuse experienced and the way her mother had managed to escape, there was still a sense of shame that her marriage had ended, meaning that divorce was out of the question for Shallini's mother. This also impacted on the way Shallini herself navigated relationships, given her understanding of the risk that potentially arose with sexual relationships. Jenny had experienced this first-hand after she was raped by her Christian boyfriend, someone who was considered an upstanding member of her church:

> there was a situation where I didn't want to have sex, and then it happened anyway. So therefore, it was [a] difficult situation. And so that whole

**156** Gendered bodies

> sexual experience is a very bad thing as far as I am concerned. So, I then didn't have a boyfriend for three years but I am with someone now, but we don't sleep together... I don't really cope with it to be honest. I am going through counselling at the moment. It is something that I have to deal with. But my way of dealing with it, my current relationship with my boyfriend is very understanding, is not to think about having sex at all, that is not on the agenda at all, it can't be.

It was only recently that Jenny had felt able to tell her mother what had happened, again a sense of shame and guilt hangs over violent experiences that are not the woman's fault. And men were not immune from violence, as participants disclosed that they had been sexually abused in childhood, for example.

### Sexual pleasure

Various seemingly contradictory discourses on sexuality and gender have existed across time and space, all with a similar effect of silencing and downplaying women's sexual pleasure. On the one hand, there is the discourse of women as the wanton seducer who is sexually vociferous and cannot be sexually satisfied. She is a threat to men and their virility. Tseëlon (1995) maps this through the myth of Pandora, who could not contain her desire and was tempted to open the box, thereby releasing death on humanity, which resonates with the perception of Eve in the Old Testament as relenting to the serpent's temptations and eating the forbidden fruit. Meanwhile, within Jewish rabbinic commentary, Lilith is understood to be Adam's first wife, who petitioned for a sexually equal relationship. When Adam refused, she leaves him, turns to Satan, and takes on a role seducing unsuspecting men. As Tseëlon explains:

> Between them, the archetypal features of the women encoded in the legends of Pandora, Eve and Lilith inform Western moral attitudes towards the woman's character and personal appearance. Together they frame the woman as cunning and gullible, untrustworthy and evil.
>
> *(1995, p. 12)*

On the other hand, there exists the discourse of the desexualised woman, who has sex not out of personal enjoyment but to do her duty to her husband (Kamitsuka, 2015). This discourse manifests in white middle-class Victorian femininity, where the Angel of the House was constructed as the good mother, but not someone who would seek out or enjoy sex. The discourses of sexual vociferousness and sexual frigidity can exist at the same time and operates on the same lines as the Mother–Whore dichotomy, or the Mary–Eve trope within Christianity. Indeed, whereas the Mother–Mary trope encourages male command of the female body – coaxing it into sexual action, thereby emphasising male proficiency and activity, the Whore–Eve trope also encourages firm control of women's sexuality, lest it gets out of control. Both discourses contribute to the silencing and downplaying of women's sexual pleasure, and both discourses promote the idea that women's bodies are there to sexually please men. Dominant understandings of sexuality within Christianity have emphasised its procreative function over and above its pleasurable elements, thereby sanctioning certain limited forms of sexual practice, such as penile penetration of the vagina, where a man's orgasm is necessary but a woman's is not (Kamitsuka, 2015).

Despite Christianity's historical emphasis on sexual denial, more recently, Evangelical cultures have focused more explicitly on maritally-derived sexual pleasure (Kamitsuka, 2015). But this engagement is gendered; assumptions are made regarding women's lack of interest in sex, or so-called frigidity. DeRogatis's (2015) study of sex manuals marketed to white American Evangelicals showed assumptions that men will be automatically sexually aroused, but women's arousal was laden with directions and instructions. Sexual difficulties become associated with the problems and unresponsiveness of women's bodies in such texts, and are rarely attributed to the male body, which retains its status as virile and sexually powerful. While much is made in Evangelical sex manuals of women ensuring they are lubricated and engage in Kegel exercises for sufficient stretch, premature ejaculation and erectile dysfunction are rarely mentioned. Instead, men are constructed as supremely virile and given the assumption that they are easily aroused, they are at risk of sexual sin if women do not police their behaviours accordingly. Therefore, in DeRogatis's account, women are to monitor their behaviour and dress carefully, and are ultimately deemed responsible for men's sexual behaviour.

Meanwhile, men are perceived as "at risk" of various sexual vices, and not just in terms of seduction by sexually promiscuous women. Jordan (2011) offers a compelling account of the historical positioning of young Christian men and boys as being especially vulnerable to various forms of desire and being easily sexually corruptible. Up until the mid-20th century, it was masturbation, rather than homosexuality, which was the core practice of concern. To engage in masturbation was to be weak and signalled degeneracy. On publication of the Kinsey report, amongst other influences, the concerns over male sexuality were relocated to homosexuality; this became the corrupting influence, although the same arguments against masturbation were effectively recycled. By the end of the 20th century and the free availability of internet pornography, the new Evangelical concern was the propensity for Christian men to be "addicted" to pornography (Perry, 2019; Thomas, 2016), with many Evangelicals understanding pornography as a form of adultery (Burke, 2016). In the context of pornography, masturbation again came to be of grave concern, leading a number of Evangelical traditions to encourage the use of male-only accountability groups (Bartkowski, 2002; Regnerus, 2007). Some groups, such as the Promise Keepers, promoted friendship bonds between men; women were deemed to be so far removed from the issue of masturbatory addiction that they were unable to understand it, rendering them unable to help. Implicit

**158** Gendered bodies

in such an account is that women are assumed not to masturbate. 'This "male problem" and the spiritual warfare it entails would seem to require a "male solution", as offered by the Promise Keepers. Women are simply "not built for that type of spiritual warfare"' (Bartkowski, 2002, p. 269). In the RYS project, both women and men watched pornography, but the rates of men's pornography use were far higher, and men were also more likely to experience a values–practice gap – that is, they used pornography, but were more likely to view this behaviour in problematic terms (Yip and Page, 2013). As these accounts indicate, it was religiously devised mechanisms that were deployed to divert attention away from pornography:

> By the time I was 15, I was well and truly hooked on masturbatory pornography… I started to work against it in a spiritual and physical sense… Started to be accountable to other people
>
> *(Mark, heterosexual Christian man)*

> We concentrate on other things, concentrate on the beauty of Allah, concentrate on the beauty of Islam and our energy goes into worship, instead of thinking just sexually, because if you have the results of masturbation and pornography all the time, because you've got addicted to it.
>
> *(Jamil, bisexual Muslim man)*

> I said to a couple of guys… we need to have an accountability group… We meet up about once a week. And we hold each other accountable.
>
> *(Stuart, bisexual Christian man)*

Such accounts tended to focus on the discourse of addiction (Thomas, 2016) and positioned masturbatory forms of pornography in terms of a permanent battle. Mark, for example, narrated his constant relapses, and the lengths he would go to in attempting to control his pornography use. For example, in an attempt to curb his pornography use, his internet browsing history was routinely sent to his pastor, so his pastor could oversee what webpages he was accessing. But in order to circumnavigate this surveillance (that Mark had himself facilitated), he took the door off his roommate's room, thereby accessing his roommate's internet facilities. A common strategy within Evangelical Christianity, therefore, as indicated by Mark and Stuart's account, was co-opting others in this battle against pornography use – typically other men – who would hold them accountable. Meanwhile, Jamil's strategy was more individualised and did not involve others. It was apparent that accountability groups were produced within certain Christian contexts and were not utilised within other religious traditions. But these accounts pointed to the way that male sexuality was situated in terms of engaging in a battle of temptation, where accessing sexual pleasure is assumed, but this was understood as needing to be channelled in very specific ways (heterosexual marriage).

Shahidian (2008) explores the complex and competing narratives around sexual pleasure within Islam, in that although sexual pleasure for women is emphasised, 'The primary concern is creating chaste-but-somewhat-satisfied women while perpetuating and enhancing men's pleasure' (2008, p. 105). Similarly, in Judaism, there is a theological emphasis on a couple's sexual pleasure in marriage, with an emphasis on husbands realising the sexual pleasure of their wife (Alpert, 2003). Although this may appear progressive when compared with the Christian denial of sexual pleasure, Alpert argues that:

> The rabbis' recognition of women's sexual needs assumes not only that women have sexual desire but also that they lack the discipline and intelligence to control it. The rabbinic tradition sees women as the source of temptation and sexual anxiety for men.
>
> *(2003, p. 182)*

This reinforces the impact of the "woman as sexual temptress" narrative, indicating that even in contexts where sexual pleasure is given greater status, these can still invoke traditional gendered scripts.

The relevance or not of virginity within religious communities, discussed previously, can also have a profound effect on how sexual pleasure is experienced. Studies of Christian and Islamic communities where women's virginity is prized discuss that women must undergo a "switch" in how they relate to their bodies (Imtoual and Hussein, 2009). Whereas before marriage women are expected to demonstrate an asexual sexuality, on marriage, they are to become sexually engaged (Freitas, 2008; Sharma, 2011). The expectation to engage sexually with a husband after years of being told that this is inappropriate (especially in contexts where self-pleasure is also decried) can have a profound effect on self-confidence and one's embodied sense of self. Imtoual and Hussein note how women blame themselves when sexual activity is less-than-perfect. This then feeds into populist stereotypes of women as being less sexually interested. Burke examines the way in which Christian internet forums become a key way for Christian wives to find practical advice and help in having a more enjoyable sex life, something she calls a 'sexual awakening' (2016, p. 108). These chat rooms are preferable over standard books on sex as they allow users to interact with each other and discuss what works. The important thing for her participants, however, is that this is undertaken in a biblical setting, where all users are promoting "godly sex".

Data from the RYS project (Yip and Page, 2013) revealed that young men and women both had anxieties about sexual encounters, but these anxieties differed. Whereas men were concerned that they were able to "perform" in sexual encounters, women were more concerned regarding whether sex would hurt, and how long it would take to adjust to sexual activity. For example, Jamie, a heterosexual Christian man disclosed that 'I don't want to be bad at [sex]' and articulated that he was 'terrified of sex'. Meanwhile, Sabrina, a heterosexual

**160** Gendered bodies

Muslim woman, said that sex 'frightens me', and Layla, a heterosexual Muslim woman who had recently attended a cervical smear test, emerged from it worried about the pain associated with sex, saying 'If it's going to be like that I'm probably not going to have sex, ever'. These narratives highlight the surrounding emphasis placed on having good and pleasurable sex. But young people did not seem to have access to resources – either within their religious communities or outside of them – to discuss these issues and to alleviate anxieties.

Technological changes such as the Pill have enabled women to be in control of contraception. The threat of pregnancy being much diminished enabled a more expansive space to explore women's sexuality, and the clitoris was "rediscovered", promoted through the commodification of women's sexual pleasure, as advocated in various women's lifestyle magazines. Although the frame of reference for women's pleasure was still narrowly defined in terms of heterosexuality, it did at least open the door to recognising women's pleasure. It could be assumed, given the way that religion is typically understood in tradition-bearing ways, that religious narratives would remain fixed and immovable to these changing trends. Indeed, this can certainly be ascertained in some contexts. Yet much accommodation to commodified sexuality has also taken place, particularly within some religious subcultures. Burke (2016) notes the popularity of online sex toy stores which are marketed especially to religious consumers. Pornographic images and references are removed from the packaging to present a more "wholesome" image, with sexual pleasure in marriage being constructed in terms of a religious and god-given mandate. Indeed, so long as it occurs within heterosexual marriage, anything sexual is on the table, with Christian Evangelicals utilising the lyrical and expansive sexuality as depicted in the *Song of Solomon* as theological justification (Burke, 2016; DeRogatis, 2015). At the same time that women's pleasure is foregrounded in these examples, through the promotion of non-vaginal practices such as oral sex and manual stimulation, as well as the use of sex toys, there still remain gender disparities and unequal balances of power. For example, DeRogatis notes how some of the Evangelical sex manuals she analysed promoted the idea that women should be constantly sexually available to men, so that although women's sexual pleasure may get a higher billing, this can be emphasised within contexts of constraint. Also limiting is that all these discussions of sexual pleasure are expected to occur in heterosexual marriage only, thereby excluding those in non-heterosexual relationships, or those who are single, who are often told to overcome any sexual feelings they have and to abstain from any sexual activity. There is also a trend, mirrored in the secular study of sexuality, where the centralisation of a woman's orgasm becomes a badge of achievement for men, so rather than it being about the promotion of women's sexual pleasure, it instead becomes about masculine performance and accomplishment, in being able to sexually satisfy a woman (Holland *et al.*, 1998).

It is also important to note that the emphasis on women's sexual pleasure in some religious contexts is restricted by classed, raced, aged, and ablest agendas. For example, Moultrie (2017) notes the way many Black American Christian women are reluctant to even recognise women's sexual pleasure as a possibility, linked with the dominant discourse depicting Black women as sexual vociferousness vis-à-vis white women. In addition, Moultrie details the historical stereotype linking Black bodies with dirt and uncleanliness, which remains impactful today, such as the high use of douching products within the Black community. As Moultrie argues, 'If one believes one's body is unclean, one is unlikely to initiate oral sex or manual stimulation of oneself or a partner' (2017, p. 119). Another impacted intersection Moultrie notes is that of age and gender, with an assumption that women over a certain age should no longer have any sexual desire. Stereotypes abound regarding the way older women should be asexual, with their motherhood and grandmother status being foregrounded, which is seen in oppositional terms to having a sexual identity. But this belies the lived reality of older women who often do still have a proclivity to have sex.

## Heteronormativity

This chapter has thus far examined the ways in which gender has an impact on the levels of religious regulation and control of one's sexual body. This section will now explore the ways in which various religious traditions have typically endorsed heteronormativity, with expectations for women and men to be heterosexual and sexually reproductive in contexts of marriage. These constructions of gendered norms have repercussions when queer individuals seek out same-sex marriage and parenthood, with heteronormative understandings therefore delegitimising their claims for equality.

### *Marriage*

Marriage has been heavily supported within many religious contexts, often linked with the control of sexuality and procreation, so that lines of inheritance are deemed legitimate. Heterosexual marriage therefore becomes a mechanism for controlling women's fertility and ensuring control of her offspring. While traditionally speaking, marriage could be considered an alliance between families, particularly for the upper classes, the 20th century saw increased propensity towards the companionate marriage, where love and mutual interest between the spouses become the foundational basis for the marriage, rather than the ambitions of wealthy families (Abbott, 2011). Therefore, the role of religion in marriage has been complicated, and has depended on the varying understandings religions have had on the role of marriage as well as how this sits with other societal institutions such as the state. Although places of worship are typically associated with spaces where weddings are solemnised, the link is by no means automatic. For example, in some social contexts, poorer Christians have not been able to afford the customary wedding rites but have cemented a monogamous partnership more informally. In some contexts, the presence of official church

**162** Gendered bodies

documents outlining proof of marriage was superseded by local customs where the newly-wed couple would parade down the street of their community to confirm their commitment. This had greater status in the eyes of the community that a marriage had taken place, rather than the formalities recorded by the church (Abbott, 2011).

In the contemporary climate, many religious traditions promote marriage as being either an expectation or an ideal. Aune (2002) considers the contradictions embedded with the notions of singleness within Christian communities. Christianity gives theological weight to singleness, in a way that is absent in the theologies of other religious traditions such as Islam and Judaism (where singleness is problematised). Yet despite Christianity having the theological resources to endorse singleness, given Jesus' own single status, Aune (2002) details how challenging single people find it to be seen legitimately by their church communities, where marriage is instead encouraged. Given the uneven gender ratios within most Christian communities, there are far more single women than single men, so this is an issue that particularly affects women. And given the Christian emphasis on remaining sexually inactive until marriage, this causes issues regarding how women negotiate expected celibacy. Such findings correlate with other religious traditions where marriage is prioritised. Imtoual and Hussein (2009), for example, emphasise the challenges that single Muslim women experience when they are expected to deny and suppress any sexual desire. And any sexual activity prior to marriage would put at risk the very potentiality of successfully finding a spouse, with this regulating women's behaviour. Because it is culturally more acceptable for men to 'sow their wild oats' (2009, p. 28), the burden falls on women to police their behaviour, all for the 'promise of a "good" marriage' (2009, p. 37). In the RYS data, the pressure for the young adults to find a suitable marriage partner was acute, with families and individuals from the religious community directly intervening, as Clare, a heterosexual Christian woman, explains:

> [M]y church at home, quite a few people I know are in the mentality that you can find your identity by having a boyfriend or husband. And when I went home at Christmas one of the older women in the church… Every time she sees me she asks me if I've found a man yet and she just talks about it as if that would be the only pursuit worth having while you are at university. Actually, I'm 20 I have a lot of fun and there's more to life than just having a boyfriend I think… I think generally people that think that it's better to be in a relationship… they feel that they are living life to the full and maybe they look at you and think you don't.

Therefore, marriage was not considered something for the individual to negotiate alone but was considered a community endeavour. This not only caused issues for heterosexuals who were not ready for marriage, but it also caused much anxiety for queer young people, as Chapter 5 emphasised. Similar to accounts already conveyed in Chapter 5, Jamil used diversionary tactics, but realised these were time-limited:

> I can delay it for so long, I can say I have studies… but when it comes to a certain age the community will look at my parents and think why aren't they getting him married, then they will figure it out.
>
> *(Jamil, bisexual Muslim man)*

Jamil could only imagine marriage in its heterosexual formation; marrying his current same-sex partner was simply unimaginable for him:

> I was thinking about it, I was like that's very selfish if I got married, I married a woman I didn't love her, I took her virginity, I give her children, and I thought that's very selfish if I married a woman for that sake… So I refused to get married… [regarding his current same-sex relationship:] I know that we can never get married, there's no Imam would marry us, and I would never get married by registry office because that's not seen as a marriage in the eyes of Allah.

Meanwhile, Abby was part of Liberal Judaism, a religious tradition which supports same-sex marriage, and Abby therefore saw no issue with imagining a future self where she was married with children, saying 'I think marriage is important… I would get married and… I would have a rabbi blessing' – thereby indicating the ways in which marriage and religious identity were integrated. At the same time, the blanket adoption of marriage by queer individuals has been critiqued for not disrupting heteronormative systems, and by creating new discriminatory hierarchies (Richardson, 2018). Overall, marriage is still highly prized in many religious traditions, with even young people feeling the pressure to conform. However, the expectations around marriage entail gendered consequences, particularly in relation to childrearing, as the next section will emphasise.

In contrast, the RGSY participants who spoke about marriage and the expectation to marry felt the pressures primarily from social norms and familial expectations; they did not express religious expectations as impacting their decisions to marry. While many saw themselves being married in the future, in some cases this was also tied to a return to religion (marriage in a church, taking their children to services), they did not feel an immediate need to "settle down" or seek out their life partner. They were content to navigate their sexual lives as they saw fit in the moment, indicating that they would think about marriage "later on".

## *Parenthood*

The sexual control of women's bodies by various institutions is connected with the ways in which motherhood is variously constructed in different societies. In most societies, motherhood is a distinct role entailing numerous responsibilities.

**164** Gendered bodies

Although motherhood expectations will differ across time and space, mothers are often seen as crucial for the reproduction of good citizens, and the ultimate production of the nation (Yuval-Davis, 1997). In this vein, certain women are deemed more suitable than others, with various techniques utilised to stop certain women from being mothers, ranging from adoption to forcible sterilisation. The forced sterilisation of Indigenous women in Canada, not as an issue of the distant past but one that has continued to occur, points to the persistent forms of discrimination in the assessment of "suitability" of Indigenous women to bear children. The issue of the role of religion in adoption processes and the forcible removal of children from unmarried mothers by religious organisations will be discussed further in Chapter 9. Meanwhile, this section will explore the broader contours of the relationship between religion and motherhood.

A pro-maternal culture pervades many religious institutions. From Bible edicts encouraging humans to be fruitful and multiply (DeRogatis, 2015) to Islamic leaders encouraging women to see themselves only as mothers (Cheruvallil-Contractor, 2016), many religions put a huge emphasis on having children, with this even being seen as a marker of good personhood. Even in the Christian tradition, where there is an equally strong theological justification given to celibacy and childlessness (Llewellyn, 2016), recent trends in many Christian spaces advocate marriage and children to all those who are able. The reproductive capacities of women's bodies can be subject to great surveillance in explicitly pro-maternal cultures, with Mishtal's (2015) research on Poland noting the Kolęda period, an annual event when priests would visit all houses in their parish, which is used as an opportunity not only to ascertain whether families are participating in the required Catholic rituals, but also about intended plans for marriage and children. This scrutiny by priests is intensified when couples are married but have no children, with priests asking forthright questions about their childless status. One of Mishtal's participants, Renata:

> became tearful when she told me that with every year the conversation with the priest is becoming more burdensome and uncomfortable... She longed for the comfort of the faith, but not the pressure of being questioned about her private life.
>
> *(2015, p. 131)*

The RYS data indicated the ways in which young adults, across religious traditions, were already shaping in their minds their future identities as mothers and fathers, as these quotes by Sikh participants indicate:

> I would like children; I haven't necessarily thought about it so much but yes, family life is quite an important thing in the Sikh faith as well, so yes ten years' time I would probably think of being married with yes maybe not kids, but maybe yes, I'm quite open to that.
>
> *(Dharam, heterosexual Sikh man)*

Gendered bodies **165**

> I would like to say that in my ideal world when I get married and you know we are both ready to have children... [I] want to make sure that he's a hands-on dad as well and it's equal; it's not me doing everything... if I've been through education and I've got degree, I've obviously got it for a reason.
>
> *(Parminder, heterosexual Sikh woman)*

Both Parminder and Dharam were part of religious traditions that placed enormous emphasis on having children, but Parminder especially noted the gendered consequences of parenthood, already expressing concern that motherhood came with greater responsibility than fatherhood (see Page and Yip, 2019). Many of the women we interviewed were very concerned about the uneven division of labour with regard to parenthood, and were already contemplating ways of negotiating this, either through delaying becoming parents or through using education and careers as a means of avoiding full-time motherhood.

Yet, despite these general trends where motherhood is valorised, often this is encouraged only in specific contexts – e.g. when one is married. Amakor (2019) notes how unmarried pregnancy generates shame in Nigerian society, with Christian families directly encouraging their unmarried daughters to seek an (illegal and dangerous) abortion. In other cases, religious traditions have been more accommodating of unmarried motherhood. In some Evangelical contexts, unmarried motherhood is tacitly welcomed as a means of demonstrating that an abortion has been avoided (McCabe, 2013). In such conservative contexts, there is a delicate balancing act between castigating unmarried motherhood as a sin, but not going too far so as to encourage abortion. However, in Amakor's research, where young women did not have an abortion, they were often put into mother and baby homes, or asked to leave the family home.

Llewellyn (2016) considers the case of Christian women who choose not to have children, and the way that religious cultures do not support their choice. For example, one participant wanted to have the blessings omitted from her marriage service, but her Catholic church refused, because being a mother is deemed essential for married women in Roman Catholic teaching. Meanwhile, women who want children but who are unable to can feel excluded from their pro-natalist religious communities. Hampshire *et al.*'s study of Muslim infertility notes how it was 'unthinkable' (2012, p. 1047) to be childless, with parenthood being deeply connected with one's identity as a Muslim. Indeed, women were at risk of divorce if they did not become pregnant soon after marriage. Meanwhile, Deifelt's (2005) research in Latin America highlights a situation where women are encouraged to have as many children as possible – even if detrimental to their health – to support the machismo culture. Religion here offers a complex role. The lack of access to contraception due to Roman Catholic Church intervention does little to alleviate the suffering. At the same time, Christian narratives offer tools of resistance, such as the equal status Jesus accorded single people and childless individuals.

## Summary

This chapter has focused on forms of sexuality regulation pertaining to reproduction and fertility, as well as sexual expression. It is clear that religion has had a significant historical contribution to the ways in which sexuality is gendered, and how fertility is interpreted and understood. Yet religious traditions do not stand still and are constantly being reinterpreted and renegotiated. As the Evangelical case indicates, as discourses of women's pleasure become more pervasive in contemporary society, religious cultures adapt new ways of interpreting sexuality, so that women's pleasure is prioritised. Similar to secular cultures, however, this may not lead to the complete erosion of unequal forms of gendered sexuality, as indicated by the strong evidence regarding the continuing salience of sexual violence. While religions are at the forefront of offering pastoral care to those experiencing sexual trauma and violence (Halstead, 2018), religious environments do not necessarily provide the support needed, and in some cases militate against the survivor of trauma and abuse, creating cultures where abuse is enabled to be perpetuated.

Meanwhile, women's bodies are at the centre of debates regarding fertility and reproductive control, with religions usually having something to say regarding reproductive desirability, and the conditions within which reproduction should occur. This often endorses heteronormative interpretations of procreation, with unequal gender burdens arising. Procreative environments often encourage marriage as the "best" location to raise children, and restrictions can be placed regarding the accessibility of contraception and abortion. From this springs gendered expectations of parenthood, with heavier burdens falling on mothers. Some traditions see the relationship between "woman" and "mother" in essentialised terms – in other words, womanhood is referenced through motherhood, denying a place for women who either choose not to have children or who cannot have children. Again, religious cultures can be impactful regarding gendered experiences, and the extent to which women are able to navigate their sexual bodies in their own terms.

# 9

# INSTITUTIONAL CONTEXTS

## Religion and state processes

### Introduction

Institutional settings are collective spaces where individuals participate in routinised and predictable practices (Goffman, 1961). As Lune argues, 'An institution is defined by the unwritten rules that everyone understands about some kind of organized behavior' (2010, p. 2). Here we are concerned with a queer feminist analysis of the power of religious institutions. An institutional organisation is one where roles and rules are embedded, often based on tradition and "common-sense" ways of doing things. In this chapter, we are therefore interested in institutional processes and practices, written and unwritten, which have contributed to the regulation and management of sexuality issues. In a number of examples cited, religious and state institutions have cooperated and been bolstered through mutual dependence.

Two theorists can help us examine what effects institutions can have in relation to religion and sexuality and can be fruitfully utilised to explore forms of regulation, power, and control through a queer feminist lens. Goffman (1961), in his fieldwork on prisons and psychiatric hospitals, coined the term "total institution", meaning the way in which an organisational culture can envelop an individual. Goffman describes a total institution as a place where 'a large number of like-situated individuals, cut off from the wider society for an appreciable period of time, together lead an enclosed, formally administered round of life' (1961, p. 11). As Clegg argues, 'Institutions are total when they surround the person at every turn: They cannot be escaped, they produce and reproduce the normalcy of life inside the institution – however abnormal it might seem from outside' (2006, p. 427). Often individuals belonging to a total institution are separated off from the outside world, with the organisation as their only reference point, and where the norms of the organisation become routinised. Surveillance becomes typical. Goffman recognised that certain religious organisations such as monasteries could be considered total institutions – but their features can be reproduced in less intense contexts. What makes the total institution distinctive is that it separates itself off from other spaces. The features of total institutions are replicated in institutions that are more permeable and loose. McPhillips (2018), for example, notes how victims of abuse in the Roman Catholic Church experience it as a total institution, as the Roman Catholic Church was the reference point for every element of life – school, home, and church. Despite not physically being cloistered behind the walls of a monastery, the power of the Church seeped through all elements of a child's life, in an encompassing and totalising experience.

Foucault examines how institutions produce disciplined subjects, with the body situated at the centre of regulatory regimes. Discipline has changed historically from physical forms of torture and pain, to systems where disciplinary expectations are internalised, so that compliance comes from within. Using Bentham's idea of the panopticon – the prison with a watchtower where the prisoner is always on show but never knows when he/she is being watched – indicates a form of internalised discipline; one self-regulates oneself. While the most extreme example of the panopticon is the prison, this correlates to other institutional systems, especially in the context of the nation state and who is considered to legitimately belong. Citizenship status is fragile, with sexuality being a particular panoptical concern of nation states. Foucault's (1976) notion of biopower connects the health of the modern nation state and the health of the population; much time is invested in *knowing* the population, through measuring life expectancy, birth and death rates, and disease. As the state started to take over functions previously undertaken by religious institutions concerning individual regulation and discipline, striving for salvation is replaced with cultivating good health and longevity, in the process creating new kinds of discipline (Bevir, 1999). Importantly, whether subscribing to the needs of a religious tradition or the state, these normatives are internally accepted, enabling institutional control of individuals through various discourses, cementing the power–knowledge nexus. Compliance is cultivated by doing what is perceived to be in one's best interests – the health check may encompass elements of discomfort, but if it stops disease from spreading, one will comply. The punishment, in this case, is suffering from a nasty disease. Confessing one's sins to the priest may engender forms of embarrassment, but by undergoing this process it ensures one's eternal soul. In this case, there is an explicit reward being invoked. As the state takes over functions previously assigned to religious institutions, it tightens its control. Yet this takes diffuse and varied forms; the organisational arms of the state are multiple and varied and these may well contradict each other. Similarly, this chapter will consider complex religious institutions where the power base is not as coherent and centralised as it first appears. This chapter will consider examples where the power regimes of religion and state become enmeshed and entangled, with implications for understanding religion and sexuality.

In sum, this chapter is focused on institutional responses to sexuality issues, therefore focusing on the context within which religious adherents live out their sexuality within particular institutional boundaries. It starts by analysing the relationship between the state and religion, recognising the complex relationships that religious institutions have with the state and its subsidiary functions such as education. This is bound up with who gets recognised as a citizen and the extent to which religions are utilised in broader functions of the state. This section will consider case studies detailing the outcomes of state–religious collaboration, such as the Magdalene laundries. The next section will focus specifically on religious discourses on sexuality, emphasising some of the statements religious institutions have issued on sexuality issues to emphasise the power that operates through institutional statements that are given certain levels of authority. The final section, institutional abuse, will focus on the ways in which institutional cultures have enabled sexual abuses of power to occur. Institutionally, religious organisations were by no means alone, with many secular organisations implicated too. But those involving religious institutions highlight particular issues worthy of attention, especially when notions of the sacred are invoked, whereby religious institutions are set on higher pedestals than most (Lynch, forthcoming).

## State–religious censure of 'problematic' bodies

The entanglements between religious organisations and other societal institutions are complex and contextual (Asad, 2003; Turner, 2011). How these relationships are teased out vary historically, also impacted by the influence of a colonial legacy. Turner (2011) argues that states today, managing neoliberal impulses, have contradictory agendas; they protect their borders from security threats, as well as ensure a labour force to manage the demands of neoliberal capitalism. This can mean that state policies are contradictory. Given the way religion has ceased to manifest itself as a private affair (Casanova, 1994), states often directly manage religions – especially Islam in Western contexts – and punitive measures can be taken if religions are understood to be a threat to state sovereignty. At the same time, Turner (2011) points out that traditional forms of religion that are associated with national identity can be deployed to support state agendas. He cites the case of Russia; the Russian Orthodox Church was out of favour during the height of the Soviet system but is now being deployed to legitimate state activities. Therefore, the relationship forged between a religion and the state will vary enormously depending on how that religious tradition is perceived, and whether that tradition consolidates the projection of the nation (see Bruce, 2003 for a broader discussion of the relationship between religion and nation states).

This section will examine how the relationships between religious institutions and the state can have far-reaching consequences for how individuals experience their sexual lives. Citizenship becomes an important barometer for the inclusion and exclusion of various bodies within the borders of the nation state. We will focus on sexual citizenship and how key constituents – women, queer

**170** Institutional contexts

people, and migrants – have been denied access to full citizenship (Richardson, 2018; Weeks, 2007). We will examine this in relation to religion and how religious institutions have been variously co-opted into state processes to control the bodies of these marginalised groups, leading in some cases to religions being associated with highly problematic and damaging practices. Using examples such as the Magdalene laundries, we will demonstrate the entangled relationships institutions have developed, underpinned by different motivations and desires, but often concerned to solve perceived or actual social problems, also embedded with ideals of the nation state and how the nation state perceived itself. At the same time, participation in such social policy endeavours also consolidated how religious institutions viewed themselves – as organisations that helped the poor and the oppressed. There are many examples where religions have willingly co-opted themselves into various schemes which, from the vantage point of our contemporary gaze, induce feelings of horror and disgust, especially in the knowledge of the abuse and suffering that individuals subject to these schemes encountered. Yet the available evidence suggests that the religious traditions involved typically understood their task in moral and upstanding terms, as a means to help the "less fortunate" (Lynch, 2016). The institutional theory previously outlined may help explain why, in some cases, this went so badly wrong.

## *Sexual and religious citizenship*

The construction of the nation state assumes a series of borders and boundaries. The nation state is an ideological construct (Yuval-Davis, 1997), a means through which a given territory projects a certain image of itself, reflected through values that are conveyed, which has much impact on how bodies within that nation state are regulated. Although citizenship predates the notion of the nation state, the two have been intimately intertwined (Tonkiss and Bloom, 2015) and citizenship has come to denote the formalisation of one's relationship to the nation state. However, the extent to which a nation state legitimates and recognises the bodies within its territories will vary. Some bodies will be subject to full exclusion – their bodies may be present within the nation state but their rights are minimal – to those who experience exclusion of some degree. Those with the most secure rights to citizenship have been white property-owning males. Meanwhile, children are deemed potential citizenship but are "not yet" considered full citizens, meaning that much power is given to the adults surrounding them. Women have historically been excluded from the key components of citizenship, even though they are crucial to the reproduction of the nation state (Richardson, 2018; Yuval-Davis, 1997). Queer people are only recently being awarded citizenship rights in Western contexts but these rights are patchy; the right to marry or raise children is still not given in many supposedly liberal and progressive locations. Indigenous communities have been routinely excluded citizenship by the nation states forged on their lands (Bloom, 2017). Meanwhile, asylum seekers continue to be precariously positioned to citizenship;

citizenship is often denied (Akin, 2017; Lewis, 2014). Citizenship itself is premised on exclusion – not everyone will be able to claim their status as a citizen within the borders that are imposed (Richardson, 2018).

How religion is implicated in citizenship inclusions and exclusions is complex and depends in part on the way that religious tradition itself is perceived. Religious traditions deemed to be threatening in some way will be subject to the greatest censure, whereas those embedded in established processes of history, tradition, and power will be given greater status (Turner, 2011). State mechanisms will be more distrustful of some groups, and will subject them to greater scrutiny. In many Western contexts, Christianity has been understood as the hallmark of citizenship, though this too has varied, such as how Catholics were denied rights to practise their faith in Protestant-dominant contexts. Some countries, such as England, have an established religious tradition (the Church of England), which has a complex interwoven relationship with state processes and mechanisms, having a role in parliamentary processes and educational provision. Given the global reach of British colonial endeavours historically, the Anglican Church generated influence across the world (McKinnon and Brittain, forthcoming). Certain religious traditions will be privileged over others. In other jurisdictions, there is an attempt to keep state and religious affairs separate, epitomised, for example, in France, where adherence to *laïcité* defines what it means to be a fully-fledged French citizen (see Davie, 2007).

In societies where religion constituted the state and the state constituted religion, religious organisations had much regulatory power – the classic example was the role that the Roman Catholic Church had in the medieval period, where even to be recognised as a citizen was constituted through church authorities. It may seem hard to locate examples of totalising institutions in a pluralistic, globalised contemporary world, but there are numerous examples where religions have a seemingly overarching hold over the norms of a society or a segment of a society, with this having an impact for how sexual lives are lived and regulated. In the Bible Belt in the United States, conservative Christian culture pervades every element of life, from shopping (godly messages on till receipts) to car stickers, to banners proclaiming Christian messages. Homosexual practices are vilified almost universally, with some churches and pastors also condemning a homosexual identity or even homosexual thoughts (Barton, 2012). Everyone is expected to be a Christian, cultivated through tight-knit communities where one's social life revolves around the church. Drawing on Foucault, Barton calls this a panoptic prison; one monitors their behaviour because at any moment you could be being watched. Barton examines the impact this pervasive and encompassing culture has on her queer participants:

> If these institutions – one's family, school, church, peers, workplace and neighbours – are all adamantly in alignment that homosexuality is an abomination to God, a rejected gay youth may literally have nowhere to turn.
>
> *(2012, p. 83)*

**172** Institutional contexts

The negative consequences include depression and anxiety, family ostracism, and attempted suicides. When religion operates as a totalising system, as a sacred canopy, this accords it great power to direct the sexual lives of individuals. Those at the margins of citizenship, who are seen to transgress the normatives of citizenship, are the ones most impacted by such regulatory regimes. The religious tradition has become a total institution, in Goffman's terms. We will now turn to various examples where the intersecting dynamics of state-religious control have impacted on various marginalised groups, including the regulation of gender, and queer sexualities, also impacting claims for asylum.

## *Regulating gender*

The exclusion of women from the social contract was considered in Chapter 7. When they have been included, this has been precarious and based on their adherence to certain sexual morality codes. The regulation of women's bodies is at the centre of citizenship concerns, given that they are constructed as the markers of communities and nations (Yuval-Davis, 1997). In many Western contexts, women have been expected to embody pious Christian femininity, epitomised through entering heterosexual marriage and becoming mothers (Brown, 2001). Women's behaviours have been heavily regulated, even through their clothing (see Chapter 7). Given that women's bodies are centrally placed to convey a nation's and community's values, symbolically representing its boundaries and borders, mechanisms will be utilised to control their behaviour, and religions have been co-opted into this regulation. The Magdalene laundries were used to contain the "sin" of unmarried motherhood, through church-run institutions, on behalf of the Irish state. The aim was to purify the sin of illegitimate sex, of which the woman (rather than the men who had impregnated them) was fully blamed. Incarceration was not necessarily premised on premarital sex, and some were sent to the laundry on the pretext that they *may* be sexually promiscuous; this fate was more likely for poor working-class girls, particularly those who were in orphanages without families to vouch for them (Titley, 2006).

The unmarried mother was the antithesis of the image that the Irish nation state wanted to project; unmarried mothers conveyed notions of shame, immorality, and an economic burden (Luddy, 2011). By the end of the 19th century, the containing workhouse was seen as the most appropriate place for them, so that they would not "contaminate" the rest of society. The margins between being considered a prostitute or an unmarried mother was a thin one – any woman with more than one illegitimate child was summarily considered a prostitute (Luddy, 2011). By the early 20th century, the Magdalen asylum system, which offered support to female prostitutes, was under rupture as the numbers of prostitutes utilising them dwindled. Thereafter, their function was often changed to instead manage increasing numbers of unmarried mothers. Numerous Christian organisations were involved in such provision, not only in Ireland but across Britain (McCormick, 2005). These spaces were envisaged as sites of training, where unmarried mothers would learn useful skills such as domestic work; after a period of weaning, the baby would be sent into foster care and the mother would find gainful employment. Yet Gott (2018) notes this was a fallacy; this was not about educational advancement, for women were being constructed as unfit for education but fit for work. When the Irish Free State was created in 1922, the unmarried mother became a negative trope for a state wanting to promote pious and domestic femininity. In its early construction, the Irish state wanted to project an idealised version of the nation through the image of the good mother, and the unmarried mother undermined this endeavour.

State authorities were concerned with the cost of providing mother and baby homes and cost-cutting exercises ensued (Luddy, 2011). The state became reliant on voluntary religious organisations to help, with state money directly funding some of these institutions. Specifically, in the case of the laundries, these were based on an economic model where they would pay for themselves – the incarcerated women would undertake the laundry work for free, with the profits facilitating the whole institution (Titley, 2006).

In direct contravention of any citizenship rights, women were often detained in these institutions long after their children had been taken away for adoption, despite there being no legal grounds for this (Luddy, 2011). Later on, the length of stay was determined by the numbers of pregnancies out of wedlock the woman had – for women with three children outside of marriage, the recommendation was an indefinite period in the institution, lest their immorality comes to "taint" wider society. As Luddy argues, 'Such a stance, though not intended to be penal, allowed for the development of an attitude that accepted detention as a means of protecting society from these reoffending women' (2011, p. 117).

This treatment was constructed as being for the good of the woman; curtailing her stay would mean her "training" would be incomplete; the intention was to recalibrate these women from fallen sinners to moral and upstanding Christian citizens (Luddy, 2011; Titley, 2006). A key aim of the religious organisations' endeavours was to offer a means of redemption, generated through hard work and discipline – 'Sin was to be washed away through penitence and by laundering – washing, scrubbing and ironing clothes' (Simpson *et al.*, 2014, p. 257). This cultivated a paradoxical environment where the rhetoric of compassion was experienced in terms of separation, unpaid labour, and back-breaking work and subject to a highly regimented regime that could include starvation and physical and verbal punishment (Gott, 2018; Simpson *et al.*, 2014; Titley, 2006). Simpson *et al.* (2014) see this as demonstrating both Goffman's total institution and Foucault's all-seeing panopticon, inculcating governance and discipline of one's body. Those who "successfully" cultivated this bodily discipline could, in some cases, be promoted to other roles and given new tasks (e.g. needlework over laundry). But this was premised on intense piety and a heightened demonstration of their spiritual devotion (Titley, 2006). Despite these efforts, such women would never be considered equal to the nuns who were their guardians.

**174** Institutional contexts

The scandal generated over unmarried mothers working in religiously instituted laundries in Ireland during the 20th century led to an apology from the Irish state (Simpson *et al.*, 2014). The management of the scandal by the Roman Catholic Church has been severely criticised; records pertaining to the laundries remain locked in archives, unable to be subject to scrutiny (Gott, 2018; McCormick, 2005). In 1996, when the president of Ireland unveiled a plaque recognising those who worked in them, church officials were conspicuously absent (Titley, 2006).

More recent gender and citizenship debates concern the inclusion of trans individuals. State conceptualisations of citizenship have typically endorsed a binary gendered system recognising only men or women (Hines, 2012). Emerging legislation, such as the Gender Recognition Act (GRA) in the UK, gives legal recognition to those who wish to change their gender status. But this is limited by insisting on a binary male–female model. Individuals who feel their gender identity is more complex are forced to formulate their identity into strict boundaries of either male or female. Those who do want to formally transition encounter many barriers in satisfying the criteria; evidence packs are scrutinised by expert panels, who need to be satisfied that the person suffers from the negatively framed medical term, "gender dysphoria" (Hines, 2012). The GRA was later reviewed due to these shortcomings. Legislation such as the GRA has given greater visibility to trans identities. Religious traditions have taken a variety of responses. The Church of England's stance offering those changing their gender identity a baptism service was followed by a backlash led by Anglican bishops who argued this practice was theologically problematic (Sherwood, 2019). Other religious traditions anxious to defend binary understandings of gender can enact forms of practice which Blyth (2018) has described as symbolically violent. This is achieved through the othering of trans individuals, and castigating them as unnatural and abnormal. Her examination of conservative Christian narratives highlights how trans identity is typically invoked as a form of sinfulness; on this basis, trans people are instructed to relinquish their trans identity, thereby denying their full humanity. More scholarship is needed to examine the experiences of trans people from the perspective of religious belonging. While some states have made some limited attempts to accept greater gender diversity, some religious traditions retain a recalcitrant or even oppositional attitude, hampering efforts for full recognition and inclusion.

## *Queer citizenship*

The "sodomite" has historically been subject to various punishments, ranging from death, life imprisonment, and hard labour regimes (Corriveau, 2011; Fone, 2000). When the term "homosexual" was coined in the late 19th century, such constructions were embedded, though 20th-century interventions started to incorporate medicalised approaches, such as hormone "therapies", in an effort to cure those with same-sex desires; the construction of sexuality was premised

Institutional contexts **175**

on "normal" and "abnormal" manifestations (Richardson, 2018). The homosexual, therefore, held the status of a non-citizen and has been varyingly associated with either criminality or disease. Indeed, such constructions remain in place in countries where homosexuality is still considered unlawful or an illness. The 2019 ILGA Report (Mendos, 2019) highlights that various countries retain the death penalty for homosexuality, including Sudan, Iran, and Saudi Arabia, with many more countries supporting prison terms. Considering various countries in Africa, Van Klinken and Chitando call this 'state sponsored homophobia' (2016, p. 1), with current legislation debated to further curtail the rights of queer people. Conservative religion is often at the centre of such implementation. This is not just about a historical overhang of an outdated law, but the continued and active cultivation of new laws or the punitive sharpening of existing laws to restrict queer people, including the Nigerian Same-Sex Marriage (Prohibition) Act of 2013 and the Anti-Homosexuality Act in Uganda of 2014. As we will later highlight, this also has an impact on those who seek asylum from countries with such punitive approaches. While many countries have decriminalised homosexuality, with some taking steps to legally protect sexuality status (Mendos, 2019), historical legacies mean that discrimination continues to be experienced even in places of legal equality (Ahmed, 2004). For example, conservative religious voices have been at the forefront of challenging notions of sexuality equality, being particularly vocal in campaigns for same-sex marriage (Hin, 2015). In citizenship terms, this means looking beyond the legal definitions over whether certain sexual acts have been decriminalised; sexuality is much broader, impacting on 'employment, immigration, housing, welfare, health' (Richardson, 2018, p. 18), among other things.

The regulation of citizenship and sexual respectability was exported through colonial expansion; in countries across Africa, monogamous heterosexuality was promoted as the most "civilised" manifestation of sexual practices (McClintock, 1995; Ndjio, 2013; Van Klinken and Obadere, 2019). In a post-colonial context, this sexual regulation continues apace, as nationhood itself is interwoven with certain types of normative sexual behaviour and religious belonging. Across the African continent, sustaining a national identity has been constituted through a commitment to heterosexuality, with religious teachings (namely Islam or Christianity) utilised to buttress this positioning (Ndjio, 2013). In a post-colonial context, "the homosexual" comes to represent an opposed threat to the nation, an imposed phenomenon from Western oppressors:

> Homosexuality is simultaneously represented as an un-African phenomenon, a disease or evil brought to Africa by whites, the most dangerous vestige of Western colonialism, and the most insidious form of neocolonialism. As a result, gays and lesbians are largely depicted as… agents of the perpetuation of Western imperialism in the black continent.
>
> *(Ndjio, 2013, p. 122)*

**176** Institutional contexts

President Obama's 2015 visit to Kenya prompted opposition marches due to fears he would push for gay rights concessions (Van Klinken, 2019); similar protests have been noted in Uganda (Bompani, 2016). Being queer, therefore, puts one's citizenship claim in peril.

Queer bodies have therefore been heavily censured, through various state apparatuses and mechanisms, such as the courts and police system. In Cameroon, police raids and court processes specifically target young people from less privileged backgrounds; individuals have been questioned at gunpoint to force a confession of one's sexual practices, imprisonment in places where sexual assault is normalised and court proceedings where defendants are associated with bestiality and perversion (Ndjio, 2013).

Religion is explicitly deployed to further these overarching narratives. Bompani (2016) examines a highly successful and numerically significant Pentecostal church in Uganda which promotes a certain vision of nationhood that is heterosexual and sexually restrained. The future of the nation depending on the strict morality of young people is buttressed through sermons. There is a firm belief that not adhering to heteronormative assumptions will lead to societal disaster and the collapse of the nation. A strong nation is therefore understood as being dependent on the exclusion of the queer body, with queer people having few legitimate spaces to occupy.

At the same time, religion can be utilised to challenge the dominant discourses; using a sacred power base (Woodhead, 2007a) can be influential in framing arguments that are not instantly "read" as Western and therefore negatively perceived in terms of neo-colonialism. For example, Van Klinken (2019) examines the forms of resistance in the context of Kenya where there is much anti-queer rhetoric; queer Kenyans make claims of sexual citizenship through creating oppositional discourses where their identities as African and Christian are aligned. He analyses the music video called *Same Love*, which uses queer iconography to foreground the legitimate queer sexual citizen. Same-sex couples are depicted accessing public park spaces normally associated with Pentecostal prayer practices, where lovers kiss and biblical verses are reclaimed, emphasising queer identities as god-given. While dominant discourses associate queer rights with a Western agenda, here the video premises its arguments on being African and Christian and arguing that these are compatible with a queer identity, and therefore emphasising an inclusive citizenship where both physical and symbolic space is reclaimed. The video, however, was banned in Kenya.

Queer people who seek asylum on the basis of their sexual orientation and persecution in their country of origin are subject to a high burden of proof at European borders, including arousal tests carried out by Czech authorities, and detailed questions about sexual practices by British authorities (Akin, 2017). Given the prescriptive ways in which sexual orientation is understood by border officials, this has placed expectations on asylum seekers to portray an identity that is easily read as a marginalised sexuality, but which reinforces essentialised understandings of sexuality. Akin calls this the 'act of translation' (2017, p. 469), with responsibility falling on asylum seekers to portray their discriminated identity in accepted terms. Lewis (2014) details the physicality of a relationship that is often required by gay asylum seekers entering the UK, where photos or videos of sexual activity is necessary to meet the threshold test. In one case, an asylum seeker who had been tortured from Malawi, a country where being gay is illegal, "proved" his sexuality through photographs of him having sex with his boyfriend. But this articulates sexuality in a particular way, premised on being sexually active, with certain types of activity being deemed as "passing the test" of an "appropriate" same-sex relationship. Lewis (2014) notes how lesbians are particularly vulnerable to disbelief; the gendered patterns of torture differ, and gang rape to punish a woman for being a lesbian is often treated by immigration officials as a result of her gender, rather than her sexuality (see also Rehaag, 2010). Immodesty concerns can make some women seeking asylum embarrassed in the face of intrusive questioning about their sexual practices, to even being potentially traumatising when sexual violence has been experienced. As Lewis argues, 'For women who perceive their sexuality as a private and deeply intimate aspect of their lives, proving their sexual orientation in the context of the political asylum process is incredibly challenging' (2014, p. 965).

These encounters with border officials occur in an environment constituted through secular terms, premised on the "bogus asylum seeker". Despite states such as the UK foregrounding queer inclusion supported through equalities legislation, examples such as this demonstrate the thinly veiled expectations of citizens who are construed as "good" sexual citizens, and the particular model of sexual citizenship that is being demanded (Lewis, 2014; Richardson, 2018).

## Religious discourses on sexuality

The discourses regulating religion and sexuality were reconstituted during the mid-20th century, as Western campaigns for gay liberation and women's liberation gained pace. These campaigns would contribute to a new understanding that religions were, in the main, sex negative, opposed to queer sexualities, and oppressive to women. This was cemented in the sets of pronouncements, official statements, and broader discourses that circulated from dominant religious sources. But understanding the relationship between religion and sexuality in this way was not inevitable. This section will examine dominant discourses – or what Jordan (2000) calls rhetoric – surrounding sexuality and religion and how institutional-led discourses formulated a pattern whereby religion comes to be associated with traditionalism and conservatism, with seemingly little to offer women or sexual minorities. As Foucault (1976) noted, however, discourses rarely operate singularly, and can simultaneously convey contradictory discourses. As Jordan (2000) argues, even when gay people are formally ostracised by a religious tradition, it does not mean that all available spaces within that tradition are closed off – indeed, there may be major differences between the rhetoric and practical experience.

**178** Institutional contexts

Religious pronouncements on sexual issues constitute powerful claims. But the extent to which such statements are heeded will depend on whether the religious tradition is centralised, and how much power is accorded to those making the pronouncements. The Roman Catholic Encyclical *Humanae Vitae* (see Chapter 8) is underpinned by the authority of the Pope, who, because of the doctrine of papal infallibility, cannot be in error. Yet its controversy is generated as much by the extent to which it is ignored by vast numbers of Catholics (Delgado, 2015). Even in centralised traditions where there is a singular authority, or at least a clear chain of command, does not mean that religious practitioners will endorse that pronouncement, or follow through its implications in their own lives. Yet the official teaching remains, with the Roman Catholic Church being well-known for its oppositional stance to contraception.

Similarly, Brittain and McKinnon (2011) note the divisions in the Anglican Communion in the lead-up to the 1998 Lambeth Conference – a meeting of the worldwide bishops of the Communion, occurring every decade. A draft Resolution outlining that homosexuality went against scripture, as well as a call for Anglicans to offer pastoral support to queer people, provoked outcry, provoking negative reaction both from liberals and conservatives. When the Episcopal Church in the United States allowed the consecration of Gene Robinson as an openly gay bishop in 2003, this provoked further disquiet. By the 2008 Lambeth Conference, a group of conservative bishops had created a separate conference altogether, Global Anglican Future Conference (GAFCON), and duly boycotted Lambeth. On occasion, religious schisms are played out on a broader stage, with little consensus from the religious authorities regarding an "official" position. This was typified in the media frenzy following an altercation between the secretary of the Lesbian and Gay Christian Movement and a bishop from Nigeria at the 1998 Lambeth Conference (Brown and Woodhead, 2016). The bishop, brandishing his Bible, shouted that God will punish homosexuals, and that in the Old Testament, homosexuals would be stoned to death. He tried to lay hands on the secretary to exorcise a homosexual demon, at which point the assembled journalists started to giggle. The mood of this display shifted from one of dire threat to amusement. This emphasises the fragility of public statements and pronouncements by religious authorities; they can, and do, backfire.

This incident highlights the global configurations surrounding sexuality, and how religious institutions that operate internationally exist in very different cultural contexts. In the Anglican Communion, this has led to tensions between Provinces, especially between sub-Saharan Africa and the Global North (McKinnon and Brittain, forthcoming). As already observed, the impact globalisation has on sexuality and religion is complex but can invoke particular understandings of homosexuality as something inherently Western, and therefore seemingly at odds with the national values of a given country (Boellstorff, 2012). These interplays are also contextually framed, for as McKinnon (2017) notes, within the context of sub-Saharan Africa where conservative Pentecostal churches gain popularity, the Anglican Church becomes negatively perceived as the "gay church", and

Institutional contexts **179**

in response, a traditionalist line is perpetuated. Global alliances have been forged between conservative American Anglicans and Global South church leaders, but this also creates tensions within the Global South, as some oppose the way that sexuality issues come to dominate the debate instead of other issues such as poverty and disease prevention (McKinnon and Brittain, forthcoming).

## *Contingent discourses*

Jordan has extensively examined Christian rhetoric on sexuality. His analysis points to the way in which sexual regulation alters over time. Whereas at one point everything from same-sex activity to nocturnal emissions was roundly condemned, nocturnal emissions faded into insignificance while "homosexuality" came to be a topic to discuss and censure. He argues that the Kinsey reports of 1948 and 1953 (1998a, 1998b) were catalysts for pushing the topic of same-sex attraction into the open, and onto the agenda of churches. Theologians and preachers alike rounded on Kinsey, especially when the report on women was published, some refusing to believe his findings could possibly depict the lives of god-fearing women who would surely not talk to strangers about their sex lives. Jordan (2011) argues that there is much slippage between the dominant discourses of the day and theological impetus – in other words, the rhetoric on homosexuality within churches can equally emerge from the domains of psychology as scripture. In the Church of England in the early 1950s, a report, *The Problem of Homosexuality*, not intended for external publication, recommended that homosexuality should be decriminalised but should also be considered unnatural. Psychology-based reasoning was also endorsed in the response. Theology was utilised only to condemn same-sex activity, framing it as sinful. The inference of such arguments was therefore to curtail the potential for homosexuality to emerge in the first place, by ensuring children were psychologically well-raised.

More progressive Christian narratives also emerged. A group of Quakers published *Towards a Quaker View of Sex* in 1963, which argued that masturbation was natural, with any ill effects created due to a guilt-induced culture. Sexuality itself was understood not in terms of sin, but as ordinary and god-ordained. Such overt religious support was, however, overshadowed by the conservative churches, galvanised to condemn homosexuality.

Jordan (2000) examines the Roman Catholic Church as a key institution which has done much to repress and silence same-sex attraction, embedded in centuries of teaching and practice, and emanating from mechanisms to discipline clergy demanding clerical obedience. There is no linear line, however, in the forms this silence and repression have taken; indeed, in an institution as powerful as the Roman Catholic Church, any change in teaching is vehemently denied, with contemporary documents referencing older texts to "prove" consistency. Jordan examines numerous Vatican-produced contemporary texts, noting how some have been interpreted as more tolerant of homosexuality. But any positive interpretations were undermined in 1986 when Cardinal Ratzinger (later Pope

**180** Institutional contexts

Benedict XVI) wrote to bishops specifying that a homosexual orientation was evil and disordered, also banning any queer groups such as Dignity from using church premises (Jordan, 2000; Primiano, 2005). The contradiction, however, is that the Church has been a space which has attracted those experiencing homo-erotic desire, bound up with the church aesthetic where elaborate vestments, poetic liturgies, and a naked Christ on the cross is foregrounded. The Church has for centuries therefore offered spaces for those it simultaneously repudiates.

Whereas for much of the 20th century conservative church approaches to homosexuality was aligned with broader state and medical discourses, by the end of the 20th century this had ruptured, as equalities legislations in respect of queer people are introduced or enhanced, and medical discourses move away from understanding homosexuality in terms of a medical disorder. Some religious traditions have been ahead of the curve and have protested against state-sanctioned criminalisation of homosexuality, promoted same-sex marriage, supported queer religious leaders, and cultivated spaces for queer people to practise their religion. Other traditions ignored the issue for as long as possible. Meanwhile, others used public spaces to protest queer rights, generating much public attention along the way. The visibility and conspicuousness in the public sphere of those vehemently opposed to queer rights can seemingly and irrevocably align religious positions as anti-homosexual, thereby overshadowing those religious traditions whose starting point has always been more inclusive, or at least became so over time. In addition, even those most opposed to homosexuality have nevertheless cultivated spaces where homoerotic desire can be experienced, even at the same time that this is highly constrained and curtailed. While most research has been focused on Christianity, emerging work has considered other religions. For example, Shah's (2018) comparative analysis of gay Muslims in the UK and Malaysia emphasises the formal and informal spaces that become available to queer Muslims. While officially many experience hostility from imams and mosques, they are able to carve out spaces of acceptance, such as the support group Imaan, which offers its own *iftaris* (breaking the fast during Ramadan) for queer Muslims.

### Interpreting the discourses: Youth voices

Within the RYS project, it was evident that religious young adults were keen to analyse the basis of religious interpretation, resisting attempts to follow certain edicts because of what a religious leader espoused. Darshan, a heterosexual Sikh, explained that he resisted scenarios where religious leaders told him what to do, as ordinarily no discussion or debate was cultivated, saying 'you can't participate… you are just listening there and it would still be the place where you follow what is being told by them'. Instead, young people emphasised their own learning, weighing up the often contested interpretations on sexuality matters, often marking a distinction between the mainstream interpretations of their religious tradition and what they personally believed. This was sometimes oriented through a personal relationship with god:

Institutional contexts **181**

I interpret the Bible in a different way. I don't think that God would necessarily condemn gay people but… Christianity wouldn't approve.

*(Leanne, Bisexual Christian woman)*

There are a lot of things in organised religion that I don't agree with and take my own stance on them.

*(Heather, heterosexual Christian woman)*

Jamil, a bisexual Muslim, had extensively analysed Qur'anic verses, and used this religious knowledge to his advantage when he encountered fellow Muslims who argued that the Qur'an forbade homosexuality, as he explains as he reflects on this conversation with a friend:

I said it does not say no in the Qur'an that homosexuality is banned, I said the acting of lusts upon men is Haram, acting upon lusts of anything is Haram, it's immodest. So he said, "Ok I can see what you think, but I still think it's Haram". I said, "Do you read the Qur'an?" He said, "No". I said, "How do you know it's Haram?" He said "Because people say". I said, "Yes, because people who are straight who hate gays will say that"… I didn't let anybody [make me] doubt what I can believe because my connection is between me and Allah.

*(Jamil, bisexual Muslim man)*

In this exchange, Jamil was critical of those who followed others without their own discernment and study of the text. When the religious text is differently recast, this can have powerful effects. As Yip argues, 'the significance of religious texts is undeniable. Even opponents with scarce theological knowledge often use clichés such as "The Bible says so" or "The Qur'an says it is wrong", to justify their stance against homosexuality' (2005, p. 49). Jamil drew upon the Sodom and Gomorrah story to argue this was about lust rather than homosexuality. This was complemented by his emotional connection with God, overshadowing the official discourses (Yip, 2005). God was a powerful ally in Jamil's recalibration in his understanding of homosexuality and Islam. Overall, then, dominant religious discourses impact on young adults' negotiation of sexual scripts available to them, but these were never absolute, and participants recognised that alternative discourses were available if they looked hard enough (Foucault, 1976). This also emphasised the lived nature of youth religiosity, where engagement with the sacred texts became part of their spiritual practice. For queer participants in particular, knowledge was power.

## Institutional sexual abuse

Sexual abuse by religious leaders has caused shockwaves across the Western world (Gleig, 2019; Keenan, 2012). Numerous religions have been implicated, but much focus has been placed on the Roman Catholic Church (Keenan, 2012; McPhillips, 2018; O'Reilly and Chalmers, 2014). The key finding is not only that trusted and esteemed priests have committed such grave offences, but that the institutional response has been equally grievous to survivors.

Childhood is constituted as a time of sexual innocence; children are not supposed to "know" about sexuality (Jackson and Scott, 2013). Meanwhile, priests are understood as following a holy vocation, underpinned by obedience and sacrifice (Peyton and Gatrell, 2013). In the Catholic context, this sacrifice incorporates celibacy (Keenan, 2012). Despite the reforms of Vatican II, the Roman Catholic Church retains a clear distinction between the laity and those ordained. Priests are seen as more holy, closer to God – especially in a context where the priest is the one who has the power to absolve one of one's sins. Priests are therefore esteemed individuals, enabling them to have a powerful societal position. When this is juxtaposed with the construction of childhood, trust is placed in the asexual priest and the child is considered safe. The marginalised role of the child impacts on their reporting capacities – strategies of abuse often relied on secrecy and an expectation that the child would not – and could not – tell (Keenan, 2012). Even when children began to tell their stories, they were not believed (Plummer, 1995). The idea that a priest could do such a thing was inconceivable. When our stories constitute our sense of self, the denial of that story is an offence on one's very identity. Brison (1999), drawing on the philosophy of John Locke, explains how Western philosophy privileges the self as constituted through the stories we tell. Selfhood is resolved through one's ability to narrativise their story, in the process demonstrating a sense of self that is seemingly stable and coherent. When one's story is not heard, this problematises one's very personhood.

Keenan (2012) argues that media tag lines, such as the "paedophile priest", oversimplifies the situation, depicting the priest himself as individually pathologised and simultaneously tainting every priest as a potential paedophile. Keenan instead argues that the clerical sex abuse crisis needs to be analysed holistically, moving beyond a concern with individualised pathology. The priest who sexually abuses a child is a particular product of a clerical system where sexual issues are not discussed and priests are ill-equipped to manage a life-long commitment to celibacy. Importantly, Keenan has gathered testimony from those priests who have sexually abused children, offering crucial insights. One startling finding was that her interviewees did not realise the damage they were inflicting on the children they were abusing. In their understanding, these children were compliant; when the children involved did not protest at their actions, this was interpreted as consent. Rather than seeing this as a problem solely with the individual, Keenan instead analyses this in relation to what the priest had been taught about sexuality. Her interviewees had often been raised in a Catholic environment where sin loomed large. Avoiding sin was paramount, but because sexuality was little-discussed, her interviewees absorbed the message that they had to avoid any sexual thoughts or practices, lest they commit a mortal sin. Yet how to practically manage this was not discussed. This silencing was further entrenched

Institutional contexts **183**

in seminary training, where sexual issues were intellectualised into theological terms, rather than emotional ones. Priests were therefore trained to individualistically not commit sin, rather than reflect on how their actions may impact on others. The priests she interviewed had started to comprehend the severity of their crimes and were appalled by how their actions had blighted the lives of their victims.

The other key element in the child sexual abuse crisis was the Church's response. Keenan's participants would disclose their actions in the confessional, often being forgiven if they promised never to do it again. But time and again they lapsed. Keenan then goes on to analyse the role that the Church itself played in perpetuating the abuse. Like understanding abusers, understanding the actions of the Church is complex too. She notes examples where bishops tried to stem what was going on but were offered no support, even encountering obstruction from the Vatican itself. At one point, a Bishop was accused of going against canon law in his attempts to recognise Church failings. More broadly, committing sexual abuse was understood as a moral failing of an individual priest rather than a systemic problem of the institution. Priests were relocated rather than directly addressing the situation. What is egregious to most is that the Church knew about the abuse far sooner, and it was only when media investigation, such as the *Boston Globe*, started to highlight the connections and patterns, that there were accusations of a cover up. Meanwhile, the Vatican localised the problem. Bishops were curtailed by authority resting with the Pope. Obedience ruled, over and above child protection issues – and this was a product of the system (Keenan, 2012). Peyton and Gatrell's analysis of the priestly body can be instrumental in understanding this. As they explain, 'The ordination of a priest disciplines and governs body and soul during every waking hour from the moment of ordination, until death… These promises require life-long and whole-hearted personal and embodied obedience in God's service, as well as an adherence to the doctrine and governance of the Church' (Peyton and Gatrell, 2013, p. 53). Obedience is embodied, and defines priesthood, entailing an ontological change on ordination. In an environment akin to a total institution (Goffman, 1961) everyone is following the same obedience principles. When obedience becomes fundamental to one's very being and lived existence, it helps explain the challenges in confronting those in authority.

The Independent Inquiry into Child Sexual Abuse (IICSA, 2018) was set up in England and Wales in 2014 to investigate a large number of institutional contexts where sexual abuse had occurred, such as councils, schools, and churches. Various factors led to this formal inquiry, but a key reason was the prolific sexual offending by celebrities such as Jimmy Saville, and the way institutions had failed to intervene (in the Saville case, even publicly funded hospitals were used for opportunistic attacks on children). The key aim of this Inquiry was to determine how and why things had gone so wrong. Its scale was ambitious, but was beset by issues – notably, the chair of the Inquiry changed four times – the first two chairs were determined as being too close to establishment ties, and therefore resigned.

**184** Institutional contexts

The Church of England is one of the religion-based case studies under investigation by IICSA, its significance heightened as the established church in England. IICSA has thus far explored the Church of England on three occasions: a 15-day hearing in March 2018, focused on the Chichester diocese, which was identified as having major safeguarding problems, where numerous clergy had been prosecuted through the courts; a five-day hearing in July 2018 focused on Peter Ball, a bishop convicted of abusing 18 young men between the 1970s and 1990s; and a hearing in July 2019, focused on the wider Anglican Church and their response to child sexual abuse. Here attention is given to the first Chichester hearing, where testimony was heard from survivors of abuse, bishops, and those involved in the processes for child protection (such as safeguarding advisors). Page (2019) undertook an analysis of these transcripts, demonstrating that the hierarchical nature of the Church was consolidated through the axes of both class and gender privilege, with these elements also intersecting. What follows is that analysis.

## *Social class*

As the established church in England, the Church already occupies a privileged societal location (Brown and Woodhead, 2016; Guest *et al.*, 2012; Page, 2017c; Paul, 1973). As Guest *et al.* explain:

> The Church of England continues to have a strong link to many elite institutions, including the public schools… law, Oxbridge colleges, Parliament, the royal family and institutions of the armed services. Indeed, the importance of religion, particularly Anglicanism, in supporting class and 'establishment' interests, is another continuing aspect of the wider cultural significance of Christianity in the UK.
>
> *(2012, p. 69)*

Bishops and archbishops continue to garner specific forms of authority, interconnected with identities bound up with class status, and where preferment often depends upon one's connections (Davies and Guest, 2007). Their status is entwined with the broader Church's elite positioning, given that 'bishops remain in the House of Lords, carry grandiose titles, officiate over public ceremony and occupy networks of civic hierarchy that remain the preserve of the privileged' (Davies and Guest, 2007, p. 107). Given the safeguarding oversight bishops had, IICSA heard testimony from numerous bishops, former archbishops, and the current incumbent, detailing the power that a diocesan bishop could wield. In her opening statement, the leading counsel to the Inquiry, Fiona Scolding QC, describes 'The diocesan bishop is king in his diocese. The power and status of the bishops is hardwired into the culture of the Church of England' (IICSA, 2018, p. 132). Evidence was presented of the enormous weight given to the opinions of archbishops and bishops. The Gibb Report (2017) criticises the then Archbishop of Canterbury, George Carey, who wrote to police in the wake of Peter Ball's questioning by police in 1993 (for which he received a caution), to say that the allegations against him were 'most unrepresentative' (2017, p. 20) of him, despite having knowledge of numerous allegations against Ball. Ball continued in ordained ministry until 2010 and was only convicted of child sexual abuse offences in 2015. The Gibb Report, and IICSA, question the undue influence such comments from an archbishop could have, given his status and power. However, the bishops and archbishops themselves presented their situation rather differently, arguing they had no formalised authority over the bishops/priests for whom they had oversight. For example, although bishops swear an oath of allegiance to the archbishop, the archbishop has no formal power to tell the bishop what to do. Meanwhile, bishops did not see themselves as in charge of the priests in their diocese, with Bishop John Hind rejecting in his testimony the idea that he was the boss of the clergy in his diocese, and contested the idea that he could operate as some kind of king. He argued he had moral authority rather than any real power. But this positioning denies the forms of authority available to the bishop. In a Weberian sense (Weber, 1968), the bishops and archbishops who gave testimony tried to distance themselves from any claim to have rational-legal authority. But the opportunities to display and perform both charismatic and traditional authority were enormous, giving them much scope for broader influence. In fact, even legal-rational authority had purchase, given that there were legal mechanisms that bishops and archbishops could utilise; they ultimately have the power – embedded in Church law – to undertake a visitation, which allows them to officially inspect an area of the Church under their control.

Priests who abused were able to utilise their class privilege to enacting that abuse. The testimony of one survivor describes his upbringing on a council estate, but unlike his peers, he obtained a place at the (selective) grammar school. He was socially isolated from his peer network, and his parents did not have the resources to help him manage this daunting encounter with the school. When the local vicar, Roy Cotton, took an interest in him, this was deemed wholly positive; he cultivated educational opportunities his family felt unable to provide. What began as using the vicar's book collection developed to numerous trips abroad, including a month-long trip around Greece on the pretext of studying classical art. The priest told hoteliers that the boy was his son; they shared a hotel room, offering prime opportunities for sexual abuse to occur. The abuse went unchecked for a decade. This abuse encounter was therefore premised on class lines, where the vicar took advantage of a marginalised working-class boy who was struggling to fit into the middle-class grammar school. Yet when attempts were made to latterly report what had happened to the Church, this survivor experienced a Church in denial, unwilling to take responsibility, resistant to offering him support such as much-needed counselling, and with senior Church figures brushing off his complaints. The Church was an unbending inflexible institution that was unwilling to prioritise his experience and perspective, to the extent that in subsequent internal Church reviews into child sexual abuse, he

**186** Institutional contexts

was further marginalised and not consulted, despite the insights he could offer. In his own words:

> The church, I feel, has continually failed me, and it's failed many others. It's been slow to change, it's been slow to accept responsibility, and, again, it's just failed to learn from those mistakes and report and share information with statutory authorities. It's put its reputation and its internal squabbles ahead of safeguarding and responding well to victims.
>
> *(IICSA, 2018, p. 107–8).*

Privilege and status were being protected, which were often demonstrated on classed lines. But this is not the only means through which individuals were marginalised, with gender too being crucial to understanding the Church's response to abuse.

## *Gendered privilege*

Women were not allowed to be bishops in the Church of England until 2014 and were barred from priesthood until 1992. This historical legacy has meant that the Church has been underpinned by a masculine-dominated culture; it is a profoundly gendered institution (Page, 2014b). Elements of the Church have struggled to accept women's ministry, with campaign groups such as Reform premised on opposing women's priesthood. Although there has been acceptance of women priests in general terms, there remains what Page has called 'pockets of opposition' (2012, p. 55), consolidated through Church organisations explicitly opposed to women's ordination. IICSA was keen to probe the extent to which the Chichester diocese perpetuated an anti-woman culture. As Peyton and Gatrell's (2013) work has already demonstrated, ordained status is powerful, demarcating a difference between the priest and the laity. But such power has been instituted as sacredly masculine (Bock, 1967), where the clergy*man* has historically held a 'sacredly ontological status' (Aldridge, 1989, p. 62). As Johnson (1992) has demonstrated, theologically, god has been situated as masculine; god has been accorded male pronouns, and related to masculine imagery. Sacrality itself has been bound up with men and their authority; women have traditionally been excluded from this sacred status, and certain sections of the Church have done much to try to maintain that exclusion (Page, 2012).

The operationalisation of sacredly masculine authority was manifest in a number of different ways. We have already noted the influence attached to the words of an archbishop. Meanwhile, the Safeguarding Officer for Chichester, Shirley Hosgood, experienced marginalisation in relation to senior clergy. While parish clergy were keen to undergo safeguarding training, resistance emerged from senior clergy. When raising serious concerns about safeguarding issues with senior clergy, some persistently ignored her emails. A formal report into safeguarding in the diocese was not initially shared with her. She was not informed

Institutional contexts **187**

by the bishop about cases of abuse that had been disclosed to him. When she made a justified recommendation that a clergy member (later convicted) who posed a safeguarding risk should have their permission to officiate removed, this recommendation was not approved by the diocesan bishop. The case of Shirley Hosgood, a specialist in safeguarding with many years' experience, gives insight into the ways that gender operated in the Chichester diocese. Despite her professional expertise, she was not ordained; she was therefore excluded from diocesan business and decision-making that directly related to her role. Not only that, but Hosgood was a woman working with a team of senior male clergy. Hosgood's account emphasises the frustration she felt working with a team of senior men, who made it extremely challenging for her to fulfil the requirements of her job in implementing safeguarding procedures and did much to undermine her role. She was also explicitly working with individuals opposed to women's ordination. Bishop Wallace Benn was a suffrage bishop in the diocese who was a member of Reform, and with whom Hosgood was required to regularly communicate with. In his own account to the Inquiry, he confirmed his theological commitment to male headship in the Church, which would see women excluded from being priests and therefore having authority over men, but he confirmed that he did not see this as applying to other areas of secular professional life. Despite this, it is clear that Benn took real issue with the authority that Hosgood had. In his own words:

> My problem with Ms Hosgood was that she went about it in quite an aggressive manner, and that caused quite a number of difficulties, not only with me, but with a number of people. (p. 44). [He is asked to specify what he means by aggressive.] I think she came with a chip on her shoulder from her previous job that bishops didn't listen to safeguarding advice and clergy didn't either. I think that affected her.
>
> *(IICSA, 2018, p. 45)*

The characterisation of women in positions of authority as being aggressive is nothing new (Cockburn, 1991), with this conceptualisation often operating as a means of treating women as out-of-place in the professional organisation (Puwar, 2004). Hosgood's own account gives credit to the argument that she was marginalised in relation to the authority mechanisms of the Church, but Benn utilises well-worn stereotypes about women in leadership to denigrate her authority, without questioning how his own behaviour contributed to Hosgood's difficulties.

It is clear from the IICSA testimonies that masculine privilege was made normative at the highest levels of the Chichester diocese, and this depended on clergy understanding themselves in sacredly masculine terms. But it is also worth highlighting the impact that gendered norms had on survivors of historical child sexual abuse. Now an adult, testimony was heard from a woman who disclosed that she and a friend were abused by Reverend Rideout, who was, at the time, an

**188** Institutional contexts

army chaplain. She was 12 years old when the case went before a court martial, understandably a very intimidating experience, and where officers holding guns were present. Nobody explained anything to her and no allowance was made for the fact that she was 12. She recalls that she felt terrified. After the court found Rideout not guilty, her family was ostracised in the community. Others in the army believed Reverend Rideout over the girls, even fundraising for his legal support. Years later, Rideout was convicted of 34 counts of indecent assault and two counts of attempted rape. This encounter demonstrates the combined forces of military and church in creating the most imposing environment for a 12-year-old girl's sensitive testimony to be heard, and then ultimately disbelieved. As her father was of a lower rank, as a sergeant, while Reverend Rideout was an officer, people felt it implausible that an officer would do this, thereby indicating the interaction of gender and class in this case.

Repeatedly, communities and parishes supported accused priests, failing to give credence to the testimonies of survivors, and being unable to believe the allegations against their friendly, personable priest. Priests were so aligned with godliness and occupying a set-apart and sacred status, parishioners could not comprehend that the priest could be capable of such vile acts. This is rooted in the sacred status that is bestowed on priests, who are seen as representatives of god on earth. And as god has been thoroughly captured as sacredly masculine (Johnson, 1992), this gives protection to men holding an ordained status. This analysis of IICSA has demonstrated the intersectional workings of class and gender privilege in firstly enabling abuse, and then creating obstacles for abuse to be reported and addressed. But the glue which ties these forms of privilege together is the way those involved are constituted as sacred.

Lynch (forthcoming) argues that one needs to examine how Christian morality is formulated in order to understand why churches such as the Church of England have failed organisationally. He argues that rather than seeing such failings being contradictory to the organisation's orientation to the sacred, godly and good, it is this very underpinning of goodness that structures their inability to successfully manage the abuse crisis. In essence, being a Christian is premised on mediating sin and redemption, with the believer trying to be of good moral standing before god, and therefore being redeemed from sin. The believer thus participates in forms of religious practice and good works so that god ultimately forgives one's sins. Church apparatus – such as its visual cultures pertaining to church buildings, vestments, and stained glass – are all premised on locating the heaven on earth, so that the church – and its representatives such as priests and bishops – come to symbolise the heavenly, and therefore the godly, and through which redemption can be achieved. This is further supported through theological understandings such as *In Persona Christi*, where the priest acts as Christ's representative on earth. Similar to the discussion above, therefore, this connection with the sacred helps explain why so much trust was placed in priests, how they were able to abuse with impunity, and why survivors themselves were not believed. What we would like to emphasise, however, is that these forms of goodness and morality have operated on layers of gendered and classed privilege. The heavenly, godly, sacred, and good have been bound up with particular kinds of embodied privileged and status-bearing masculinity (Page, 2017c) – indeed, *In Persona Christi* has been utilised as a reason for why women cannot be priests, for women, the argument contends, cannot represent the maleness of Christ. Therefore, the moral meaning-making that Lynch (forthcoming) persuasively argues explains the abuse crisis within which Christianity has to be understood as constituted through gendered and classed privilege, which operate as systems of power that marginalise the survivor.

## Summary

This chapter has demonstrated the operationalisation of power within institutional contexts, and the extent to which religious organisations operate as "total institutions" (Goffman, 1961). While much of the chapter has focused on Christian institutions, we have also emphasised that religions do not act in isolation but also contribute to broader sexuality discourses, in conjunction with other societal institutions, and even supporting the arms of the state. Indeed, although the relationship between states and religious organisations is complex and contextual, it is clear that in many examples, each has supported the other, with dominant discourses often promoting the powerful censure of individuals. Therefore, when considering the institutional context of a religious tradition, this is mediated with other social institutions, and impacted by the religious tradition's status vis-à-vis the state. Yet the continued knowledge emerging of religious institutional harms perpetuated has led to a loss of credibility as a moral authority. This corresponds with major shifts in attitudes towards gender and queer rights in the late 20th and early 21st centuries, so that religions are constituted as forces for harm in sexual lives, and religions become dominantly framed as sex-negative. Although the implications of this negativity are well-founded, it can let secular institutions "off the hook", so that emancipatory potential is premised in secular terms. Yet, as the examples of those seeking asylum show, secular institutions too promote harms and injustices to those at the edges of societal belonging. Meanwhile, beyond the West, in other countries historically impacted by colonialism and trying to cultivate new national identities in neo-colonial contexts, the promotion of queer-positive rhetoric is deemed inherently Western, and against the principles of the nation. This generates new discourses aligned with conservatism and buttressed through religious teachings so that queer people living in such contexts are denied a space in the nation state, and are instead subject to harassment, imprisonment, and even death. But religion is a complex resource, and although many examples surface of its alignment with conservative causes, there do remain instances where religious narratives are used to contest the dominant discourses in operation.

# CONCLUSION

## Managing religion and sexualities

The aim of this book has been to provide an assessment on research into religion and sexuality, drawing on our own significant projects. To do this, we have advocated a queer feminist lens, thereby prioritising an understanding of power dynamics and research hierarchies, and the implications for gendered and queer bodies. While maintaining a queer feminist lens as our preferred framing, we have articulated that a number of key conceptual areas significantly assist in understanding the relationship between religion and sexuality, which complement this queer feminist approach.

Firstly, we argue that an embodied approach is important in recognising that real bodies are impacted by the varying discourses that circulate. In some contexts, this puts queer and certain gender bodies in grave peril, such as when the state considers homosexuality an illegal act or when abortion is deemed illicit, or when a trans identity is not accepted – in such cases, trans individuals may be assaulted, and queer people and women seeking abortions may be arrested and imprisoned. In other contexts, legal frameworks have put accommodations in place, though often these too contain their own embedded discriminations. Religions often have something to say in either supporting or contesting state-sanctioned regulation. Bodies are crucial to understanding sexuality and religion – bodies are marked through circumcision for religious ends (Barras and Dabby, 2014), special clothing is utilised to convey sexual modesty (Pedwell, 2011) – and it is real bodies that engage in intimate sexual acts. We have noted how religious discourse has an impact on the levels and types of access people have to contraception and abortion, the extent to which sexual violence and abuse is taken seriously, and whether sexual pleasure is sanctioned. We have examined the extent to which queer bodies come to be accepted or not, and the mechanisms for inclusion and exclusion, such as controversial religiously

**192** Conclusion

sanctioned conversion "therapies" aimed at eradicating homosexual relationships and engagements.

Understanding the emplacement of bodies relates to our second concept, that of space. Bodies occupy spaces, but those spaces are not neutral, nor are they simply "there" to be occupied. Instead, spaces are created; certain bodies are made welcome and are allowed to be deemed in place; other spaces are crafted to exclude other bodies (Puwar, 2004). Whether that be queer bodies, children, women, asylum seekers, or indigenous communities – we have included numerous examples throughout the book of these spatial processes of inclusion and exclusion, such as how whole geographical areas can constitute a total institution, excluding the queer body (e.g. Barton's [2012] work on the Bible Belt and how hostility to queer people is commonplace). Equally, we have noted how certain gender bodies – those displaying a short skirt or a bra strap in church (Moultrie, 2017; Sharma, 2011) are made to feel uncomfortable until those bodies conform to the expected morality standards. While queer-affirming religious spaces may enable broader forms of inclusion, this is not absolute either; even spaces premised on welcoming all may ultimately exclude, such as how trans people and bisexuals have felt marginalised, and where gay men's experiences can take centre stage.

Meanwhile, bodies move through space in a lifecourse pattern, constructed as straight time (Boellstorff, 2007; Wilcox, 2009), and where individuals are expected to follow a typical pattern of getting married and having children. The dominance of straight time is our third concept. Anyone who falls "short" – e.g. having children outside of marriage, not having children within marriage, forming a same-sex partnership, forming a polyamorous relationship, or not wanting to form any sort of sexual relationship – is treated with suspicion and as "against the norm". While religions have typically endorsed the straight time narrative, religious traditions are complex entities, often with various and competing discourses available. For example, there is a strong tradition within Christianity endorsing singleness, thereby giving alternative options (Aune, 2002). Meanwhile, many Buddhist approaches challenge straight time formulations (Page and Yip, 2017b).

The configuration of bodies in space and time indicates a broader organising system, that of heteronormativity, our fourth concept. We have cited many examples in this book where religions have buttressed and supported heteronormative formulations – where heterosexuality is taken as the norm – also highlighting whether the campaigns for same-sex marriage inclusion are also premised on heteronormative lines, and thereby exclude those wanting to practise ethically grounded non-monogamous relationships (Page and Yip, 2017b). The particular emphasis many religious traditions place on marking out marriage and procreation and including them as sacredly endorsed rites of passage means that religions are implicated in heteronormative formulations, which also excludes those who do not want to have children (Llewellyn, 2016) or those who cannot have children (O'Donnell, 2019).

Embedded in all of this is a concern with power and regulation – our fifth conceptual concern. We have utilised Foucault (1976), who, although he did not gender his account in any significant way, is still a highly productive starting point for understanding religion and sexuality (Ramazanoglu, 1993). His notion of power as something that circulates, rather than operating in zero-sum and totalising terms, highlights how discursive techniques can be deployed to help determine the prominent frame of reference. Sexuality is something configured in these discursive techniques, so that sexuality claims, bound up within a particular power–knowledge nexus making certain thoughts and ideas meaningful and believable – become 'powerful sets of assumptions... governing... social and cultural practices' (Baxter, 2003, p. 7). In contemporary configurations of sexuality discourses, biopower comes to the fore, where social institutions make themselves responsible for mapping and monitoring the population. Certain subjects are formulated in the process, where much purchase is placed on one's own responsibilisation (technologies of the self) for complying with the requirements of biopower.

Contemporary discursive formulations also position religion in particular ways. We have noted how religion comes to be considered something that is tradition-bearing, outdated, and opposed to sexuality equalities (Scott, 2018; White, 2016). The configuration of the religious–secular is our sixth conceptual issue, and that the dominant discourse endorsing the secular as the epitome of freedom and sexual liberation while religion positions itself against sexual equality is an erroneous one. We have noted how secular contexts continue to discriminate against queer and gendered bodies, as well as highlighting how, although positioning religion as negative towards sexuality can be justified, this is not the whole story, with religious traditions offering complex and varied repositories for providing alternative and inclusive narratives. The discourse perpetuating the idea of religion as the site of unfreedom, and, conversely, the secular as the site of liberty and freedom, also problematises those who are religious and queer, leading to the oft-heard sentiment – can you even be religious and queer (Page and Yip, forthcoming)? Instead, it is purposeful to interrogate what broader purposes are served by perpetuating this simplistic understanding of religion (Scott, 2018).

This leads nicely to our seventh conceptual issue, regarding how we understand religion. We have put much emphasis on advocating for a lived religion approach, whose starting point is captured by McGuire:

> Scholars of religion, especially sociologists, must reexamine their assumptions about individuals' religious lives. What might we discover if, instead of looking at affiliation or organizational participation, we focused first on individuals, the experiences they consider most important, and the concrete practices that make up their personal religious experience and expression? What if we think of religion, at the individual level, as an ever-changing, multifaceted, often messy—even contradictory—amalgam

**194** Conclusion

of beliefs and practices that are not necessarily those religious institutions consider important?

*(2008, p. 4)*

Lived religion therefore enables us to account for the queer religious person, in their own terms, and understanding their own experience, while also considering this in relation to the broader discursive power dynamics within which their subjectivity is experienced. This bottom-up approach to understanding religion does not foreground the views and perspectives of religious authorities – nor those seeming authoritative texts, but instead refocuses our attention on the meanings and practices generated by individuals themselves, and how this engagement with something called religion is often negotiated in complex ways.

This connects up with our eighth conceptual issue, that of identity. A lived religion approach foregrounds a concern with identity, and how identities are navigated in various ways. For our purposes, our key focus has been the navigation of religious and sexual identities. Although there are many different ways of understanding identities, identities are contextually forged and are often premised on how we "speak" our identities through the narratives and the stories that we tell (Plummer, 1995). We have emphasised that sociologists have often privileged narrativised forms of methods (the speaking subject) in understanding identity, but that other methods can be utilised to emphasise the varying components to identity (such as some forms of visual methods).

Finally, our identities are not evenly experienced, but operate in broader power dynamics, as the above discussion has demonstrated. This leads us to emphasise the importance of intersectional understandings of religion and sexuality (Page and Yip, forthcoming; Young and Shipley, 2020). Intersectionality focuses on identity as mediated through an assemblage of facets, such as class, ethnicity, sexuality, gender, ability, age, and religion. The way in which these facets interact will have a profound impact on one's resulting experience, and the extent to which one is incorporated or denied space. Therefore, intersectionality is a crucial mechanism for moving identity beyond a concern with individual experience to how those experiences collectively forge particular forms of social inequality. This approach deems it as too simplistic to explain inequity in singular terms – e.g. in terms of classism or racism. But instead it recognises how inequalities are forged in mutually constitutive ways, thereby foregrounding complexity (Brah and Phoenix, 2004; Collins and Bilge, 2016; Mirza, 2013).

In conclusion, this book should not be considered the last word on the topic of religion and sexuality. What we have drawn together here relates to our own experience, expertise, and knowledge of the field, but new studies and research findings are emerging all the time, refocusing our analysis over time. There has certainly been a proliferation of studies taking into account religion and sexuality in recent years, but the field is by no means a saturated one (Yip and Page, forthcoming; Young and Shipley, forthcoming). There is far more work to be done and avenues to be explored. We have barely scratched the surface in understanding how trans people are situated in religious discourses. There is very little material on asexuality and bisexuality, with a predominant focus on lesbian and gay sexualities. We also need to be mindful of analysing heterosexuality and how it comes to take dominant forms in religious discourses. Much work we have considered here has focused on Christianity. In our own projects, we have tried to move the focus to include a greater range of religious identities, but there is still so much work to be done in this regard. While an increasing number of studies have started to focus on queer Muslims (Goh, 2018; Hamzić, 2012; Jaspal, 2014; Kugle, 2013; Rahman, 2014; Shah, 2018; Shannahan, 2009; Yip, 2005), it is still the case that the identities of gay men are typically prioritised. There is hardly any material on, for example, Sikh sexualities (though do see Sehmi, 2018). In terms of the lifecourse, far more focus has been placed on young people, religion, and sexuality (Freitas, 2008; Regnerus, 2007; Young and Shipley, 2020; Yip and Page, 2013). More interrogation is needed of mid- and later life, and how sexuality is religiously configured. This also includes a greater understanding of same-sex individuals raising children in religious environments. The geographical expansion of our research investigation is also necessary. So much sexuality and religion research emerges from North America, followed by Western Europe. There are pockets of scholarship broader than this (Amakor, forthcoming; Boellstorff, 2005; Chan and Huang, 2014; Goh, 2018; Jaspal, 2014; Lazzara, forthcoming; Shah, 2018, among others), but further work of this kind is to be strongly welcomed. Equally, more work is needed on how masculinity and sexuality intersect in relation to religion. Finally, we have also highlighted some of the methodological challenges and opportunities in this field, and how innovative methods could be more fruitfully deployed to help us in our investigative endeavours. We consider this book to be part of an ongoing conversation and we are excited regarding where the field will head next.

# BIBLIOGRAPHY

Abbott, D.A. and Dalla, R.L. (2008). "It's a Choice, Simple as That": Youth Reasoning for Sexual Abstinence or Activity. *Journal of Youth Studies*, 11(6): 629–49.

Abbott, E. (2011). *A History of Marriage*. London: Duckworth Overlook.

Adamczyk, A. and Felson, J. (2006). Friends' Religiosity and First Sex. *Social Science Research*, 35(4): 924–47.

Ahmed, L. (1992). *Women and Gender in Islam: Historical Roots of a Modern Debate*. London: Yale University Press.

Ahmed, S. (2004). *The Cultural Politics of Emotion*. Edinburgh: Edinburgh University Press.

Ahmed, S. (2013). Making Feminist Points. https://feministkilljoys.com/2013/09/11/making-feminist-points/. Accessed 05.08.19.

Akin, D. (2017). Queer Asylum Seekers: Translating Sexuality in Norway. *Journal of Ethnic and Migration Studies*, 43(3): 458–74.

Aldridge, A. (1989). Men, Women and Clergymen: Opinion and Authority in a Sacred Organization. *The Sociological Review*, 37(1): 43–64.

Aldridge, J. (2014). Working with Vulnerable Groups in Social Research: Dilemmas by Default and Design. *Qualitative Research*, 14(1): 112–30.

Alpert, R. (2003). Sex in Jewish Law and Culture. In: D.W. Machacek and M.M. Wilcox (Eds.), *Sexuality and the World's Religions*. Santa Barbara, CA: ABC-CLIO: 177–202.

Althaus-Reid, M. (2003). *The Queer God*. London: Routledge.

Amakor, G.O. (2019). Unmarried Young Mothers in South-Eastern Nigeria: Attitudes and Experiences. Unpublished PhD. Birmingham: Aston University.

Amakor, G.O. (forthcoming). Contraceptive Use by Young Unmarried Mothers in Nigeria: An Intersectional Analysis. In: S. Page and A.K.T. Yip (Eds.), *Intersecting Religion and Sexuality: Sociological Perspectives*. Leiden: Brill.

Ammerman, N.T. (2014). *Sacred Stories, Spiritual Tribes: Finding Religion in Everyday Life*. Oxford: OUP.

Ammerman, N.T. and Williams, R.R. (2012). Speaking of Methods: Eliciting Religious Narratives through Interviews, Photos, and Oral Diaries. *Annual Review of the Sociology of Religion*, 3(3): 117–34.

Anderson, E. and McCormack, M. (2016). *The Changing Dynamics of Bisexual Men's Lives: Social Research Perspectives*. Basel: Springer.

Apetrei, S. (2010). *Women, Feminism and Religion in Early Enlightenment England*. Cambridge: Cambridge University Press.

AP News. (2018). New Kansas Law Allows Agencies to Refuse LGBT Adoptions. May 18, 2018. https://www.apnews.com/27fde90b032e4ddab2b05bfe622fa22a. Accessed 01.29.19.

Archer, L.S. (1990). In Thy Blood Live: Gender and Ritual in the Judaeo-Christian Tradition. In: A. Joseph (Ed.), *Through the Devil's Gateway: Women, Religion and Taboo*. London: SPCK: 22–49.

Asad, T. (2003). *Formations of the Secular: Christianity, Islam, Modernity*. Stanford: Stanford University Press.

Attwood, F. (2009). Introduction: The Sexualization of Culture. In: F. Attwood (Ed.), *Mainstreaming Sex: The Sexualization of Western Culture*. London: I.B. Tauris: xiii–xxiv.

Aune, K. (2002). *Single Women: Challenge to the Church?* Carlisle: Paternoster Press.

Aune, K., Sharma, S. and Vincett, G. (Eds.), (2008). *Women and Religion in the West: Challenging Secularization*. Farnham: Ashgate.

Avishai, O. (2008). "Doing Religion" in: A Secular World: Women in Conservative Religions and the Question of Agency. *Gender and Society*, 22(4): 409–33.

Avishai, O. (2012). Contesting Sex-Restrictive Sexual Narratives from Within: Jewish Laws of Menstrual Purity and Orthodox Sexual Anxieties. In: S. Hunt and A.K.T. Yip (Eds.), *The Ashgate Research Companion to Contemporary Religion and Sexuality*. Farnham: Ashgate: 275–88.

Bagnoli, A. (2009). Beyond the Standard Interview: The Use of Graphic Elicitation and Arts-Based Methods. *Qualitative Research*, 9(5): 547–70.

Barnard, I. (2004). *Queer Race: Cultural Interventions in the Racial Politics of Queer Theory*. New York: Peter Lang.

Barras, A. and Dabby, D. (2014). Only Skin Deep: Revising the Secular Narrative through Circumcision. In: H. Shipley (Ed.), *Globalized Religion and Sexual Identity: Contexts, Contestations, Voices*. Leiden: Brill: 86–106.

Barrett-Fox, R. and Yip, A.K.T. (forthcoming). Crosses and Crossroads: American Conservative Christianity's Anti-Intersectionality Discourse and the Erasure of LGBTQ+ Believers'. In: S. Page and A.K.T. Yip (Eds.), *Intersecting Religion and Sexuality: Sociological Perspectives*. Leiden: Brill. Page numbers forthcoming.

Bartkowski, J.P. (2002). Breaking Walls, Raising Fences: Masculinity, Intimacy, and Accountability among the Promise Keepers. In: C.L. Williams and A. Stein (Eds.), *Sexuality and Gender*. Oxford: Blackwell Publishers: 259–70.

Barton, B. (2012). *Pray the Gay Away: The Extraordinary Lives of Bible Belt Gays*. New York: New York University Press.

Baxter, J. (2003). *Positioning Gender in Discourse: A Feminist Methodology*. Basingstoke: Palgrave Macmillan.

Beaman, L.G. (2002). Aboriginal Spirituality and the Legal Construction of Freedom of Religion. *Journal of Church and State*, 44(1): 135–49.

Beardsley, C. (2015). Unacknowledged Shamans? On Revisiting Camille Paglia's Suggestion That Modern Transsexual People Should Resort to Poets Rather than to Surgeons: Religion, Spirituality and Trans People's Wellbeing. *Variant Sex and Gender, Religion and Wellbeing Conference*, 19th June, University Of Exeter.

Bearman, P. and Brückner, H. (2001). Promising the Future: Virginity Pledges and First Intercourse. *Journal of American Sociology*, 106(4): 859–912.

**198** Bibliography

Beattie, T. (2004). Religious Identity and the Ethics of Representation: The Study of Religion and Gender in the Secular Academy. In: U. King and T. Beattie (Eds.), *Gender, Religion and Diversity: Cross-Cultural Perspectives.* London: Continuum: 65–78.

Beckford, J.A. (2003). *Social Theory and Religion.* Cambridge: Cambridge University Press.

Begun, S. and Walls, N.E. (2015). Pedestal or Gutter: Exploring Ambivalent Sexism's Relationship with Abortion Attitudes. *Affilia*, 30(2): 200–15.

Bernhardt-House, P.A. (2012). Reinforcing Binaries, Downgrading Passions: Bisexual Invisibility in Mainstream Queer Christian Theology. In: L. Hutchins and H.S. Williams (Eds.), *Sexuality, Religion and the Sacred: Bisexual, Pansexual and Polysexual Perspectives.* Abingdon: Routledge: 22–31.

Berry, D. (2004). Internet Research: Privacy, Ethics and Alienation: An Open Source Approach. *Internet Research*, 14(4): 323–32.

Bethmont, R. (2019). Blessing Same-Sex Unions in the Church of England: The Liturgical Challenge of Same-Sex Couples' Demand for Equal Marriage Rites. *Journal of Anglican Studies*, 17(2): 148–67.

Bevir, M. (1999). Foucault, Power and Institutions. *Political Studies*, XLVII(2): 345–59.

Beyer, P.F. (2008). From Far and Wide: Canadian Religious and Cultural Diversity in Global/Local Context. In: L.G. Beaman and P. Beyer (Eds.), *Religion and Diversity in Canada.* Leiden: Brill Academic Press: 9–40.

Beyer, P.F. and Ramji, R. (2013). *Growing Up Canadian: Muslims, Hindus, Buddhists.* Montreal and Kingston: McGill-Queen's University Press.

Bloom, T. (2017). Members of Colonised Groups, Statelessness and the Right to Have Rights. In: T. Bloom, K. Tonkiss and P. Cole (Eds.), *Understanding Statelessness.* Abingdon: Routledge: 153–72.

Blyth, C. (2018). Sticks and Stones: Anti-Trans Discourses and Conservative Christianity. *New Zealand Association for the Study of Religions*, 29th–30th November, University of Auckland,.

Blyth, C., Colgan, E. and Edwards, K.B. (Eds.), (2018a), *Rape Culture, Gender Violence, and Religion: Christian Perspectives.* Cham: Palgrave MacMillan.

Blyth, C., Colgan, E. and Edwards, K.B. (Eds.), (2018b). *Rape Culture, Gender Violence, and Religion: Biblical Perspectives.* Cham: Palgrave MacMillan.

Blyth, C., Colgan, E. and Edwards, K.B. (Eds.), (2018c). *Rape Culture, Gender Violence, and Religion: Interdisciplinary Perspectives.* Cham: Palgrave MacMillan.

Bock, E.W. (1967). The Female Clergy: A Case of Professional Marginality. *The American Journal of Sociology*, 72(5): 531–9.

Boellstorff, T. (2005). *The Gay Archipelago: Sexuality and Nation in Indonesia.* Princeton, NJ: Princeton University Press.

Boellstorff, T. (2007). When Marriage Falls: Queer Coincidences in Straight Time. *A Journal of Lesbian and Gay Studies*, 13(2–3): 227–48.

Boellstorff, T. (2012). Some Notes on New Frontiers of Sexuality and Globalisation. In: P. Aggleton, P. Boyce, H. Moore and R. Parker (Eds.), *Understanding Global Sexualities: New Frontiers.* London: Routledge: 171–85.

Bompani, B. (2016). 'For God and for My Country': Pentecostal-Charismatic Churches and the Framing of a New Political Discourse in Uganda. In: A. Van Klinken and E. Chitando (Eds.), *Public Religion and the Politics of Homosexuality in Africa.* London: Routledge: 19–34.

Boswell, J. (1980). *Christianity, Social Tolerance and Homosexuality: Gay People in Western Europe from the Beginning of the Christian Era to the Fourteenth Century.* Chicago, IL: University of Chicago Press.

## Bibliography  199

Bowie, F. (2000). *The Anthropology of Religion: An Introduction*. Oxford: Blackwell.

Brah, A. and Phoenix, A. (2004). Ain't I a Woman? Revisiting Intersectionality. *Journal of International Women's Studies*, 5(3): 75–86.

Braidotti, R. (2008). In Spite of the Times: The Postsecular Turn in Feminism. *Theory, Culture and Society*, 25(6): 1–24.

Braidotti, R. (2011). *Nomadic Subjects: Embodiment and Sexual Difference in Contemporary Feminist Theory*. New York: Columbia University Press.

Brasher, B.E. (1997). My Beloved is All Radiant: Two Case Studies of Congregational-Based Christian Fundamentalist Female Enclaves and the Religious Experiences they Cultivate Among Women. *Review of Religious Research*, 38(3): 231–46.

Brintnall, K.L. (2016). Introduction: Embodied Religion. In: K.L. Brintnall (Ed.), *Religion: Embodied Religion*. Farmington Hills, MI: MacMillan Reference USA: xv–xxxi.

Brison, S.J. (1999). Trauma Narratives and the Remaking of the Self. In: M. Bal, J. Crewe and L. Spitzer (Eds.), *Acts of Memory: Cultural Recall in the Present*. Hanover: Dartmouth College: 39–54.

Brittain, C.C. and McKinnon, A. (2011). Homosexuality and the Construction of "Anglican Orthodoxy": The Symbolic Politics of the Anglican Communion. *Sociology of Religion*, 72(3): 351–73.

Brotman, S. and Ryan, B. (2004). An Intersectional Approach to Queer Health Policy and Practice: Two-Spirit People in Canada. In: J.A. Rummens (Ed.). *Intersections of Diversity*, 3(1): 4–30. Montreal: Association for Canadian Studies.

Brown, A. and Woodhead, L. (2016). *That Was the Church That Was*. London: Bloomsbury.

Brown, C., Costley, C., Friend, L. and Varey, R. (2010). Capturing Their Dream: Video Diaries and Minority Consumers. *Consumption Markets and Culture*, 13(2): 419–36.

Brown, C.G. (2001). *The Death of Christian Britain: Understanding Secularisation 1800–2000*. London: Routledge.

Browne, K. (2010). Queer Spiritual Spaces: Conclusion. In: K. Browne, S.R. Munt and A.K.T. Yip (Eds.), *Queer Spiritual Spaces: Sexuality and Sacred Places*. Farnham: Ashgate.

Browne, K. (2016). Queer Quantification or Queer(y)ing Quantification. In: K. Browne and C.J. Nash (Eds.), *Queer Methods and Methodologies: Intersecting Queer Theories and Social Science Research*. London: Routledge: 231–49.

Browne, K., Munt, S.R. and Yip, A.K.T. (Eds.), (2010). *Queer Spiritual Spaces: Sexuality and Sacred Places*. Farnham: Ashgate.

Browne, K. and Nash, C.J. (2016). Queer Methods and Methodologies. In: K. Browne and C.J. Nash (Eds.), *Queer Methods and Methodologies: Intersecting Queer Theories and Social Science Research*. London: Routledge: 1–23.

Bruce, S. (2003). *Politics and Religion*. Cambridge: Polity Press.

Bryman, A. (2004). *Social Research Methods*, 2nd edition. Oxford: Oxford University Press.

Bryman, A. (2012). *Social Research Methods*, 4th edition. Oxford: Oxford University Press.

Burke, K. (2016). *Christians Under Covers: Evangelicals and Sexual Pleasure on the Internet*. Oakland, CA: University of California Press.

Butler, J. (1990). *Gender Trouble: Feminism and the Subversion of Identity*. New York: Routledge.

Butler, J. (1993). *Bodies That Matter: On the Discursive Limits of "Sex"*. New York: Routledge.

Cahill, C. (2007). Including Excluded Perspectives in Participatory Action Research. *Design Studies*, 28(3): 325–40.

**200** Bibliography

Calder, G. (2014). Conclusion: "To the Exclusion of All Others"– Polygamy, Monogamy, and the Legal Family in Canada. In: G. Calder and L.G. Beaman (Eds.), *Polygamy's Rights and Wrongs*. Vancouver: UBC Press: 215–33.

Campbell, A. (2014). Plus Ça Change? In: G. Calder and L.G. Beaman (Eds.), *Polygamy's Rights and Wrongs*. Vancouver: UBC Press: 21–45.

Carillo, H. and Hoffman, A. (2018). Straight with a Pinch of Bi: The Construction of Heterosexuality as an Elastic Category among Adult US Men. *Sexualities*, 21(1–2): 90–108.

Carpenter, L.M. (2005). *Virginity Lost: An Intimate Portrayal of First Sexual Experiences*. New York: New York University Press.

Carpenter, L.M. (2010). Gendered Sexuality Over the Life Course: A Conceptual Framework. *Sociological Perspectives*, 53(2): 155–78.

Carrette, J. and King, R. (2005). *Selling Spirituality: The Silent Takeover of Religion*. London: Routledge.

Carter, S. (2008). *The Importance of Being Monogamous: Marriage and Nation Building in Western Canada to 1915*. Alberta: University of Alberta Press.

Casanova, J. (1994). *Public Religions in the Modern World*. Chicago, IL: University of Chicago Press.

Cavanagh, S.L. (2007). *Sexing the Teacher: School Sex Scandals and Queer Pedagogies*. Vancouver: UBC Press.

Chan, S.H. and Huang, P. (2014). Religion and Homosexuality in Contemporary China: Debates, Identity and Voices. In: H. Shipley (Ed.), *Globalized Religion and Sexual Identity: Contexts, Contestations, Voices*. Leiden: Brill: 170–92.

Cheruvallil-Contractor, S.M. (2016). Motherhood as Constructed by Us: Muslim Women's Negotiations from a Space That Is Their Own. *Religion and Gender*, 6(1): 9–28.

Chinwuba, N. (2014). 'They Go Burn in Hell!' Exploring How African MSM Negotiate Religion and Sexuality in Canada. In: H. Shipley (Ed.), *Globalized Religion and Sexuality: Contexts, Contestations, Voices*. Leiden: Brill: 256–75.

Church of England. (1991). *Issues in Human Sexuality*. London: Church House Publishing.

Clegg, S.R. (2006). Why is Organization Theory So Ignorant? The Neglect of Total Institutions. *Journal of Management Inquiry*, 15(4): 426–30.

Clements, B. (2015). *Religion and Public Opinion in Britain: Continuity and Change*. New York: Palgrave MacMillan.

Cockburn, C. (1991). *In the Way of Women: Men's Resistance to Sex Equality in Organizations*. Basingstoke: Macmillan Education.

Cokely, C.L. (2005). Someday My Prince Will Come: Disney, the Heterosexual Imaginary and Animated Film. In: C. Ingraham (Ed.), *Thinking Straight: The Power, the Promise, and the Paradox of Heterosexuality*. London: Routledge: 167–81.

Colgan, E. (2018). Let Him Romance You: Rape Culture and Gender Violence in Evangelical Christian Self-Help Literature. In: C. Blyth, E. Colgan and K.B. Edwards (Eds.), *Rape Culture, Gender Violence, and Religion: Christian Perspectives*. Cham: Palgrave MacMillan: 9–26.

Collins, P.H. and Bilge, S. (2016). *Intersectionality*. Cambridge: Polity Press.

Combahee River Collection. (1977). A Black Feminist Statement. In: B. Guy-Sheftall (Ed.), *Words of Fire: An Anthology of African-American Feminist Thought*. New York: The New Press: 232–40.

Cornwall, S.M. (2013). *Theology and Sexuality*. Norwich: SCM Press.

Cornwall, S.M. (2019). Healthcare Chaplaincy and Spiritual Care for Trans People: Envisaging the Future. *Health and Social Care Chaplaincy*, 7(1): 8–27.

Corriveau, P. (2011). *Judging Homosexuals: A History of Gay Persecution in Quebec and France*. Vancouver: UBC Press.

Cossman, B. (2007). *Sexual Citizens: The Legal and Cultural Regulation of Sex and Belonging.* Redwood City, CA: Stanford University Press.

Cossman, B. and Ryder, B. (2001). What Is Marriage-Like Like? The Irrelevance of Conjugality. *Journal of Family Law*, 18(2): 269–326.

Creek, S.J. (2014). Mindful of the Words Spoken: The Shifting Narratives and Identity Work of Former Ex-gays. In: Y. Taylor and R. Snowdon (Eds.), *Queering Religion, Religious Queers*. London: Routledge: 137–56.

Crenshaw, K. (1989). Demarginalizing the Intersection of Race and Sex: A Black Feminist Critique of Antidiscrimination Doctrine, Feminist Theory and Antiracist Politics. *University of Chicago Legal Forum*, 1(8): 139–67.

Cuthbert, K. and Taylor, Y. (2018). Queer Liveability: Inclusive Church-Scenes. *Sexualities*, 22(5–6): 951–68.

Daniels, B. (2016). Queer Theory. In: K.L. Brintnall (Ed.), *Religion: Embodied Religion*. Farmington Hills, MI: MacMillan: 289–308.

Daniels, M. (2012). Not Even on the Page: Freeing God from Heterocentrism. In: L. Hutchins and H.S. Williams (Eds.), *Sexuality, Religion and the Sacred: Bisexual, Pansexual and Polysexual Perspectives*. Abingdon: Routledge: 12–21.

Davidman, L. (1991). *Tradition in a Rootless World: Women Turn to Orthodox Judaism*. London: University of California Press.

Davie, G. (2007). *The Sociology of Religion: A Critical Agenda*. London: Sage.

Davie, G. and Starkey, C. (2019). The Lincoln Letters: A Study in Institutional Change. *Ecclesial Practices*, 6(1): 44–64.

Davies, D. (2011). *Emotion, Identity and Religion: Hope, Reciprocity, and Otherness*. Oxford: Oxford University Press.

Davies, D. and Guest, M. (2007). *Bishops, Wives and Children: Spiritual Capital Across the Generations*. Aldershot: Ashgate.

Day, A. (2011). *Believing in Belonging: Belief and Social Identity in the Modern World*. Oxford: Oxford University Press.

Day, A. and Lee, L. (2014). Making Sense of Surveys and Censuses: Issues in Religious Self-Identification. *Religion*, 44(3): 345–56.

D'Costa, G. (2007). Queer Trinity. In: G. Loughlin (Ed.), *Queer Theology: Rethinking the Western Body*. Malden, MA: Blackwell Publishing: 269–79.

Deifelt, W. (2005). Beyond Compulsory Motherhood. In: P.B. Jung, M.E. Hunt and R. Balakrishnan (Eds.), *Good Sex: Feminist Perspectives from the World's Religions*. London: Rutgers University Press: 96–112.

Delaney, J., Lupton, M.J. and Toth, E. (1988). *The Curse: A Cultural History of Menstruation*, 2nd edition. Chicago, IL: University of Illinois Press.

Delap, L. and Morgan, S. (2013). Introduction: Men, Masculinities and Religious Change in Post-Christian Britain. In: L. Delap and S. Morgan (Eds.), *Men, Masculinities and Religious Change in Twentieth-Century Britain*. Basingstoke: Palgrave MacMillan: 1–29.

Delgado, T. (2015). Beyond Procreativity: Heterosexuals Queering Marriage. In: K.T. Talvacchia, M.F. Pettinger and M. Larrimore, (Eds.), *Queer Christianities: Lived Religion in Transgressive Forms*. New York: New York University Press: 91–102.

Denzin, N.K. and Lincoln, Y.S. (2011). *The Sage Handbook of Qualitative Research*. London: Sage.

DeRogatis, A. (2015). *Saving Sex: Sexuality and Salvation in American Evangelicalism*. Oxford: Oxford University Press.

## 202 Bibliography

Detamore, M. (2016). Queer(y)ing the Ethics of Research Methods. In: K. Browne and C.J. Nash (Eds.), *Queer Methods and Methodologies: Intersecting Queer Theories and Social Science Research.* London: Routledge: 167–82.

De Zordo, S., Mishtal, J. and Anton, L. (2017). Introduction. In: S. De Zordo, J. Mishtal and L. Anton (Eds.), *A Fragmented Landscape: Abortion Governance and Protest Logics in Europe.* New York: Berghahn: 1–19.

Dialmy, A. (2010). Sexuality and Islam. *The European Journal of Contraception and Reproductive Health Care*, 15(3): 160–8.

Diamond, L.M. (2003). Was it a Phase? Young Women's Relinquishment of Lesbian/Bisexual Identities over a 5-year Period. *Journal of Personality and Social Psychology*, 84(2): 352–64.

Douglas, M. (1966). *Purity and Danger: An Analysis of Concept of Pollution and Taboo.* Abingdon: Routledge.

Dudink, S. (2016). A Queer Nodal Point: Homosexuality in Dutch Debates on Islam and Multiculturalism. *Sexualities*, 20(1–2): 3–23.

Duggan, L. (2002). The New Homonormativity: The Sexual Politics of Neoliberalism. In: R. Castronovo and D.D. Nelson (Eds.), *Materializing Democracy: Toward a Revitalized Cultural Politics.* Durham: Duke University Press: 175–94.

Duggan, L. (2003). *The Twilight of Equality? Neoliberalism, Cultural Politics, and the Attack on Democracy.* Boston, MA: Beacon Press.

Duits, L. and Van Zoonen, L. (2006). Headscarves and Porno-chic: Disciplining Girls' Bodies in the European Cultural Society. *European Journal of Women's Studies*, 13(2): 103–17.

Eisner, E. (2008). Art and Knowledge. In: J.G. Knowles and A.L. Cole (Eds.), *Handbook of the Arts in Qualitative Research: Perspectives, Methodologies, Examples, and Issues.* London: Sage: 71–81.

Elliott, R. and Jankel-Elliott, N. (2003). Using Ethnography in Strategic Consumer Research. *Qualitative Market Research: An International Journal*, 6(4): 215–23.

Epstein, D., O'Flynn, S. and Telford, D. (2003). *Silenced Sexualities in Schools and Universities.* Stoke on Trent: Trentham Books.

Ezzy, D. (2014). *Sex, Death and Witchcraft: A Contemporary Pagan Festival.* London: Bloomsbury.

Fallon, B. (2018). Violence of Mind, Body and Spirit: Spiritual and Religious Responses Triggered by Sexual Violence During the Rwandan Genocide. In: C. Blyth, E. Colgan and K.B. Edwards (Eds.), *Rape Culture, Gender Violence, and Religion: Interdisciplinary Perspectives.* Cham: Palgrave MacMillan: 71–86.

Fernando, M. (2017). Intimacy Surveilled: Religion, Sex, and Secular Cunning. In: D.L. Boisvert and C. Daniel-Hughes (Eds.), *The Bloomsbury Reader in Religion, Sexuality, and Gender.* London: Bloomsbury: 231–39.

Fielder, B. and Ezzy, D. (2018). *Lesbian, Gay, Bisexual and Transgender Christians: Queer Christians, Authentic Selves.* London: Bloomsbury.

Finch, J. (1993). 'It's Great to Have Someone to Talk to'. Ethics and Politics of Interviewing Women. In: M. Hammersley (Ed.), *Social Research - Philosophy, Politics and Practice.* London: Sage: 166–80.

Fone, B. (2000). *Homophobia: A History.* New York: Picador.

Forna, A. (1998). *Mother of All Myths: How Society Moulds and Constrains Mothers.* London: HarperCollins.

Foucault, M. (1976). *The History of Sexuality: I.* London: Penguin Books.

Freitas, D. (2008). *Sex and the Soul: Juggling Sexuality, Spirituality, Romance and Religion on America's College Campuses.* Oxford: Oxford University Press.

# Bibliography 203

Friedman, M.S., Marshal, M.P., Guadamuz, T.E., Wei, C., Wong, C.F., Saewyc, E.M. and Stall, R. (2011). A Meta-analysis of Disparities in Childhood Sexual Abuse, Parental Physical Abuse, and Peer Victimization among Sexual Minority and Sexual Nonminority Individuals. *American Journal of Public Health*, 101(8): 1481–94.

Fumia, D. (2007). 'I. Do' Belong in Canada. In D. Cheal (Ed.), *Canadian Families Today: New Perspectives*. Don Mills: Oxford University Press: 177–93.

Furlong, M. (1984). Introduction: Feminine in the Church. In: M. Furlong (Ed.), *Feminine in the Church*. London: SPCK: 1–10.

Furlong, M. (1988). Introduction to Mirror to the Church: Reflections on Sexism. In: M. Furlong (Ed.), *Mirror to the Church: Reflections on Sexism*. London: SPCK: 1–16.

Gaddini, K. (forthcoming). Practising Purity: How Single Evangelical Women Negotiate Sexuality. In: S. Page and A.K.T. Yip (Eds.), *Intersecting Religion and Sexuality: Sociological Perspectives*. Leiden: Brill.

Gahan, L. (2016). 'I Will Be Married in the Eyes of God': Religious Same-Sex Attracted Young People Reimagining their Future. In: S. Sharma and D. Llewellyn (Eds.), *Religion, Equalities and Inequalities*. Farnham: Routledge: 198–209.

Gandhi, K. (2015). Here's Why I Ran the London Marathon on the First Day of My Period – and Chose Not to Wear a Tampon. *Independent*, August 14, 2015. https://www.independent.co.uk/voices/comment/heres-why-i-ran-the-london-marathon-on-the-first-day-of-my-period-and-chose-not-to-wear-a-tampon-10455176.html. Accessed 24.01.19.

Geertz, C. (1993). *The Interpretations of Cultures*. London: Fontana Press.

Geiringer, D. (2019). *The Pope and the Pill: Sex, Catholicism and Women in Post-War England*. Manchester: Manchester University Press.

Gerhards, J. (2010). Non-Discrimination Towards Homosexuality: The European Union's Policy and Citizens' Attitudes Towards Homosexuality in 27 European Countries. *International Sociology*, 25: 5–28.

Gibb, M. (2017). *The Independent Peter Ball Review: An Abuse of Faith*. https://www.churchofengland.org/more/safeguarding/safeguarding-news-statements/independent-report-churchs-handling-peter-ball-case. Accessed 25.05.19.

Giddens, A. (1991). *Modernity and Self-Identity: Self and Society in the Late Modern Age*. Cambridge: Polity Press.

Giddens, A. (1992). *The Transformation of Intimacy: Sexuality, Love, and Eroticism in Modern Societies*. Cambridge: Polity Press.

Gill, S. (1994). *Women and the Church of England: From the Eighteenth Century to the Present*. London: SPCK.

Gleason, M. (1999). *Normalizing the Ideal: Psychology, Schooling, and the Family in Postwar Canada*. Toronto: University of Toronto Press.

Gleig, A. (2012). Queering Buddhism or Buddhist De-Queering? Reflecting on Differences Amongst Western LGBTQI Buddhists and the Limits of Liberal Convert Buddhism. *Theology and Sexuality*, 18(3): 198–214.

Gleig, A. (2019). *American Dharma: Buddhism beyond Modernity*. New Haven, CT: Yale University Press.

Goddard, A. (2015). Theology and Practice in Evangelical Churches. In: A. Thatcher (Ed.), *The Oxford Handbook of Theology, Sexuality, and Gender*. Oxford: Oxford University Press: 377–94.

Goffman, E. (1959). *The Presentation of Self in Everyday Life*. London: Penguin Books.

Goffman, E. (1961). *Asylums: Essays on the Social Situation of Mental Patients and Other Inmates*. London: Penguin Books.

**204** Bibliography

Goffman, E. (1963). *Stigma: Notes on the Management of Spoiled Identity.* London: Penguin Books.

Goh, J. (2018). *Living Out Sexuality and Faith: Body Admissions of Malaysian Gay and Bisexual Men.* London: Routledge.

Goldenberg, N. (2007). What's God Got to Do with It?- A Call for Problematizing Basic Terms in the Feminist Analysis of Religion. *Feminist Theology*, 15(3): 275–88.

Gorman-Murray, A., Johnston, L. and Waitt, G. (2016). Queer(Ing) Communication in Research Relationships. In: K. Browne and C.J. Nash (Eds.), *Queer Methods and Methodologies: Intersecting Queer Theories and Social Science Research.* London: Routledge: 97–112.

Gott, C. (2018). Unfit for Education, Fit for Work: Magdalene Laundries within the Irish Educational System. *Sociology of Religion Study Group Annual Conference: Religion and Education*, 10th–12th July, University of Strathclyde.

Gray, E.R. and Thumma, S. (2005a). Introduction. In: S. Thumma and E.R. Gray (Eds.), *Gay Religion.* Walnut Creek, CA: Altamira: xi–xvi.

Gray, E.R. and Thumma, S. (2005b). The Gospel Hour: Liminality, Identity, and Religion in a Gay Bar. In: S. Thumma and E.R. Gray (Eds.), *Gay Religion.* Walnut Creek, CA: Altamira: 285–301.

Graybill, B. and Arthur, L.B. (1999). The Social Control of Women's Bodies in Two Mennonite Communities. In: L.B. Arthur (Ed.), *Religion, Dress and the Body.* Oxford: Berg: 9–30.

Green, A.I. (2010). Queer Unions: Same-Sex Spouses Marrying Tradition and Innovation. *Canadian Journal of Sociology*, 35(3): 399–436.

Greenough, C. (2018). Visual Intimacies: Faith, Sexuality, Photography. *Sexuality and Culture*, 22(4): 1516–26.

Greil, A.L. and Davidman, L. (2007). Religion and Identity. In: J.A. Beckford and N.J. Demerath III (Eds.), *The SAGE Handbook of the Sociology of Religion.* London: Sage: 549–65.

Griffith, R.M. (1997). *God's Daughters: Evangelical Women and the Power of Submission.* London: University of California Press.

Grosz, E. (2005). *Time Travels: Feminism, Nature, Power.* Durham, NC: Duke University Press.

Guest, M., Olson, E. and Wolffe, J. (2012). Christianity: Loss of Monopoly. In: L. Woodhead and R. Catto (Eds.), *Religion and Change in Modern Britain.* London: Routledge: 57–78.

Guillemin, M. (2004). Understanding Illness: Using Drawings as a Research Method. *Qualitative Health Research*, 14(2): 272–89.

Hall, D. (forthcoming). Geographical Mobility, Sexual Identities and Personal Stories: Complexities of LGBT Christians' Activism in Poland. In: S. Page and A.K.T. Yip (Eds.), *Intersecting Religion and Sexuality: Sociological Perspectives.* Leiden: Brill.

Hall, K.D. (2002). *Lives in Transition: Sikh Youth as British Citizens.* Philadelphia, PA: University of Pennsylvania Press.

Hall, S. (1980). Encoding/Decoding. In: S. Hall (Ed.), *Culture, Media, Language: Working Papers in Cultural Studies, 1972-79.* London: Hutchinson: 128–38.

Halperin, D. (1995). *Saint Foucault: Towards a Gay Hagiography.* Oxford: Oxford University Press.

*Halpern v. Canada (AG)*, [2003] O.J. No. 2268.

Halstead, P. (2018). There Are No Winners Here: A Pastor's Response to Date Rape in the Church. In: C. Blyth, E. Colgan and K.B. Edwards (Eds.), *Rape Culture, Gender Violence, and Religion: Christian Perspectives.* Cham: Palgrave MacMillan: 177–94.

Hammers, C. and Brown III, A.D. (2004). Towards a Feminist-Queer Alliance: A Paradigmatic Shift in the Research Process. *Social Epistemology*, 18(1): 85–101.

Hampshire, K.R., Blell, M.T. and Simpson, B. (2012). 'Everybody is Moving on': Infertility, Relationality and the Aesthetics of Family among British-Pakistani Muslims. *Social Science and Medicine*, 74(7): 1045–52.

Hamzić, V. (2012). The Resistance from an Alterspace: Pakistani and Indonesian Muslims beyond the Dominant Sexual and Gender Norms. In: P. Nynäs and A.K.T. Yip (Eds.), *Religion, Gender and Sexuality in Everyday Life*. Farnham: Ashgate: 17–35.

Hanemann, R.W. (2016). Educating Catholics for a Liberal Society: An Ethnographic Study of Religious Transmission. Unpublished PhD. Canterbury: University of Kent.

Harley, D.A. (2016). The Role of Religious and Faith Communities in Addressing the Needs of LGBT Elders. In: D.A. Harley and P.B. Teaster (Eds.), *Handbook of LGBT Elders*. New York: Springer: 525–44.

Harley, D.A., Gassaway, L. and Dunkley, L. (2016). Isolation, Socialization, Recreation, and Inclusion of LGBT Elders. In: D.A. Harley and P.B. Teaster (Eds.), *Handbook of LGBT Elders*. New York: Springer: 563–81.

Harvey, G. (2013). *Food, Sex and Strangers: Understanding Religion as Everyday Life*. Durham, NC: Acumen.

Harvey, L. and Gill, R. (2011). Spicing It Up: Sexual Entrepreneurs and the Sex Inspectors. In: R. Gill and C. Scharff (Eds.), *New Femininities: Postfeminism, Neoliberalism and Subjectivity*. Basingstoke: Palgrave Macmillan: 52–67.

Hastrup, K. (1993). The Semantics of Biology: Virginity. In: S. Ardener (Ed.), *Defining Females: The Nature of Women in Society*. Oxford: Berg: 34–50.

Heckert, J. (2016). Intimacy with Strangers/Intimacy with Self. In: K. Browne. and C.J. Nash (Eds.), *Queer Methods and Methodologies: Intersecting Queer Theories and Social Science Research*. London: Routledge: 41–53.

Heelas, P. and Woodhead, L. (2005). *The Spiritual Revolution: Why Religion is Giving Way to Spirituality*. Oxford: Blackwell Publishing.

Helmick, R.G. (2014). *The Crisis of Confidence in the Catholic Church*. London: Bloomsbury.

Helminiak, D. (2000). *What the Bible Really Says about Homosexuality*. Alamo, TX: Alamo Square Press.

Hesse-Biber, S.N. (2007). The Practice of Feminist In-Depth Interviewing. In: S.N. Hesse-Biber and P.L. Leavy (Eds.), *Feminist Research Practice: A Primer*. London: Routledge: 111–48.

Heyes, J. (2019). Postsecular RSE? Reimagining the Relationship between Sexuality Education and Religion. *Statutory Relationships and Sex Education: Issues of Cultural and Moral Diversity, British Educational Research Association Conference*, 28th June, University of Birmingham.

Hidayatullah, A. (2003). Islamic Conceptions of Sexuality. In: D.W. Machacek and M.M. Wilcox (Eds.), *Sexuality and the World's Religions*. Santa Barbara, CA: ABC-CLIO: 255–92.

Hin, L.W. (2015). "I'm Not Homophobic, I'm Chinese": Hong Kong Canadian Christians and the Campaign against Same-Sex Marriage. In: P.D. Young, H. Shipley and T.J. Trothen (Eds.), *Religion and Sexuality: Diversity and the Limits of Tolerance*. Vancouver: UBC Press: 67–92.

Hines, S. (2012). Stirring It Up – Again: A Politics of Difference in the New Millennium. In: S. Hines and Y. Taylor (Eds.), *Sexualities: Past Reflections, Future Directions*. New York: Palgrave MacMillan: 186–205.

**206** Bibliography

Hobbs, V. (2018). Rape Culture in Sermons on Divorce. In: C. Blyth, E. Colgan and K.B. Edwards (Eds.), *Rape Culture, Gender Violence, and Religion: Interdisciplinary Perspectives*. Cham: Palgrave MacMillan: 87–110.

Hogan, L. (2015). Conflicts within the Roman Catholic Church. In: A. Thatcher (Ed.), *The Oxford Handbook of Theology, Sexuality, and Gender*. Oxford: Oxford University Press: 323–39.

Holland, J., Ramazanoglu, C., Sharpe, S. and Thomson, R. (1998). *The Male in the Head: Young People, Heterosexuality and Power*, 2nd edition. London: The Tufnell Press.

Hooghe, M., Claes, E., Harell, A., Quintelier, E. and Dejaeghere, Y. (2010). Anti-Gay Sentiment among Adolescents in Belgium and Canada: A Comparative Investigation into the Role of Gender and Religion. *Journal of Homosexuality*, 57(3): 384–400.

Hooghe, M. and Meeusen, C. (2013). Is Same-Sex Marriage Legislation Related to Attitudes Toward Homosexuality? Trends in Tolerance of Homosexuality in European Countries Between 2002 and 2010. *Sexuality Research and Social Policy*, 10(4): 258–68.

hooks, b. (2000). *Feminist Theory: From Margin to Center*. London: Pluto Press.

Hookway, N. (2008). Entering the Blogosphere: Some Strategies for Using Blogs in Social Research. *Qualitative Research*, 8(1): 91–113.

Hornsby-Smith, M.P. (1987). *Roman Catholics in England*. Cambridge: Cambridge University Press.

Howson, A. (2005). *Embodying Gender*. London: Sage.

Hunt, S. (2010). *The Library of Essays on Sexuality and Religion: Judaism and Islam*. Aldershot: Ashgate.

Hunt, S.J. and Yip, A.K.T. (Eds.), (2012). *The Ashgate Research Companion to Contemporary Religion and Sexuality*. Farnham: Ashgate.

Ibbitson, J. (2018). LBGTQ Seniors Fear Renewed Discrimination in Long-Term Care. *Globe and Mail*. https://www.theglobeandmail.com/politics/article-lgbtq-seniors-fe ar-renewed-discrimination-in-long-term-care/. Accessed 23.03.19.

Independent Inquiry into Child Sexual Abuse (IICSA) (2018). *Child Sexual Abuse in the Anglican Church*. https://www.iicsa.org.uk/investigations/investigation-into-failin gs-by-the-anglican-church. Accessed 25.01.19.

Imtoual, A. and Hussein, S. (2009). Challenging the Myth of the Happy Celibate: Muslim Women Negotiating Contemporary Relationships. *Contemporary Islam*, 3(1): 25–39.

Ingraham, C. (1999). *White Weddings: Romancing Heterosexuality in Popular Culture*. London: Routledge.

Isherwood, L. (2007). *The Fat Jesus: Feminist Explorations in Boundaries and Transgressions*. London: Darton, Longman and Todd.

Isherwood, L. and Stuart, E. (1998). *Introducing Body Theology*. Sheffield: Sheffield Academic Press.

Jackson, S. (2006). Gender, Sexuality and Heterosexuality: The Complexity (and Limits) of Heteronormativity. *Feminist Theory*, 7(1): 105–21.

Jackson, S., Jieyu, L. and Juhyun, W. (Eds.), (2008). *East Asian Sexualities: Modernity, Gender and New Sexual Cultures*. London: Zed Books.

Jackson, S. and Scott, S. (2002). Introduction: The Gendering of Sociology. In: S. Jackson and S. Scott (Eds.), *Gender: A Sociological Reader*. London: Routledge: 1–26.

Jackson, S. and Scott, S. (2010). *Theorizing Sexuality*. Maidenhead: Open University Press.

Jackson, S. and Scott, S. (2013). Childhood. In: G. Payne (Ed.), *Social Divisions*, third edition. Basingstoke: Palgrave Macmillan: 164–81.

Jakobsen, J.R. and Pellegrini, A. (2004). *Love the Sin: Sexual Regulation and the Limits of Religious Tolerance*. Boston, MA: Beacon Press.

Bibliography **207**

Jakobsen, J.R. and Pellegrini, A. (Eds.), (2008). *Secularisms*. Durham, NC: Duke University Press.

Jamieson, L. (2002). Intimacy Transformed? A Critical Look at the 'Pure Relationship'. In: C.L. Williams and A. Stein (Eds.), *Sexuality and Gender*. Oxford: Blackwell Publishers: 456–67.

Jantzen, G.M. (2005). Good Sex: Beyond Private Pleasure. In: P.B. Young, M.E. Hunt and R. Balakrishnan (Eds.), *Good Sex: Feminist Perspectives from the World's Religions*. London: Rutgers University Press: 3–19.

Jaspal, R. (2012). 'I Never Faced Up To Being Gay': Sexual, Religious and Ethnic Identities among British Indian and British Pakistani Gay Men. *Culture, Health and Sexuality: An International Journal for Research, Intervention and Care*, 14(7): 767–80.

Jaspal, R. (2014). Sexuality, Migration and Identity among Gay Iranian Migrants to the UK. In: Y. Taylor and R. Snowdon (Eds.), *Queering Religion, Religious Queers*. London: Routledge: 44–60.

Johnson, E.A. (1992). *She Who Is: The Mystery of God in Feminist Theological Discourse*. New York: Crossroad Publishing Company.

Johnson, P., Vanderbeck, R. and Falcetta, S. (2017). *Religious Marriage of Same-Sex Couples: A Report on Places of Worship in England and Wales Registered for the Solemnization of Same-Sex Marriages*, SSRN. https://ssrn.com/abstract=3076841 Accessed 1.08.19.

Jordan, M.D. (1997). *The Invention of Sodomy in Christian Theology*. Chicago, IL: University of Chicago Press.

Jordan, M.D. (2000). *Homosexuality in Modern Catholicism: The Silence of Sodom*. Chicago, IL: University of Chicago Press.

Jordan, M.D. (2011). *Recruiting Young Love: How Christians Talk about Homosexuality*. Chicago, IL: University of Chicago Press.

Jordan, M.D. (2015). *Convulsing Bodies: Religion and Resistance in Foucault*. Stanford: Stanford University Press.

Joy, M. (2017). Women's Journeys in the Study of Religion: Adventures in Gender, Postmodernism, Postcolonialism and Globalization. *Journal of the British Association for the Study of Religions*, 19: 55–73.

Jung, P.B. (2005). Sanctifying Women's Pleasure. In: P.B. Jung, M.E. Hunt and R. Balakrishnan (Eds.), *Good Sex: Feminist Perspectives from the World's Religions*. London: Rutgers University Press: 77–95.

Jung, P.B., Hunt, M.E. and Balakrishnan, R. (Eds.), (2005). *Good Sex: Feminist Perspectives from the World's Religions*. London: Rutgers University Press.

Kamitsuka, M.D. (2015). Sexual Pleasure. In: A. Thatcher (Ed.), *The Oxford Handbook of Theology, Sexuality, and Gender*. Oxford: Oxford University Press: 505–22.

Keenan, Marie (2012). *Child Sexual Abuse and the Catholic Church: Gender, Power, and Organizational Culture*. Oxford: Oxford University Press.

Keenan, Michael (2006). *Fishers of Men: An Exploration of the Identity Negotiations of Gay Male Anglican Clergy*. Unpublished. PhD, Nottingham: Nottingham Trent University.

Keenan, Michael (2009). The Gift (?) that Dare Not Speak its Name: Exploring the Influence of Sexuality on the Professional Performances of Gay Male Anglican Clergy. In: S.J. Hunt (Ed.), *Contemporary Christianity and LGBT Sexualities*. Farnham: Ashgate: 23–37.

Kilmer, J.J. (2014). Reconceiving and Recontextualizing Religious Identity: Lesbian Mothers and Transracial Adoption. In: Y. Taylor and R. Snowdon (Eds.) *Queering Religion, Religious Queers*. London: Routledge: 269–85.

King, A. (2016a). Troubling Identities? Examining Older Lesbian, Gay and Bisexual People's Membership Categorisation Work and its Significance. In: E. Peel and R.

## 208 Bibliography

Harding (Eds.), *Ageing & Sexualities: Interdisciplinary Perspectives*. Farnham: Ashgate: 163–82.

King, A. (2016b). Queer Categories: Queer(y)ing the Identification 'Older Lesbian, Gay and/or Bisexual (LGB) Adults' and its Implications for Organizational Research, Policy and Practice. *Gender, Work and Organization*, 23(1): 7–18.

King, M., Semylen, J., See Tai, S., Killaspy, H., Osborn, D., Popelyuk, D. and Nazareth, I. (2008). A Systematic Review of Mental Disorder, Suicide, and Deliberate Self Harm in Lesbian, Gay, and Bisexual People. *Biomedical Central Psychiatry*, 8(7): 1–17.

Kinsey, A. (1998a). *Sexual Behavior in the Human Male*. Philadelphia, PA: Saunders.

Kinsey, A. (1998b). *Sexual Behavior in the Human Female*. Philadelphia, PA: Saunders.

Kinsman, G.W. (1996). *The Regulation of Desire: Homo and Hetero Sexualities*. Montréal: Black Rose Books.

Kitzinger, J. (1995). Introducing Focus Groups. *British Medical Journal*, 311(7000): 299–302.

Klesse, C. (2007). *The Spectre of Promiscuity: Gay Male and Bisexual Non-Monogamies and Polyamories*. Aldershot: Ashgate.

Knott, K. (2005). *The Location of Religion: A Spatial Analysis*. London: Equinox.

Koenig, H.G., King, D.E. and Carson, V.B. (2001). *Handbook of Religion and Health*. Oxford/New York: Oxford University Press.

Kolysh, S. (2017). Straight Gods, White Devils: Exploring Paths to Non-Religion in the Lives of Black LGBTQ People. *Secularism and Nonreligion*, 6(2): 1–13.

Koralewska, I. (2018). Lessons on Abortion: The Roman Catholic Church vs. Individual Experiences – A Case Study of Polish Religious Women Who Performed Abortion. *Sociology of Religion Study Group Annual Conference: Religion and in Education*, 10th–12th July, University of Strathclyde.

Kugle, S. (2013). *Living Out Islam: Voices of Gay, Lesbian, and Transgender Muslims*. New York: NYU Press.

Lalich, J. and McLaren, K. (2010). Inside and Outcast: Multifaceted Stigma and Redemption in the Lives of Gay and Lesbian Jehovah's Witnesses. *Journal of Homosexuality*, 57(10): 1303–33.

Lawler, S. (2002). Narrative in Social Research. In: T. May (Ed.), *Qualitative Research in Action*. London: Sage: 242–58.

Lawler, S. (2008). *Identity: Sociological Perspectives*. Cambridge: Polity Press.

Lazzara, M. (forthcoming). Our Lives from a Different Perspective: How Chinese and Taiwanese Gay and Lesbian Individuals and their Parents Navigate Confucian Beliefs. In: S. Page and A.K.T. Yip (Eds.), *Intersecting Religion and Sexuality: Sociological Perspectives*. Leiden: Brill.

Letherby, G. (2003). *Feminist Research in Theory and Practice*. Buckingham: Open University Press.

Levy, D. and Lo, J. (2013). Transgender, Transsexual, and Gender Queer Individuals with a Christian Upbringing: The Process of Resolving Conflict between Gender Identity and Faith. *Journal of Religion & Spirituality*, 32(1): 60–83.

Lewis, R. (2015). *Muslim Fashion: Contemporary Style Cultures*. Durham: Duke University Press.

Lewis, R.A. (2014). 'Gay? Prove It': The Politics of Queer Anti-deportation Activism. *Sexualities*, 17(18): 958–75.

Llewellyn, D. (2016). Maternal Silences: Motherhood and Voluntary Childlessness in Contemporary Christianity. *Religion and Gender*, 6(1): 64–79.

Lofton, K. (2016). Religion and Sexuality. In: K.L. Brintnall (Ed.), *Religion: Embodied Religion*. Farmington Hills, MI: MacMillan: 19–34.

Bibliography **209**

Loughlin, G. (2007). Omphalos. In: G. Loughlin (Ed.), *Queer Theology: Rethinking the Western Body*. Malden, MA: Blackwell Publishing: 115–27.

Lowe, P. (2016). *Reproductive Health and Maternal Sacrifice: Women, Choice and Responsibility*. London: Palgrave MacMillan.

Lowe, P. and Hayes, G.A. (2019). Anti-Abortion Clinic Activism, Civil Inattention, and the Problem of Gendered Harassment. *Sociology*, 53(2): 330–46.

Lowe, P. and Page, S. (2019). On the Wet Side of the Womb: The Construction of Mothers in Anti-Abortion Activism in England and Wales. *European Journal of Women's Studies*, 26(2): 165–80.

Lowe, P. and Page, S. (forthcoming). *Anti-Abortion Activism in the UK: Understanding Religion, Gender and Reproductive Rights in the Public Sphere*. Bradford: Emerald.

Luddy, M. (2011). Unmarried Mothers in Ireland, 1880–1973. *Women's History Review*, 20(1): 109–26.

Lune, H. (2010). *Understanding Organizations*. Cambridge: Polity Press.

Lupton, D. (2013). *The Social Worlds of the Unborn*. Basingstoke: Palgrave.

Lynch, G. (2016). *Remembering Child Migration: Faith, Nation-Building and the Wounds of Charity*. London: Bloomsbury.

Lynch, G. (forthcoming). 'To See A Sinner Repent is a Joyful Thing': Moral Cultures and the Sexual Abuse of Children in the Christian Church. In: A. Strhan, D. Hennig and J. Robbins (Eds.), *The Social Life of Ethics: Ethical Life Between Social Theory and Philosophy*. London: Bloomsbury.

MacDougall, B. and Short, D. (2010). Religion-based Claims for Impinging on Queer Citizenship. *Dalhousie Law Journal*, 33(2): 133–60.

Macke, K.E. (2014). Que(e)rying Methodology to Study Church-Based Activism: Conversations in Culture, Power, and Change. In: Y. Taylor and R. Snowdon (Eds.), *Queering Religion, Religious Queers*. London: Routledge: 13–30.

Maguire, H., McCartan, A., Nash, C.J. and Browne, K. (2018). The Enduring Field: Exploring Researcher Emotions in Covert Research with Antagonistic Organisations. *Area*, 51(2): 299–306.

Mahmood, S. (2005). *Politics of Piety: The Islamic Revival and the Feminist Subject*. Princeton, NJ: Princeton University Press.

Mahmood, S. (2011). Religion, Feminism, and Empire: The New Ambassadors of Islamophobia. In: L.M. Alcoff and J.D. Caputo (Eds.), *Feminism, Sexuality, and the Return of Religion*. Bloomington, IN: Indiana University Press: 77–102.

Marchal, J.A. (2016). Trans ★ and Intersex Studies. In: K.L. Brintnall (Ed.), *Religion: Embodied Religion*. Farmington Hills, MI: MacMillan Reference USA: 309–24.

Masci, D. (2018). American Religious Groups Vary Widely in Their Views of Abortion. http://www.pewresearch.org/fact-tank/2018/01/22/american-religious-groups-vary-widely-in-their-views-of-abortion/. Accessed 25.01.18.

McCabe, J. (2013). Tea with Mother: Sarah Palin and the Discourse of Motherhood as a Political Ideal. *Imaginations*, 4(2): 70–90.

McClintock, A. (1995). *Imperial Leather: Race, Gender and Sexuality in the Colonial Contest*. New York: Routledge.

McCormick, L. (2005). Sinister Sisters? The Portrayal of Ireland's Magdalene Asylums in Popular Culture. *Popular Culture, Cultural and Social History*, 2(3): 373–79.

McGarry, M. (2008). 'The Quick, the Dead, and the Yet Unborn': Untimely Sexualities and Secular Hauntings. In: J.R. Jakobsen and A. Pellegrini (Eds.), *Secularisms*. Durham: Duke University Press: 247–79.

McGuire, M.B. (1990). Religion and the Body: Rematerializing the Human Body in the Social Sciences of Religion. *Journal for the Scientific Study of Religion*, 29(3): 283–96.

**210** Bibliography

McGuire, M.B. (2008). *Lived Religion: Faith and Practice in Everyday Life*. Oxford: Oxford University Press.

McKenzie, L. (2015). *Getting By: Estates, Class and Culture in Austerity Britain*. Bristol: Policy Press.

McKinnon, A. (2017). Socrel Member Interview, *Socrel News Issue 5*. https://www.britsoc.co.uk/media/24597/socrelnews-issue-5.pdf. Accessed 12.10.18. .

McKinnon, A. and Brittain, C.C. (forthcoming) Anglican Disputes over Sexuality in the Intersection of Global Power Relations: Accounts from African Church Leaders. In: S. Page and A.K.T. Yip (Eds.), *Intersecting Religion and Sexuality: Sociological Perspectives*. Leiden: Brill.

McKinnon, A. and Trzebiatowska, M. (2014). Introduction: Thinking Theoretically in the Sociology of Religion. In: A. McKinnon and M. Trzebiatowska (Eds.), *Sociological Theory and the Question of Religion*. Burlington, NJ: Ashgate: 1–18.

McLaughlin, J., Casey, M.E. and Richardson, D. (2006). Introduction: At the Intersection of Feminist and Queer Debates. In: D. Richardson, J. McLaughlin and M.E. Casey (Eds.), *Intersections between Feminist and Queer Theory*. Cham: Palgrave MacMillan: 1–18.

McLelland, M. (2005). Inside Out: Queer Theory and Popular Culture. *Musicological Society of Australia National Workshop Proceedings: Aesthetics and Experience in Music Performance*, Cambridge Scholars Press: 268–81.

McLeod, H. (2007). *The Religious Crisis of the 1960s*. Oxford: Oxford University Press.

McPhillips, K. (2018). The Royal Commission Investigates Child Sexual Abuse: Uncovering Cultures of Sexual Violence in the Catholic Church. In: C. Blyth, E. Colgan and K.B. Edwards (Eds.), *Rape Culture, Gender Violence, and Religion: Christian Perspectives*. Cham: Palgrave MacMillan: 53–71.

Mellor, P.A. and Shilling, C. (1997). *Re-Forming the Body: Religion, Community and Modernity*. London: Sage.

Mellor, P.A. and Shilling, C. (2014). *Sociology of the Sacred: Religion, Embodiment and Social Change*. London: Sage.

Mendos, L.R. (2019). State-Sponsored Homophobia, ILGA Report. https://ilga.org/downloads/ILGA_Sexual_Orientation_Laws_Map_2019.pdf. Accessed 21.05.08.

Menendez, A.J. (1996). *Church and State in Canada*. Amherst, NY: Prometheus Books.

Mies, M. (1993). Towards a Methodology for Feminist Research In: M. Hammersley (Ed.), *Social Research - Philosophy, Politics and Practice*. London: Sage: 64–82.

Miller, P. (2014). *Good Catholics: The Battle over Abortion in the Catholic Church*. London: University of California Press.

Millman, M. and Kanter, R.M. (1987). Introduction to Another Voice: Feminist Perspectives on Social Life and Social Science. In: S. Harding (Ed.), *Feminism and Methodology*. Milton Keynes: Open University Press: 29–36.

Mirza, H.S. (2013). 'A Second Skin': Embodied Intersectionality, Transnationalism and Narratives of Identity and Belonging among Muslim Women in Britain. *Women's Studies International Forum*, 26: 5–15.

Mishtal, J. (2015). *The Politics of Morality: The Church, the State, and Reproductive Rights in Postsocialist Poland*. Athens, OH: Ohio University Press.

Mishtal, J. (2017). Quietly 'Beating the System': The Logics of Protest and Resistance under the Polish Abortion Ban. In: S. De Zordo, J. Mishtal and L. Anton (Eds.), *A Fragmented Landscape: Abortion Governance and Protest Logics in Europe*. New York: Berghahn: 226–44.

Mizock, L. and Mueser, K.T. (2014). Employment, Mental Health, Internalized Stigma, and Coping with Transphobia among Transgender Individuals. *Psychology of Sexual Orientation and Gender Diversity*, 1(2): 146–58.

Monro, S. (2015). *Bisexuality: Identities, Politics, and Theories*. London: Palgrave Macmillan.

Monture-Angus, P. (1995). *Thunder in My Soul: A Mohawk Woman Speaks*. Winnipeg: Fernwood Publishing.

Morrow, V. (1998). If You Were a Teacher, It Would Be Harder to Talk to You: Reflections on Qualitative Research with Children in School. *International Journal of Social Research Methodology: Theory and Practice*, 1(4): 297–313.

Moultrie, M. (2017). *Passionate and Pious: Religious Media and Black Women's Sexuality*. Durham and London: Duke University Press.

Muhammad, N.A., Shamsuddin, K., Sulaiman, Z., Amin, R.M. and Omar, K. (2017). Role of Religion in Preventing Youth Sexual Activity in Malaysia: A Mixed Methods Study. *Journal of Religion and Health*, 56(6): 1916–29.

Munson, Z.W. (2002). *The Making of Pro-Life Activists*. London: University of Chicago Press.

Munt, S.R. (2010). Queer Spiritual Spaces. In: K. Browne, S.R. Munt and A.K.T. Yip (Eds.), *Queer Spiritual Spaces: Sexuality and Sacred Places*. Farnham: Ashgate: 1–33.

Mustanski, B.S., Garofalo, R. and Emerson, E.M. (2010). Mental Health Disorders, Psychological Distress, and Suicidality in a Diverse Sample of Lesbian, Gay, Bisexual and Transgender Youths. *American Journal of Public Health*, 100(12): 2426–32.

Mutler, A. (2019). Same-Sex Couples in Romania Face Hostility as They Challenge Discrimination, RadioFreeEurope. https://www.rferl.org/a/same-sex-couples-in-romania-face-hostility-as-they-challenge-discrimination/30057755.html. Accessed 02.09.2019.

Namaste, K. (1994). The Politics of Inside/Out: Queer Theory, Poststructuralism, and a Sociological Approach to Sexuality. *Sociological Theory*, 12(2): 220–31.

Nash, C.J. (2016). Queer Conversations. In: K. Browne and C.J. Nash (Eds.), *Queer Methods and Methodologies: Intersecting Queer Theories and Social Science Research*. London: Routledge: 129–42.

Nason-Clark, N., Fisher-Townsend, B., Holtmann, C. and McMullin, S. (2018). *Religion and Intimate Partner Violence: Understanding the Challenges and Proposing Solutions*. Oxford: Oxford University Press.

Ndjio, B. (2013). Sexuality and Nationalist Ideologies in Post-Colonial Cameroon. In: S. Wieringa and H. Sivori (Eds.), *The Sexual History of the Global South: Sexual Politics in Africa, Asia, and Latin America*. London: Zed Books: 120–43.

Neitz, M.J. (2000). Queering the Dragonfest: Changing Sexualities in a Post-Patriarchal Religion. *Sociology of Religion*, 61(4): 369–91.

Neitz, M.J. (2003). Dis/location: Engaging Feminist Inquiry in the Sociology of Religion. In: M. Dillon (Ed.), *Handbook of the Sociology of Religion*. Cambridge: Cambridge University Press: 276–93.

O'Brien, M. (1981). *The Politics of Reproduction*. London: Routledge.

O'Donnell, K. (2019). Reproductive Loss: Toward a Theology of Bodies. *Theology and Sexuality*, 25(1–2): 146–59.

O'Donohue, W. and Caselles, C.E. (1993). Homophobia: Conceptual, Definitional, and Value Issues. *Journal of Psychopathology and Behavioral Assessment*, 15(3): 177–95.

O'Rand, A.M. (1996). The Cumulative Stratification of the Life Course. In: R.H. Binstock and L.K. George (Eds.), *Handbook of Aging and the Social Sciences*. San Diego, CA: Academic Press: 188–207.

O'Reilly, J.T. and Chalmers, M.S.P. (2014). *The Clergy Sex Abuse Crisis and the Legal Responses*. Oxford: Oxford University Press.

Oakley, A. (1981). Interviewing Women: A Contradiction in Terms In: H. Roberts (Ed.), *Doing Feminist Research*. London: Routledge: 30–61.

## 212 Bibliography

Orel, N.A. (2014). Investigating the Needs and Concerns of Lesbian, Gay, Bisexual, and Transgender Older Adults: The Use of Qualitative and Quantitative Methodology. *Journal of Homosexuality*, 61(1): 53–78.

Orsi, R. (2007). *Between Heaven and Earth: The Religious Worlds People Make and the Scholars Who Study Them*. Princeton, NJ: Princeton University Press.

Page, S. (2010). *Femininities and Masculinities in the Church of England: A Study of Priests as Mothers and Male Clergy Spouses*. Unpublished PhD. Nottingham: University of Nottingham.

Page, S. (2011). Negotiating Sacred Roles: A Sociological Exploration of Priests Who Are Mothers. *Feminist Review*, 97(1): 92–109.

Page, S. (2012). Femmes, Mères et Prêtres dans l'Église d'Angleterre: Quels Sacerdoces. *Travail, Genre et Sociétés*, 27(1): 55–71.

Page, S. (2013). Feminist Faith Lives? Exploring Perceptions of Feminism among Two Anglican Cohorts. In: N. Slee, F. Porter and A. Phillips (Eds.), *The Faith Lives of Women and Girls: Qualitative Research Perspectives*. Farnham: Ashgate: 51–63.

Page, S. (2014a). Sexuality and Christianity: Understanding the Attitudes and Negotiations of Young Adults in the UK. In: G. Vincett and E. Obinna (Eds.), *Christianity in the Modern World: Changes and Controversies*. Farnham: Ashgate: 95–118.

Page, S. (2014b). The Scrutinised Priest: Women in the Church of England Negotiating Professional and Sacred Clothing Regimes. *Gender, Work and Organization*, 21(4): 295–307.

Page, S. (2015). Sex Talk: Discussion and Meaning-Making among Religious Young Adults. In: M.K. Smith, N. Stanton and T. Wylie (Eds.), *Youth Work and Faith: Debates, Delights and Dilemmas*. Lyme Regis: Russell House: 70–84.

Page, S. (2016a). Counter-Normative Identities: Religious Young Adults Subverting Sexual Norms. In: F. Stella, Y. Taylor, T. Reynolds and A. Rogers (Eds.), *Sexuality, Citizenship and Belonging: Trans-National and Intersectional Perspectives*. London: Routledge: 199–217.

Page, S. (2016b). Navigating Equality: Religious Young Women's Perceptions of Gender and Sexuality Equality. In: L. Gemzöe, M. Keinänen and A. Maddrell (Eds.), *Contemporary Encounters in Gender and Religion*. Basingstoke: Palgrave: 131–50.

Page, S. (2016c). Double Scrutiny at the Vicarage: Clergy Mothers, Expectations and the Public Gaze. In: V. Reimer (Ed.), *Angels on Earth: Mothering, Religion and Spirituality*. Bradford, Canada: Demeter Press: 17–38.

Page, S. (2017a). Lived Religion and Sexuality: Future Directions. In: L. Doggett and A. Arat (Eds.), *Foundations and Futures in the Sociology of Religion*. London: Routledge: 83–98.

Page, S. (2017b). Exploring Young Adults' Faith Lives through Video Diaries: Consent, Voice and Power. In: N. Slee, F. Porter and A. Phillips (Eds.), *Researching Female Faith: Qualitative Research Methods*. London: Routledge: 98–112.

Page, S. (2017c). Anglican Clergy Husbands Securing Middle-Class Gendered Privilege through Religion. *Sociological Research Online*, 22(1). http://www.socresonline.org.uk /22/1/10.html. Accessed 20.12.2017.

Page, S. (2018). Religion, Attitudes to Abortion, and Women's Embodied Rights. *The 24th Nordic Conference in the Sociology of Religion*, 1st–3rd August, University of Oslo.

Page, S. (2019). The Independent Inquiry into Child Sexual Abuse (IICSA) and the Church of England: Denials, Apologies and Accountability in a Sacred Institution. *Australian Association for the Study of Religion*, 5th–6th December, University of Newcastle, Australia.

Page, S. (forthcoming). Religion and Intimate Life: Marriage, Family, Sexuality. In: E. Tomalin and C. Starkey (Eds.), *Religions, Gender and Society*. London: Routledge.

# Bibliography    213

Page, S. and Yip, A.K.T. (2012a). Hindu, Muslim and Sikh Young Adults: Gendered Practices in the Negotiation of Sexuality and Relationship. In: P. Nynäs and A.K.T. Yip (Eds.), *Religion, Gender and Sexuality in Everyday Life*. Farnham: Ashgate: 51–69.

Page, S. and Yip, A.K.T. (2012b). Religious Young Adults Recounting the Past: Narrating Sexual and Religious Cultures in School. *Journal of Beliefs and Values*, 33(3): 405–15.

Page, S. and Yip, A.K.T. (2017a). Gender Equality and Religion: A Multi-Faith Exploration of Young Adults' Narratives. *European Journal of Women's Studies*, 24(3): 249–65.

Page, S. and Yip, A.K.T. (2017b). *Understanding Young Buddhists: Living Out Ethical Journeys*. Leiden: Brill.

Page, S. and Yip, A.K.T. (2019). The Gendering of Heterosexual Religious Young Adults' Imagined Futures. *Journal of Contemporary Religion*, 34(2): 253–73.

Page, S. and Yip, A.K.T. (forthcoming). Intersecting Religion and Sexuality: Contributing to an Unfinished Conversation. In: S. Page and A.K.T. Yip (Eds.), *Intersecting Religion and Sexuality: Sociological Perspectives*. Leiden: Brill.

Page, S., Yip, A.K.T. and Keenan, Michael. (2012). Risk and the Imagined Future: Young Adults Negotiating Religious and Sexual Identities. In: S. Hunt and A.K.T. Yip (Eds.), *The Ashgate Research Companion to Contemporary Religion and Sexuality*. Farnham: Ashgate: 255–70.

Pargament, K.I. (1997). *The Psychology of Religion and Coping: Theory, Research, Practice*. New York/London: Guilford Press.

Parveen, N. (2019). Birmingham Anti-LGBT Protestors Banned from School by Injunction. *The Guardian*, June 11, 2019. https://www.theguardian.com/uk-news /2019/jun/11/birmingham-anti-lgbt-protesters-banned-school-injunction. Accessed 21.09.19.

Pateman, C. (1988). *The Sexual Contract*. Cambridge: Polity.

Paul, L. (1973). *A Church by Daylight*. London: Geoffrey Chapman.

Peart, A. (2008). Women and Ministry within the British Unitarian Movement. In: I. Jones, K. Thorpe and J. Wootton (Eds.), *Women and Ordination in the Christian Churches: International Perspectives*. London: Continuum: 102–12.

Pedwell, C. (2011). The Limits of Cross-Cultural Analogy: Muslim Veiling and 'Western' Fashion and Beauty Practices. In: R. Gill and C. Scharff (Eds.), *New Femininities: Postfeminism, Neoliberalism and Subjectivity*. Basingstoke: Palgrave Macmillan: 188–99.

Pells, K. (2012). 'Rights are Everything We Don't Have': Clashing Conceptions of Vulnerability and Agency in the Daily Lives of Rwandan Children and Youth. *Children's Geographies*, 10(4): 427–40.

Perry, S. (2019). *Addicted to Lust: Pornography in the Lives of Conservative Protestants*. Oxford: Oxford University Press.

Pew Research Centre. (2014). Global Morality. https://www.pewresearch.org/global/ interactives/global-morality/. Accessed 17.03.2018.

Peyton, N. and Gatrell, C. (2013). *Managing Clergy Lives: Obedience, Sacrifice, Intimacy*. London: Bloomsbury.

Pilcher, K. (2016). *Erotic Performance and Spectatorship: New Frontiers in Erotic Dance*. London: Routledge.

Pilcher, K. (forthcoming). Living an "Orgasmic" Life: The Spiritual and Religious Journeys of Practitioners of Orgasmic Meditation. In: S. Page and K. Pilcher (Eds.), *Embodying Religion, Gender and Sexualities*. London: Routledge.

Plummer, K. (1995). *Telling Sexual Stories: Power, Change and Social Worlds*. London: Routledge.

Plummer, K. (2003). *Intimate Citizenship: Private Decisions and Public Dialogue*. Montreal: McGill-Queen's University Press.

**214** Bibliography

Power, K. (2014). Talking Sexuality: Religious Identity Construction in Rural Canada. In: H. Shipley (Ed.), *Globalized Religion and Sexuality: Contexts, Contestations, Voices.* Leiden: Brill Academic Press: 62–85.

Primiano, L.N. (2005). The Gay God of the City: The Emergence of the Gay and Lesbian Ethnic Parish. In: S. Thumma and E.R. Gray (Eds.), *Gay Religion.* Walnut Creek, CA: Altamira: 7–29.

Puar, J.K. (2007). *Terrorist Assemblages: Homonationalism in Queer Times.* Durham: Duke University Press.

Puwar, N. (2004). *Space Invaders: Race, Gender and Bodies Out of Place.* Oxford: Berg.

Rahman, M. (2014). *Homosexualities, Muslim Cultures and Modernity.* Basingstoke: Palgrave MacMillan.

Rahman, M. and Jackson, S. (2010). *Gender and Sexuality: Sociological Approaches.* Cambridge: Polity Press.

Ramazanoglu, C. (1993). Introduction: Up Against Foucault - Explorations of Some Tensions Between Foucault and Feminism. In: C. Ramazanoglu (Ed.), *Up Against Foucault - Explorations of Some Tensions Between Foucault and Feminism.* London: Routledge: 1–25.

Ramazanoglu, C. and Holland, J. (2002). *Feminist Methodology: Challenges and Choices.* London: Sage Publications.

Raphael, M. (1996). *Thealogy and Embodiment: The Post-Patriarchal Reconstruction of Female Sacrality.* Sheffield: Sheffield Academic Press.

Raphael, M. (1999). *Introducing Thealogy: Discourse on the Goddess.* Sheffield: Sheffield Academic Press.

Rasmussen, M.L. (2004). Safety and Subversion: The Production of Sexualities and Genders in School Spaces. In: M.L. Rasmussen, E. Rofes and S. Talfurt (Eds.), *Youth and Sexualities: Pleasure, Subversion and Insubordination in and Out of Schools.* Basingstoke: Palgrave MacMillan: 131–52.

Rasmussen, M.L. and Leahy, D. (2018). Young People, Publics, and Counterpublics in School-Based Education on Gender and Sexuality: An Australian Story. In: S. Talburt (Ed.), *Youth Sexualities: Public Feelings and Contemporary Cultural Politics.* Santa Barbara, CA: Praeger Publishers: 61–81.

Reeves, S., Kuper, A. and Hodges, B.D. (2008). Qualitative Research Methodologies: Ethnography. *British Medical Journal,* 337(7668): 512–14.

Regnerus, M.D. (2007). *Forbidden Fruit: Sex and Religion in the Lives of American Teenagers.* Oxford: Oxford University Press.

Rehaag, S. (2010). Bisexuals Need Not Apply: A Comparative Appraisal of Refugee Law and Policy in Canada, the United States, and Australia. *The International Journal of Human Rights,* 13(2–3): 415–36.

Remafedi, G., Farrow, J.A. and Deisher, R.W. (1991). Risk Factors for Attempted Suicide in Gay and Bisexual Youth. *Pediatrics,* 87(6): 869–75.

Rich, A. (1980). Compulsory Heterosexuality and Lesbian Existence. *Signs,* 5(4): 631–60.

Richardson, D. (2018). *Sexuality and Citizenship.* Cambridge: Polity Press.

Richardson, D. and Monro, S. (2012). *Sexuality, Equality and Diversity.* Basingstoke: Palgrave MacMillan.

Robinson, J. (2009). *Bluestockings.* London: Penguin Books.

Rosenfeld, D. (2009). Heteronormativity and Homonormativity as Practical and Moral Resources: The Case of Lesbian and Gay Elders. *Gender and Society,* 23(5): 617–38.

Rubin, G. (1993). Thinking Sex: Notes for a Radical Theory of the Politics of Sexuality. In: H. Abelove, M.A. Barale and D. Halperin (Eds.), *The Lesbian and Gay Studies Reader.* New York: Routledge: 143–79.

## Bibliography 215

Rundall, E. and Vecchietti, V. (2010). (In)Visibility in the Workplace: The Experiences of Trans-Employees in the UK. In: S. Hines and T. Sanger (Eds.), *Transgender Identities: Toward a Social Analysis of Gender Diversity*. London: Routledge: 127–52.

SAGE (Services & Advocacy for GLBT Elders). (2014). *Out & Visible: The Experiences and Attitudes of Lesbian, Gay, Bisexual and Transgender Older Adults, Ages: 45–75*. www.sageusa.org/resource-posts/out-visible-the-experiences-and-attitudes-of-lesbian-gay-bisexual-and-transgender-older-adults-ages-45-75-by-the-numbers-full-report/. Accessed 19.03.2019.

Savage, S., Collins-Mayo, S., Mayo, B. and Cray, G. (2006). *Making Sense of Generation Y: The World View of 15–25 Year Olds*. London: Church House Publishing.

Scharff, C. (2012). *Repudiating Feminism: Young Women in a Neoliberal World*. Farnham: Ashgate.

Scherrer, K.S. (2008). Coming to an Asexual Identity: Negotiating Identity, Negotiating Desire. *Sexualities*, 11(5): 621–41.

Schnoor, R.E. (2003). *Finding One's Place: Ethnic Identity Construction among Gay Jewish Men*. Unpublished PhD. Montreal: McGill University.

Schoeffel, P., Boodoosingh, R. and Percival, G.S. (2018). It's All About Eve: Women's Attitudes to Gender-Based Violence in Samoa. In: C. Blyth, E. Colgan and K.B. Edwards (Eds.), *Rape Culture, Gender Violence, and Religion: Interdisciplinary Perspectives*. Cham: Palgrave MacMillan: 9–31.

Schwartz, L. (2010a). The Bible and the Cause: Freethinking Feminists vs Christianity, England, 1870–1900. *Women: A Cultural Review*, 21(3): 266–78.

Schwartz, L. (2010b). Freethought, Free Love and Feminism: Secularist Debates on Marriage and Sexual Morality, England c. 1850–1885. *Women's History Review*, 19(5): 775–93.

Scott, J.W. (2018). *Sex and Secularism*. Princeton, NJ: Princeton University Press.

Scott, S. and Dawson, M. (2015). Rethinking Asexuality: A Symbolic Interactionist Perspective. *Sexualities*, 18(1/2): 3–19.

Sedgwick, E.K. (2008). *Epistemology of the Closet*, 2nd edition. Berkeley, CA: University of California Press.

Sehmi, M.S. (2018). British Asian Sikh Attitudes towards the Sikh LGBT Community and the Anand Karaj (Wedding Ceremony). *Contemporary Sikhism, CCISC event held at Aston University*, 9th March, Birmingham.

Selby, J.A. (2014). Polygamy in the Parisian Banlieues. In: G. Calder and L.G. Beaman (Eds.), *Polygamy's Rights and Wrongs*. Vancouver: UBC Press: 120–41.

Semple, R.A. (2010). Professionalising Their Faith: Women, Religion and the Cultures of Mission and Empire. In: S. Morgan and J. de Vries (Eds.), *Women, Gender and Religious Cultures in Britain, 1800–1940*. London: Routledge: 117–37.

Shah, S. (2018). *The Making of a Gay Muslim: Religion, Sexuality and Identity in Malaysia and Britain*. Cham: Palgrave MacMillan.

Shah, S. (forthcoming). Ethnicity, Gender and Class in the Experiences of Gay Muslims. In: S. Page and A.K.T. Yip (Eds.), *Intersecting Religion and Sexuality: Sociological Perspectives*. Leiden: Brill.

Shahidian, H. (2008). Contesting Discourses of Sexuality in Post-Revolutionary Iran. In: P. Ikkaracan (Ed.), *Deconstructing Sexuality in the Middle East: Challenges and Discourses*. Aldershot: Ashgate: 101–38.

Shalhoub-Kevorkian, N. (2008). Towards a Cultural Definition of Rape: Dilemmas in Dealing with Rape Victims in Palestinian Society. In: P. Ikkaracan (Ed.), *Deconstructing Sexuality in the Middle East: Challenges and Discourses*. Aldershot: Ashgate: 177–98.

## 216 Bibliography

Shannahan, D.S. (2009). Sexual Ethics, Marriage, and Sexual Autonomy: The Landscapes for Muslimat and Lesbian, Gay, Bisexual, and Transgendered Muslims. *Contemporary Islam*, 3(1): 59–78.

Sharma, S. (2008). When Young Women Say 'Yes': Exploring the Sexual Selves of Young Canadian Women in Protestant Churches. In: K. Aune, S. Sharma and G. Vincett (Eds.), *Women and Religion in the West: Challenging Secularization*. Aldershot: Ashgate: 71–82.

Sharma, S. (2011). *Good Girls, Good Sex: Women Talk about Church and Sexuality*. Halifax &Winnipeg: Fernwood Publishing.

Sheff, E. (2006). Poly-Hegemonic Masculinities. *Sexualities*, 9(5): 621–42.

Shepherd, C.A. (2019). *Bisexuality and the Western Christian Church: The Damage of Silence*. Cham: Palgrave MacMillan.

Sherwood, H. (2019). Church of England Plan for Welcoming Trans People Under Fire. *The Guardian*, 29 January. https://www.theguardian.com/world/2019/jan/29/church-england-plan-welcoming-trans-people-under-fire-clergy-lay-members-bishops-withdraw-guidance. Accessed 13.09.19.

Shilling, C. (1993). *The Body and Social Theory*. London: Sage.

Shipley, H. (2014). Religious and Sexual Orientation Intersections in Education and Media: A Canadian Perspective. *Sexualities*, 17(5–6): 512–28.

Shipley, H. (2015). The Spaces in Between: Religious and Sexual Intersections in Education. In: L.G. Beaman and L. Van Arragon (Eds.), *Issues in Religion and Education: Whose Religion?* Leiden: Brill Academic Press: 211–30.

Shipley, H. (2018a). Religion, Secularism and Sexuality Education: The Politics of Ideology in Canada. In: A.K.T. Yip and F. Sanjakdar (Eds.), *Critical Pedagogy, Sexuality Education, and Young People*. New York: Peter Lang Publishers: 19–34.

Shipley, H. (2018b). Apathy or Misunderstanding?: Youth's Reflections on Their Religious Identity in Canada. In: P. Gareau, S. Bullivant and P. Beyer (Eds.), *Youth, Religion and Identity in a Globalizing Context. International Perspectives*. Leiden: Brill Academic Press: 191–210.

Shipley, H. (2019). Experiencing Religious and Sexual Diversity in Ontario's Schools. In: E. Arweck and H. Shipley (Eds.), *Young People and the Diversity of (Non)Religious Identities in International Perspective*. London: Springer: 241–58.

Shipley, H. (forthcoming). Sites of Resistance: LGBTQI+ Experiences at Trinity Western University. *Canadian Journal of Law and Society*.

Shipley, H. and Young, P.D. (2014). Values and Attitudes: How are Youth Integrating Religion and Sexuality in their Daily Lives? In: H. Shipley (Ed.), *Globalized Religion and Sexual Identity: Contexts, Contestations, Voices*. Leiden: Brill Academic Press: 276–94.

Shipley, H. and Young, P.D. (2017a). Religion, Youth and Queer Identities in Canada. In: M. Jaime (Ed.), *Sexual Diversity and Religions*. Lima, Peru: PEG/Diversities Publishing: 219–34.

Shipley, H. and Young, P.D. (2017b). Christianity, Gender and Identity among Canadian Youth. In: S. Hunt (Ed.), *The Brill Handbook of Global Christianity*. Leiden: Brill Academic Press: 327–45.

Shipley, H. and Young, P.D. (forthcoming). Bisexuality, (Non)Religion and Spirituality in Canadian Young Adults. In: A.K.T. Yip and A. Toft (Eds.), *Bisexuality, Spirituality and Identity. Page Numbers*. London: Routledge: 11–28.

Short, D. (2013). *Don't Be So Gay!: Queers, Bullying, and Making Schools Safe*. Vancouver: UBC Press.

Simpson, A.V., Clegg, S.R., Lopes, M.P., Cunha, E., Rego, A. and Pitsis, T. (2014). Doing Compassion or Doing Discipline? Power Relations and the Magdalene Laundries. *Journal of Political Power*, 7(2): 253–74.

Siraj, A. (2012). Looking 'In' from the 'Outside': The Methodological Challenges of Researching Minority Ethnic Gay Men and Lesbian Women. In: S. Hunt and A.K.T. Yip (Eds.), *The Ashgate Research Companion to Religion and Sexuality*. Farnham: Ashgate: 59–71.

Slee, N., Porter, F. and Phillips, A. (Eds.), (2018). *Researching Female Faith: Qualitative Research Methods*. Abingdon: Routledge.

Smith, M. (1999). *Lesbian and Gay Rights in Canada: Social Movements and Equality-Seeking, 1971–1995*. Toronto: University of Toronto Press.

Stan, L. and Turcescu, L. (2011). Religion and Politics in Romania: From Public Affairs to Church-State Relations. *Journal of Global Initiatives: Policy, Pedagogy, Perspective*, 6(2): 97–108.

Stella, F., Taylor, Y., Reynolds, T. and Rogers, A. (Eds.), (2016). *Sexuality, Citizenship and Belonging: Trans-National and International Perspectives*. London: Routledge.

Stringer, M. (2000). Of Gin and Lace: Sexuality, Liturgy and Identity among Anglo-Catholics in the Mid-Twentieth Century. *Theology and Sexuality*, 7(13): 35–54.

Stuart, E. (2015). The Theological Study of Sexuality. In: A. Thatcher (Ed.), *The Oxford Handbook of Theology, Sexuality, and Gender*. Oxford: Oxford University Press: 18–31.

Sullivan, W. (2009). *Prison Religion: Faith-Based Reform and the Constitution*. Princeton, NJ: Princeton University Press.

Taylor, Y. (2011). Complexities and Complications: Intersections of Class and Sexuality. In: Y. Taylor, S. Hines and M. Casey (Eds.), *Theorizing Intersectionality and Sexuality*. Basingstoke: Palgrave Macmillan: 37–55.

Taylor, Y. (2016). The "Outness" of Queer. In: K. Browne and C.J. Nash (Eds.), *Queer Methods and Methodologies: Intersecting Queer Theories and Social Science Research*. London: Routledge: 69–83.

Taylor, C. and Peter, T. (2011). Every Class in Every School: Final Report on the First National Climate Survey on Homophobia, Biphobia, and Transphobia in Canadian Schools. *EGALE Canada*. http://archive.egale.ca/EgaleFinalReport-web.pdf. Accessed 18.12.2011.

Taylor, Y., Hines, S. and Casey, M. (2011). Introduction. In: Y. Taylor, S. Hines and M. Casey (Eds.), *Theorizing Intersectionality and Sexuality*. Basingstoke: Palgrave Macmillan: 1–12.

Taylor, Y. and Snowdon, R. (2013). *Queering Religion, Religious Queers*. London: Routledge.

Taylor, Y. and Snowdon, R. (2014a). Making Space for Young Lesbians in Church? Intersectional Sites, Scripts, and Sticking Points. *Journal of Lesbian Studies*, 18(4): 393–414.

Taylor, Y. and Snowdon, R. (2014b). Mapping Queer, Mapping Me: Visualizing Queer Religious Identity. In: H. Shipley (Ed.), *Globalized Religion and Sexual Identity: Contexts, Contestations, Voices*. Leiden: Brill: 295–312.

Terry, G. (2012). "I'm Putting a Lid on that Desire": Celibacy, Choice and Control. *Sexualities*, 15(7): 871–89.

Thomas, J.N. (2016). The Development and Deployment of the Idea of Pornography Addiction within American Evangelicalism. *Sexual Addiction and Compulsivity*, 23(2–3): 182–95.

Thomson, R. (2011). *Unfolding Lives: Youth, Gender and Change*. London: Policy Press.

## 218 Bibliography

Thornton, A. (1988). Reciprocal Influences of Family and Religion in a Changing World. In: D.L. Thomas (Ed.), *The Religion and Family Connection: Social Science Perspectives.* Provo, UT: Religious Studies Center: Brigham Young University: 27–50.

Thumma, S. (1991). Negotiating a Religious Identity: The Case of the Gay Evangelical. *Sociological Analysis,* 52(4): 333–47.

Thumma, S. and Gray, E.R. (Eds.), (2005). *Gay Religion.* Walnut Creek, CA: Altamira.

Tisdall, K. and Punch, S. (2012). Not so 'New'? Looking Critically at Childhood Studies. *Children's Geographies,* 10(3): 249–64.

Titley, B. (2006). Heil Mary: Magdalen Asylums and Moral Regulation in Ireland. *History of Education Review,* 35(2): 1–15.

Toft, A. (2012). Bisexuality and Christianity: Negotiating Disparate Identities in Church Life. In: S. Hunt and A.K.T. Yip (Eds.), *The Ashgate Research Companion to Contemporary Religion and Sexuality.* Farnham: Ashgate: 189–203.

Toft, A. (2014). Re-imagining Bisexuality and Christianity: The Negotiation of Christianity in the Lives of Bisexual Women and Men. *Sexualities,* 17(5–6): 546–64.

Toft, A. and Yip, A.K.T. (2018). Intimacy Negotiated: The Management of Relationships and the Construction of Personal Communities in the Lives of Bisexual Women and Men. *Sexualities,* 21(1–2): 233–50.

Tonkiss, K. and Bloom, T. (2015). Theorising Noncitizenship: Concepts, Debates and Challenges. *Citizenship Studies,* 19(8): 837–52.

Truth, S. (1851). *Look at Me! Ain't I a Woman.* https://www.thesojournertruthprojec t.com/. Accessed 14.08.2019.

Tseëlon, E. (1995). *The Masque of Femininity: The Presentation of Woman in Everyday Life.* London: Sage.

Turner, B.S. (1983). *Religion and Social Theory.* London: Heinemann Educational Books.

Turner, B.S. (2008). *The Body and Society,* 3rd edition. London: Sage.

Turner, B.S. (2011). *Religion and Modern Society: Citizenship, Secularisation and the State.* Cambridge: Cambridge University Press.

Tweed, T.A. (2006). *Crossing and Dwelling: A Theory of Religion.* London: Harvard University Press.

Uecker, J.E., Angotti, N. and Regnerus, M.D. (2008). Going Most of the Way: 'Technical Virginity' among American Adolescents. *Social Science Research,* 37(4): 1200–15.

Vaggione, J.M. (2002). Paradoxing the Secular in Latin America: Religion, Gender and Sexuality at the Crossroads. *Transregional Center for Democratic Studies Journal,* 3(8): 1–19.

Valentine, G. (2007). Theorizing and Researching Intersectionality: A Challenge for Feminist Geography. *The Professional Geographer,* 59(1): 10–21.

Valverde, M. (2006). A New Entity in the History of Sexuality: The Respectable Same-Sex Couple. *Feminist Studies,* 32(1): 155–162.

Van Klinken, A. (2015). Queer Love in a 'Christian Nation': Zambian Gay Men Negotiating Sexual and Religious Identities. *Journal of the American Academy of Religion,* 83(4): 947–64.

Van Klinken, A. (2019). Citizenship of Love: The Politics, Ethics and Aesthetics of Sexual Citizenship in a Kenyan Gay Music Video. In: A. Van Klinken and E. Obadare (Eds.), *Christianity, Sexuality and Citizenship in Africa.* Abingdon: Routledge: 94–109.

Van Klinken, A. and Chitando, E. (2016). Introduction: Public Religion, Homophobia and the Politics of Homosexuality in Africa. In: A. Van Klinken and E. Chitando (Eds.), *Public Religion and the Politics of Homosexuality in Africa.* London: Routledge: 1–16.

Van Klinken, A. and Obadare, E. (2019). Christianity, Sexuality and Citizenship in Africa: Critical Intersections. In: A. Van Klinken and E. Obadare (Eds.), *Christianity, Sexuality and Citizenship in Africa*. Abingdon: Routledge: 1–12.

Vatican Congregation for Catholic Education. (2019). *Male and Female He Created Them: Towards a Path of Dialogue on the Question of Gender Theory in Education*. http://www.vatican.va/roman_curia/congregations/ccatheduc/index.htm. Accessed 04.09.19.

Vincett, G. (2008). *Feminism and Religion: A Study of Christian Feminists and Goddess Feminists in the UK*. Unpublished PhD. Lancaster: Lancaster University.

Vincett, G., Sharma, S. and Aune, K. (2008). Introduction: Women, Religion and Secularization: One Size Does Not Fit All. In: K. Aune, S. Sharma and G. Vincett (Eds.), *Women and Religion in the West: Challenging Secularization*. Aldershot: Ashgate: 1–19.

Von Benzon, N. and Van Blerk, L. (2017). Research Relationships and Responsibilities: 'Doing' Research with 'Vulnerable' Participants: Introduction to the Special Edition. *Social and Cultural Geography*, 18(7): 895–905.

Warner, M. (2002). *The Trouble with Normal*. Cambridge: Harvard University Press.

Warwick, I.P., Aggleton, P. and Douglas, N. (2001). Playing It Safe: Addressing the Emotional and Physical Health of Lesbian and Gay Pupils in the UK. *Journal of Adolescence*, 24(1): 129–40.

Weber, M. (1968). *Economy and Society: An Outline of Interpretive Sociology*. New York: Bedminster Press.

Weeks, J. (2007). *The World We Have Won: The Remaking of Erotic and Intimate Life*. Abingdon: Routledge.

Weeks, J. (2011). *The Languages of Sexuality*. London: Routledge.

Weeks, J. (2014). *Sex, Politics and Society: The Regulations of Sexuality Since 1800*, 3rd edition. London: Routledge.

Weingarten, K. (2012). Impossible Decisions: Abortion, Reproductive Technologies, and the Rhetoric of Choice. *Women's Studies: An Inter-disciplinary Journal*, 41(3): 263–81.

Weitz, T.A. (2010). Rethinking the Mantra that Abortion Should be 'Safe, Legal, and Rare'. *Journal of Women's History*, 22(3): 161–72.

Whitaker, R. and Horgan, G. (2017). Abortion Governance in the New Northern Ireland. In: S. De Zordo, J. Mishtal and L. Anton (Eds.), *A Fragmented Landscape: Abortion Governance and Protest Logics in Europe*. New York: Berghahn: 245–65.

White, H.R. (2012). Virgin Pride: Born Again Faith and Sexual Identity in the Faith-Based Abstinence Movement. In: S. Hunt and A.K.T. Yip (Eds.), *The Ashgate Research Companion to Contemporary Religion and Sexuality*. Farnham: Ashgate: 241–53.

White, H.R. (2015). *Reforming Sodom: Protestants and the Rise of Gay Rights*. Chapel Hill, NC: University of North Carolina Press.

White, H.R. (2016). History. In: K.L. Brintnall (Ed.), *Religion: Embodied Religion*. Farmington Hills, MI: MacMillan Reference USA: 205–16.

Wiering, J. (2017a). The Curious Case of the Condom: Reflections on Sexual Enchantment in the Netherlands. *Sociology of Religion Study Group Annual Conference: On the Edge? Centres and Margins in the Sociology of Religion*, 12th–14th July, University of Leeds.

Wiering, J. (2017b). There is a Secular Body: Introducing a Material Approach to the Secular. *Secularism and Nonreligion*, 6(8): 1–11.

Wilcox, M.M. (2003). Innovation in Exile: Religion and Spirituality in Lesbian, Gay, Bisexual, and Transgender Communities. In: D.W. Machacek and M.M. Wilcox (Eds.), *Sexuality and the World's Religions*. Santa Barbara, CA: ABC-CLIO: 323–57.

**220** Bibliography

Wilcox, M.M. (2009). *Queer Women and Religious Individualism*. Bloomington, IN: Indiana University Press.

Wilcox, M.M. (2018a). *Queer Nuns: Religion, Activism and Serious Parody*. New York: New York University Press.

Wilcox, M.M. (2018b). Religion is Already Transed: Religious Studies is not (yet) Listening. *Journal of Feminist Studies in Religion*, 34(1): 84–8.

Wilkins, A. (2008). *Wannabes, Goths and Christians: The Boundaries of Sex, Style and Status*. Chicago, IL: University of Chicago Press.

Wilmot, A. (2007). In Search of a Question on Sexual Identity. *62nd Annual Conference for the American Association of Public Opinion Research*. https://ons.gov.uk. Accessed 24.09.19.

Wilson, J. (2017). Mindfulness Makes you a Better Lover: Mindful Sex and the Adaptation of Buddhism to New Cultural Desires. In: D. McMahan and E. Braun (Eds.), *Meditation, Buddhism, and Science*. Oxford: Oxford University Press: 152–72.

Winder, T.J.A. (2015). 'Shouting it Out': Religion and the Development of Black Gay Identities. *Qualitative Sociology*, 38(4): 375–94.

Woodhead, L. (2001). Feminism and the Sociology of Religion: From Gender-blindness to Gendered Difference. In: R.K. Fenn (Ed.), *The Blackwell Companion to Sociology of Religion*. Oxford: Blackwell Publishing: 67–84.

Woodhead, L. (2007a). Gender Difference in Religious Practice and Significance. In: J.A. Beckford and N.J. Demerath III (Eds.), *The SAGE Handbook of the Sociology of Religion*. London: Sage: 566–86.

Woodhead, L. (2007b). Sex and Secularization. In: G. Loughlin (Ed.), *Queer Theology: Rethinking the Western Body*. Malden, MA: Blackwell Publishing: 230–44.

Woodhead, L. (2008). 'Because I'm Worth It': Religion and Women's Changing Lives in the West. In: K. Aune, S. Sharma and G. Vincett (Eds.), *Women and Religion in the West: Challenging Secularization*. Aldershot: Ashgate: 147–61.

Woodhead, L. (2013). *Religion and Personal Life*. London: Darton, Longman and Todd.

Yip, A.K.T. (1997). Attacking the Attacker: Gay Christians Talk Back. *British Journal of Sociology*, 48(1): 113–127.

Yip, A.K.T. (2003). The Self as the Basis of Religious Faith: Spirituality of Gay, Lesbian and Bisexual Christians. In: G. Davie, P. Heelas and L. Woodhead (Eds.), *Predicting Religion: Christian, Secular and Alternative Futures*. Aldershot: Ashgate: 135–46.

Yip, A.K.T. (2004a). Negotiating Space with Family and Kin in Identity Construction: The Narratives of British Non-heterosexual Muslims. *The Sociological Review*, 52(3): 336–50.

Yip, A.K.T. (2004b). Embracing Allah and Sexuality? South Asian Non-Heterosexual Muslims in Britain. In: K.A. Jacobsen (Ed.), *South Asians in the Diaspora: Histories and Religious Traditions*. Leiden: Brill: 294–310.

Yip, A.K.T. (2005). Queering Religious Texts: An Exploration of British Non-Heterosexual Christians' and Muslims' Strategies of Constructing Sexuality-Affirming Hermeneutics. *Sociology*, 39(1): 47–65.

Yip, A.K.T. (2008). Researching Lesbian, Gay, and Bisexual Christians and Muslims: Some Thematic Reflections. *Sociological Research Online*, 13(1). http://www.socresonline.org.uk/13/1/5.html. Accessed 21.08.18.

Yip, A.K.T. (2011). Homophobia and Ethnic Minority Communities in the United Kingdom. In: L. Trappolin, A. Gasparini and R. Wintemute (Eds.), *Confronting Homophobia in Europe: Social and Legal Perspectives*. Oxford: Hart Publishing: 107–30.

Yip, A.K.T. (2015). When Religion Meets Sexuality: Two Tales of Intersection. In: P.D. Young, H. Shipley and T.J. Trothen (Eds.), *Religion and Sexuality: Diversity and the Limits of Tolerance*. Vancouver: UBC Press: 119–40.

Yip, A.K.T. and Page, S. (2013). *Religious and Sexual Identities: A Multi-Faith Exploration of Young Adults*. Farnham: Ashgate.

Yip, A.K.T. and Page, S. (2014). Religious Faith and Heterosexuality: A Multi-Faith Exploration of Young Adults. *Research in the Social Scientific Study of Religion*, 25: 78–108.

Yip, A.K.T. and Page, S. (forthcoming). Bisexual Erasure and Religious Spaces: Experiences of Young Adults in the United Kingdom. In: A.K.T. Yip and A. Toft (Eds.), *Bisexuality, Religion and Spirituality: Critical Perspectives*. Abingdon: Routledge: 49–67.

Young, P.D. (2012). *Religion, Sex and Politics: Christian Churches and Same-Sex Marriage in Canada*. Winnipeg: Fernwood Press.

Young, P.D. (2015). Who Speaks for Religion? In: L. Beaman and L. Van Arragon (Eds.), *Issues in Religion and Education: Whose Religion?* Leiden: Brill Academic Press: 305–20.

Young, P.D. (2019). Influences of Religion on the Sexual Attitudes and Practices of Canadian Youth: The Case of Premarital Sex. In: P. Gareau, S. Bullivant and P. Beyer (Eds.), *Youth, Religion, and Identity in a Globalizing Context: International Perspectives*. Leiden: Brill Academic Press: 66–77.

Young, P.D. and Shipley, H. (2014). Belief, Not Religion: Youth Negotiations of Religious Identity in Canada. In: J. Wyn and H. Cahill (Eds.), *Handbook on Child and Youth Studies*. London: Springer: 861–73.

Young, P.D. and Shipley, H. (2020). *Identities under Construction: Religion, Gender and Sexuality among Youth in Canada*. Montreal: McGill-Queen's University Press.

Young, P.D. and Shipley, H. (forthcoming). Gender Fluidity, Sexuality and Religion. In: S. Page and A.K.T. Yip (Eds.), *Intersecting Religion and Sexuality: Sociological Perspectives*. Leiden: Brill.

Young, P.D., Shipley, H. and Cuthbertson, I. (2016). Religion, Gender and Sexuality among Youth in Canada: Some Preliminary Findings. In: A. Macdonald (Ed.). special issue of *Bulletin for the Study of Religion*, 45(1): 17–26.

Yuval-Davis, N. (1997). *Gender and Nation*. London: Sage.

Zachs, M. (2015). The Significance of Ancient Jewish Spiritual and Ritualistic Practices for Gender Non-conforming. *Variant Sex and Gender, Religion and Wellbeing Conference*, 19th June, University Of Exeter.

Zuckerman, P. (2012). *Faith No More: Why People Reject Religion*. Oxford: Oxford University Press.

# INDEX

Abbott, Douglas A. 137
Abbott, Elizabeth 161–2
abortion 146–7, 150–4, 165–6, 191
abortion clinics 7, 46, 151–2
Adamczyk, Amy 102, 137–8
adoption 97, 99, 106, 127, 164, 173
adultery 77, 118, 157
Africa 175–6, 178
age: and identity 11, 14, 68, 72; and
    intersectionality 70, 161, 194; and
    milestones 102, 104, 116–17, 163; and
    older generations 107–8; and research
    considerations 71, 85, 91
Ahmed, Leila 135, 150
Ahmed, Sara 11, 175
Akin, Deniz 171, 176
Aldridge, Alan 186
Aldridge, Jo 71
Alpert, Rebecca 159
Althaus-Reid, Marcella 64
Amakor, George 55, 63, 85, 165, 195
Ammerman, Nancy T. 3, 58–61, 87
Anderson, Eric 121
anti-abortion activism 7, 56, 61, 81–2
Apetrei, Sarah 133
Archer, Leonie. S. 141
Asad, Talal 169
asexual/ asexuality 74, 108, 120, 124–6,
    159, 161, 182
asylum seekers 170–2, 175–7, 189
attitudes 77–9, 173–4
Attwood, Feona 55
Aune, Kristin 13, 97, 99, 162, 192

Australia 25, 65, 117, 132
authority: and agency 53; and gender
    19, 23, 39, 114–15, 130, 132, 134,
    142, 186–7; and moral authority 189;
    religious 5, 13, 31–2, 36, 78, 89–90,
    148–9, 153, 169, 178, 183–5; and
    research: 72, 75; and sacred masculinity
    186–7; and theology 65; and tradition
    20; and Weber: 11, 185
Avishai, Orit 142–3

Bagnoli, Anna 85
Barnard, Ian 4
Barras, Amélie 191
Barrett-Fox, Rebecca 63
Bartkowski, John P. 157–8
Barton, Bernadette 43–4, 50, 55, 69,
    113–15, 117, 171–2, 192
Baxter, Judith 193
BDSM (bondage and discipline, sadism
    and masochism) 83
Beaman, Lori G. 4, 9
Beardsley, Christina 123
Bearman, Peter S 102, 138
Beattie, Tina 11
Beckford, James A. 3, 5, 10, 14
Begun, Stephanie 152
belonging: and exclusions 25; and gender
    115; and queer individuals 112; and
    religion 30–2, 58, 76, 153, 175; and
    secularization 36; and trans identity 174
Bernhardt-House 123
Berry, David M 80, 88

## Index

Bethmont, Rémy 110
Bevir, Mark 168
Beyer, Peter F 98, 100
Bible Belt 50, 55, 113–15, 171, 192
bicurious 74
biopower 37–9, 168, 193
birth: and gender 24; and the lifecourse 14, 16, 100–1; and regulation 38–9, 133, 142, 168; and relationship to sexuality 1
birth control pill 137, 147–50, 160
bisexuality: and discrimination 66, 118–22; and identity 49, 73–4; and marginalisation 3, 43, 96, 105, 114, 192, 195; and relationship to LGBT 3, 108; and religion 48, 121
Bloom, Tendayi 170
Blyth, Caroline 122, 154, 174
body: and Butler 52; and clothing 139–41; and discipline 29; exclusion of queer bodies 176, 192; and Foucault 37–8, 168, 173; and gender 129–30, 133–4, 136, 139, 156–7; and goddess spiritualities 17–18; and Goffman 54, 173; and piety 52–3; and pregnancy 84; and reproductive technology 18–19, 152; and sacrality 143; and sexualisation 34; *see also* embodiment; menstruation
Bock E. Wilbur 186
Boellstorff, Tom 11, 15–16, 178, 192, 195
Bompani, Barbara 176
Boswell, John 99
Bowers v. Hardwick 32
Bowie, Fiona 143
Brah, Avtar 194
Braidotti, Rosi 18, 24–6, 48
Brasher, Brenda 69
Brintnall, Kent L. 1, 3, 26, 46, 144
Brison, Susan J. 182
British Common Law 97
Brittain, Christopher C. 105, 178
Brokeback Mountain 96, 109
Brotman, Shari 112
Brown, Andrew 178, 184
Brown, Callum G. 13, 30–1, 132, 172
Brown, Charis 87
Browne, Kath 65, 69–70, 73, 91, 112
Bruce, Steve 169
Bryman, Alan 72, 88
Buddhism: and sexuality 17, 121, 125, 137, 192; and commodification 58; and ethnicity 115
bullying 101, 108, 118
Burke, Kelsey 57, 89, 157, 159–60
Butler, Judith 37, 50–3, 55, 63–4, 71

Cahill, Caitlin 71
Calder, Gillian 126
Cameroon 176
Campbell, Angela 126
Canada: and education 101, 117; and gender 31, 164; and Indigenous communities 112, 164; and legislation 2, 97–8, 117, 126; and the RGSY project 7, 71, 83, 86, 100–1, 135–6; and same-sex marriage 84; and secularization 4
Capitalism 19–20, 38, 169
Carillo,Héctor 120–1
Carpenter, Laura M 101–3, 135–8
Carrette, Jeremy 56
Carter, Sarah 97
Casanova, José 32, 37, 169
Cavanagh, Sheila L. 95, 109
celibacy: attitudes towards 124; definition 124; and the lifecourse 105; and relationship to sexuality 1, 3; and religion 135, 162, 164, 182; and the straight time account 125
Chan, Shun Hing 195
Cheruvallil-Contractor, Sariya 164
childbearing *see* pregnancy
Chinwuba, Nesochi 72
Christ/Jesus 24, 162, 165, 180, 189
Christianity: and colonialism 100, 130–4, 171, 175; and conservatism 63; and dominance 6, 12, 68, 76, 92, 180, 195; and gender 21, 23–4, 30–1, 156–7, 186–9; and homonegative discourse 44; and homosexuality 6, 89, 181; and institutional sexual abuse 181–9; and neutralization 34–5; and polygamy 126; and pornography 157–8; and queer inclusivity 66; and secularisation 29, 36, 112; and secularism 4–5; and sex 32–3; and singleness 162, 192; and social class 184–6; and sodomy 64; and virginity 135, 138
Church of England: and bisexuality 122; and contraception 147, 149; and homosexuality 179; and the Independent Inquiry into Child Sexual Abuse 7, 8, 183–9; and motherhood 8; and queer clergy 51, 89; and relationship to the state 171; and same sex marriage 105, 110; and trans identity 123, 174; and women's priesthood 142;
Church of the Latter-Day Saints 126
church-state separation 33–4
Civil Marriage Act (2005) Canada 97–8

**224** Index

Clegg, Stewart R. 167
Clements, Ben 76
clergy abuse *see* institutional abuse
clothing 18, 134, 138–41, 144, 172, 191
Cockburn, Cynthia 187
Cokely, Carrie L. 95
Colgan, Emily 154
Collins, Patricia Hill 61–3, 194
colonialism–colonization: and
    Christianity 6, 100, 130–4, 170–1;
    and Indigenous communities 112; and
    neo-colonialism 189; and sexuality
    175–6
Combahee River Collective 61
coming out/Coming out narratives 16,
    49–50, 94, 96, 114–16
commodified identities 42, 55–8
compulsory heterosexuality 40, 94
condom 66, 150–1
confession 38, 45, 49, 67, 176, 183
consumerism/ consumption 22, 30, 42,
    55–8, 95–6, 160
contraception: and abortion 153; and
    attitudes towards 77, 150–1; and
    Catholicism 39, 45, 137; 147–9, 165,
    178; and the Church of England 147;
    definition 147; and Evangelicalism 149;
    and gender 160 (*see also* birth control
    pill; condom); and Islam 149–50; in the
    19th century 147; and state control 63,
    96; in the 20th century 137, 147
conversion therapy 74, 113
Cornwall, Susannah 105, 123, 135
Corriveau, Patrice 174
Cossman, Brenda 97, 108
Creek, S. J. 113
Crenshaw, Kimberlé Williams 61–2, 70
Cuthbert, Karen 65
Cuthbertson, Ian 9
Czech Republic 176

Daniels, Brandy 64
Daniels, Martha 3, 114, 122–3
Davidman, Lynn 69
Davie, Grace 34, 89–90, 171
Davies, Douglas 141, 184
Day, Abby 73, 75, 78
D'Costa, Gavin 64
death: and abortion 152; and embodiment
    21; and gender 156; and the lifecourse
    14, 16, 39, 101; and menstruation
    141; as punishment 174–5, 178; and
    regulation 38–9, 168; and sexuality
    43, 152
death penalty 175, 178, 189

decriminalization (of homosexuality)
    175, 179
Deifelt, Wanda 165
Delaney, Janice 136, 141, 143
Delap, Lucy 147
Delgado, Teresa 178
Denzin, Norman K. 73, 80
DeRogatis, Amy 57, 89, 138, 149, 157,
    160, 164
Derrida, Jacques 52
Detamore, Mathias 81
De Zordo, Silvia 153
Dialmy, Abdessamad 100, 135–6, 150
Diamond Lisa M. 120
disability 59–60, 62, 67
discipline 96, 111, 119, 168, 173, 179
discourse: and ethnicity 161; and gender
    129–30, 138, 142, 156–7; and human
    rights 108; and identity 52; and
    methods 88–9; and poststructuralism
    25, 38–9, 44–5, 69, 168; and religion
    6, 15, 24, 29, 31–2, 39, 44, 59–60,
    71, 81, 84, 98, 102, 130, 132, 142,
    144, 176–81, 191–2, 195; and the
    secular/secularism 4, 17, 35–6, 97,
    193; and sexualities 29, 31, 38, 45, 71,
    83–4, 152, 156–7, 176–81, 193; and
    violence 154
divorce 20–1, 36, 77, 154–5, 165
domestic violence 13, 42, 83, 146, 154–5
Douglas, Mary 136, 139, 144
dualism 12, 23–4, 27–8, 122–3, 134
Dudink, Stefan 78
Duggan, Lisa 2, 41–3, 75, 95, 128
Duits, Linda 140–1
Durkheim, Emile 11, 30

Egypt 52–4
Eisner, Elliot 85
Elliott, Richard 80
embodiment: and Christianity
    21–4; and definition 19, 24–5; and
    economic systems 20; and Foucault
    37–9; and gender 20–1, 23–6, 74,
    139, 144–5, 159; and importance
    191; and priesthood 183; and religion
    26–7, 59–60; and research 82; and
    secularization 21; and sexuality 22;
    *see also* body; clothing
England, Wales and Scotland 2, 105,
    117–18
Enlightenment 35, 129–30, 133
Epstein, Debbie 118
equality: and attitudes 75; gender 35,
    133, 153; and national identity 43, 77;

and queer 14, 35, 54, 94, 108, 127–8, 161, 175; and and religion 45, 193; and same-sex marriage 101, 105, 127–8
ethnicity: assumed 12; and gender 56, 139, 144, 160–1; and intersectionality 14, 62, 70, 194; and sexuality 41, 114–15, 160–1;and theory/research 12, 68, 72, 86–7, 91
ethnography 7, 18, 66, 80–2
Eucharist 141–2
Europe: and border control 176; and Christianity 4–5; and control of religion 25, 35, 43; and gender 141; privileged 12, 195; surveys 76–8
Evangelical: attitudes 151; gender 133; historic 132; and queer worship 80; and sexuality 57, 89, 105, 121, 135, 138, 149, 154, 157–8, 160, 165
evangelicalism 57, 132, 138
Ezzy, Douglas 18

Fallon, Breann 154–4
family: and "coming out" 50, 104; and diversity 109; and dominant constructions 2, 95–7, 101, 106, 117, 130; and gender 136; and honour 138; and influence 78; and inheritance/ primogeniture 31; and rejection 65, 112–13, 115–16, 165, 171–2; and the sacred 13; and stigma 54; and values 32
family planning *see* contraception
femininity: contemporary 137; and 1960s sexual liberation 13, 30; Victorian 131–4, 156–7
feminism: campaigns 108, 133; perspectives 97, 132–3, 146; relationship to queer 69–70, 73, 91, 191; secular 35; and theology 114
Fernando, Mayanthi 34
fertility: attitudes 151; gender 153, 165–6; and goddess spiritualities 143; and regulation 38, 147–8, 161; and religion 19; and social class 130; and technology 146, 148
Fielder, Bronwyn 65–6
Finch, Janet 69, 92
First Nations spirituality 4
first wave feminism 133
focus groups 8, 70, 75, 82–5
Fone, Byrne 40, 94, 174
Forna, Aminatta 116
foster care 173
Foucault, Michel 19–20, 29, 37–9, 44–5, 49, 52, 64, 89, 96, 168, 171, 173, 177, 181, 193

France 34, 37, 171
Freitas, Donna 138, 159, 195
Friedman, Mark S. 101
Fumia, Doreen 94
Furlong, Monica 23, 141

Gaddini, Katie 69
Gahan, Luke 105–6
Gandhi, Kiran 144
gay: and adoption 106; and definition 15, 49–50, 73–4; and education 118–20; and exclusion 43; and legal cases 32–3; and the LGBT acronym 2–3; and marginalization 96–7; and post-colonialism 175–7; privileged 6, 42–3, 192, 195; and religion 48, 51, 54–5, 71, 80–1, 90, 103, 113–16, 125, 171, 180–1; and research considerations 83–4
gay liberation movement 2, 117, 177–8
gay pride 24, 46
Geertz, Clifford J. 80
Geiringer, David 30, 32, 148–9
gender: and citizenship 174; definitions 52, 74, 91; equality/ inequality 22, 26, 35, 37, 44, 65, 114–15, 133, 153, 177, 186–9; gender-based violence 13, 42, 83, 146, 154–6, 186–9; gender conformity/norms/roles 2, 8, 21, 57, 71, 78, 93–5, 99, 101, 129–31, 134–5, 138, 161; gender diversity/ fluid/ fluidity 12, 48, 74, 91, 100, 106, 108, 122–4, 174 gender identity 74, 117; gender nonbinary 74, 95, 123–4; and heterosexuality 40, 58, 94–6, 101–2, 149, 161–5; ignored 12–13, 30, 73; and intersectionality 34, 62–3, 70, 72, 86–7, 107, 112, 131–2; and patriarchy/regulation 18, 172–4; and performativity 52–4; and pleasure 156–61; relationship to queer 69–70; and the sacred/profane 23–4, 133, 141–4
genderfuck 66–7
Gender Recognition Act 174
Gerhards, Jürgen 78
Gibb, Moira 184–5
Giddens, Anthony 21, 47, 55
Gill, Sean 132, 147
Gleason, Mona 94
Gleig, Ann 115, 181
globalization 14–15, 178
Goddard, Andrew 149
goddess spirituality 17–18, 23, 36, 143
Goffman, Erving 19, 50–2, 54–5, 119, 167–8, 172–3, 183, 189

**226** Index

Goh, Joseph 195
Goldenberg, Naomi 3
"good" sex 22–3, 95, 137
Gorman-Murray, Andrew 72
Gott, Chloe 90, 173–4
Gray, Edward R 48, 80
Graybill, Beth 139–40
Green, Adam I. 77
Greenough, Christopher 85
Greil, Arthur L. 47
Griffith, R. Marie 69
Grosz, Elizabeth 16–17
Guest, Mathew 137, 149, 184
Guillemin, Marilys 86

Hall, Dorota 123
Hall, Stuart 4
Hall Kathleen D. 138
Halperin, David 96
Halpern v. Canada 98
Halstead, Philip 166
Hammers, Corie 68, 91
Hampshire, Katherine R. 165
Hamzić, Vanja 195
Hanemann, Rachel W. 119
Harley, Debra A. 108
Harvey, Graham 37
Harvey, Laura 137
Hastrup, Kirsten 135–6
Hayes, Graeme 9
Heckert, Jamie 74
Heelas, Paul 31, 56
Helmick, Raymond G. 137, 148–9
Helminiak, Daniel A. 99–100
Hesse-Biber, Sharlene 82
heteronormativity: and age 108;
    definition 40–1, 44, 93–7, 129; and
    gender 102, 135, 161–5; and legal cases
    32–4, 99; as an organising system 2, 26,
    42, 53, 91, 192; and queer theory 64;
    and religion 14, 24, 41, 65–6, 97–100,
    119; and reproduction 18; and same-sex
    marriage 75; and straight time 16, 101,
    104, 109
heterosexuality: and attitudes 75, 78; and
    dominant constructions 2–3, 33, 40,
    48–50, 73–4, 93–7, 101, 122, 192; and
    gender 31, 52, 160; as a hierarchy 19,
    32, 40, 44, 71–3, 95, 99–100, 175; and
    inequality 23; and queer theory 63–4,
    69–70; and regulation 24, 31, 98–9,
    104, 176; and researcher positionality
    83–4 ; and secular institutions 41; and
    sodomy 33; and young people 14, 83,
    100–3, 118

"heterosexual time" 95, 109
Heyes, Joshua 117
Hidayatullah, Aysha 149–50
hijra 12
Hin, Lee Win 175
Hinduism 12, 124, 139, 155
Hines, Sally 174
HIV/AIDS 43, 96, 117, 155
Hobbs, Valerie 154
Hogan, Linda 149
Holland, Janet 160
Home 14, 65, 82–3, 115–6
homonationalism 29, 40, 43–4
homonegativity 40, 44, 118–9
homonormativity 41–4, 65–6, 127–8
homophobia: critique of 40; and
    Indigenous communities 112; and
    schooling 118–19; and the state 175;
    and religion 6, 43–4, 55, 63
homosexual/heterosexual binary 2, 73,
    94–100
homosexuality: and attitudes 75–9; and
    Christianity 5–6, 32, 54–5, 64–5,
    89, 98–100, 114, 171–2, 178–80; and
    condemnation 36, 54, 94, 96, 171–2;
    emergence of the term 5–6, 38, 50,
    74, 174–5; and homophobia 40; and
    Islam 65, 100, 103, 181; and the Kinsey
    Report 157, 179; and the law 33, 175;
    LGBT acronym 2–3; and punishment
    175; relationship to heterosexuality 2,
    73–4, 94, 96–7; and same–sex marriage
    105; and school/education 117–19; and
    sodomy 33, 38
Hooghe, Marc 75
hooks, bell 14, 26
Hookway, Nicholas 89
Hornsby-Smith, Michael P. 147
Howson, Alexandra 19, 52
Humanae Vitae 32, 148–9, 178
Hunt, Stephen J. 69, 100, 135

Ibbitson, John 108
identity: and definition 47–67, 91; and
    gender 22, 25–6, 52–4, 164–5, 174;
    and intersectionality 14, 61–3, 70, 72,
    107; and nationhood 34, 39, 43, 153,
    169, 175, 189; and religion 4, 11–12,
    16–17, 23, 30–1, 34, 36–7, 51, 58–61,
    63–7, 71, 75, 80, 100, 112–14, 163; and
    research 81–6, 88; and sexualities 3,
    15–17, 22, 36–7, 42–3; 50, 54–8, 63–7,
    71, 73–4, 80, 93, 95–100, 104–5, 108,
    112–14, 116, 120–6, 163, 176
imagined future 17

Imtoual, Alia 105, 136, 159, 162
Independent Inquiry into Child Sexual
   Abuse (IICSA) 7–8, 183–9
in-depth interviews 82–5
India 12
Indigenous 28, 112, 164, 170, 192
Ingraham, Chrys 95
inheritance, laws of 19–21, 44, 161
insider/outsider research 72, 81
institutional abuse 181–9
institutions: definition 167–8; and
   knowledge 4; and religion 3–4, 27,
   31, 36–7, 61, 66, 98, 112, 123–4, 153,
   169–81; and sexual abuse 7–8, 181–9;
   and sexualities 2, 29, 36, 38, 40, 95,
   98–9; and the state 34, 39–40, 44, 130,
   161, 163–4, 169–77
intersectionality: and child sexual
   abuse 184, 188; and colonialism
   131; definition 61; and identity 62,
   72; importance 14, 63, 194–5; and
   inequality 42, 114–15; and methods 87;
   and queer feminist 70, 91; in research
   34, 62–3, 107–8, 161; roots 61–2; and
   the state 172
intersex 3, 127
intimate partner violence see domestic
   violence
Iran 43, 175
Ireland 45, 137, 172–4
Isherwood, Lisa 23–4, 135, 141
Islam: attitudes 77–8; and clothing
   140; and contraception 150–1; and
   doing research 83–4; and gender
   25, 31, 34–5, 52–3, 105, 140, 162,
   164–5; and intersectionality 62; and
   menstruation 142; and polygamy 126;
   and procreation 17; and queer 25,
   42–4, 48, 65, 71, 81, 90, 100; 116–17,
   175, 180–1, 195; and securitisation 71,
   169; and sexual pleasure 158–60, 162;
   and virginity 135–6; 138–9
Islamophobia 43

Jackson, Stevi 11–12, 40, 50, 93,
   116–17, 182
Jakobsen, Janet 4–5, 32–5, 97
Jamieson, Lynn 47
Jantzen, Grace 131, 137
Jaspal, Rusi 116, 195
Jehovah's Witnesses 90, 114, 151
Johnson, Elizabeth A. 186, 188
Johnson, Paul 105
Jordan, Mark D. 44, 64, 89, 98–9, 114,
   157, 177, 179–80

Joy, Morny 13
Judaism: and celibacy 135; and gender
   123, 156; and legal cases 33; and
   menstruation 141–2; and queer 16–17,
   48, 100, 105, 107, 115, 163; and sexual
   pleasure 100, 159; singleness 162
Jung, Patricia Beattie 22–4

Kamitsuka, Margaret D. 156–7
Keenan, Marie 181–3
Keenan, Michael 9, 50–1
Kenya 176
Kilmer, Julie J. 106–7
King, Andrew 108
King, Michael 101
Kinsey, Alfred 2, 157, 179
Kinsman, Gary 97
Kitzinger, Jenny 85
Klesse, Christian 117
Knott, Kim 14–15, 26–7
Koenig, Harold G. 4
Kolysh, Simone 112
Koralewska, Inga 153
Kugle, Scott 195

Laïcité 34, 171
Lalich, Janja 90
Lawler, Steph 48–52, 55
Lazzara, Emmanuele 195
lesbian: and gender 115, 177; and identity
   50; and the LGBT acronym 2–3,
   121–2, 195; and marginalization 40,
   43, 73, 96–7, 175; and punishment
   177; and recognition 15, 42, 120; and
   religion 16, 48, 63, 90, 98, 125
Lesbian and Gay Christian Movement 178
Letherby, Gayle 68, 91
Levy, Denise 123
Lewis, Rachel A. 171, 177
Lewis, Reina 141
LGBT: as an acronym 2–3; LGBT rights
   43; LGBT+ support and opposition
   groups 81, 84, 90, 113–14
LGBTQI 8
Liberal Jews/ Liberal Judaism 105, 107,
   115, 163
lifecourse/ lifecourse model: challenged
   101, 103; and exclusion 105; and older
   generations 107–9; and religion 14, 99;
   and sexuality 16, 192
lived religion: benefit of 193–4; and
   complexity 91; definition 3, 5, 58–9,
   98; and embodiment 27; and research
   80–2, 87; and sexuality 10, 59–61,
   99–101

**228** Index

Llewellyn, Dawn 93, 99, 164–5, 192
Lofton, Kathryn 5
Loughlin, Gerard 64
Lowe, Pam 7, 9, 19, 56–7, 61, 81–2, 138, 147, 151–3
Luddy, Maria 172–3
Lune, Howard 167
Lupton, Deborah 152
Luther, Martin 21
Lynch, Gordon 169–70, 188–9

McCabe, Janet 165
McClintock, Anne 130–2, 175
McCormick, Leanne 172, 174
MacDougall, Bruce 97
McGarry, Molly 97
McGuire, Meredith B. 1, 3, 5, 27, 58–9, 60, 98, 111, 193
Macke, Karen E. 69, 91
McKenzie, Lisa 41
McKinnon, Andrew 10, 12, 105, 171, 178–9
McLaughlin, Janice 69–70
McLelland, Mark J. 96
McLeod, Hugh 149, 152
McPhillips, Kathleen 168, 182
Magdalene laundries 137, 169–70, 172–4
Maguire, Heather 81
Mahmood, Saba 35, 52–4, 140
Malaysia 71, 81, 88, 180
Malinowski, Bronisław 80
Marchal, Joseph A. 12
marriage: and children 106–7, 127; and Christianity 36, 39, 138, 164–5; and contraception 147, 149; and expectations 36, 40, 104–6, 116, 192; and gender 54, 130, 133, 139, 149, 155, 161–2, 173; heterosexual 2, 56–7, 95, 97–9, 146, 172; idealized 31–2; and Islam 165; and the lifecourse 16–17, 101, 135; and plural forms 97–8, 126; same-sex 2, 16, 42, 44, 75–7, 84, 97–9, 127, 162–3, 175, 180, 192; and sexual acts 24, 56–7, 78, 100–3, 137–8, 158–60
Marx, Karl 11, 19, 30
Masci, David 151
masculinity: binary understandings 1, 124, 134; and Christianity 30; and control 52, 97, 160; and dominant constructions 69–70, 145, 153–4; and god 186; and the sacred 186–9
masturbation 2–3, 57, 77, 98, 157–8, 179
media 4, 8, 34, 45, 55–6, 78, 88, 97, 178, 182–3

media analysis 88
medicine 130; medical 38, 45, 51, 58, 94, 123, 151–2, 174, 180
Mellor, Philip A. 11, 21–3
memory work 49; *see also* narrative identity
Mendos, Lucas R. 175
Menendez, Albert J. 97
menstruation 19, 23, 49, 86, 134, 141–3, 145
Métis 4, 112
Metropolitan Community Church (MCC) 36, 65, 66, 69, 114, 123
middle-class 30, 42, 59, 63, 69, 81, 130–4, 144, 156, 185
Mies, Maria 73
migration 36, 116
Miller, Patricia 45, 114, 147–9
Millman, Marcia 73
mindfulness 58
mindful sex 58
mind maps 85
Mirza, Heidi S. 71, 194
Mishtal, Joanna 29, 39, 153, 164
mixed methods 77, 87–8, 91
Mizock, Lauren 107
modesty 129, 137, 139–40, 191; immodesty 177
monogamy 32, 42, 122, 126
monosexism/monosexist 122
Monro, Surya 3, 43, 120
Monture-Angus, Patricia 112
Mormon/s/ism 97, 126, 151
Morrow, Virginia 85
motherhood 8, 17, 21, 147, 161, 163–6, 172; *see also* birth; childbearing
Moultrie, Monique 69, 71, 139, 160–1, 192
Mueser, Kim T. 107
Muhammad, Noor A. 88
Munson, Ziad W. 61, 152
Munt, Sally 112
Muslim women 25, 31, 34, 52, 105, 140, 142, 151, 162
Mustanski, Brian S. 101
Mutler, Alison 77

Namaste, Ki 96
narrative identity 49, 84
Nash, Catherine J. 69–70, 72–4, 91
Nason-Clark, Nancy 13, 154
nation state 37, 97, 117, 168–70, 172, 189
national identity/ies 34, 39, 43, 153, 169, 175, 189
national surveys 75–7

natural family planning 148–9
Ndjio, Basile 175–6
Neitz, Mary Jo 3, 13, 69
neoliberal/ism 41–3, 56, 169
Netherlands 78, 151
Nigeria 2, 31, 45, 55, 63, 85, 178
nomadic body/subject 24–5
nonbinary 95, 123–4
North America 12, 28, 195
nuns– queer 66–7, 173

Oakley, Ann R. 69
Obergefell v. Hodges 99
O'Brien, Mary 133, 141
O'Donnell, Karen 192
O'Donohue, William 40
online: communities 57, 90;
    discussions 89
opposite-sex attraction 95, 121–2, 124
oral sex 23, 83, 160–1
O'Rand, Angela M. 107
O'Reilly, James T. 182
Orel, Nancy A. 108
organisation/s 5, 7, 9, 45, 78–81, 88,
    97, 98, 113, 138, 146–7, 164, 167–73,
    186–7, 189
orgasm 83, 146, 157, 160
orgasmic meditation 58
Orsi, Robert 58–61, 98

Pagan/s 18, 126
Page, Sarah-Jane 7–9, 14, 17, 23, 37, 48,
    50–1, 56–7, 59, 61–3, 67, 70, 72, 74,
    79, 81, 85–8, 93, 98, 100, 102–5, 116,
    118–19, 121, 124, 126–7, 136–8, 141–2,
    150–2, 158–9, 165, 184, 186, 189,
    192–5
panopticon 168, 173
parenthood 147, 161, 163, 165–6
Pargament, Kenneth I. 4
participant-observation 80
Parveen, Nazia 117
Pateman, Carole 20, 130
patriarchy 11, 13, 18, 20, 41, 130, 133
Paul, Leslie 184
Peart, Ann 133
Pedwell, Carolyn 140, 191
Pells, Kirrily 71
performativity 50, 52–3, 55, 63, 67,
    81, 124
Perry, Samuel 157
personhood 51, 130, 152, 164, 182
Peter, Tracey 101, 108, 111
Pew Research Centre 77–8, 151
Peyton, Nigel 183, 186

piety 24, 26, 30, 47, 49, 52–4, 132, 133,
    134, 137, 139–40, 142, 144, 173
Pilcher, Katy 58, 69, 91
place 3, 11, 18, 25, 51, 65, 91, 100, 109,
    114–15, 167, 172, 192
place of worship 68, 76, 105, 180
Plummer, Ken 40, 49, 86, 91, 95,
    182, 194
pluralistic 171
plural relationships 96–7; see also
    marriage; polyamory; polygamy
Poland 29, 39, 45, 123, 153, 164
politics 4, 25–6, 42, 49, 53
polyamory/ous 96, 108, 119–20,
    126–8, 192
polygamy 34, 105, 126
Pope Francis 106
population control 38
pornography 23, 55, 77, 157–8
post-secular/ity 26–7
poststructuralist feminists 25, 53
power 10–67, 146–189
Power, Kate 84
power dynamics 10–67, 146–189
power-knowledge 10–67, 146–189
prayer 4, 22, 24, 61, 110, 114, 149,
    151, 176
pregnancy 19, 84–5, 137–9, 143, 147,
    160, 165
Pride events 24, 46
Primiano, Leonard N. 180
prison 2, 39, 43, 105, 167, 168, 171,
    174–6, 189, 191
private sphere 13, 30, 34, 36, 129, 130,
    131, 133
privilege 17, 19, 23, 26, 32, 35, 36, 40, 44,
    62–3, 67–72, 83, 85–6, 91–2, 96, 100,
    144, 171, 176, 182, 184–9, 194
procreation 19, 99, 101, 149, 161,
    166, 192
profane 3, 139, 142
Promise Keepers 157–8
Protestant/ism 4, 9, 11, 21, 32, 97, 147,
    149, 152, 171
psychiatric hospitals 167
psychology 4, 179
Puar, Jasbir K 43–4
puberty 101
public sphere 24–5, 32, 34, 36–7, 51, 130,
    133–4, 141, 180
Punch, Samantha 71
pure relationship 21, 22
purity 30, 56, 131, 134–5, 137–9, 144
purity balls 138
Puwar, Nirmal 187, 192

**230** Index

Quakers 105, 126, 149, 179
qualitative/research 7, 8, 71, 73–5, 78, 85, 87, 91, 148, 152
queer-affirming 69, 79, 114, 192
queer experiences 112
queer feminist 68–71, 91, 93, 109, 111, 129, 146, 167, 191
queering/queer religion 63, 65–7
queer theology 64
queer theory 12, 47, 55, 63–4
questionnaires 7, 70, 73, 75, 78–80, 85, 88; *see also* surveys

racial hierarchies 12, 44, 131–2
racial identities 6, 34, 112
racism/ist 63, 114, 116, 118, 131, 194
Rahman, Momin 135, 195
Ramazanoglu, Caroline 37, 91, 193
Ramji, Rubina 100
rape 83, 85, 98, 135, 146, 153–5, 177, 188
Raphael, Melissa 17–18, 23, 143–4
Rasmussen, Mary Lou 112, 117
Reeves, Scott 80
reflexivity 11, 70–2, 81–2
Regnerus, Mark D. 77, 102, 157, 195
Rehaag, Sean 177
religion, category of 4
Religion, Gender, and Sexuality Among Youth in Canada Project (RGSY) 7, 71, 73–4, 78, 79, 82, 86, 88, 102, 111, 113, 116, 119, 120, 123, 124, 127, 135, 140, 163
Religion, Youth and Sexuality Project (RYS) 6, 7, 71–4, 78, 79, 82–3, 86, 88, 100, 102–4, 106, 107, 109, 111, 115, 118–26, 135–8, 140, 142–3, 150, 155, 158–9, 162, 164, 180
religionfuck 66
religious culture 13, 56, 107, 124, 137, 145, 165–6
religious leaders 5, 46, 115, 132, 134, 152, 180–1
religious nones/ non-religion 4, 112
religious studies 1, 6
Remafedi, Gary 101
reproduction 16, 18, 20, 21, 32, 56, 58, 94, 101, 106, 109, 137, 153, 164, 166, 170
reproductive 11, 18, 26, 29, 39, 45, 61, 94, 95, 109, 125, 131, 133, 146–7, 152, 153, 161, 164, 166
reproductive sex 95
reproductive technologies 26
The Respectable Same-Sex Couple (RSSC) 96, 101

rhetoric 43, 106, 173, 176–7, 179, 189
Rich, Adrienne 94
Richardson, Diane 2, 3, 40, 42, 43, 64, 95, 119, 125, 163, 170–1, 175, 177
rights 15, 24, 29, 32, 35, 37, 42–5, 61, 94–7, 105, 108, 117, 127–8, 130, 146, 152, 153, 170–3, 175–6, 180, 189
rituals 16, 18, 39, 60, 99, 123, 142
Robinson, Jane 130
Roman Catholic Church 19, 20, 32, 34, 38, 39, 44–5, 66, 114, 123, 137, 141, 147–8, 165, 168, 171, 174, 178–9, 182
Romania 77
Romer v. Evans 33
Rosenfeld, Dana 108
Rubin, Gayle 95
Rundall, Em 107
Russia/n 169
Ryder, Bruce 97

sacredly masculine authority 186–7
sacred text 64–5, 181
safe school programme 117
safe sex 66, 138, 151
SAGE (Services & Advocacy for GLBT Elders 108
salvation 38, 168
same-sex attraction 50, 179
Samoa 154
Saudi Arabia 175
Savage, Sara 135
Scharff, Christina 20
Scherrer, Kristin S 124
Schnoor, Randal F 48, 100
Schoeffel, Penelope 154
school/ing 8, 34, 71, 101, 111–12, 116–19, 120, 135, 150, 168, 171, 185
Schwartz, Laura 133
Scott, Joan Wallach 15, 34, 35, 97, 193
Scott, Sue 2, 11, 12, 93, 116–17, 124, 182
secular culture 23–4, 93, 109, 122, 126, 143, 145, 166
secularisation 10, 13, 14, 20, 29–30, 32, 35–6, 45
secularism 4, 5, 35–6
Sedgwick, Eve K. 73
Sehmi, Mandeep S. 195
Selby, Jennifer A. 34, 126
self-harm 38, 101, 116, 172
semi-structured interviews 7, 8, 73, 80, 82, 88, 90
Semple, Rhonda A. 132
sensitive topics (research) 70, 79, 82, 88
separation of church and state 32, 34, 97, 127

Index **231**

settler colonial violence 112
sex before marriage 36, 59, 102, 135, 137–8
sex education 71, 117, 138, 153
sex education curriculum 71, 117
sex manuals 57, 89, 146, 157, 160
sex toys 55, 57, 160
sexual abuse 7–9, 60, 83, 146, 154, 169, 181–7
sexual abuse survivors 60, 83, 184
sexual attraction 129
sexual citizen/ship 42, 125, 169, 176–7
sexual difference 25, 96–7, 129, 130, 134
sexual diversity 44, 77, 79, 95–6, 98, 100, 101, 108, 117
sexuality–definition 1, 2, 33, 74, 94, 95, 120, 125, 160
sexuality equality 119, 175, 193
sexuality– regulation 24, 29, 34, 37, 41, 97, 99, 172
sexual minorities–mainstreaming 96
sexual orientation 33, 48, 63, 77, 84, 94–5, 97, 108, 176–7, 180
sexual pleasure 100, 146, 148, 156–61, 191
sexual regulation 23, 34, 175, 179
sexual rights 37, 146
sexual sin 38, 55, 157
sexual stories 49
sexual violence 146, 154–5, 166
Shah, Shanon 42–3, 62, 71, 81, 98, 114, 180, 195
Shahidian, Hammed 159
Shalhoub-Kevorkian, Nadera 136, 154
Shannahan, Dervla S 48, 90, 195
Sharma, Sonya 31, 69, 135, 139, 159, 192
Sheff, Elisabeth 126
Shepherd, Carol A. 122
Sherwood, Harriet 174
Shilling, Chris 11, 21–3
Shipley, Heather 7, 8, 14, 69, 71–5, 79, 86, 88, 98, 100–1, 111, 117, 120–3, 126, 194–5
Short, Donn 97, 108
Simpson, A. V. 173–4
sin 21, 24, 38, 157, 165, 172–3, 179, 182, 188
single mothers 42
Siraj, Asifa 72
Sisters of Perpetual Indulgence 66
Slee, Nicola 69
smear tests 83, 160
Smith, Miriam 108
Snowdon, Ria 84
social class 11, 14, 34, 68, 70, 91, 107, 144, 147, 184
social isolation 118

social normatives 93, 124
social norms 19, 99, 108, 111, 163
sociological theory 11, 19
sodomy 6, 32, 33, 64, 89, 94, 98
space–safe 66, 111, 112, 120
Stan, Lavinia 77
status quo 132, 133
Stella, Francesca 10
stereotypes 58, 74, 93, 99, 116, 130, 139, 159, 161, 187
sterilisation 151, 164
stigma 47, 49, 53–5, 90, 102, 107
straight time 16, 17, 93, 95, 100, 104–6, 109, 111, 125, 192
Stringer, Martin 99
structured interviews 73, 82
Stuart, Elizabeth 23–4, 124, 135, 141
subjective turn 31
Sudan 175
suicide *see* self-harm
Sullivan, Winnifred Fallers 9
surveillance 34, 37–9, 41, 96, 132, 138, 144, 158, 164, 167
surveys 72–9; *see also* questionnaires

taboo 102, 141, 143
Taylor, Catherine 91, 101, 108, 111
Taylor, Yvette 36, 62, 63, 65, 70, 72, 84–6, 98, 112, 115
teenagers 77, 138
Terry, Gareth 124
text analysis 90
Thatcher, Margaret 117
thealogy 18
therapeutic culture 58, 98
Thomas, Jeremy N. 157–8
Thomson, Rachel 115
Thornton, Arland 147
Thumma, Scott 48, 55, 69, 80, 114
Tisdall, E. Kay M 71
Titley, Brian 173–4
Toft, Alex 48, 120, 122
tolerance 33, 43, 75
Tonkiss, Katherine 170
trans identity 3, 43, 48–9, 66, 74, 95, 107–8, 111, 120, 122–4, 127, 128, 174, 191–2, 195
Trinity Western University Community Covenant 8
Truth, Sojourner 61
Tseëlon, Efrat 156
Turner, Bryan S. 11, 19–22, 45, 133, 169, 171
Tweed, Thomas 14, 25
two-spirited 112

**232** Index

Uecker, Jeremy E. 135
Uganda 2, 175–6
United Kingdom (UK) 1, 6–7, 11, 31, 41, 56, 71, 81, 83–4, 86, 100, 104–5, 112, 117, 138, 148, 152, 156–7, 174, 177, 180, 184
United States (USA) 32–4, 37, 41–3, 48, 50, 56, 63, 66, 99, 108, 113, 114, 126, 138, 146, 148, 152, 154, 171, 178

Vaggione, Juan Marco 32
Valentine, Gill 62
values 31–3, 36, 53, 76, 78, 81, 84, 89, 98–100, 102, 109, 117, 131, 134, 158, 170, 172, 178
Valverde, Mariana 95–6, 101, 128
Van Klinken, Adriaan 2, 175–6
Vatican 122, 137, 148–9, 179, 182–3
Vecchietti, Vincent 107
veiling practices 35, 140
Viagra 58
Victorian femininity 30, 131–2, 134, 144, 156
Victorian masculinity 134
video diary/ies 7, 83, 85–8
Vincett, Giselle 13, 30, 46, 143
violence 13, 38, 42, 49, 61, 70, 83, 108, 112–13, 115, 116, 118, 122, 146, 154–6, 166, 177, 191
virginity 31, 56, 93, 101–3, 129, 134–9, 141, 159, 163
virginity pledges 102, 138
visible difference 2, 24, 96, 117, 131
visual methods 85–7, 194
Von Benzon, Nadia 71

Warner, Michael 114
war on terror 43
Warwick, Ian P. 118
Weber, Max 11, 13, 19, 22, 30, 185

Weeks, Jeffrey 40, 71, 100–1, 116, 117, 132–3, 137, 147, 149, 170
Weingarten, Karen 153
Weitz, Tracy A. 153
Whitaker, Robin 153
White, Heather 5, 56–7, 62, 64, 98, 138, 193
whiteness 6, 12, 25, 30, 33, 42, 44, 61, 63, 112, 131–4, 144, 156–7, 161, 170, 175
white wedding 95
Wiering, Jelle 151
Wilcox, Melissa M. 16, 36–7, 66–9, 80, 93, 95, 109, 111–12, 114, 123, 192
Wilmot, Amanda 73
Wilson, Jeff 58
Winder, Terrell J. A. 80–1
women's ordination 186–7
Woodhead, Linda 12, 13, 31, 32, 36, 56, 69, 76, 152, 176, 178, 184
workplace 31, 41, 48, 107, 130, 171

Yip, Andrew Kam-Tuck 7, 14, 17, 31, 36–7, 40, 48, 50, 54, 62, 63, 65, 67, 69–75, 79, 85–6, 88, 93, 98, 100, 102–4, 106, 116, 118–22, 136–8, 142, 150, 158–9, 165, 181, 192–5
yoga 56
Young, Pamela Dickey 7, 14, 73–4, 79, 86, 88, 98, 100–1, 111, 120–1, 123, 126, 194–5
young people 14, 56, 71, 74, 85–6, 91, 100, 101, 104–5, 108, 112–13, 115, 120, 126–7, 137, 160, 162–3, 176, 180, 195
youth 6, 17, 63, 77, 80, 83–5, 101–5, 108, 112, 117, 120, 126, 135, 138, 171, 180–1
Yuval-Davis, Nira 170, 172

Zachs, Maxwell 123
Zambia 84
Zuckerman, Phil 31